# THE PILOT AND THE PASSENGER

# THE PILOT
# AND
# THE PASSENGER

### Essays on Literature, Technology, and Culture in the United States

## Leo Marx

New York   Oxford

OXFORD UNIVERSITY PRESS

1988

Oxford University Press

Oxford   New York   Toronto
Delhi   Bombay   Calcutta   Madras   Karachi
Petaling Jaya   Singapore   Hong Kong   Tokyo
Nairobi   Dar es Salaam   Cape Town
Melbourne   Auckland

and associated companies in
Beirut   Berlin   Ibadan   Nicosia

Copyright © 1988 by Leo Marx

Published by Oxford University Press, Inc.,
200 Madison Avenue, New York, New York 10016

Oxford is a registered trademark of Oxford University Press

Library of Congress Cataloging-in-Publication Data
Marx, Leo, 1919–
The pilot and the passenger.
1. American literature—History and criticism. 2. Literature and
technology—United States. 3. Literature and society—United States.
I. Title
PS121.M28   1987   810'.9   87-11051
ISBN 0-19-504875-X

9 8 7 6 5 4 3 2 1

Printed in the United States of America
on acid-free paper

*For Stephen, Andrew, and Lucy*

# CONTENTS

Introduction, ix

### PART I

The Vernacular Tradition in American Writing, 3
The Pilot and the Passenger: Landscape Conventions
    and the Style of *Huckleberry Finn,* 18
Mr. Eliot, Mr. Trilling, and *Huckleberry Finn,* 37
Melville's Parable of the Walls, 54
Henry Thoreau
    Excursions, 76
    The Two Thoreaus, 83
Robert Frost: A Literary Life, 101

### PART II

The Machine in the Garden, 113
Literature, Technology, and Covert Culture (with
    Bernard Bowron and Arnold Rose), 127
American Institutions and Ecological Ideals, 139
The Neo-Romantic Critique of Science, 160

American Literary Culture and the Fatalistic
    View of Technology, 179
The Puzzle of Anti-Urbanism in American
    Literature, 208


PART III

F. O. Matthiessen
    The Teacher, 231
    "Double Consciousness" and the Cultural
        Politics of an American Critic, 239
"Noble Shit": The Uncivil Response of American
    Writers to Civil Religion, 261
Susan Sontag's "New Left Pastoral": Notes on
    Revolutionary Pastoralism, 291
The American Revolution and the American Landscape, 315
Irving Howe: The Pathos of the Left in the Reagan
    Era, 337
Acknowledgments, 349
Index, 351

# Introduction

The essays in this volume were published over a period of some thirty-seven years (between 1950 and 1987), and except for a few minor corrections and reformulations, they are reprinted here in their original form. The circumstances of their first publication are indicated in the bibliographical note that follows. Although each was conceived as a self-contained piece of cultural history or criticism, they derive a degree of unity from their common subject: the representation and interpretation of American experience.

The essays derive a further measure of unity from the contextual mode of interpretation they exemplify. A tacit assumption of this literary-historical approach, as practiced by certain scholars and critics of what has been called the "myth and symbol school" within American studies,[1] is the idea of culture as a cognitive, meaning-generating con-

---

1. The term "myth and symbol school," along with its derogatory overtones, derives from Bruce Kuklick's influential 1972 essay, "Myth and Symbol in American Studies," *American Quarterly,* 24, 435-50. According to Kuklick and other critics with social scientific and positivistic inclinations, the work of the "school" is too subjective, mentalistic, or literary, which is to say (1) that it imputes too much determinative efficacy to ideas, books, or cultural formations, and (2) that it is insufficiently precise, systematic, quantitative or, in a word, objective. The historians and critics who have been identified with the "school" include Daniel Aaron, R. W. B. Lewis, Charles Sanford, Henry Nash Smith, Alan Trachtenberg,

text. This conception is very much like that held by Victor Turner, Clifford Geertz, and other symbolic anthropologists. As Geertz defines it, a culture "consists of socially established structures of meaning"; these structures are conceptual frameworks or templates that enable members of the culture to interpret the signs and symbols, practices and events that constitute their direct experience, and thereby to participate in the unending argument about meanings, values, and purposes that helps to set a society's course of change.[2]

In practice, however, anthropologists and Americanists deploy the concept of culture in significantly different ways. Anthropologists, perhaps because of their long-standing preoccupation with relatively small, homogeneous, preindustrial societies, have tended to emphasize the cohering, unifying aspects of culture, whereas students of the American past and present with whom I have been associated tended to emphasize the dissonant, conflictual, self-contradictory aspects. Indeed, I believe that many of my colleagues who practice this contextual method share, as I do, Lionel Trilling's conviction that the very form of a modern culture's existence "is struggle, or at least debate—it is nothing if not dialectic."[3] This explains why so much of our work involves the elucidation of conflicts between radically opposed views of the same persons, events, institutions, policies, and practices.

In accordance with this dialectical view of culture, the outlook of any individual also may be said to consist of several overlapping, partly conflicting belief systems: religious, class (socio-economic), political, regional, racial, ethnic, gender, vocational, or generational. In recent years, in fact, Americanists' sense of the pluralistic or what today might be called, after the Russian critic M. M. Bakhtin, the "dialogic" character of culture, has become so strong as to cast serious doubt on the valid-

John William Ward, and myself. The "myth and symbol" method also has been associated with a more inclusive "paradigm" that allegedly characterizes the work (in addition to those mentioned) of V. L. Parrington, Perry Miller, F. O. Matthiessen, Richard Hofstadter, Louis Hartz, and Marvin Meyers. See, e.g., " 'Paradigm Dramas' in American Studies: A Cultural and Historical History of the Movement," *American Quarterly*, 31 (1979), 293-337.

2. "Thick Description: Toward an Interpretive Theory of Culture," *The Interpretation of Cultures* (New York: Basic Books, 1973), p. 12; Victor Turner, *Dramas, Fields, and Metaphors* (Ithaca: Cornell University Press, 1974).

3. Lionel Trilling, "Reality in America," *The Liberal Imagination: Essays on Literature and Society* (New York: Anchor Books, 1950), p. 7.

ity of such synthetic cultural studies as Henry Nash Smith's *Virgin Land* (1950), Richard Slotkin's *Regeneration Through Violence* (1973), Ann Douglas's *The Feminization of American Culture* (1977), or Sacvan Bercovitch's *The American Jeremiad* (1978)—studies which presume to generalize about American society and culture as a whole. Put differently, this awareness of the culture's multilayered, fragmented character has made problematic the very existence of anything like a single, coherent, unified *national* culture. (To be sure, several of the works mentioned were written in the light of the "dialogic" character of the culture, but their authors nonetheless ventured to generalize on the basis of purportedly decisive conflicts of meaning, value, or purpose.) Hence the rise of a "new" social history, sometimes called "history from below" or "micro-history," with its commitment to more modest, empirical studies, and its emphasis on the role of class, especially the working class, in American society, and hence, too, the proliferation of sub-fields like Labor History, Black Studies, Women's Studies, Hispanic Studies, Popular Culture Studies, etc.

According to Bakhtin, who would apply the dialogic concept to the analysis of all works of art and expression, the meaning of any utterance is governed by the operation of "heteroglossia," the distinctive, ever-changing character of the context—social, historical, political, literary, meteorological—in a specific time and place. All of which makes it necessary for historians and critics of culture to heed (1) the constant interaction, or dialogue, between meanings; (2) the inescapable primacy of the context over any particular text or, in other words, the dubious character of all claims for the autonomy of texts; and (3) the essentially "dialogical" character of culture as a totality.[4] Novel as this terminology may sound, the essence of Bakhtin's theory would not have come as a surprise to Herman Melville or Mark Twain, whose masterworks, *Moby-Dick* and *Adventures of Huckleberry Finn,* are brilliant studies (and expressions) of "heteroglossia."

The cogency of the dialectical theory, as applied to American cultural history, is suggested by the strong hold that contradictory versions of the myth of national origins continue to have on the collective imagination. For at least five centuries (beginning long before the establish-

4. M. M. Bakhtin, *The Dialogic Imagination,* ed. Michael Holquist (Austin: University of Texas Press, 1981).

ment of permanent colonies in the New World) variants of essentially the same narrative core—stories of the transit of Europeans to America—have served to represent distinct interpretations of our national beginning, some of them with diametrically opposed implications. Thus the trans-Atlantic migration of white settlers has been represented both as a triumph of "civilization" over wild, undeveloped nature (or "barbarism"), and as a recovery of "the natural"—a liberating retreat—from the oppressive, overdeveloped, hierarchical societies of the Old World. From time to time each version of the founding myth has been updated and, in the process, partially transformed. In the early nineteenth century, for example, Daniel Boone figured as the hero of antithetical legends. In one Boone was apotheosized as "the standard-bearer of civilization and refinement"; in the other he was depicted as "the child of nature who fled into the wilderness before the advance of settlement."[5]

At roughly the same time, different groups accommodated each version of the myth to distinct, even contradictory, conceptions of history. Certain Americans, especially those most committed to rapid industrial development, attached the story of the conquest of the North American continent by advance parties of European civilization to the idea of progress, fulcrum of what soon would become the dominant secular world view of industrial societies: the belief that history is a record of the steady, cumulative, continuous, and (for its most ardent exponents) predestined expansion of knowledge of (and power over) nature. At the same time, a dissident minority blended its own critical, dissident, or "romantic" response to the onset of industrial capitalism with the opposed representation of the trans-Atlantic migration as a redemptive retreat from the corrupt Old World. This recoil from industrialization lent new vitality and meaning to the sophisticated yearning for simplicity that always had been a central feature of the pastoral mode in the arts. Here, as elsewhere, the psychic root of pastoralism was the desire, in the face of the growing complexity and power of organized society, to disengage from the dominant culture and to seek the basis for

5. Henry Nash Smith, *Virgin Land: The American West as Symbol and Myth* (Cambridge: Harvard University Press, 1950), p. 55; another compelling example of this dialectical analysis of American culture-heroes is John William Ward's essay, "The Meaning of Lindbergh's Flight," *American Quarterly*, 10 (1958), 3-16, reprinted in his *Red, White, and Blue* (New York: Oxford University Press, 1969), pp. 21-37.

a simpler, more harmonious way of life "closer" (as we say) to "nature."[6]

Today opposed groups of Americans have invested this old conflict of ideas with new meanings. In current debates on environmental issues, for example, spokespersons for industry routinely invoke the progressive version of the myth in defence of their own interests. They reject programs for the protection of the environment on the ground that they are obstacles to "progress," or to the realization of "the American dream" as measured by economic growth—by accelerating rates of technological innovation, production, and consumption. On the other hand, the environmentalists, "greens," and others who assert the primacy of essentially noneconomic, "quality of life" measures of collective well-being, tend to invoke concepts of balance—of equilibrium between socio-economic institutions and the environment—which prove, on examination, to be modern variants of the ancient pastoral ideal of "harmony with nature."

My aim in sketching these recurrent appropriations and transformations of the myth of American origins is to suggest how the dialectical concept of culture can help to map historical terrain. But the abstract quality of the sketch should alert us to an obvious pitfall of this historical method. It can lead the practitioner to impute excessive determinative power to "ideology," using the term in its broad non-Marxist sense as embracing ideas, images, mentalities, languages, or, in a word, thought. Work of this kind (including my own, no doubt) often seems to imply that a disembodied mental formation is, or could be, an independent agent of change—a primary driving force of history.

I don't believe that it can be, but neither do I doubt that cultural formations have, so to speak, their own internal, quasi-autonomous history, or that that history can be written without falling into the trap of reification. What cultural critics and historians need above all, if they are to avoid that trap, is an imagination at once literary and sociological. It entails, among other things, a recognition of two obvious but

6. I examine some aspects of this conflict of world views in *The Machine in the Garden: Technology and the Pastoral Ideal in America* (New York: Oxford University Press, 1964); for a recent reassessment of that argument, see my essay, "Pastoralism in America," in Sacvan Bercovitch and Myra Jehlen, eds., *Ideology and Classic American Literature* (Cambridge: Cambridge University Press, 1986), pp. 36-69.

often slighted facts: first, that ideas only can acquire determinative power when adhered to by significant social groups, and second, that a group's thinking often is revealed as clearly by its discursive practices, its stylistic habits, and the figurative forms it favors, as by express ideas.

All of this suggests that the various manifestations of cultural conflict are related to each other like a nest of Chinese boxes. Beginning with the psycho-social embodiment of the conflict in individuals (the smallest box), an analysis would trace the conflict to its relatively impersonal (or less personal), formal, and aesthetic expression in discrete works of thought and expression (an intermediate size box), and then outward to the clash of encompassing socio-economic and ideological formations (the largest box).[7]

From the standpoint of the dialectical theory, in any case, sharp divisions within the culture are not defects—not impediments to the realization of its creative potentialities. On the contrary, in much of the work done by the Americanists in question,[8] conflicts of meaning and value prove to be a stimulus to intellectual vitality and innovation. A nice illustration of this generative power can be found in the circumstances surrounding Samuel Clemens's greatest invention—the distinctive, supple, evocative prose style of *Huckleberry Finn*. He contrived the style in the course of an effort to resolve a conflict of the sort I have been discussing—one whose importance later was to be famously discovered

7. Of course the problem of accurately delineating the relationships between (1) cultural or ideological and (2) "material" or socio-economic (class) formations is far more complex and difficult than this statement suggests. By now the standard (or "vulgar") ways of applying the Marxist "base and superstructure" model to that relationship have been discredited, as have all notions of a direct, one-to-one linkage, a "reflecting" or simply mimetic relationship, between the two realms. Indeed, Daniel Bell has made a strong case for the recent development of a radical disjunction between American culture and what he calls the "techno-economic order." In his view the increasingly interdependent and rationalized "techno-economic order" is, on balance, a unifying or at least non-disruptive force, whereas the culture, especially its most dynamic and innovative (avant-garde) elements, tends (especially at the national level) to be a source of conflict, disaffection, and disunity. See *The Cultural Contradictions of Capitalism* (New York: Basic Books, 1976).

8. I am thinking of such works as Perry Miller's *The New England Mind*, (1939), F. O. Matthiessen's *American Renaissance* (1941), Henry Nash Smith's *Virgin Land* (1950), Lionel Trilling's *The Liberal Imagination* (1950), R. W. B. Lewis's *The American Adam* (1955), John William Ward's *Andrew Jackson: Symbol for an Age* (1955), and Alan Trachtenberg's *The Incorporation of America* (1982).

by George Santayana. In his 1911 Berkeley lecture on the Genteel Tradition, Santayana ascribed the prevalence of the conflict between the genteel and vernacular mindsets in the United States to the fact that it is
"a country with two mentalities, one a survival of the beliefs and standards of the fathers, the other an expression of the instincts, practices,
and discoveries of the younger generations."[9]

As Mark Twain tells the story in *Old Times on the Mississippi,* the
clash between the genteel and the vernacular mentalities first became a
problem for him during his initiation into the art of steamboat piloting. Before completing his apprenticeship on the eve of the Civil War,
he had shared the passengers' enthusiasm for the beauty of the Mississippi Valley landscape. They saw it as a series of pretty pictures. The
young pilot associated this viewpoint with the dominant Eastern culture,
which is to say, with wealth, status, power, and with the most cultivated,
refined taste in the arts. When he first traveled the river he too had
seen "pretty pictures" on all sides. But then, as he learned the pilots'
way of seeing beneath the water's surface, the river became a new and
"wonderful book" to him. Now, instead of delighting in the reflections
of a splendid sunset on the water, he saw in almost every pleasing detail of line or color a sign of hidden menace: a bluff reef or dangerous
current or new snag. The passengers could not read the esoteric language of this book (so far as they were concerned, in fact, it was written in a "dead language"), but it delivered its most telling secrets to
him. He was exhilarated by his new knowledge, though in gaining it he
claims to have lost something too. He was no longer able to enjoy the
pretty pictures, or as he grandly puts it, the "romance and the beauty
were all gone from the river."

Back of this characteristically hoked-up account—at one point the
confused pilot compares his situation to that of a doctor whose medical
knowledge prevents him from appreciating the physical charms of
women—there was a real problem that Samuel Clemens faced as a
writer. It stemmed from his dissatisfaction with a received, elevated
style of landscape description like that favored by the passengers. Here,
incidentally, long before the idea was made fashionable by the struc-

9. "The Genteel Tradition in American Philosophy," *The Genteel Tradition,
Nine Essays by George Santayana* (Cambridge: Harvard University Press, 1967),
p. 39.

turalist critics of the 1960s and their heirs, the deconstructionists, he represents the landscape—the visible world—as a "text" constituted by the language in which people register their perceptions of it. Thus his parodic "pretty pictures" (hackneyed "texts" fashioned in a tired picturesque idiom) expose a particular way of depicting the Mississippi landscape as the imposition of a foreign, shopworn aesthetic on a fresh native subject; it projects on to the natural world the Easterners' imported, privileged, leisure-class mentality. Yet the spare, matter-of-fact, technical language of the pilots did not suit Clemens's needs any better. The truth is that neither discourse, the pilots' or the passengers', enabled him to convey his own powerful response to the beauty of the Mississippi Valley. In his effort to resolve this dilemma, he forged, out of the Southwestern idiom, the incomparable vernacular style of *Huckleberry Finn,* or so I attempt to demonstrate in "The Pilot and the Passenger."

The essays that follow are divided into three groups. Those in Part One are about particular writers, texts, and literary conventions. Recent perturbations in the world of literary criticism can be taken to imply that we must choose between our respect for the aesthetic integrity of works of imaginative literature and our recognition of their embeddedness in culture, but I wrote these essays on the assumption that such a choice is unnecessary. Although the dialectic of American culture is not their express subject, it makes itself felt in all that follows. "The Vernacular Tradition" was my first attempt to deal with cultural divisions embodied in language. In the essays on Melville, Thoreau, and Mark Twain, I explore the ways in which individual writers defined the salient conflicts of the culture. The remarkable thing about nineteenth-century American literature is that so many of the accomplished writers were, as Lionel Trilling put it, "repositories of the dialectic of their times—they contained both the yes and the no of their culture . . ."[10]

The essays in Part Two move to wider parameters of the dialectic, especially to certain conflicts generated by the dynamism of science, technology, and urban industrial capitalism generally. But here the con-

10. "Reality in America," p. 7.

spicuous definitions of the opposing forces often cut across, even contradict, Santayana's distinction between the genteel and the vernacular
mentalities. Although the latter, as exemplified, say, by Mark Twain's
mentor, Mr. Bixby, the veteran pilot in *Old Times on the Mississippi,*
exhibited a certain practical, technical flair—the homegrown familiarity
with various technologies associated with the artisan, the mechanic, the
Yankee jack-of-all-trades—that vernacular technical style finally was too
anti-theoretical, rule-of-thumb, even anti-intellectual, to be easily reconciled with the more radically innovative, synthesizing, transformative
aspects of certain crucial sciences and technologies imported from Europe. In American literary culture, accordingly, the steam engine, the
factory system, the industrial city—or for that matter, Darwinian theory
and late nineteenth-century physics—often were perceived as foreign,
discordant, intrusive forces. The critique of science and technology that
characterized the adversary culture of the 1960s (and since) had its
roots in that nineteenth-century romantic-pastoral response to the alleged imperialism of instrumental rationality.

The essays in Part Three deal with particular cruxes—practitioners,
themes, problems—of our twentieth-century cultural criticism. They reflect my interest in the complicated and, I think, quite distinctive relations between writers, critics, and the political left in the United States.
Susan Sontag's book about Vietnam thus exemplifies the curious native
blend of pastoralism and left-wing radicalism in the ideology of the
1960s' dissident Movement. A similar note of native American anar-
chism also may be heard in the refreshingly irreverent, skeptical literary
responses to the solemnities of American civil religion; they remind
us that the vernacular has been an invaluable resource for our most
gifted writers, especially for their resolute nay-saying in the face of semi-
official religious rhetoric and its nationalistic pieties.

But it has not been easy for writers, artists, and intellectuals to sustain such a critical position. The important work of F. O. Matthiessen
and Irving Howe, two critics on the left who rejected each other's politics, reveals some of the difficulties that beset those who try to fashion
a responsible, consistently critical, radically democratic cultural criticism in the United States. The Marxist mainstream of left-wing radical
thought, as it came to us from Europe, has not been readily adaptable
to the special circumstances of American politics in the late twentieth

century. Nonetheless, the work of socialists like Matthiessen and Howe carries on the tradition of Van Wyck Brooks, Lewis Mumford, and V. L. Parrington, who prepared the way for academic American studies, and who never doubted that the significance of our central literature is enhanced when read in the context of continuing efforts to make our's a more just, a more democratic society.

# Bibliographical Note

"The Vernacular Tradition in American Literature: Walt Whitman and Mark Twain," was first published in *Die Neuren Sprachen,* Frankfurt, 1958.

"The Pilot and the Passenger: Landscape Conventions and the Style of *Huckleberry Finn,*" was first published in *American Literature,* 1956.

"Mr. Eliot, Mr. Trilling, and *Huckleberry Finn,*" was first published in *The American Scholar,* 1953.

"Melville's Parable of the Walls" was first published in *The Sewanee Review,* 1953.

"Excursions" was first published as the Introduction to Henry Thoreau, *Excursions* (New York: Corinth Books, 1962.)

"The Two Thoreaus" was first published in *The New York Review of Books,* 1978.

"Robert Frost: A Literary Life," was first published in *The London Review of Books,* 1985.

"The Machine in the Garden" was first published in *The New England Quarterly,* 1956.

"Literature, Technology, and Covert Culture" was first published (as "Literature and Covert Culture") in *American Quarterly,* 1957.

"American Institutions and Ecological Ideals" was first published in *Science,* 1970.

"The Neo-Romantic Critique of Science" was first published as "Reflections on the Neo-Romantic Critique of Science" in *Daedelus,* 1978.

"American Literary Culture and the Fatalistic View of Technology" was first published in *Alternative Futures,* 1978.

"The Puzzle of Anti-Urbanism in American Literature" was first published in *Literature and the Urban Experience, Essays on the City and Literature,* eds. Michael C. Jaye and Ann Chalmers Watts (New Brunswick, New Jersey, Rutgers University Press, 1981).

"The Teacher" was first published in *Monthly Review,* 1950.

"Double Consciousness and the Cultural Politics of an American Critic" was first published as "Double Consciousness and the Cultural Politics of F. O. Matthiessen" in *Monthly Review,* 1983.

"Susan Sontag's 'New Left Pastoral': Notes on Revolutionary Pastoralism" was first published in *Literature in Revolution,* eds. George Abbott White and Charles Newman (New York: Holt, Rinehart and Winston, 1972).

" 'Noble Shit': The Uncivil Response of American Writers to Civil Religion in America" was first published in *The Massachusetts Review,* 1973.

"The American Revolution and the American Landscape" was first published in *America's Continuing Revolution,* ed., Stephen J. Tonsor (Washington, D.C.: American Enterprise Institute for Public Policy Research, 1975).

"Irving Howe: The Pathos of the Left in the Reagan Era," was first published in *The New York Review of Books,* 1987.

# PART I

# The Vernacular Tradition
# in American Literature

From the beginning writers have had much less trouble finding an American subject than a mode appropriate to its expression. In 1620 Willam Bradford recognized an inevitable subject even before he stepped off the *Mayflower*. Gazing toward the forbidding shore he asked, in effect, "What is to be the fate of civilized man in this prehistoric landscape?" Later the question was reformulated. Writers like James Fenimore Cooper, Nathaniel Hawthorne, and Henry James asked, "What does it mean to be an American?" Around this theme they elaborated an infinitely complex art. To get at the meaning of American experience they submitted the native character to the test of Europe. They created a drama of cultural contrast. What gave their work its American stamp was their vivid awareness of certain cultural differences.

And yet, having said all that, we are not satisfied that we have settled the old problem: what *is* different, after all, about American literature? Granted that the "international theme" is American, can a particular subject ever make for a lasting distinction between one national literature and another? If we ask what is different about German literature, we know very well the first answer to expect: it is written in German. But the language of Cooper is not all that different from the language of Scott, and with Cooper's generation the boundary between British and American literature remains uncertain. When we come to "Song of Myself" or *Huckleberry Finn*, however, the line is much more distinct. That may explain why Walt Whitman and Mark Twain are so widely respected, nowadays, as the two great seminal figures of modern American writing. They establish, once and for all, the literary usefulness of the native idiom. With it they fashioned a vernacular mode or, if you will, a national style. This style marks a major difference between English and American literature.

But I do not mean to suggest, as many contemporary critics do, a violent opposition between two strains in American writing. In *The Complex Fate,* for example, Marius Bewley deplores the influence of Whitman and Twain, seeing in it a narrow chauvinism, a kind of literary isolationism in marked contrast to the scope and subtlety of Hawthorne and James. My own view is quite different. The styles of Whitman and Twain seem to me to serve as a measure, even an embodiment, of the very cultural differences that preoccupy Hawthorne and James. The image of America that we find in the work of Hawthorne and James, though depicted from another angle, is really the same image we find in Whitman and Twain. All these writers were concerned with what it means to be an American; all felt—though in different degrees to be sure—the tension between the possibilities and the dangers of the new society. And not one was a narrow chauvinist. Much of Mr. Bewley's contempt for the work of Whitman and Twain derives, I believe, from a mistaken conception of the vernacular tradition.

To see what is contained in that tradition—if the word can be used to describe so rebellious a state of mind—let us first consider Walt Whitman.

When Whitman's first poems were taking shape, America was preoccupied with the slavery problem—another rather distinctive American subject. Whitman's contemporaries turned out a large volume of poetry about slavery. Here is a fair sample by the most popular poet of the age, Henry Wadsworth Longfellow:

### The Slave in the Dismal Swamp

In dark fens of the Dismal Swamp
The hunted Negro lay;
He saw the fire of the midnight camp,
And heard at times a horse's tramp
And a bloodhound's distant bay.

Where will-o'-the-wisps and glow-worms shine,
        In bulrush and in brake;
Where waving mosses shroud the pine,
And the cedar grows, and the poisonous vine
        Is spotted like the snake;

Where hardly a human foot could pass,
        Or a human heart would dare,
On the quaking turf of the green morass
He crouched in the rank and tangled grass,
        Like a wild beast in his lair.

A poor old slave, infirm and lame;
        Great scars deformed his face;
On his forehead he bore the brand of shame,
And the rags, that hid his mangled frame,
        Were the livery of disgrace.

All things above were bright and fair,
        All things were glad and free;
Lithe squirrels darted here and there,
And wild birds filled the echoing air
        With songs of Liberty!

On him alone was the doom of pain,
        From the morning of his birth;
On him alone the curse of Cain
Fell, like a flail on the garnered grain,
        And struck him to the earth!

Now consider these lines from Section 10 of "Song of Myself":

The runaway slave came to my house and stopt outside,
I heard his motions crackling the twigs of the woodpile,
Through the swung half-door of the kitchen I saw him limpsy
    and weak,
And went where he sat on a log and led him in and assured him,
And brought water and fill'd a tub for his sweated body and
    bruis'd feet,

And gave him a room that enter'd from my own, and gave him
   some coarse clean clothes,
And remember perfectly well his revolving eyes and his awk-
   wardness,
And remember putting plasters on the galls of his neck and
   ankles;
He staid with me a week before he was recuperated and pass'd
   north,
I had him sit next me at table, my fire-lock lean'd in the corner.

One might use this comparison to demonstrate the difference between good and bad poetry. But that is not my purpose. The point is
that Longfellow's poem was written in a hackneyed literary language
then still thought in America to be poetic. To get near his subject
Whitman felt it necessary to dispense with the entire apparatus of such
poetry: not only the diction, but the meter and rhyme as well. Indeed,
he went further than that; he dispensed with the poet. By this I
mean that in Longfellow's poem the traditional calling of the man of
letters is obtrusive. The words carry our thoughts not to a slave in a
swamp, but to a man using the special equipment reserved for men
of letters when they write poems. In Whitman's lines, on the contrary,
the poet disappears. Like Huckleberry Finn, the "I" of Whitman's
poem is at once the hero and the poet. That is to say, both Whitman
and Twain resorted to the old device of the persona—the first-person
narrator—and the result was a new sort of immediacy. The American
subject was brought up closer than it ever had been before. The device
was old, but the particular persona was new. Whitman's hero is the
product of a new sort of culture, and appropriately enough, he speaks
a new language.

There is no need to insist that Whitman's language literally was the
spoken language of his time. Indeed, we can be sure that it was not.
What matters is that at his best he succeeds in creating the illusion
that a certain kind of man is speaking. In his case the illusion probably
stems from the cadence, and the absence of traditional meter and
rhyme, rather than from the diction. In any event, his poetry is nearer
to the spoken language of Americans than our poetry had ever got

before. I do not mean to impute any absolute superiority to the use
of spoken language in poetry. That depends upon the particular aims
of the writer. But given Whitman's problem, his desire to convey ideas
and emotions for which the standard manner of poetry was inappropriate, the vernacular was a source of immense vitality. To see this one
only has to compare:

> In dark fens of the Dismal Swamp
> The hunted Negro lay;

with:

> I heard his motions crackling the twigs of the woodpile,
> Through the swung half-door of the kitchen I saw him limpsy
>     and weak.

What is most striking here is the extraordinary sense of immediacy
that the vernacular mode conveys. We see Longfellow's subject through
a murk of tired images: "like a wild beast in his lair"; to Whitman he
is a man with "sweated body and bruis'd feet." Everyone knows that
the more specific image is likely to be the more evocative. But why
does one writer seize it while another avoids it? Longfellow says of
the slave, "great scars deformed his face." Whitman says, "And remember putting plasters on the galls of his neck and ankles." The fact
is that Whitman imagines a completely different relation to the black
man, one that takes us back of language to something more fundamental, to the kind of persona Whitman felt impelled to employ. He
is a man "hankering, gross, mystical, nude." He is aggressively un-
genteel, and he thinks about the slave in a very different way from
Longfellow.

> In all people I see myself, none more and not one a barley-corn
>     less,
> And the good or bad I say of myself I say of them.

Given this sort of hero, Whitman can introduce details once thought
to lie outside the bounds of respectable poetry. Among other things,

the vernacular made possible a long step forward in the candor of modern writing, as in Whitman's daring treatment of sexuality.

There is another kind of immediacy that results from the use of the vernacular narrator. That is the way meaning comes to us here by what Whitman called "indirection" rather than by use of personification, abstraction, or, for that matter, direct statement. Longfellow finds it necessary to tell us of the slave, "on him alone the curse of Cain / Fell . . ." Whitman avoids comment. He first describes the relations between his mythic hero and the slave, and then at the end he casually mentions the gun in the corner. The image *is* the meaning; it is a perfect expression of the democratic hero's relaxed but militant egalitarianism. Right here, incidentally, Whitman anticipates the kind of ironic understatement that was to become a dominant accent of twentieth-century American poetry.

But it must not be thought that a mere technical device enables Whitman to convey so much in so little. If he does not need to proclaim the solidarity between the two men, it is because he can describe it so vividly. That is, the style has been called forth as a fitting expression of something else, an ideal human situation, indeed a kind of model society. The slave and the hero exemplify the egalitarian community of Whitman's imagination. It is a society that stands in relation to the actual society as vernacular language does to the stock elevated language of poetry. All of Whitman's poetry exalts this conception. It is the same sort of community that Mark Twain later sets up aboard a Mississippi raft. Here is the core of the American vernacular. It is not simply a style, but a style with a politics in view. The style is a vehicle for the affirmation of an egalitarian faith so radical that we can scarcely credit it today. It sweeps aside received notions of class and status—and of literature. In Whitman's mind all these inherited forms are identified with Europe.

This is where the problem of chauvinism arises. There can be no question that Whitman celebrates America at the expense of Europe and the past. Of course the notion that stylistic elegance was the literary counterpart of European political oppression arose in America long before Whitman. In 1787, for example, Royall Tyler had expressed this prejudice in his play *The Contrast*; speaking of aristocratic titles, ornaments, and manners, Tyler said:

> Our free-born ancestors such arts despis'd;
> Genuine sincerity alone they priz'd;
> Their minds, with honest emulation fir'd,
> To solid good—not ornament—aspir'd . . .

Constance Rourke has shown how this "contrast theme" runs through our native humor. By Whitman's time the animus against a European style of life had been strengthened by the repeated European sneer against the crudities of American culture. To establish his identity the American is impelled to defy tradition:

> I too am not a bit tamed, I too am untranslatable,
> I sound my barbaric yawp over the roofs of the world.

Now granted that as a view of human experience there are serious limitations to this Whitmanian yawp, it does not seem to me that chauvinism is one of them. Whitman does not celebrate the vernacular hero because he is an American, but the other way around. It is because he is "untranslatable" that the American must be allowed to have his say in his own idiom. He is a new kind of man, and the socio-political conditions which brought him into being may (at least theoretically) be reproduced anywhere. In reality the vernacular character is international. Hence Whitman's attitude is not to be confused with what Mr. Bewley calls "literary isolationism." To see that, one has only to read what Whitman had to say later in *Democratic Vistas,* when he thought that America was betraying the egalitarian ideal. Like Hawthorne and James, he put his country to a severe test. It was not the same test they used, but it was exacting nevertheless. In point of fact it proved finally to be too exacting.

Curiously enough, Whitman represents that side of the vernacular tradition which drew its inspiration from Europe in the first place. We know that he was inspired by Emerson, who recognized what American poets needed to do, even if he was not the man to do it. And behind Emerson, of course, we are led directly to England, and the revolution in poetry Wordsworth had announced fifty-five years before *Leaves of Grass,* in the Preface to the second edition of *Lyrical Ballads* in 1800.

This is not to imply that in Whitman we have a simple case of delayed literary influence, of what is sometimes called "cultural lag."
Whitman went much further than Wordsworth, and he did so largely
because American conditions imparted a special intensity to Wordsworthian doctrine. Was it a good thing for poets to escape the refine-
ments of civilization, to catch impulses from the vernal wood? Then
how lucky to be an American poet! Was it true that Wordsworth's
country neighbors spoke a language more vivid and precise, hence
more poetic than the language of cultivated men? Again, this idea
touched an American in ways unimaginable to an English poet. In
America the exaltation of what Wordsworth called "humble and rustic
life" could not be received as a mere program for poetry. By Whitman's time it had already become something like a national ethos. In
the defiant accent of Whitman's hero we recognize how far we have
come from Wordsworth's simple peasants.


> Who goes there? hankering, gross, mystical, nude;
> How is it I extract strength from the beef I eat?
> What is a man anyhow? what am I? what are you?
> .  .  .
> I wear my hat as I please indoors or out.
> Why should I pray? why should I venerate and be ceremonious?
> Having pried through the strata, analyzed to a hair, counsel'd
>     with doctors and calculated close,
> I find no sweeter fat than sticks to my own bones.


This boast is a self-portrait of Whitman's democratic man. It is a revealing and ironic fact that the average American reader preferred
Longfellow's poetry. Whether this had anything to do with Whitman's
style, his success or failure in catching the popular tone of voice, is a
question that is probably unanswerable. In any event Whitman was
never persuaded that he was speaking the truly distinctive native idiom,
but he had a good idea where that idiom was likely to arise. "Today,"
he wrote in 1871, "doubtless, the infant genius of American poetic expression . . . lies sleeping far away, happily unrecognized and unin-
jur'd by the coteries, the art-writers, the talkers and critics of the sa-

loons, or the lecturers in the colleges—lies sleeping, aside, unrecking itself, in some western idiom . . ."


This brings me to Mark Twain and the other or frontier side of the vernacular tradition. His mature style, the very essence of his humor, is grounded in a sensitivity to language as an index of cultural difference. He felt that the distinguishing trait of the American story was its emphasis upon *manner* rather than matter. That also explains why Mark Twain was so exasperated by the work of James Fenimore Cooper. For him reading Cooper was like listening to a tone-deaf man trying to sing. "He keeps near the tune," said Twain, "but it is *not* the tune. . . . you perceive what he is intending to say, but you also perceive that he doesn't *say* it." In other words Cooper, like Longfellow, had spoiled a fine subject by encasing it in a foreign idiom. As it happens it was Twain's chosen subject, so he had a special reason for wanting to dispose of Cooper. Fitness of language to subject was a cardinal point in the literary ethic of Mark Twain. He felt that Cooper achieved his blurred effect by virtue of his unfailing instinct for the *approximate* word. As his best work suggests, the *precise* word for Twain was the word spoken by his native hero himself.

Twain's feeling for language was in large measure derived from the oral tradition of the West. The frontiersman was a celebrated boaster. He screamed his barbaric yawp to call attention to his strength and to his many triumphs over nature. The vocabulary of the boast was itself a form of triumph: it displayed his dexterity and ingenuity with language: "Mister . . . I can whip my weight in wild cats, and ride straight thro' a crab apple orchard on a flash of lightning—clear meat axe disposition—the best man, if I an't, I wish I may be tetotaciously exfluncated." The Western man's idiom made him conspicuous, and sometimes it made him feel a fool. Actually, he was sensitive about it, and his tall tale was in part an effort to get his own back from those who mocked his barbaric speech. We see this clearly in T. B. Thorpe's classic, "The Big Bear of Arkansas" (1841)—a story which belongs to the long line of American hunting fantasies which include Melville's *Moby-Dick*, Faulkner's "The Bear," Hemingway's *Old Man and the Sea*, and Mailer's *Why Are We in Vietnam?* Here the Western narrator introduces his tale with a brief account of his visit to the big city, from which he is returning. There he had met some gentlemen who interrogated him about his home state, Arkansas. But they did not speak his language, and when they asked him about "game" in Arkansas he mistook them and told about "poker, and high-low-jack." They laughed at him, and called him green. "Strangers," he says he told them, "if you'd asked me *how we got our meat* in Arkansaw, I'd a told you at once . . . Game, indeed, that's what city folks call it . . ." With this prelude, he launches his boastful story. Of course he tells it in the same vernacular idiom that had marked him for a rustic dolt in the eyes of gentlemen. But he has learned that his speech is his identity, and now he will use it to glorify himself at the expense of those who patronize him. Here again is the hostility, the chip-on-the-shoulder defiance of what pretends to be a superior culture that so often animates the vernacular style.

In *Huckleberry Finn* Mark Twain exploits similar misunderstandings on the part of his Western hero for similar purposes. For example, in reporting the king's funeral oration, Huck says that he "slobbers out a speech, all full of tears and flapdoodle, about its being a sore trial for him and his poor brother to lose the *diseased,* and to miss seeing *diseased* alive." Clearly, this joke has two edges. We are intended to laugh at Huck's ignorance, to be sure; the real butt, however, is the pompous euphemism, the respectable burial rhetoric which Huck fails to recognize for what it is. This is a minor example of the satiric device that Mark Twain uses throughout. In the magnificent description of the Grangerford house he turns it against all the pretensions of refinement associated with the sort of people Huck calls the "quality." He has never been in such a nice house before, and he is impressed. He admires everything from the brass doorknob to Emmeline Grangerford's poetry. But at the same time his keen eye makes it possible for us to see how spurious it all is: "On the table in the middle of the room was a kind of a lovely crockery basket that had apples and oranges and peaches and grapes piled up in it, which was much redder and yellower and prettier than real ones is, but they warn't real because you could see where pieces had got chipped off and showed the white chalk, or whatever it was, underneath."

Huck is less certain about the pictures on the walls: "They was different from any pictures I ever see before—blacker, mostly, than is common. One was a woman in a slim black dress, belted small under the armpits, with bulges like a cabbage in the middle of the sleeves, and a large black scoop-shovel bonnet with a black veil, and white slim ankles crossed about with black tape, and very wee black slippers, like a chisel, and she was leaning pensive on a tombstone on her right elbow, under a weeping willow, and her other hand hanging down her side holding a white handkerchief and a reticule, and underneath the picture it said 'Shall I Never See Thee More Alas.'" In conclusion, Huck says: "These was all nice pictures, I reckon, but I didn't somehow seem to take to them, because if ever I was down a little they always give me the fan-tods." (When reading these words to a European audience one feels the need to provide a gloss on "fan-tods." Not that Americans necessarily can define the word with precision. It is not even to be found in the *Dictionary of Americanisms*. But a native audience can be relied on to get the point.) The passage contains the recurrent pattern of the book: Huck knows how he is supposed to feel about many things, but he cannot always feel that way.

Much the same thing happens to his feelings about Jim and obedience to the laws enforcing the slave system. He knows that he should pray for divine help to return Jim to his "rightful owner," and occasionally this knowledge takes possession of his will, as in the moral crisis of the book—when he writes to Miss Watson to tell her of Jim's presence. But having written the letter, Huck says: "[I] got to thinking over our trip down the river; and I see Jim before me all the time: in the day and in the night-time, sometimes moonlight, sometimes storms, and we a-floating along, talking and singing and laughing. But somehow I couldn't seem to strike no places to harden me against him, but only the other kind. I'd see him standing my watch on top of his'n, 'stead of calling me, so I could go on sleeping; and see him how glad he was when I come back out of the fog . . . and at last I struck the time I saved him by telling the men we had smallpox aboard, and he was so grateful, and said I was the best friend old Jim ever had in the world, and the *only* one he's got now; and then I happened to look around and see that paper. It was a close place. I took it up and held it in my hand. I was a-trembling, because I'd got to decide, forever, betwixt two things, and I knowed it." Here, at the level of social morality, is the same distinction Huck had felt in the Grangerford house. Indeed, the respectable values of society prove to be like the lovely crockery basket of fruit that "warn't real because you could see where pieces had got chipped off and showed the white chalk, or whatever it was, underneath." In the crisis Huck finally is forced to choose between two things: the demands of the crockery culture and those of the provisional community he and Jim have established aboard the raft.

In the background we can still discern the contrast theme in slightly modified form. In Mark Twain's novel the young barbarian is compared to a spurious local culture. But in the moral geography of America, this sentimental elegance is associated with the culture of the Eastern seaboard, which in turn is but an American extension of European civilization. In *Huckleberry Finn* the vernacular humor also is used against the old European targets. The two rogues, the Duke and the Dauphin, are the crockery royalty that serves to expose the real thing:

> "Don't it s'prise you [Jim asks] de way dem kings carries on, Huck?"
> "No," I says, "it don't."
> "Why don't it, Huck?"
> "Well, it don't, because it's in the breed. I reckon they're all alike."
> "But, Huck, dese kings o' ourn is reglar rapscallions; dat's jist what dey is; dey's reglar rapscallions."
> "Well, that's what I'm a-saying; all kings is mostly rapscallions, as fur as I can make out."
> "Is dat so?"

Mark Twain pushes this republican piety right back to the genesis of the contrast theme, the American Revolution itself: "You don't know kings, Jim, but I know them; and this old rip of ourn is one of the cleanest I've struck in history. Well, Henry he takes a notion he wants to get up some trouble with his country. How does he go at it—give notice?—give the country a show? No. All of a sudden he heaves all the tea in Boston Harbor overboard, and whacks out a declaration of independence, and dares them to come on. That was *his* style—he never give anybody a chance."

So far I have talked about the vernacular style of *Huckleberry Finn* in its negative aspect, that is, its aggressive uses. But in this book we also find an affirmation, the hero's self-exaltation: "Well," says Huck, "the days went along, and the river went down between its banks again; and about the first thing we done was to bait one of the big hooks with a skinned rabbit and set it and catch a catfish that was as big as a man, being six foot two inches long, and weighed over two hundred pounds." Actually, there is not much of this sort of thing in *Huckleberry Finn*. The reason is that the entire book, in its total conception, is a Westerner's boast. He is telling the story in his own idiom, hence the tale is a celebration of his point of view from beginning to end. Like Whitman's hero, Huck is a rebellious, democratic barbarian. He lies, he steals, he prefers magic to religion, he identifies his interests with those of escaped slaves, and above all he speaks the vernacular. The largest boast of *Huckleberry Finn* is reserved for the language itself—its capacity to take on the dignity of art, to replace the elevated style of Longfellow or Cooper.

The vernacular style bears many marks of its plebeian origin. For example, it has been peculiarly useful in expressing a preoccupation with process, with the way things are done. By its very nature a genteel style implies an invidious distinction between intellectual and manual work. But the vernacular hero does not honor the distinction, and moreover his practical rhetoric denies its significance: "Well, last I *pulled* out some of my hair, *and blooded* the ax good, *and stuck* it on the back side, *and slung* the ax in the corner. Then I *took* up the pig *and held* him to my breast with my jacket (so he couldn't drip) till I got a good piece below the house *and then dumped* him into the river. Now I thought of something else. So *I went and got* the bag of meal and my old saw out of the canoe, *and fetched* them to the house. *I took* the bag to where it used to stand, *and ripped* a hole in the bottom of it with the saw . . . ." What we have here is a meticulous rendering, one by one, of physical actions or manipulations. A series of verbs (here italicized) is strung together, largely by the word "and," and the total effect is an immediate impression of a process. The writer takes it for granted that we are as interested in *how* the hero does things as in *what* he does. From this passage one can make a direct link to the style of many of our modern writers, for instance Ernest Hemingway describing how Nick Adams baits a fishhook.

Vernacular narration is the key to Mark Twain's style just as it is the key to Whitman's. Twain uses a naive character and his naive language to convey a highly complicated state of mind. But the point of view and the idiom finally are inseparable: together they form a style. And it is this style that lends immediacy to the affirmation without which the book would be morally empty. Huck compresses his whole conception of felicity into one sentence: "It's lovely," he says, "to live on a raft." Actually there are two separate but analogous ideals implied in Huck's pastoral emotion here. The first is a relation between men (it is in a sense political), while the other is a relation between man and nature (it is religious or, if you will, metaphysical).

The political ideal is freedom, freedom *from* the oppression of society, and freedom *to* establish the egalitarian community. The escaped slave and the son of the village drunkard set up their model society on the raft. "What you want," says Huck, "above all things, on a raft, is for everybody to be satisfied, and feel right and kind toward the others." This sort of community can exist only on the river, insulated from the surrounding society, and even there it is terribly vulnerable. Rogues take over the raft, a steamboat smashes into it, and the river's current carries it steadily toward the slave society its occupants want to escape. But vulnerability, after all, is appropriate to what is essentially a utopian conception. The pastoral impulse that leads the vernacular hero to renounce the existing society is much stronger, needless to say, than the impulse to create a new one.

Although the vernacular ideal of the raft turns upon human solidarity, it derives its ultimate support from another sort of solidarity—one which is given to us only indirectly, by way of the lyrical strain in the book: "Sometimes we'd have that whole river all to ourselves for the longest time. Yonder was the banks and the islands, across the water; and maybe a spark—which was a candle in a cabin window; and sometimes on the water you could see a spark or two—on a raft or a scow, you know; and maybe you could hear a fiddle or a song coming over from one of them crafts. It's lovely to live on a raft. We had the sky up there, all speckled with stars, and we used to lay on our backs and look up at them, and discuss about whether they was made or only just happened." In such passages Mark Twain manages to convey a feeling of belonging to the physical universe comparable to the feeling of community aboard the raft. That is, he suggests a grand analogy between the political and metaphysical relations within the novel. The vernacular thereby receives its final sanction from nature itself. It is a fitting sanction for a literary style developed in a new society in a prehistoric landscape.

The vernacular style is a distinctive achievement of American culture. But this is not to say that it has served to convey anything like an adequate view of experience, or that it has yet given America a great literature. Its creativity came from the radical program of freedom it affirmed, but like any such program, it demands an exceptional discipline. The writer who works in the vernacular takes great risks. To see this we have only to recall those excesses of uncontrolled improvisation that mar the work of Whitman and Twain. This literary barbarism follows from the rejection of inherited forms and theories. It is of course a symptom of primitivism, and along with it we get what is perhaps the chief defect of the vernacular mode—its unremitting anti-intellectualism. This seems to me a more valid point of attack than chauvinism. In defying the constraints and oppression identified with the European past, our writers also have tended to ignore the achievements of the trained intellect. This familiar primitivist bias has retained its affinity to the mode in our time. It seems to have followed the style from Walt Whitman to Carl Sandburg, from Mark Twain to Ernest Hemingway.

But it is one thing to charge the vernacular with an anti-intellectual bias, and quite another to think it (as Mr. Bewley does) "uncritically acceptant" of America. In Hawthorne and James criticism arose from a comparison of America to tradition, to the past. In Whitman and Twain, on the other hand, the criticism was based on egalitarian standards. It came from a comparison of an actual America with an idealized democratic vision of the nation's destiny. That is what led to the writing of such uncompromising works as *Democratic Vistas, A Connecticut Yankee,* and "The Man That Corrupted Hadleyburg." From the beginning the vernacular was more than a literary technique—it was a view of experience. When the style first emerged it was nourished by a political faith that we can scarcely imagine nowadays. Since that time the history of the vernacular has been a history of its fragmentation. The technique has been separated from the belief it originally was designed to affirm. But that is another story.

# The Pilot and the Passenger: Landscape Conventions and the Style of *Huckleberry Finn*

Nowadays it is not necessary to argue the excellence of Mark Twain's *Adventures of Huckleberry Finn*. Everyone seems to agree that it is a great book, or in any event one of the great American books. But we are less certain about what makes it great. Why is it in fact more successful than most of Mark Twain's other work? No one would claim that it is free of his typical faults. It descends here and there to sentimentality, buffoonery, and (particularly in the closing chapters) just plain juvenility. Nonetheless we persist in regarding the novel as a masterpiece. How are we to account for its singular capacity to engage us? One persuasive answer to the question has been to say that the book's excellence in large measure follows from the inspired idea of having the western boy tell his own story in his own idiom.[1] From that seminal idea, it may be said, many of the book's virtues—the convincing sense of life, the fresh lyricism, the wholeness of point of view—follow as the plant from the seed. This approach is persuasive, but it is easier to assert than to demonstrate. My purpose is to establish

1. Today this view is something of a commonplace, and there would be no point in attempting to assign priorities. Much of my appreciation of its importance, however, I owe to Henry Nash Smith, and to the illuminating study by Paul Stewart Schmidt, "Samuel Clemens's Technique as a Humorist, 1857-1872," unpublished Ph.D. thesis, University of Minnesota, 1951.

certain ways in which the use of the narrator contribute to the novel's greatness.

The point to begin with is that it is Huckleberry Finn's story. And what he imparts to it, in a word, is style. The style is unique. To get a vivid impression of its uniqueness one need only compare the novel with *Life on the Mississippi* and *The Adventures of Tom Sawyer,* the other books in which Clemens re-creates the world of the Mississippi Valley. The three are linked in many ways, but above all by geography. In each the landscape is a primary source of unity and meaning. The same countryside, indeed sometimes the same scene, is described in each. Take, for example, the lyrical description of the dawn in *Huckleberry Finn,* the passage beginning, "Two or three days and nights went by; I reckon I might say they swum by, they slid along so quiet and smooth and lovely." This celebrated piece of writing, recently cited as exemplifying our national manner in prose,[2] may serve as a measure of stylistic achievement. As it happens, a similar description of the sunrise is to be found in each of the other Mississippi books. (All three passages are reprinted at the end of this essay, and to follow the argument they should be read at once.) Anyone who reads them in sequence will, I am confident, be struck by the superiority of the *Huckleberry Finn* version. I mean later to discuss the grounds for this judgment; here it is only necessary to recognize the difference. It is an impressive difference, and one which obviously turns upon narrative method or, if you will, style. The distinguishing mark of style in turn is language.

But to say this is not to answer the original question. To say that vernacular narration is a distinctive feature of *Huckleberry Finn* is one thing; it is quite another to account for Mark Twain's success with that technique. After all, we know that he used it elsewhere without comparable results. Moreover, it means nothing to contend that the novel is great because it is written in the native idiom unless, that is, we mean to impute an intrinsic or absolute value to the vernacular. That would be ridiculous. What we want to know, then, is why this method worked best for Clemens at this juncture. I assume that only a strong need can have called forth so original a style.

2. "The Emergence of a National Style," *Times Literary Supplement,* Sept. 17, 1954, pp. xii-xiv.

One of Clemens's persistent motives, clearly, was to convey a certain experience of his native landscape. *Adventures of Huckleberry Finn* is, among other things, the fulfillment of a powerful pastoral impulse. Probably no one needs to be told that. But what is perhaps less obvious is that the vernacular style made possible the expression of emotions Clemens had long been working to put into words. The three attempts to depict the sunrise on the Mississippi reveal something of that liberating process. In each case the "theme" is the same: the observer's sense of the beauty and harmony of nature. But for some reason, in the *Huckleberry Finn* version Clemens manages to create for us what, in the other two, he had only been able to describe. When, in reading the three passages consecutively, we come to the last, a sudden release of imaginative energy makes itself felt. The whole experience comes into bright focus. Sentences flow in perfect cadence, without strain or stilted phrase or misplaced word. It is as if the shift to the vernacular had removed some impediment to fullest expression.

I

What the impediment was Clemens reveals in "Old Times on the Mississippi." This series of articles written for the *Atlantic Monthly* in 1875 was his first sustained effort to represent the valley society he had known before the Civil War. In those chapters which now comprise the first volume of *Life on the Mississippi* his theme is "learning the river." Here the narrator recalls his initiation into a unique western mystery: Mississippi piloting. He makes clear that this vocation has to be learned by an apprentice on the spot; no books, no school, no theory can equip him. What he has to learn is a new language—indeed a language of nature. It is not simply the abstract technique of piloting, but a particular piece of western geography which he must possess. He has to "know the river" by day and night, heading upstream and heading downstream. He must memorize the landscape. It is this knowledge which will forever distinguish him from the uninitiated. When ignorant passengers gaze at the face of the water they see "nothing but . . . pretty pictures."[3] But when the trained pilot

3. (New York, 1906), p. 83. The account of the sunset is on pp. 82-85.

looks at the river the river tells its "mind" to him. Nature, he explains, has been made to deliver him "its most cherished secrets." This experience is exhilarating, and in re-creating it Clemens managed to impart the exhilaration to his prose. (Notice that the second volume, which lacks the theme, is dull by comparison.) Yet—and here the problem arises—the narrator confesses that in acquiring the new lore he loses something too: the "grace, the beauty, the poetry" of the majestic river. It is gone. In learning the matters of fact necessary to his Western vocation the pilot loses, or so he thinks, the capacity to enjoy the beauty of the landscape.

To illustrate his dilemma he compares two ways of experiencing a sunset on the river. It is a brilliant sunset. First he describes it as, in his innocence, he once might have enjoyed it. At that time he would have observed "soft distances," "dissolving lights," and "graceful curves." The painter's terms are significant. In much of Clemens's work we find landscapes similarly framed, noble pictures seen as through a "Claude glass." For instance, Venice, in *Innocents Abroad*, is like "a beautiful picture—very soft and dreamy and beautiful."[4] Or of Lake Tahoe, in *Roughing It*, we are told that a "circling border of mountain domes, clothed with forests, scarred with landslides, cloven by cañons and valleys, and helmeted with glittering snow, fitly framed and finished the noble picture."[5] Clemens obviously was working within the convention of the picturesque. Yet it should be added at once that he was not comfortable in that mode. He often betrays his dissatisfaction by making comedy of the elevated style. In *Innocents Abroad* he allows a description of a Mediterranean vista to reach grandiose rhetorical heights. Then he quickly destroys the illusion with a revealing and self-conscious gag: "[Copyright secured according to law.]"[6] A similar impulse, in *Roughing It*, leads him to say, of a "majestic panorama," that "nothing helps scenery like ham and eggs."[7] Clemens was a writer of travel books and he recognized, as these remarks indicate, that the established idiom of landscape portrayal could not bear steady exposure to the observed natural fact. But if that style, at least when most ele-

4. (New York, 1906), I, 281.
5. (New York, 1906), I, 186.
6. I, 134.
7. I, 148.

gant, was ludicrous, how was a writer to convey the loveliness of scenery? Clemens manifestly did not know. He resorted again and again to the conventional mode, using it straight as well as for burlesque.

Returning now to the sunset in "Old Times," we find that Clemens uses a language as trite as the paintings he must have had in mind. The pilot, discussing the lost beauty of the scene, says that he once would have enjoyed the sight of boughs that "glowed like flame" and trails upon the water that "shone like silver." This vocabulary is the literary counterpart of the painter's picturesque, an appropriately conventional medium for a conventional idea of beauty. In the presence of nature the pilot stands "like one bewitched" in a "speechless rapture." But this ecstasy was what he felt before his initiation. Afterward, ". . . if that sunset scene had been repeated, I should have looked upon it without rapture, and should have commented upon it inwardly after this fashion: 'This sun means that we are going to have wind to-morrow; that floating log means that the river is rising, small thanks to it; that slanting mark on the water refers to a bluff reef which is going to kill somebody's steamboat one of these nights. . . . that silver streak in the shadow of the forest is the "break" from a new snag. . . .' " And so on. Beauty, the pilot infers, is for those who see only the surface of nature. Behind every perception of the beautiful there is a fact of another sort. And once he knows the facts "the romance and beauty . . . [are] all gone from the river."

Of course it may be said that this is merely another statement of a familiar modern conflict between two modes of perception, one analytic and instrumental, the other emotive and aesthetic. So it is. But to dispose of the issue thus is to miss the special significance the alternatives had for Sam Clemens. In *Life on the Mississippi* each way of apprehending the river characterizes a particular mode of life. One might say a particular culture. One culture is exemplified by the uninitiated spectators and the ignorant novice pilot; the other is reflected in the melancholy wisdom of the older man who tells the story. There are many differences between these two ways of life, but the most important is the relation to nature fostered by each. The passengers are strangers to the river. They lack the intimate knowledge of its physical character a pilot must possess. As spectators, well-trained to appreciate painted landscapes, they know what to look for. They enjoy the play of light on the water. This aesthetic response to nature, given the American geography, Clemens inevitably associates with the cultivated, urban East. But the pilot, on the other hand, is of the West, and his calling such that he can scarcely afford to look upon the river as a soft and beautiful picture. He is responsible for the steamboat. To navigate safely he must keep his mind on the menacing "reality" masked by the trail that shines like silver.

The pilot's dilemma is a recurrent theme of our nineteenth-century literature. It was an age which attributed special meaning to the landscape, particularly in America. At the level of popular culture images of the landscape were used to depict a national destiny as glorious and beautiful as the surface of the Mississippi at sunset.[8] The nation's scenic splendor was a sign of divine blessing. At the same time, however, this chosen people was engaged in transforming the landscape it celebrated, and in fact subjecting it to the same instrumental method the pilot had learned. Hence it is understandable, quite apart from the influence of European philosophy or literature, that many of our writers were concerned with the penalties and perils attendant upon piercing Nature's mask. Melville's Ahab, driven by a compulsion to penetrate the ocean of mere appearance, also fears he may find "naught beyond."[9] Like the pilot, however, he cannot turn back. For both men the need arises as an almost inescapable consequence of native callings. In *Walden* we find the identical symbolic motif. Again the water's surface is a metaphoric boundary between the beautiful and another possible reality. When Thoreau, submitting faith to a test, fills a glass with the "matchless and indescribable light blue" water of the pond, he finds that it is in fact colorless.[10] Throughout the century the alleged values of nature, including its beauty, disappear when considered too curiously. When the pilot's keen eye penetrates the silvery trail he sees the menacing snag. There are two ways of regarding the Mississippi, just as, in *Moby-Dick* there are "gentle thoughts" above the Pacific's

8. Henry Nash Smith calls my attention to this account of sunset on the river: "When the sun went down it turned all the broad river to a national banner laid in gleaming bars of gold and purple and crimson; and in time these glories faded out in the twilight and left the fairy archipelagoes reflecting their fringing foliage in the steely mirror of the stream" (Clemens and Warner, *The Gilded Age,* New York, 1906, I, 42).

9. Chap. xxxvi, "The Quarter-Deck."

10. Chap. ix, "The Ponds."

surface, and murderous sharks and leviathans below.[11] Ahab and the pilot are committed to knowing; they can only lament the sacrifice, as Ahab put it, of "low enjoyment" for a "higher perception."[12] The bedeviling question of the age, however, was whether that perception was indeed higher.

This was not, for Clemens, an abstract philosophical issue. It would be wrong to think of him, standing at an artist's proper remove, playfully manipulating an interesting theme. For him the dilemma had a more compelling and practical urgency: it was a matter of style. He faced it as a writer of prose, and it was as a writer (he was no theorist) that he finally came to grips with it. His solution, if that is the correct word, was implicit in the choice of Huckleberry Finn as narrator of his own adventures.

II

In 1875, when Clemens began work on the Mississippi material, the problem of landscape description became more acute. Writing about the country he had known as a boy and pilot was not quite the same as writing about Venice or Lake Tahoe. Here, for one thing, the picturesque convention was even less appropriate. We may guess that his feeling for his native landscape was such that he aimed at a greater fidelity to experience than the standard mode allowed. But what was the alternative? As he apparently felt, the choice was between the sentimental views of the passengers and the analytical attitude of the pilot, between a lush picture and mere matters of fact. It was an impossible choice. If *Huckleberry Finn* is any indication, what Clemens wanted was to affirm the landscape's beauty *in its actuality*. To do so, though he surely did not realize it, he had to do nothing less than fashion a literary style. The three versions of the dawn on the river help us to understand something of that process.

In *Tom Sawyer*, which he wrote soon after "Old Times," we see

11. Chap. cxxxii, "The Symphony."
12. Chap. xxxvii, "Sunset." The rest of the passage is of some interest in view of Melville's symbolization of the same conflict with the same images: "Oh! time was, when as the sunrise nobly spurred me, so the sunset soothed. No more. This lovely light, it lights not me; all loveliness is anguish to me, since I can ne'er enjoy. Gifted with the high perception, I lack the low enjoying power. . . ."

the new mode taking shape. Here we have certain obvious holdovers from the older landscape tradition in the hackneyed use of personification and the sense of the event as pictorial spectacle. "The marvel of Nature shaking off sleep and going to work unfolded itself to the musing boy." On the other hand, the effort to include sharp detail is a gauge of Clemens's need to break out of the painter's style. The microscopic focus upon the green worm is well outside the picturesque, which dealt with the general, not the particular; with the remote, not the near; and with a genteel notion of the beautiful, not worms. In the older mode man was an onlooker or, in the pilot's language, a passenger. (Human figures are rare, or in any case of little consequence, in picturesque landscapes.) But the worm's journey over Tom blends the boy into the fabric of nature, and points toward the well-nigh baptismal immersion of Huck and Jim in the river. Nevertheless, in *Tom Sawyer* the older tradition remains dominant and finally reasserts itself. The passage culminates in a coda of gaudy pictorial banality: "All Nature was wide awake and stirring, now; long lances of sunlight pierced down through the dense foliage far and near, and a few butterflies came fluttering upon the scene."

Clemens finished *Tom Sawyer* in 1875. "I perhaps made a mistake," he remarked to Howells, "in not writing it in the first person."[13] The following year he began *Adventures of Huckleberry Finn*. After he completed roughly four hundred manuscript pages (or about the first sixteen of forty-two chapters) his inspiration waned and he abandoned the project for several years.[14] Then, in 1882, he made a trip back to the river as the basis for the second volume of *Life on the Mississippi*. He finished it in 1883. It is an uneven, hasty, and loosely put-together volume. But

13. July 5, 1875, *Mark Twain's Letters*, ed. Albert Bigelow Paine (New York, 1917), I, 258. Actually, Bernard De Voto has demonstrated that an early version of *Tom Sawyer* was written in the first person. It is now called "Boy's Manuscript," and probably dates from the years 1870-1872. See *Mark Twain at Work* (Cambridge, Mass., 1942), pp. 3-9. The ms itself is reprinted on pp. 25-44. This ms seems to support my contention that first-person narration itself is no key to the superiority of *Huckleberry Finn*. De Voto rightly calls this first attempt at fiction "crude and trivial, false in sentiment, clumsily farcical, an experiment in burlesque with all its standards mixed" (p 7). The fact is that Clemens here used the technique in a thoroughly mechanical fashion. Though the boy is supposed to be talking, his words do not actually reveal a boy's attitude, as in *Huckleberry Finn,* but rather that of a bemused adult observing childish behavior.

14. For the chronology I am following De Voto, *Mark Twain at Work.*

it illuminates the complex relationship between history and style: "The majestic bluffs that overlook the river . . . charm one with the grace and variety of their forms, and the soft beauty of their adornment. The steep, verdant slope . . . is topped by a lofty rampart of broken, turreted rocks, . . . exquisitely rich and mellow in color—mainly dark browns and dull greens, but splashed with other tints."[15] Again we have a painting with all the picturesque niceties, not excepting the castle. There are sleepy villages, stealthy rafts, and white steamers too. It is a glimpse of the old river, a scene "as tranquil and reposeful as dreamland." But then, suddenly, the "unholy train comes tearing along . . . with its devil's war-whoop and the roar and thunder of its rushing wheels." The railroad, emblem of industrial power, is the demon of the entire volume. It destroys steamboating and the pilot's vocation and the natural beauty of the valley. And in the same stroke it renders the established landscape convention obsolete. Clemens, in this remarkable passage, admits as much. He describes the train, in a metaphor whose concealed term is a picturesque canvas, "ripping the sacred solitude to rags and tatters." The second volume of *Life on the Mississippi* marks the passing of a way of life, a mode of apprehending nature, and by inference, a literary style.

### III

The increasing obsolescence of the style becomes apparent when we compare the two accounts of the dawn which Clemens wrote after his return to the river.

The first is in *Life on the Mississippi*. The narrator pretends to be a reporter on the spot. What he gives us, however, is another formal landscape painting, "one of the fairest and softest pictures imaginable." Of course it may be said that the style has a certain appropriateness. Clemens in this case actually was a kind of reporter, an official visitor from the East. Yet the passage scarcely succeeds as reporting; it might pass for a description of the dawn on the Rhine or the Amazon. Nor does it fit another role the narrator intermittently assumes, that of the ex-pilot who knows the score. His command of piloting is carefully avoided in honor of the "picture," as if beauty really requires the

15. P. 432.

suppression of knowledge. There is no danger, no thought of treacherous snags. All is beautiful, "soft and rich and beautiful." Compared with the dawn in *Tom Sawyer* this is writing of a conventional order.

Indeed it represents a regression to a divided universe in which beauty and reality are hermetically separated. Nothing makes this compartmentalization of life plainer than the paragraph which follows the sunrise passage. There we find that although no snags are permitted to mar the sunrise, they have not ceased to haunt the pilot.

> We had the Kentucky Bend country in the early morning—scene of a strange and tragic accident in the old times. Captain Poe had a small stern-wheel boat, for years the home of himself and his wife. One night the boat struck a snag in the head of Kentucky Bend, and sank with astonishing suddennness; water already well above the cabin floor when the captain got aft. So he cut into his wife's stateroom from above with an ax; she was asleep in the upper berth, the roof a flimsier one than was supposed; the first blow crashed down through the rotten boards and clove her skull.

There is no way, within the convention, to treat the beautiful and the murderous river as one. The style imposes a hopeless bifurcation of experience. In the second half of *Life on the Mississippi*, consequently, the past and the present, the beautiful and the actual, the benign and the tragic are discrete compartments of life. The result is a disorderly patchwork.

What happens next is, for an understanding of the creative process, the most illuminating part of the story. For apparently the disheartening journey, so perfunctorily reported in the one book, inspired Clemens to go back to work on his masterpiece. It had reinvigorated the pastoral impulse. He had described how the older and by now idealized society of the valley was being torn apart by the new industrial power. But the unfinished manuscript offered him a chance to render it whole.[16]

16. According to De Voto, Clemens stopped work on the manuscript just after describing the steamboat—its "long row of wide-open furnace doors shinning like red-hot teeth"—colliding with the raft. Clearly the boat is a monstrous embodiment of the forces menacing freedom in this idyllic valley society. The fact that Clemens stopped work at this point is highly suggestive. One might infer that the dilemma posed by the industrial transformation of the society had been acting upon his imagination from the first, but that he had not yet settled upon the literary form of his response. For a parallel in the genesis of Hawthorne's fiction, see "The Machine in the Garden," *NEQ*, 29 (March, 1956), 27-42.

In art he might achieve a unified vision of the world he had seen being destroyed in fact. But this was not simply a matter of turning his attention to the past. Just as important was the technique of vernacular narration he had fashioned. It was a style which at last made possible a genuine celebration of the landscape.

These circumstances help to explain the extraordinary lyrical intensity of *Huckleberry Finn,* of which the sunrise is but one example.

There are countless descriptions in literature of the sun coming up across a body of water, but it is inconceivable that a substitute exists for this one. It is unique in diction, rhythm, and tone. Certainly when we place it alongside the earlier versions we see at once how vital point of view can be. In *Life on the Mississippi,* the narrator, who is also supposed to be on the scene, self-consciously pictures the dawn for a distant audience. He stands apart and reports; his explicit aim is to tell his readers why they should believe him when he says that the scene is "enchanting." Huck, on the other hand, is a participant, at times literally immersed in the river he is telling about. Hence the immediacy of his account. The scene is described in concrete details, but they come to us as subjective sense impressions. Time itself is transformed; it takes on the attributes of the landscape, and the days and nights *swim* by. All the narrator's senses are alive, and through them a high light is thrown upon the distinctiveness of the particulars. Furthermore, Huck is not, as in the two earlier versions, committed to any abstract conception of the scene. He sets out merely to tell how he and Jim put in their time. Because he has nothing to "prove" there is room in his account for *all* the facts. Nothing is fixed, absolute, or perfect. The passage gains immensely in verisimilitude from his repeated approximations: "soon as night was *most* gone," "*nearly always* in the dead water," "a *kind of* dull line," "*sometimes* you could hear," "*but sometimes* not that way." Nature, too, is in process: "the daylight *come,*" "paleness *spreading* around," "river *softened* up," "mist *curl* up," "east *reddens* up," "breeze *springs* up." Both subject and object are alive; the passage has more in common with a motion picture than with a landscape painting.

Huck, moreover, "belongs" to this landscape in that his language is native to it. Perhaps this fact, above all, accounts for the exquisite freshness of these lines. Sunrises have not changed much since Homer sang of the rosy-fingered dawn, but here is the first one ever described in this idiom. What is distinctive about it, in other words, ultimately derives from the historical distinctiveness of the narrator, his speech, and the culture from which both emerge. But particularly his speech, for that is the raw material of this art, and we delight in the incomparable fitness of subject and language. Observe, for example, the three successive efforts to convey the solitude and silence at dawn. (It was the "sacred solitude" that the railroad tore to tatters.) Compare "deep pervading calm and silence of the woods," "eloquence of silence," "not a sound anywheres—perfectly still—just like the whole world was asleep, only sometimes the bullfrogs a-cluttering, maybe." The first is merely commonplace; "eloquence of silence" is neat and fine, and has the merit of compression and (to invoke a currently popular critical test) paradox. The phrase is so good, in fact, that it has often been used. Yet relative novelty is not the main point. There is nothing novel about "just like the whole world was asleep" either. On the contrary, both phrases are familiar; the difference is that our familiarity with one comes from the written, indeed the printed, word, and the other from the spoken word. One bears the unmistakable mark of a man bent on making phrases; it is literary; the other sounds like a boy talking. The same may be said of several other parallels, such as "the birds were fairly rioting"; "jubilant riot of music"; "the songbirds just going it." Much of the superior power of *Huckleberry Finn* must be ascribed to the voice of the boy experiencing the event. Of course no one ever really spoke such concentrated poetry, but the illusion that we are hearing the spoken word is an important part of the total illusion of reality. The words on the page carry our attention to life, not to art, and that after all is what gives pleasure to most readers.

My purpose, I repeat, is not to exalt vernacular narration as a universally superior technique. Each writer discovers methods best suited to the sense of life he must (if he is to succeed) create. In this case, however, the vernacular method liberated Sam Clemens. When he looked at the river through Huck's eyes he was suddenly free of certain arid notions of what a writer should write. It would have been absurd to have had Huck Finn describe the Mississippi as a sublime landscape painting.

Accordingly Clemens, in spite of his evident effort to convey the beauty of the sunrise, permits Huck to report that "by and by you could see a streak on the water which you know by the look of the streak that there's a snag there in the swift current which breaks on it and makes the streak look that way." He is endowed with the knowledge of precisely those matters of fact which had seemed to impair the pilot's sense of beauty. Huck now accepts that fearful principle of nature responsible for the death of Captain Poe's wife. Now at last, through the consciousness of the boy, the two rivers are one. Mingled with the loveliness of the scene are things not so lovely: murderous snags, wood piled by cheats, and—what could be less poetic?—the rank smell of dead fish. Huck is not the innocent traveler, yet neither is he the initiated pilot. He sees the snags, but they do not spoil his pleasure. In his person Clemens reaches back to a primal mode of perception undisturbed by the tension between art and science. It does not occur to Huck to choose between beauty and utility. His willingness to accept the world as he finds it, without anxiously forcing meanings upon it, lends substance to the magical sense of peace the passage conveys. When the lights of the river form a continuum with the stars, the boy's sense of belonging reaches the intensity of a religious experience; the two on the raft face the mystery of the creation with the equanimity of saints: "It's lovely to live on a raft. We had the sky up there, all speckled with stars, and we used to lay on our backs and look up at them, and discuss about whether they was made or only just happened."

IV

The passion we feel here may be compared only with love. It is not the conventional sentiment of the early landscapes, but the love of an object as it exists, in all its gloriously imperfect actuality. Indeed, this sequence of Clemens's attitudes toward the landscape is comparable, in several respects, to an intricate love relationship. In all three of the Mississippi books his deep feeling for the landscape is evident. But at first, as the pilot in *Life on the Mississippi* reveals, a conflict blocks its full expression. He tells of a violent shift from one extreme conception of nature to another. At first the landscape is sheer perfection— soft, rich, and beautiful; then it suddenly comes to seem a merely indifferent, if not hostile, force. After having been submissive and adoring, he now is wary and aggressive. But in *Huckleberry Finn* there is no trace of either attitude. Here the narrator feels neither adoration nor hostility. The boy gives us a full account of his experience of nature, sensations unpleasant as well as pleasant, matters of fact and matters of feeling, objects attractive and repellent. At dawn on the river Huck knows neither anxiety nor guilt, but an intense feeling of solidarity with the physical universe.[17]

It is obvious that this capacity for realistic affirmation coincides with the disappearance, however temporary, of the earlier conflict. Needless to say, the conflict was no mere fiction. It was vital to Clemens, as it was endemic in a society at once so passionately committed to—and at war with—nature. As a writer, however, he felt the destructive consequences of this tension most acutely in his work. It was impossible to do justice to American experience by treating nature, in the conventional manner, as benign and beautiful. Clemens knew better, and his continuing impulse was to parody the accepted mode. To him the landscape, no matter how lovely, concealed a dangerous antagonist. He knew that nature had to be watched, resisted and—when possible—subdued. Unfortunately this often meant its obliteration as an object of beauty, hence of love. Nothing impressed this upon Clemens with

17. How revealing that Clemens, who seldom if ever was able to depict a mature love relation, should have been able to express this passion only in the words of an adolescent. Those interested in a psychological analysis of his work should examine this highly suggestive material. Notice, for example, the unmistakable sexual connotations of the two attitudes toward landscape. On the beautiful surface nature has obvious feminine characteristics (softness, dimples, graceful curves), but the subsurface is represented by objects with strongly masculine overtones (logs, bluff reefs, menacing snags). In Melville the symbolism is explicit. For instance, in the passage from "The Symphony" (see above), the air is "pure and soft" and has a "woman's look," while in the waters beneath the sea rush mighty leviathans and sharks, the "murderous thinkings of a masculine sea." Perhaps these sexual identifications are the key to the alternating submission and aggression noted in Clemens's treatment of the landscape (an object, finally, of love)—as if he were projecting an inner conflict. Henry A. Murray has made the point about Melville ("In Nomine Diaboli," *NEQ*, 24 (Dec., 1951), 435-52. Of course Melville and Clemens were not alone, among our 19th-century writers, in presenting an apparent antithesis between (feminine) beauty and (masculine) reality. The subject would seem to warrant close examination, particularly in view of the frequency with which social scientists have noted the conflict between aggressive competitiveness and a desire to yield as peculiarly characteristic of American society. See, e.g., Franz Alexander, *Our Age of Unreason* (Philadelphia, 1942); Arnold W. Green, "The Middle-Class Male Child and Neurosis," *American Sociological Review*, 2 (Feb., 1946), 31-41; Karen Horney, *The Neurotic Personality of Our Time* (New York, 1937).

such force as what he saw happening to the Mississippi Valley in 1882.

In the uncompleted manuscript of *Huckleberry Finn*, to which he then returned with renewed imaginative vigor, he found a solution. Here was a tale told by a boy who—granted his age, his education, and the time he lived—could not possibly feel the anxiety Clemens felt. To Huck nature was neither an object of beauty nor the raw material of progress. Or, rather, it was both. He was as tough and practical as the pilot, and as sensitive to color and line as an artist; he kept his eye on dangerous snags, but he did not lose his sense of the river's loveliness. Moreover, he spoke a language utterly unlike the stilted vocabulary of the literary cult of nature. His speech, never before used in a sustained work of fiction, was as fresh and supple as his point of view. The interaction of a narrative technique and the heightened emotion to which that technique lent expression helps account for the singular power of the sunrise passage. Behind the mask of Huck Finn, Clemens regained that unity of thought and feeling he felt himself, along with his contemporaries, to be losing.

But this is not to say that Clemens had suddenly thought his way out of the dilemma. We have only to read his later work to see that he had not. What he did was to discover a way around it—a sublimation, as it were, of the conflict. The discovery came to him not conceptually, but spontaneously, in the practice of his art. For all the intricacies of a problem at once psychological, philosophical, and historical, the "solution" was simple and primarily aesthetic. In one sense it consisted merely of placing himself behind the mask of a narrator for whom the problem did not exist. This device, however, was only the first step; it provided a point of view—an ideological, not an aesthetic truth. The more difficult task was to endow this viewpoint, for which there existed no appropriate style, with literary vitality, with a semblance of life. He accomplished this by maintaining a fidelity to the experience of his narrator so disciplined that it cut beneath established conventions. The point of view became a style. Unfortunately, Clemens did not realize the dimensions of this achievement. But since his time many of our best writers, responding to pressures not unlike those he felt, have recognized the usefulness of the mode he devised.

Nor was the vernacular style useful only to depict landscape. Most of the book is as fine, in various ways, as the sunrise passage. Clemens not only fashioned a vital style, he sustained it. Its merit was the product not so much of technical virtuosity as of the kinds of truth to which it gave access. *Adventures of Huckleberry Finn* contains insights neither a pilot nor a passenger could have had. It is a book, rare in our literature, which manages to suggest the lovely possibilities of life in America without neglecting its terrors.

## Mark Twain: The Three Dawns

I

When Tom awoke in the morning, he wondered where he was. He sat up and rubbed his eyes and looked around. Then he comprehended. It was the cool gray dawn, and there was a delicious sense of repose and peace in the deep pervading calm and silence of the woods. Not a leaf stirred; not a sound obtruded upon great Nature's meditation. Beaded dewdrops stood upon the leaves and grasses. A white layer of ashes covered the fire, and a thin blue breath of smoke rose straight into the air. Joe and Huck still slept.

Now, far away in the woods a bird called; another answered; presently the hammering of a woodpecker was heard. Gradually the cool dim gray of the morning whitened, and as gradually sounds multiplied and life manifested itself. The marvel of Nature shaking off sleep and going to work unfolded itself to the musing boy. A little green worm came crawling over a dewy leaf, lifting two-thirds of his body into the air from time to time and "sniffing around," then proceeding again—for he was measuring, Tom said; and when the worm approached him, of its own accord, he sat as still at a stone, with his hopes rising and falling, by turns, as the creature still came toward him or seemed inclined to go elsewhere; and when at last it considered a painful moment with its curved body in the air and then came decisively down upon Tom's leg and began a journey over him, his whole heart was glad—for that meant that he was going to have a new suit of clothes—without the shadow of a doubt a gaudy piratical uniform. Now a procession of ants appeared, from nowhere in particular, and when about their labors; one struggled manfully by with a dead spider five times as big as itself in its arms, and lugged it straight up a tree-trunk. A brown spotted lady-bug climbed the dizzy height of a grass-blade, and Tom bent down close to it and said, "Lady-bug, lady-bug, fly away home, your house is on fire, your children's alone," and she took wing and went off to see about it—which did not surprise the boy, for he knew of old that this insect was credulous about conflagrations, and he had practised upon its simplicity more than once. A tumblebug came next, heaving sturdily at its ball, and Tom touched the creature, to see it shut its legs against its body and pretend to be dead. The birds were fairly rioting by this time. A catbird, the Northern mocker, lit in a tree over Tom's head, and trilled out her imitations of her neighbors in a rapture of enjoyment; then a shrill jay swept down, a flash of blue flame, and stopped on a twig almost within the boy's reach, cocked his head to one side and eyed the strangers with a consuming curiosity; a gray squirrel and a big fellow of the "fox" kind came scurrying along, sitting up at intervals to inspect and chatter at the boys, for the wild things had probably never seen a human being before and scarcely knew whether to be afraid or not. All Nature was wide awake and stirring, now; long lances of sunlight pierced down through the dense foliage far and near, and a few butterflies came fluttering upon the scene.—*The Adventures of Tom Sawyer*, Chapter XIV.


II

I had myself called with the four-o'clock watch, mornings, for one cannot see too many summer sunrises on the Mississippi. They are enchanting. First, there is the eloquence of silence; for a deep hush broods everywhere. Next, there is the haunting sense of loneliness, isolation, remoteness from the worry and bustle of the world. The dawn creeps in stealthily; the solid walls of black forest soften to gray, and vast stretches of the river open up and reveal themselves; the water is glass-smooth, gives off spectral little wreaths of white mist, there is not the faintest breath of wind, nor stir of leaf; the tranquillity is profound and infinitely satisfying. Then a bird pipes up, another follows, and soon the pipings develop into a jubilant riot of music. You see none of the birds; you simply move through an atmosphere of song which seems to sing itself. When the light has become a little stronger, you have one of the fairest and softest pictures imaginable. You have the intense green of the massed and crowded foliage near by; you see it paling shade by shade in front

of you; upon the next projecting cape, a mile off or more, the tint
has lightened to the tender young green of spring; the cape beyond
that one has almost lost color, and the furthest one, miles away under the horizon, sleeps upon the water a mere dim vapor, and hardly
separable from the sky above it and about it. And all this stretch of
river is a mirror, and you have the shadowy reflections of the leafage
and the curving shores and the receding capes pictured in it. Well,
that is all beautiful; soft and rich and beautiful; and when the sun
gets well up, and distributes a pink flush here and a powder of gold
yonder and a purple haze where it will yield the best effect, you
grant that you have seen something that is worth remembering.—*Life
on the Mississippi,* Chapter **XXX**.

III

Two or three days and nights went by; I reckon I might say they
swum by, they slid along so quiet and smooth and lovely. Here is the
way we put in the time. It was a monstrous big river down there—
sometimes a mile and a half wide; we run nights, and laid up and
hid daytimes; soon as night was most gone we stopped navigating
and tied up—nearly always in the dead water under a towhead; and
then cut young cottonwoods and willows, and hid the raft with
them. Then we set out the lines. Next we slid into the river and had
a swim, so as to freshen up and cool off; then we set down on the
sandy bottom where the water was about knee-deep, and watched
the daylight come. Not a sound anywheres—perfectly still—just like
the whole world was asleep, only sometimes the bullfrogs a-cluttering, maybe. The first thing to see, looking away over the water, was
a kind of dull line—that was the woods on t'other side; you couldn't
make nothing else out; then a pale place in the sky; then more paleness spreading around; then the river softened up away off, and
warn't black any more, but gray; you could see little dark spots
drifting along ever so far away—trading-scows, and such things; and
long black streaks—rafts; sometimes you could hear a sweep screak-
ing; or jumbled-up voices, it was so still, and sounds come so far;
and by and by you could see a streak on the water which you know
by the look of the streak that there's a snag there in a swift current
which breaks on it and makes that streak look that way; and you see
the mist curl up off of the water, and the east reddens up, and the
river, and you make out a log cabin in the edge of the woods, away

on the bank on t'other side of the river, being a wood-yard, likely,
and piled by them cheats so you can throw a dog through it anywheres; then the nice breeze springs up, and comes fanning you from
over there, so cool and fresh and sweet to smell on account of the
woods and the flowers; but sometimes not that way, because they've
left dead fish laying around, gars and such, and they do get pretty
rank; and next you've got the full day, and everything smiling in
the sun, and the song-birds just going it!

A little smoke couldn't be noticed now, so we would take some
fish off of the lines and cook up a hot breakfast. And afterwards we
would watch the lonesomeness of the river, and kind of lazy along,
and by and by lazy off to sleep. Wake up by and by, and look to see
what done it, and maybe see a steamboat coughing along up-stream,
so far off towards the other side you couldn't tell nothing about her
only whether she was a stern-wheel or side-wheel; then for about an
hour there wouldn't be nothing to hear nor nothing to see—just solid
lonesomeness. . . .

Sometimes we'd have that whole river all to ourselves for the
longest time. Yonder was the banks and the islands, across the
water; and maybe a spark—which was a candle in a cabin window;
and sometimes on the water you could see a spark or two—on a raft
or a scow, you know; and maybe you could hear a fiddle or a song
coming over from one of them crafts. It's lovely to live on a raft.
We had the sky up there, all speckled with stars, and we used to lay
on our backs and look up at them, and discuss about whether they
was made or only just happened. Jim he allowed they was made,
but I allowed they happened; I judged it would have took too long
to *make* so many. Jim said the moon could 'a' *laid* them; well, that
looked kind of reasonable, so I didn't say nothing against it, because
I've seen a frog lay most as many, so of course it could be done. We
used to watch the stars that fell, too, and see them streak down. Jim
allowed they'd got spoiled and was hove out of the nest.—*Adventures of Huckleberry Finn,* Chapter XIX.

# Mr. Eliot, Mr. Trilling, and *Huckleberry Finn*

> In the losing battle that the plot fights with the characters, it often takes a cowardly revenge. Nearly all novels are feeble at the end. This is because the plot requires to be wound up. Why is this necessary? Why is there not a convention which allows a novelist to stop as soon as he feels muddled or bored? Alas, he has to round things off, and usually the characters go dead while he is at work, and our final impression of them is through deadness.
>
> E. M. FORSTER

The *Adventures of Huckleberry Finn* has not always occupied its present high place in the canon of American literature. When it was first published in 1885, the book disturbed and offended many reviewers, particularly spokesmen for the genteel tradition.[1] In fact, a fairly accurate inventory of the narrow standards of such critics might be made simply by listing epithets they applied to Clemens's novel. They called it vulgar, rough, inelegant, irreverent, coarse, semi-obscene, trashy, and vicious.[2] So much for them. Today (we like to think) we know the true worth of the book. Everyone now agrees that *Huckleberry Finn* is

1. I use the term "genteel tradition" as George Santayana characterized it in his address "The Genteel Tradition in American Philosophy," first delivered in 1911 and published the following year in his *Winds of Doctrine*. Santayana described the genteel tradition as an "old mentality" inherited from Europe. It consists of the various dilutions of Christian theology and morality, as in transcendentalism—a fastidious and stale philosophy of life no longer revelant to the thought and activities of the United States. "America," he said, "is a young country with an old mentality." (Later references to Santayana also refer to this essay.)
2. For an account of the first reviews, see A. L. Vogelback, "The Publication and Reception of *Huckleberry Finn* in America," *American Literature,* 11 (Nov. 1939), 260-72.

a masterpiece: it is probably the one book in our literature about which highbrows and lowbrows can agree. Our most serious critics praise it. Nevertheless, a close look at what two of the best among them have recently written will likewise reveal, I believe, serious weaknesses in current criticism. Today the problem of evaluating the book is as much obscured by unqualified praise as it once was by parochial hostility.

I have in mind essays by Lionel Trilling and T. S. Eliot.[3] Both praise the book, but in praising it both feel obligated to say something in justification of what so many readers have felt to be its great flaw: the disappointing "ending," the episode which begins when Huck arrives at the Phelps place and Tom Sawyer reappears. There are good reasons why Mr. Trilling and Mr. Eliot should feel the need to face this issue. From the point of view of scope alone, more is involved than the mere "ending"; the episode comprises almost one-fifth of the text. The problem, in any case, is unavoidable. I have discussed *Huckleberry Finn* in courses with hundreds of college students, and I have found only a handful who did not confess their dissatisfaction with the extravagant mock rescue of Nigger Jim and the denouement itself. The same question always comes up: "What went wrong with Twain's novel?" Ernest Hemingway has an answer. After his celebrated remark to the effect that all modern American literature stems from *Huckleberry Finn,* Hemingway adds: "If you read it you must stop where the Nigger Jim is stolen from the boys. That is the real end. The rest is cheating." Even Bernard De Voto, whose wholehearted commitment to Clemens's genius is well known, has said of the ending that "in the whole reach of the English novel there is no more abrupt or more chilling descent."[4] Mr. Trilling and Mr. Eliot do not agree. They both attempt, and on similar grounds, to explain and defend the conclusion.

Of the two, Mr. Trilling makes the more moderate claim for Clemens's novel. He does admit that there is a "falling off" at the end; nevertheless he supports the episode as having "a certain formal aptness." Mr. Eliot's approval is without serious qualification. He al-

---

3. Eliot's essay is the introduction to the edition of *Huckleberry Finn* published by Chanticleer Press, New York, 1950. Trilling's is the introduction to an edition of the novel published by Rinehart (New York, 1948), and later reprinted in his *The Liberal Imagination* (New York: Viking, 1950).

4. *Mark Twain at Work* (Cambridge: Harvard University Press, 1942), p. 92.

lows no objections, asserts that "it is right that the mood of the end of the book should bring us back to the beginning." I mean later to discuss their views in some detail, but here it is only necessary to note that both critics see the problem as one of form. And so it is. Like many questions of form in literature, however, this one is not finally separable from a question of "content," of value, or, if you will, of moral insight. To bring *Huckleberry Finn* to a satisfactory close, Clemens had to do more than find a neat device for ending a story. His problem, though it may never have occurred to him, was to invent an action capable of placing in focus the meaning of the journey down the Mississippi.

I believe that the ending of *Huckleberry Finn* makes so many readers uneasy because they rightly sense that it jeopardizes the significance of the entire novel. To take seriously what happens at the Phelps farm is to take lightly the entire downstream journey. What is the meaning of the journey? With this question all discussion of *Huckleberry Finn* must begin. It is true that the voyage down the river has many aspects of a boy's idyl. We owe much of its hold upon our imagination to the enchanting image of the raft's unhurried drift with the current. The leisure, the absence of constraint, the beauty of the river—all these things delight us. "It's lovely to live on a raft." And the multitudinous life of the great valley we see through Huck's eyes has a fascination of its own. Then, of course, there is humor—laughter so spontaneous, so free of the bitterness present almost everywhere in American humor that readers often forget how grim a spectacle of human existence Huck contemplates. Humor in this novel flows from a bright joy of life as remote from our world as living on a raft.

Yet along with the idyllic and the epical and the funny in *Huckleberry Finn,* there is a coil of meaning which does for the disparate elements of the novel what a spring does for a watch. The meaning is not in the least obscure. It is made explicit again and again. The very words with which Clemens launches Huck and Jim upon their voyage indicate that theirs is not a boy's lark but a quest for freedom. From the electrifying moment when Huck comes back to Jackson's Island and rouses Jim with the news that a search party is on the way, we are meant to believe that Huck is enlisted in the cause of freedom. "Git up and hump yourself, Jim!" he cries. "There ain't a minute to lose.

They're after us!" What particularly counts here is the *us*. No one is after Huck; no one but Jim knows he is alive. In that small word Clemens compresses the exhilarating power of Huck's instinctive humanity. His unpremeditated identification with Jim's flight from slavery is an unforgettable moment in American experience, and it may be said at once that any culmination of the journey which detracts from the urgency and dignity with which it begins will necessarily be unsatisfactory. Huck realizes this himself, and says so when, much later, he comes back to the raft after discovering that the Duke and the King have sold Jim:

> "After all this long journey . . . here it was all come to nothing, everything all busted up and ruined, because they could have the heart to serve Jim such a trick as that, and make him a slave again all his life, and amongst strangers, too, for forty dirty dollars."

Huck knows that the journey will have been a failure unless it takes Jim to freedom. It is true that we do discover, in the end, that Jim is free, but we also find out that the journey was not the means by which he finally reached freedom.

The most obvious thing wrong with the end, then, is the flimsy contrivance by which Clemens frees Jim. In the end we discover not only that Jim has been a free man for two months, but that his freedom has been granted by old Miss Watson. If this were only a mechanical device for terminating the action, it might not call for much comment. But it is more than that: it is a significant clue to the import of the last ten chapters. Remember who Miss Watson is. She is the Widow's sister whom Huck introduces in the first pages of the novel. It is she who keeps "pecking" at Huck, who tries to teach him to spell and to pray and to keep his feet off the furniture. She is an ardent proselytizer for piety and good manners, and her greed provides the occasion for the journey in the first place. She is Jim's owner, and he decides to flee only when he realizes that she is about to break her word (she cannot resist a slave trader's offer of eight hundred dollars) and sell him down the river away from his family.

Miss Watson, in short, is the Enemy. If we except a predilection for physical violence, she exhibits all the outstanding traits of the valley society. She pronounces the polite lies of civilization that suffocate Huck's spirit. The freedom which Jim seeks, and which Huck and Jim temporarily enjoy aboard the raft, is accordingly freedom *from* everything for which Miss Watson stands. Indeed, the very intensity of the novel derives from the discordance between the aspirations of the fugitives and the respectable code for which she is a spokesperson. Therefore, her regeneration, of which the deathbed freeing of Jim is the unconvincing sign, hints a resolution of the novel's essential conflict. Perhaps because this device most transparently reveals that shift in point of view which he could not avoid, and which is less easily discerned elsewhere in the concluding chapters, Clemens plays it down. He makes little attempt to account for Miss Watson's change of heart, a change particularly surprising in view of Jim's brazen escape. Had Clemens given this episode a dramatic emphasis appropriate to its function, Miss Watson's bestowal of freedom upon Jim would have proclaimed what the rest of the ending actually accomplishes—a vindication of persons and attitudes Huck and Jim had symbolically repudiated when they set forth downstream.

It may be said, and with some justice, that a reading of the ending as a virtual reversal of meanings implicit in the rest of the novel misses the point—that I have taken the final episode too seriously. I agree that Clemens certainly did not intend us to read it so solemnly. The ending, one might contend, is simply a burlesque upon Tom's taste for literary romance. Surely the tone of the episode is familiar to readers of Mark Twain. The preposterous monkey business attendant upon Jim's "rescue," the careless improvisation, the nonchalant disregard for commonsense plausibility—all these things should not surprise readers of Twain or any low comedy in the tradition of "Western humor." However, the trouble is, first, that the ending hardly comes off as burlesque: it is *too* fanciful, *too* extravagant; and it is tedious. For example, to provide a "gaudy" atmosphere for the escape, Huck and Tom catch a couple of dozen snakes. Then the snakes escape.

> "No, there warn't no real scarcity of snakes about the house for a considerable spell. You'd see them dripping from the rafters and places every now and then; and they generly landed in your plate, or down the back of your neck. . . ."

Even if this were *good* burlesque, which it is not, what is it doing here? It is out of keeping; the slapstick tone jars with the underlying seriousness of the voyage.

*Huckleberry Finn* is a masterpiece because it brings Western humor to perfection and yet transcends the narrow limits of its conventions. But the ending does not. During the final extravaganza we are forced to put aside many of the mature emotions evoked earlier by the vivid rendering of Jim's fear of capture, the tenderness of Huck's and Jim's regard for each other, and Huck's excruciating moments of wavering between honesty and respectability. None of these emotions are called forth by the anticlimatic final sequence. I do not mean to suggest that the inclusion of low comedy per se is a flaw in *Huckleberry Finn*. One does not object to the shenanigans of the rogues; there is ample precedent for the place of extravagant humor even in works of high seriousness. But here the case differs from most which come to mind: the major characters themselves are forced to play low comedy roles. Moreover, the most serious motive in the novel, Jim's yearning for freedom, is made the object of nonsense. The conclusion, in short, is farce, but the rest of the novel is not.

That Clemens reverts in the end to the conventional manner of Western low comedy is most evident in what happens to the principals. Huck and Jim become comic characters; that is much more serious ground for dissatisfaction than the unexplained regeneration of Miss Watson. Remember that Huck has grown in stature throughout the journey. By the time he arrives at the Phelps place, he is not the boy who had been playing robbers with Tom's gang in St. Petersburg the summer before. All he has seen and felt since he parted with Tom has deepened his knowledge of human nature and of himself. Clemens makes a point of Huck's development in two scenes which occur just before he meets Tom again. The first describes Huck's final capitulation to his own sense of right and wrong: "All right, then, I'll *go* to Hell." This is the climactic moment in the ripening of his self-knowledge. Shortly afterward, when he comes upon a mob riding the Duke and the King out of town on a rail, we are given his most memorable insight into the nature of man. Although these rogues had subjected Huck to every indignity, what he sees provokes this precocious comment:

"Well, it made me sick to see it; and I was sorry for them poor pitiful rascals, it seemed like I couldn't ever feel any hardness against
them any more in the world. It was a dreadful thing to see. Human
beings can be awful cruel to one another."

The sign of Huck's maturity here is neither the compassion nor the
skepticism, for both had been marks of his personality from the first.
Rather, the special quality of these reflections is the extraordinary
combination of the two, a mature blending of his instinctive suspicion
of human motives with his capacity for pity.

But at this point Tom reappears. Soon Huck has fallen almost completely under his sway once more, and we are asked to believe that the
boy who felt pity for the rogues is now capable of making Jim's capture
the occasion for a game. He becomes Tom's helpless accomplice, submissive and gullible. No wonder that Clemens has Huck remark, when
Huck first realizes Aunt Sally has mistaken him for Tom, that "it was
like being born again." Exactly. In the end, Huck regresses to the subordinate role in which he had first appeared in *The Adventures of Tom
Sawyer*. Most of those traits which made him so appealing a hero now
disappear. He had never, for example, found pain or misfortune amusing. At the circus, when a clown disguised as a drunk took a precarious
ride on a prancing horse, the crowd loved the excitement and danger;
"it warn't funny to me, though," said Huck. But now, in the end, he
submits in awe to Tom's notion of what is amusing. To satisfy Tom's
hunger for adventure he makes himself a party to sport which aggra-
vates Jim's misery.

It should be added at once that Jim doesn't mind too much. The fact
is that he has undergone a similar transformation. On the raft he was an
individual, man enough to denounce Huck when Huck made him the
victim of a practical joke. In the closing episode, however, we lose sight
of Jim in the maze of farcical invention. He ceases to be a man. He
allows Huck and "Mars Tom" to fill his hut with rats and snakes," and
every time a rat bit Jim he would get up and write a line in his journal
whilst the ink was fresh." This creature who bleeds ink and feels no
pain is something less than human. He has been made over in the
image of a flat stereotype: the submissive stage-Negro. These antics

divest Jim, as well as Huck, of much of his dignity and individuality.[5]

What I have been saying is that the flimsy devices of plot, the discordant farcical tone, and the disintegration of the major characters all betray the failure of the ending. These are not aspects merely of form in a technical sense, but of meaning. For that matter, I would maintain that this book has little or no formal unity independent of the joint purpose of Huck and Jim. What components of the novel, we may ask, provide the continuity which links one adventure with another? The most important is the unifying consciousness of Huck, the narrator, and the fact that we follow the same principals through the entire string of adventures. Events, moreover, occur in a temporal sequence. Then there is the river; after each adventure Huck and Jim return to the raft and the river. Both Mr. Trilling and Mr. Eliot speak eloquently of the river as a source of unity, and they refer to the river as a god. Mr. Trilling says that Huck is "the servant of the river-god." Mr. Eliot puts it this way: "The River gives the book its form. But for the River, the book might be only a sequence of adventures with a happy ending." This seems to me an extravagant view of the function of the neutral agency of the river. Clemens had a knowledgeable respect for the Mississippi and, without sanctifying it, was able to provide excellent reasons for Huck's and Jim's intense relation with it. It is a source of food and beauty and terror and serenity of mind. But above all, it provides motion; it is the means by which Huck and Jim move away from a menacing civilization. They return to the river to continue their journey. The river cannot, does not, supply purpose. That purpose is a facet of their consciousness, and without the motive of escape from society, *Huckleberry Finn* would indeed "be only a sequence of adventures." Mr. Eliot's remark indicates how lightly he takes the quest for freedom. His somewhat fanciful exaggeration of the river's role is of a piece with his neglect of the theme at the novel's center.

That theme is heightened by the juxtaposition of sharp images of contrasting social orders: the microcosmic community Huck and Jim establish aboard the raft and the actual society which exists along the Mississippi's banks. The two are separated by the river, the road to

5. For these observations on the transformation of Jim in the closing episodes, I am indebted to the excellent unpublished essay by Mr. Chadwick Hansen on the subject of Clemens and Western humor.

freedom upon which Huck and Jim must travel. Huck tells us what the river means to them when, after the Wilks episode, he and Jim once again shove their raft into the current: "It *did* seem so good to be free again and all by ourselves on the big river, and nobody to bother us." The river is indifferent. But its sphere is relatively uncontaminated by the civilization they flee, and so the river allows Huck and Jim some measure of freedom at once, the moment they set foot on Jackson's Island or the raft. Only on the island and the raft do they have a chance to practice that kind of brotherhood of which they are capable. "Other places do seem so cramped and smothery," Huck explains, "but a raft don't. You feel mighty free and easy and comfortable on a raft." The main thing is freedom.

On the raft the escaped slave and the white boy try to practice their code: "What you want, above all things, on a raft, is for everybody to be satisfied, and feel right and kind towards the others." This simple credo constitutes the paramount affirmation of *Adventures of Huckleberry Finn,* and it obliquely aims a devastating criticism at the existing social order. It is a creed which Huck and Jim bring to the river. It neither emanates from nature nor is it addressed to nature. Therefore I do not see that it means much to talk about the river as a god in this novel. The river's connection with this high aspiration for man is that it provides a means of escape, a place where the code can be tested. The truly profound meanings of the novel are generated by the impingement of the actual world of slavery, feuds, lynching, murder, and a spurious Christian morality upon the ideal of the raft. The result is a tension which somehow demands release in the novel's ending.

But Clemens was unable to effect this release and at the same time control the central theme. The unhappy truth about the ending of *Huckleberry Finn* is that the author, having revealed the tawdry nature of the culture of the great valley, yielded to its essential complacency. The general tenor of the closing scenes, to which the token regeneration of Miss Watson is merely one superficial clue, amounts to just that. In fact, this entire reading of *Huckleberry Finn* merely confirms the brilliant insight of George Santayana, who many years ago spoke of American humorists, of whom he considered Mark Twain an outstanding representative, as having only "half escaped" the genteel tradition. Santayana meant that men like Clemens were able to "point to what contradicts it in the facts; but not in order to abandon the genteel tradition, for they have nothing solid to put in its place." This seems to me the real key to the failure of *Huckleberry Finn.* Clemens had presented the contrast between the two social orders but could not, or would not, accept the tragic fact that the one he had rejected was an image of solid reality and the other an ecstatic dream. Instead he gives us the cozy reunion with Aunt Polly in a scene fairly bursting with approbation of the entire family, the Phelpses included.

Like Miss Watson, the Phelpses are almost perfect specimens of the dominant culture. They are kind to their friends and relatives; they have no taste for violence; they are capable of devoting themselves to their spectacular dinners while they keep Jim locked in the little hut down by the ash hopper, with its lone window boarded up. (Of course Aunt Sally visits Jim to see if he is "comfortable," and Uncle Silas comes in "to pray with him.") These people, with their comfortable Sunday-dinner conviviality and the runaway slave padlocked nearby, are reminiscent of those solid German citizens we have heard about in our time who tried to maintain a similarly *gemütlich* way of life within virtual earshot of Buchenwald. I do not mean to imply that Clemens was unaware of the shabby morality of such people. After the abortive escape of Jim, when Tom asks about him, Aunt Sally replies: "Him? . . . the runaway nigger? . . . They've got him back, safe and sound, and he's in the cabin again, on bread and water, and loaded down with chains, till he's claimed or sold!" Clemens understood people like the Phelpses, but nevertheless he was forced to rely upon them to provide his happy ending. The satisfactory outcome of Jim's quest for freedom must be attributed to the benevolence of the very people whose inhumanity first made it necessary.

But to return to the contention of Mr. Trilling and Mr. Eliot that the ending is more or less satisfactory after all. As I have said, Mr. Trilling approves of the "formal aptness" of the conclusion. He says that "some device is needed to permit Huck to return to his anonymity, to give up the role of hero," and that therefore "nothing could serve better than the mind of Tom Sawyer with its literary furnishings, its conscious romantic desire for experience and the hero's part, and its ingenious schematization of life. . . ." Though more detailed, this is essentially akin to Mr. Eliot's blunt assertion that "it is right that the

mood at the end of the book should bring us back to that of the beginning." I submit that it is wrong for the end of the book to bring us
back to that mood. The mood of the beginning of *Huckleberry Finn*
is the mood of Huck's attempt to accommodate himself to the ways of
St. Petersburg. It is the mood of the end of *The Adventures of Tom
Sawyer,* when the boys had been acclaimed heroes, and when Huck
was accepted as a candidate for respectability. That is the state in which
we find him at the beginning of *Huckleberry Finn*. But Huck cannot
stand the new way of life, and his mood gradually shifts to the mood
of rebellion which dominates the novel until he meets Tom again. At
first, in the second chapter, we see him still eager to be accepted by the
nice boys of the town. Tom leads the gang in re-enacting adventures he
has culled from books, but gradually Huck's pragmatic turn of mind
gets him in trouble. He has little tolerance for Tom's brand of make-
believe. He irritates Tom. Tom calls him a "numbskull," and finally
Huck throws up the whole business:

> "So then I judged that all that stuff was only just one of Tom Saw-
> yer's lies. I reckoned he believed in the A-rabs and the elephants, but
> as for me I think different. It had all the marks of a Sunday school."

With this statement, which ends the third chapter, Huck parts company with Tom. The fact is that Huck has rejected Tom's romanticizing
of experience; moreover, he has rejected it as part of the larger pattern
of society's make-believe, typified by Sunday school. But if he cannot
accept Tom's harmless fantasies about the A-rabs, how are we to believe
that a year later Huck is capable of awestruck submission to the far
more extravagant fantasies with which Tom invests the mock rescue of
Jim?

After Huck's escape from his "pap," the drift of the action, like
that of the Mississippi's current, is *away* from St. Petersburg. Huck
leaves Tom and the A-rabs behind, along with the Widow, Miss Watson, and all the pseudo-religious ritual in which nice boys must partake.
The return, in the end, to the mood of the beginning therefore means
defeat—Huck's defeat; to return to that mood *joyously* is to portray
defeat in the guise of victory.

Mr. Eliot and Mr. Trilling deny this. The overriding consideration
for them is form—form which seems largely to mean symmetry of

structure. It is fitting, Mr. Eliot maintains, that the book should come full circle and bring Huck once more under Tom's sway. Why? Because it begins that way. But it seems to me that such structural unity is *imposed* upon the novel, and therefore is meretricious. It is a jerry-built structure, achieved only by sacrifice of characters and theme. Here the controlling principle of form apparently is unity, but unfortunately a unity much too superficially conceived. Structure, after all, is only one element—indeed, one of the more mechanical elements—of unity. A unified work must surely manifest coherence of meaning and clear development of theme, yet the ending of *Huckleberry Finn* blurs both. The eagerness of Mr. Eliot and Mr. Trilling to justify the ending is symptomatic of that absolutist impulse of our critics to find reasons, once a work has been admitted to the highest canon of literary reputability, for admiring every bit of it.

What is perhaps most striking about these judgments of Mr. Eliot's and Mr. Trilling's is that they are patently out of harmony with the basic standards of both critics. For one thing, both men hold far more complex ideas of the nature of literary unity than their comments upon *Huckleberry Finn* would suggest. For another, both critics are essentially moralists, yet here we find them turning away from a moral issue in order to praise a dubious structural unity. Their efforts to explain away the flaw in Clemens's novel suffer from a certain narrowness surprising to anyone who knows their work. These facts suggest that we may be in the presence of a tendency in contemporary criticism which the critics themselves do not fully recognize.

Is there an explanation? How does it happen that two of our most respected critics should seem to treat so lightly the glaring lapse of moral imagination in *Huckleberry Finn?* Perhaps—and I stress the conjectural nature of what I am saying—perhaps the kind of moral issue raised by *Huckleberry Finn* is not the kind of moral issue to which today's criticism readily addresses itself. Today our critics, no less than our novelists and poets, are most sensitively attuned to moral problems which arise in the sphere of individual behavior. They are deeply aware of sin, individual infractions of our culture's Christian ethic. But my impression is that they are, possibly because of the strength of the reaction against the mechanical sociological criticism of the thirties, less sensitive to questions of what might be called social or political morality.

By social or political morality I refer to the values implicit in a social system, values which may be quite distinct from the personal morality of any given individual within the society. Now *Adventures of Huckleberry Finn,* like all novels, deals with the behavior of individuals. But one mark of Clemens's greatness is his deft presentation of the disparity between what people do when they behave as individuals and what they do when forced into roles imposed on them by society. Take, for example, Aunt Sally and Uncle Silas Phelps, who consider themselves Christians, who are by impulse generous and humane, but who happen also to be staunch upholders of certain degrading and inhuman social institutions. When they are confronted with an escaped slave, the imperatives of social morality outweigh all pious professions.

The conflict between what people think they stand for and what social pressure forces them to do is central to the novel. It is present to the mind of Huck and, indeed, accounts for his most serious inner conflicts. He knows how he feels about Jim, but he also knows what he is expected to do about Jim. This division within his mind corresponds to the division of the novel's moral terrain into the areas represented by the raft on the one hand and society on the other. His victory over his "yaller dog" conscience therefore assumes heroic size: it is a victory over the prevailing morality. But the last fifth of the novel has the effect of diminishing the importance and uniqueness of Huck's victory. We are asked to assume that somehow freedom can be achieved in spite of the crippling power of what I have called the social morality. Consequently the less importance we attach to that force as it operates in the novel, the more acceptable the ending becomes.

Moreover, the idea of freedom, which Mr. Eliot and Mr. Trilling seem to slight, takes on its full significance only when we acknowledge the power which society exerts over the minds of men in the world of *Huckleberry Finn.* For freedom in this book specifically means freedom from society and its imperatives. This is not the traditional Christian conception of freedom. Huck and Jim seek freedom not from a burden of individual guilt and sin, but from social constraint. That is to say, evil in *Huckleberry Finn* is the product of civilization, and if this is indicative of Clemens's rather too simple view of human nature, nevertheless the fact is that Huck, when he can divest himself of the taint of social conditioning (as in the incantatory account of sunrise on the river), is entirely free of anxiety and guilt. The only guilt he actually knows arises from infractions of a social code. (The guilt he feels after playing the prank on Jim stems from his betrayal of the law of the raft.) Huck's and Jim's creed is secular. Its object is harmony among men, and so Huck is not much concerned with his own salvation. He repeatedly renounces prayer in favor of pragmatic solutions to his problems. In other words, the central insights of the novel belong to the tradition of the Enlightenment. The meaning of the quest itself is hardly reconcilable with that conception of human nature embodied in the myth of original sin. In view of the current fashion of reaffirming man's innate depravity, it is perhaps not surprising to find the virtues of *Huckleberry Finn* attributed not to its meaning but to its form.

But "if this was not the right ending for the book," Mr. Eliot asks, "what ending would have been right?" Although this question places the critic in an awkward position (he is not always equipped to re-write what he criticizes), there are some things which may justifiably be said about the "right" ending of *Huckleberry Finn*. It may be legitimate, even if presumptuous, to indicate certain conditions which a hypothetical ending would have to satisfy if it were to be congruent with the rest of the novel. If the conclusion is not to be something merely tacked on to close the action, then its broad outline must be immanent in the body of the work.

It is surely reasonable to ask that the conclusion provide a plausible outcome to the quest. Yet freedom, in the ecstatic sense that Huck and Jim knew it aboard the raft, was hardly to be had in the Mississippi Valley in the 1840s, or, for that matter, in any other known human society. A satisfactory ending would inevitably cause the reader some frustration. That Clemens felt such disappointment to be inevitable is borne out by an examination of the novel's clear, if unconscious, symbolic pattern. Consider, for instance, the inferences to be drawn from the book's geography. The river, to whose current Huck and Jim entrust themselves, actually carries them to the heart of slave territory. Once the raft passes Cairo, the quest is virtually doomed. Until the steamboat smashes the raft, we are kept in a state of anxiety about Jim's escape. (It may be significant that at this point Clemens found himself unable to continue work on the manuscript, and put it aside for several years.) Beyond Cairo, Clemens allows the intensity of that anxiety to diminish, and it is probably no accident that the fainter it becomes, the more he falls back upon the devices of low comedy. Huck and Jim make no serious effort to turn north, and there are times (during the Wilks episode) when Clemens allows Huck to forget all about Jim. It is as if the author, anticipating the dilemma he had finally to face, instinctively dissipated the power of his major theme.

Consider, too, the circumscribed nature of the raft as a means of moving toward freedom. The raft lacks power and maneuverability. It can only move easily with the current—southward into slave country. Nor can it evade the mechanized power of the steamboat. These impotencies of the raft correspond to the innocent helplessness of its occupants. Unresisted, the rogues invade and take over the raft. Though it is the symbolic focus of the novel's central affirmations, the raft provides an uncertain and indeed precarious mode of traveling toward freedom. This seems another confirmation of Santayana's perception. To say that Clemens only half escaped the genteel tradition is not to say that he failed to note any of the creed's inadequacies, but rather that he had "nothing solid" to put in its place. The raft patently was not capable of carrying the burden of hope Clemens placed upon it.[6] (Whether this is to be attributed to the nature of his vision or to the actual state of American society in the nineteenth century is another interesting question.) In any case, the geography of the novel, the raft's powerlessness, the goodness and vulnerability of Huck and Jim, all prefigure a conclusion quite different in tone from that which Clemens gave us. These facts constitute what Hart Crane might have called the novel's "logic of metaphor," and this logic—probably inadvertent—actually takes us to the underlying meaning of *Adventures of Huckleberry Finn*. Through the symbols we reach a truth which the ending obscures: the quest cannot succeed.

Fortunately, Clemens broke through to this truth in the novel's last sentences:

6. Gladys Bellamy (*Mark Twain as a Literary Artist*, Norman: University of Oklahoma Press, 1950, p. 221) has noted the insubstantial, dream-like quality of the image of the raft. Clemens thus discusses travel by raft in *A Tramp Abroad:* "the motion of the raft is . . . gentle, and gliding, and smooth, and noiseless; it calms down all feverish activities, it soothes to sleep all nervous . . . impatience; under its restful influence all the troubles and vexations and sorrows that harass the mind vanish away, and existence becomes a dream . . . a deep and tranquil ecstasy."

"But I reckon I got to light out for the territory ahead of the rest, because Aunt Sally she's going to adopt me and civilize me, and I can't stand it. I been there before."

Mr. Eliot properly praises this as "the only possible concluding sentence." But one sentence can hardly be advanced, as Mr. Eliot advances this one, to support the rightness of ten chapters. Moreover, if this sentence is right, then the rest of the conclusion is wrong, for its meaning clashes with that of the final burlesque. Huck's decision to go west ahead of the inescapable advance of civilization is a confession of defeat. It means that the raft is to be abandoned. On the other hand, the jubilation of the family reunion and the proclaiming of Jim's freedom create a quite different mood. The tone, except for these last words, is one of unclouded success. I believe this is the source of the almost universal dissatisfaction with the conclusion. One can hardly forget that a bloody civil war did not resolve the issue.

Should Clemens have made Huck a tragic hero? Both Mr. Eliot and Mr. Trilling argue that that would have been a mistake, and they are very probably correct. But between the ending as we have it and tragedy in the fullest sense, there was vast room for invention. Clemens might have contrived an action which left Jim's fate as much in doubt as Huck's. Such an ending would have allowed us to assume that the principals were defeated but alive, and the quest unsuccessful but not abandoned. This, after all, would have been consonant with the symbols, the characters, and the theme as Clemens had created them—and with history.

Clemens did not acknowledge the truth his novel contained. He had taken hold of a situation in which a partial defeat was inevitable, but he was unable to—or unaware of the need to—give imaginative substance to that fact. If an illusion of success was indispensable, where was it to come from? Obviously Huck and Jim could not succeed by their own efforts. At this point Clemens, having only half escaped the genteel tradition, one of whose preeminent characteristics was an optimism undaunted by disheartening truth, returned to it. *Why* he did so is another story, having to do with his parents and his boyhood, with his own personality and his wife's, and especially with the character of his audience. But whatever the explanation, the faint-hearted ending of *Adventures of Huckleberry Finn* remains an important datum in the record of American thought and imagination. It has been noted before, both by critics and non-professional readers. It should not be forgotten now.

To minimize the seriousness of what must be accounted a major flaw in so great a work is, in a sense, to repeat Clemens's failure of nerve. This is a disservice to criticism. Today we particularly need a criticism alert to lapses of moral vision. A measured appraisal of the failures and successes of our writers, past and present, can show us a great deal about literature and about ourselves. That is the critic's function. But he cannot perform that function if he substitutes considerations of technique for considerations of truth. Not only will such methods lead to errors of literary judgment, but beyond that, they may well encourage comparable evasions in other areas. It seems not unlikely, for instance, that the current preoccupation with matters of form is bound up with a tendency, by no means confined to literary quarters, to shy away from painful answers to complex questions of political morality. The conclusion to *Adventures of Huckleberry Finn* shielded both Clemens and his audience from such an answer. But we ought not to be as tender-minded. For Huck Finn's besetting problem, the disparity between his best impulses and the behavior the community attempted to impose upon him, is as surely ours as it was Twain's.

# Melville's Parable of the Walls

Dead,
25. Of a Wall . . .: Unbroken, unrelieved by breaks or interruptions; absolutely uniform and continuous.

*New English Dictionary*

In the spring of 1851, while still at work on *Moby-Dick*, Herman Melville wrote his celebrated "dollars damn me" letter to Hawthorne:

> In a week or so, I go to New York, to bury myself in a third-story room, and work and slave on my "Whale" while it is driving through the press. *That* is the only way I can finish it now—I am so pulled hither and thither by circumstances. The calm, the coolness, the silent grass-growing mood in which a man *ought* always to compose,—that, I fear, can seldom be mine. Dollars damn me. . . . My dear Sir, a presentiment is on me,—I shall at last be worn out and perish. . . . What I feel most moved to write, that is banned,—it will not pay. Yet, altogether, write the *other* way I cannot.

He went on and wrote the "Whale" as he felt moved to write it; the public was apathetic and most critics were cool. Nevertheless Melville stubbornly refused to return to the *other* way, to his more successful earlier modes, the South Sea romance and the travel narrative. In 1852 he published *Pierre,* a novel even more certain not to be popular. And this time the critics were vehemently hostile. Then, the following year, Melville turned to shorter fiction. "Bartleby the Scrivener," the first of his stories, dealt with a problem unmistakably like the one Melville had described to Hawthorne.

There are excellent reasons for reading "Bartleby" as a parable having to do with Melville's own fate as a writer. To begin with, the story *is* about a kind of writer, a "copyist" in a Wall Street lawyer's office. Furthermore, the copyist is a man who obstinately refuses to go on doing the sort of writing demanded of him. Under the circumstances there can be little doubt about the connection between Bartleby's dilemma and Melville's own. Although some critics have noted the autobiographical relevance of this facet of the story, a close examination of the parable reveals a more detailed parallel with Melville's situation than has been suggested.[1] In fact the theme itself can be described in a way which at once establishes a more precise relation. "Bartleby" is not only about a writer who refuses to conform to the demands of society, but it is, more relevantly, about a writer who forsakes conventional modes because of an irresistible preoccupation with the most baffling philosophical questions. This shift of Bartleby's attention is the symbolic equivalent of Melville's own shift of interest between *Typee* and *Moby-Dick*. And it is significant that Melville's story, read in this light, does not by any means proclaim the desirability of the change. It was written in a time of deep hopelessness, and as I shall attempt to show, it reflects Melville's doubts about the value of his recent work.

Indeed, if I am correct about what this parable means, it has immense importance, for it provides the most explicit and mercilessly self-critical statement of his own dilemma that Melville has left us. Perhaps it is because "Bartleby" reveals so much of his situation that Melville took such extraordinary pains to mask its meaning. This may explain why he chose to rely on symbols which derive from his earlier work, and to handle them with so light a touch that only the reader who comes to the story after an immersion in the other novels can be expected to see how much is being said here. Whatever Melville's motive may have been, I believe it may legitimately be accounted a grave defect of the parable that we must go back to *Typee* and *Moby-Dick* and

1. The most interesting interpretations of the story are those of Richard Chase and Newton Arvin. Chase stresses the social implications of the parable in his *Herman Melville, A Critical Study* (New York, 1949), pp. 143-49. Arvin describes "Bartleby" as a "wonderfully intuitive study in what would now be called schizophrenia . . ." in his *Herman Melville* (New York, 1950), pp. 240-42. Neither Chase nor Arvin makes a detailed analysis of the symbolism of the walls. E. S. Oliver has written of the tale as embodying Thoreau's political ideas in "A Second Look at 'Bartleby'," *College English* (May, 1945), 431-39.

*Pierre* for the clues to its meaning. It is as if Melville had decided that the only adequate test of a reader's qualifications for sharing so damagaing a self-revelation was a thorough reading of his own work.

I

"Bartleby the Scrivener" is a parable about a particular kind of writer's relations to a particular kind of society. The subtitle, "A Story of Wall Street," provides the first clue about the nature of the society. It is a commercial society, dominated by a concern with property and finance. Most of the action takes place in Wall Street. But the designation has a further meaning: as Melville describes the street it literally becomes a walled street. The walls are the controlling symbols of the story, and in fact it may be said that this is a parable of walls, the walls which hem in the meditative artist and for that matter every reflective man. Melville also explicitly tells us that certain prosaic facts are "indispensable" to an understanding of the story. These facts fall into two categories: first, details concerning the personality and profession of the narrator, the center of consciousness in this tale, and more important, the actual floor-plan of his chambers.

The narrator is a Wall Street lawyer. One can easily surmise that at this unhappy turning point in his life Melville was fascinated by the problem of seeing what his sort of writer looked like to a representative American. For his narrator he therefore chose, as he did in "Benito Cereno," which belongs to the same period, a man of middling status with a propensity for getting along with people, but a man of distinctly limited perception. Speaking in lucid, matter-of-fact language, this observer of Bartleby's strange behavior describes himself as comfortable, methodical, and prudent. He has prospered; he unabashedly tells of the praise with which John Jacob Astor has spoken of him. Naturally, he is a conservative, or as he says, an "eminently *safe*" man, proud of his snug traffic in rich men's bonds, mortgages, and deeds. As he tells the story we are made to feel his mildness, his good humor, his satisfaction with himself and his way of life. He is the sort who prefers the remunerative though avowedly obsolete sinecure of the Mastership of Chancery, which has just been bestowed upon him when the action starts, to the exciting notoriety of the courtroom. He wants only to be left alone; nothing disturbs his complacency until Bartleby appears. As a spokesman for the society he is well chosen; he stands at its center and performs a critical role, unraveling and retying the invisible cords of property and equity which intertwine in Wall Street and bind the social system.

The lawyer describes his chambers with great care, and only when the plan of the office is clearly in mind can we find the key to the parable. Although the chambers are on the second floor, the surrounding buildings rise above them, and as a result only very limited vistas are presented to those inside the office. At each end the windows look out upon a wall. One of the walls, which is part of a sky-light shaft, is *white*. It provides the best light available, but even from the windows which open on the white wall the sky is invisible. No direct rays of the sun penetrate the legal sanctum. The wall at the other end gives us what seems at first to be a sharply contrasting view of the outside world. It is a lofty brick structure within ten feet of the lawyer's window. It stands in an everlasting shade and is *black* with age; the space it encloses reminds the lawyer of a huge black cistern. But we are not encouraged to take this extreme black and white, earthward and skyward contrast at face value (readers of *Moby-Dick* will recall how illusory colors can be), for the lawyer tells us that the two "views," in spite of their colors, have something very important in common: they are equally "deficient in what landscape painters call 'life.'" The difference in color is less important than the fact that what we see through each window is only a wall.

This is all we are told about the arrangement of the chambers until Bartleby is hired. When the lawyer is appointed Master in Chancery he requires the services of another copyist. He places an advertisement, Bartleby appears, and the lawyer hastily checks his qualifications and hires him. Clearly the lawyer cares little about Bartleby's previous experience; the kind of writer wanted in Wall Street need merely be one of the great interchangeable white-collar labor force. It is true that Bartleby seems to him peculiarly pitiable and forlorn, but on the other hand the lawyer is favorably impressed by his neat, respectable appearance. So sedate does he seem that the boss decides to place Bartleby's desk close to his own. This is his first mistake; he thinks it will be useful to have so quiet and apparently tractable a man within easy call. He does not understand Bartleby then or at any point until their difficult relationship ends.

When Bartleby arrives we discover that there is also a kind of wall inside the office. It consists of the ground-glass folding-doors which separate the lawyer's desk, and now Bartleby's, from the desks of the other employees, the copyists and the office boy. Unlike the walls outside the windows, however, this is a social barrier men can cross, and the lawyer makes a point of telling us that he opens and shuts these doors according to *his* humor. Even when they are shut, it should be noted, the ground glass provides at least an illusion of penetrability quite different from the opaqueness of the walls outside.

So far we have been told of only two possible views of the external world which are to be had from the office, one black and the other white. It is fitting that the coming of a writer like Bartleby is what makes us aware of another view, neither black nor white, but a quite distinct third view which is now added to the topography of the Wall Street microcosm.

> I placed his desk close up to a small side-window in that part of the room [a corner near the folding-doors]—a window which originally had afforded a lateral view of certain grimy back yards and bricks, but which, owing to subsequent erections, commanded at present no view at all, though it gave some light. Within three feet of the panes was a wall, and the light came down from far above, between two lofty buildings, as from a very small opening in a dome. Still further to a satisfactory arrangement, I procured a high green folding screen, which might entirely isolate Bartleby from my sight, though not remove him from my voice. And thus, in a manner, privacy and society were conjoined.

Notice that of all the people in the office Bartleby is to be in the best possible position to make a close scrutiny of a wall. His is only three feet away. And although the narrator mentions that the new writer's window offers "no view at all," we recall that he has, paradoxically, used the word "view" a moment before to describe the walled vista to be had through the other windows. Actually every window in the office looks out upon some sort of wall; the important difference between Bartleby and the others is that he is closest to a wall. Another notable difference is implied by the lawyer's failure to specify the color of Bartleby's wall.

Apparently it is almost colorless, or blank. This also enhances the new man's ability to scrutinize and know the wall which limits his vision; he does not have to contend with the illusion of blackness or whiteness. Only Bartleby faces the stark problem of perception presented by the walls. For him external reality thus takes on some of the character it had for Ishmael, who knew that color did not reside in objects, and therefore saw beyond the deceptive whiteness of the whale to "a colorless, all-color of atheism." As we shall see, only the nature of the wall with which the enigmatic Bartleby is confronted can account for his strange behavior later.

What follows (and it is necessary to remember that all the impressions we receive are the lawyer's) takes place in three consecutive movements: Bartleby's gradually stiffening resistance to the Wall Street routine, then a series of attempts by the lawyer to enforce the scrivener's conformity, and finally, society's punishment of the recalcitrant writer.

During the first movement Bartleby holds the initiative. After he is hired he seems content to remain in the quasi-isolation provided by the "protective" *green* screen and to work silently and industriously. This screen, too, is a kind of wall, and its color, as will become apparent, means a great deal. Although Bartleby seems pleased with it and places great reliance upon it, the screen is an extremely ineffectual wall. It is the flimsiest of all the walls in and out of the office; it has most in common with the ground-glass door—both are "folding," that is, susceptible to human manipulation.

Bartleby likes his job, and in fact at first seems the exemplar of the writer wanted by Wall Street. Like Melville himself in the years between *Typee* and *Pierre,* he is an ardent and indefatigable worker; Bartleby impresses the lawyer with probably having "been long famished for something to copy." He copies by sunlight and candle-light, and his employer, although he does detect a curiously silent and mechanical quality in Bartleby's behavior, is well satisfied.

The first sign of trouble is Bartleby's refusal to "check copy." It is customary for the scriveners to help each other in this dull task, but when Bartleby is first asked to do it, to everyone's astonishment, he simply says that he prefers not to. From the lawyer's point of view "to verify the accuracy of his copy" is an indispensable part of the writer's job. But evidently Bartleby is the sort of writer who is little concerned with the detailed accuracy of his work, or in any case he does not share the lawyer's standards of accuracy. This passage is troublesome because the words "verify accuracy" seem to suggest a latter-day conception of "realism." For Melville to imply that what the public wanted of him in 1853 was a kind of "realism" is not plausible on historical grounds. But if we recall the nature of the "originals" which the lawyer wants impeccably copied, not to mention Melville's own abhorence of proof-reading, the incident makes sense. These documents are mortgages and title-deeds, and they incorporate the official version of social (property) relations as they exist at the time. It occurs to the lawyer that "the mettlesome poet, Byron" would not have acceded to such a demand either. And like the revolutionary poet, Bartleby apparently cares nothing for "common usage" or "common sense"—a lawyer's way of saying that this writer does not want his work to embody a faithful copy of human relations as they are conceived in the Street.

After this we hear over and over again the reiterated refrain of Bartleby's nay-saying. To every request that he do something other than copy he replies with his deceptively mild, "I would prefer not to." He adamantly refuses to verify the accuracy of copy, or to run errands, or to do anything but write. But it is not until much later that the good-natured lawyer begins to grasp the seriousness of his employee's passive resistance. A number of things hinder his perception. For one thing he admits that he is put off by the writer's impassive mask (he expresses himself only in his work); this and the fact that there seems nothing "ordinarily human" about him saves Bartleby from being fired on the spot. Then, too, his business preoccupations constantly "hurry" the lawyer away from considering what to do about Bartleby. He has more important things to think about; and since the scrivener unobtrusively goes on working in his green hermitage, the lawyer continues to regard him as a "valuable acquisition."

On this typically pragmatic basis the narrator has become reconciled to Bartleby until, one Sunday, when most people are in church, he decides to stop at his office. Beforehand he tells us that there are several keys to this Wall Street world, four in fact, and that he himself has one, one of the other copyists has another, and the scrub woman has the third. (Apparently the representative of each social stratum has its own key.) But there is a fourth key he cannot account for. When he

arrives at the office, expecting it to be deserted, he finds to his amaze-
ment that Bartleby is there. (If this suggests, however, that Bartleby
holds the missing key, it is merely an intimation, for we are never actually provided with explicit evidence that he does, a detail which serves
to underline Melville's misgivings about Bartleby's conduct throughout
the story). After waiting until Bartleby has a chance to leave, the lawyer enters and soon discovers that the scrivener has become a permanent
resident of his Wall Street chambers, that he sleeps and eats as well as
works there.

At this strange discovery the narrator feels mixed emotions. On the
one hand the effrontery, the vaguely felt sense that his rights are being
subverted, angers him. He thinks his actual identity, manifestly inseparable from his property rights, is threatened. "For I consider that
one . . . is somehow unmanned when he tranquilly permits his hired
clerk to dictate to him, and order him away from his own premises."
But at the same time the lawyer feels pity at the thought of this man
inhabiting the silent desert that is Wall Street on Sunday. Such abject
friendlessness and loneliness draws him, by the bond of common humanity, to sympathize with the horrible solitude of the writer. So horri-
rible is this solitude that it provokes in his mind a premonitory image
of the scrivener's "pale form . . . laid out, among uncaring strangers,
in its shivering winding sheet." He is reminded of the many "quiet
mysteries" of the man, and of the "long periods he would stand looking out, at his pale window behind the screen, upon the *dead brick
wall.*" The lawyer now is aware that death is somehow an important
constituent of that no-color wall which comprises Bartleby's view of
reality. After this we hear several times of the forlorn writer immobi-
lized in a *"dead*-wall revery." He is obsessed by the wall of death which
stands between him and a more ample reality than he finds in Wall
Street.

The puzzled lawyer now concludes that Bartleby is the victim of an
"innate" or "incurable" disorder; he decides to question him, and if
that reveals nothing useful, to dismiss him. But his efforts to make
Bartleby talk about himself fail. Communication between the writer and
the rest of Wall Street society has almost completely broken down. The
next day the lawyer notices that Bartleby now remains permanently fixed
in a "dead-wall revery." He questions the writer, who calmly announces

that he has given up all writing. "And what is the reason?" asks the lawyer. "Do you not see the reason for yourself?" Bartleby enigmatically replies. The lawyer looks, and the only clue he finds is the dull and glazed look of Bartleby's eyes. It occurs to him that the writer's "unexampled diligence" in copying may have had this effect on his eyes, particularly since he has been working near the dim window. (The light surely is very bad, since the wall is only three feet away.) If the lawyer is correct in assuming that the scrivener's vision has been "temporarily impaired" (Bartleby never admits it himself) then it is the proximity of the colorless dead-wall which has incapacitated him. As a writer he has become paralyzed by trying to work in the shadow of the philosophic problems represented by the wall. From now on Bartleby does nothing but stand and gaze at the impenetrable wall.

Here Melville might seem to be abandoning the equivalence he has established between Bartleby's history and his own. Until he chooses to have Bartleby stop writing and stare at the wall the parallel between his career as a writer and Bartleby's is transparently close. The period immediately following the scrivener's arrival at the office, when he works with such exemplary diligence and apparent satisfaction, clearly corresponds to the years after Melville's return to America, when he so industriously devoted himself to his first novels. And Bartleby's intransigence ("I prefer not to") corresponds to Melville's refusal ("Yet . . . write the *other* way I cannot") to write another *Omoo,* or, in his own words, another "beggarly 'Redburn.'" Bartleby's switch from copying what he is told to copy to staring at the wall is therefore, presumably, the emblematic counterpart to that stage in Melville's career when he shifted from writing best-selling romances to a preoccupation with the philosophic themes which dominate *Mardi, Moby-Dick,* and *Pierre.* But the question is, can we accept Bartleby's merely passive staring at the blank wall as in any sense a parallel to the state of mind in which Melville wrote the later novels?

The answer, if we recall who is telling the story, is yes. This is the lawyer's story, and in his eyes, as in the eyes of Melville's critics and the public, this stage of his career *is* artistically barren; his turn to metaphysical themes *is* in fact the equivalent of ceasing to write. In the judgment of his contemporaries Melville's later novels are no more meaningful than Bartleby's absurd habit of staring at the dead-wall.

Writing from the point of view of the Wall Street lawyer, Melville accepts the popular estimate of his work and of his life.[2] The scrivener's trance-like stare is the surrealistic device with which Melville leads us into the nightmare world where he sees himself as his countrymen do. It is a world evoked by terror, and particularly the fear that he may have allowed himself to get disastrously out of touch with actuality. Here the writer's refusal to produce what the public wants is a ludicrous mystery. He loses all capacity to convey ideas. He becomes a prisoner of his own consciousness. "Bartleby the Scrivener" is an imaginative projection of that premonition of exhaustion and death which Melville had described to Hawthorne.

To return to the story. With his decision to stop copying, the first, or "Bartleby," movement ends. For him writing is the only conceivable kind of action, and during the rest of his life he is therefore incapable of action or, for that matter, of making any choice except that of utter passivity. When he ceases to write he begins to die. He remains a fixture in the lawyer's chamber, and it is the lawyer who now must take the initiative. Although the lawyer is touched by the miserable spectacle of the inert writer, he is a practical man, and he soon takes steps to rid himself of the useless fellow.

He threatens Bartleby, but the writer cannot be frightened. He tries to bribe him, but money holds no appeal for Bartleby. Finally he conceives what he thinks is a "masterly" plan; he will simply convey to the idle writer that he "assumes" Bartleby, now that he has ceased to be productive, will vacate the premises. But when he returns to the office after having communicated this assumption, which he characteristically thinks is universally acceptable, he finds Bartleby still at his window. This "doctrine of assumptions," as he calls it, fails because he and the writer patently share no assumptions whatsoever about either human behavior or the nature of reality. However, if Bartleby refuses to accept the premises on which the Wall Street world operates, he also refuses to leave. We later see that the only escape available to Bartleby is by way of prison or death.

2. It is not unreasonable to speculate that Melville's capacity for entertaining this negative view of his work is in fact a symptom of his own doubts about it. Was there some truth to the view that he was merely talking to himself? He may have asked himself this question at the time, and it must be admitted that this fear, a least in the case of *Pierre* and *Mardi,* is not without basis in fact.

Bartleby stays on, and then an extraordinary thing happens. After yet another abortive attempt to communicate with the inarticulate scrivener the narrator finds himself in such a state of nervous indignation that he is suddenly afraid he may murder Bartleby. The fear recalls to his mind the Christian doctrine of charity, though he still tends, as Melville's Confidence Man does later, to interpret the doctrine according to self-interest: it pays to be charitable. However, this partial return to a Christian view leads him on toward metaphysical speculation, and it is here that he finds the help he needs. After reading Jonathan Edwards on the will and Joseph Priestley on necessity, both Christian determinists (though one is a Calvinist and the other on the road to Unitarianism), he becomes completely reconciled to his relationship with Bartleby. He infers from these theologians that it is his fate to furnish Bartleby with the means of subsistence. This excursion in Protestant theology teaches him a kind of resignation; he decides to accept the inexplicable situation without further effort to understand or alleviate the poor scrivener's suffering.

At this point we have reached a stasis and the second, or "lawyer's" movement ends. He accepts his relation to Bartleby as "some purpose of an allwise Providence." As a Christian he can tolerate the obstinate writer although he cannot help him. And it is an ironic commentary on this fatalistic explanation of what has happened that the lawyer's own activities from now on are to be explicitly directed not, insofar as the evidence of the story can be taken as complete, by any supernatural force, but rather by the Wall Street society itself. Now it seems that it is the nature of the social order which determines Bartleby's fate. (The subtitle should be recalled; it is after all Wall Street's story too.) For the lawyer admits that were it not for his professional friends and clients he would have condoned Bartleby's presence indefinitely. But the sepulchral figure of the scrivener hovering in the background of business conferences causes understandable uneasiness among the men of the Street. Businessmen are perplexed and disturbed by writers, particularly writers who don't write. When they ask Bartleby to fetch a paper and he silently declines, they are offended. Recognizing that his reputation must suffer, the lawyer again decides that the situation is intolerable. He now sees that the mere presence of a writer who does not accept Wall Street assumptions has a dangerously inhibiting effect upon business. Bartleby seems to cast a gloom over the office, and more disturbing, his attitude implies a denial of all authority. Now, more clearly than before, the lawyer is aware that Bartleby jeopardizes the sacred right of private property itself, for the insubordinate writer in the end may "outlive" him and so "claim possession . . . [of his office] by right of perpetual occupancy" (a wonderful touch!). If this happens, of course, Bartleby's unorthodox assumptions rather than the lawyer's will eventually dominate the world of Wall Street. The lawyer's friends, by "relentless remarks," bring great pressure to bear upon him, and henceforth the lawyer is in effect an instrument of the great power of social custom, which forces him to take action against the non-conforming writer.

When persuasion fails another time, the only new stratagem which the lawyer can conceive is to change offices. This he does, and in the process removes the portable green screen which has provided what little defense Bartleby has had against his environment. The inanimate writer is left "the motionless occupant of a naked room." However, it soon becomes clear to the lawyer that it is not so easy to abdicate his responsibility. Soon he receives a visit from a stranger who reports that the scrivener still inhabits the old building. The lawyer refuses to do anything further. But a few days later several excited persons, including his former landlord, confront him with the news that Bartleby not only continues to haunt the building, but that the whole structure of Wall Street society is in danger of being undermined. By this time Bartleby's rebellion has taken on an explicitly revolutionary character: "Everyone is concerned," the landlord tells the lawyer, "clients are leaving the offices; some fears are entertained of a mob. . . ."

Fear of exposure in the public press now moves the lawyer to seek a final interview with the squatter. This time he offers Bartleby a series of new jobs. To each offer the scrivener says no, although in every case he asserts that he is "not particular" about what he does; that is, all the jobs are equally distasteful to him. Desperate because of his inability to frighten Bartleby's "immobility into compliance," the lawyer is driven to make a truly charitable offer: he asks the abject copyist to come home with him. (The problem of dealing with the writer gradually brings out the best in this complacent American.) But Bartleby does not want charity; he prefers to stay where he is.

Then the narrator actually escapes. He leaves the city, and when he returns there is word that the police have removed Bartleby to the Tombs as a vagrant. (He learns that even physical compulsion was unable to shake the writer's impressive composure, and that he had silently obeyed the orders of the police.) There is an official request for the lawyer to appear and make a statement of the facts. He feels a mixture of indignation and approval at the news. At the prison he finds Bartleby standing alone in the "inclosed grass-platted yards" silently facing a high wall. Renewing his efforts to get through to the writer, all the lawyer can elicit is a cryptic "I know where I am." A moment later Bartleby turns away and again takes up a position "fronting the dead-wall." The wall, with its deathlike character, completely engages Bartleby. Whether "free" or imprisoned he has no concern for anything but the omnipresent and impenetrable wall. Taking the last resort of the "normal" man, the lawyer concludes that Bartleby is out of his mind.

A few days pass and the lawyer returns to the Tombs only to find that they have become, for Bartleby, literally a tomb. He discovers the wasted figure of the writer huddled up at the base of a wall, dead, but with his dim eyes open.

In a brief epilogue the lawyer gives us a final clue to Bartleby's story. He hears a vague report which he asserts has a "certain suggestive interest"; it is that Bartleby had been a subordinate clerk in the Dead Letter Office at Washington. There is some reason to believe, in other words, that Bartleby's destiny, his appointed vocation in this society, had been that of a writer who handled communications for which there were no recipients—PERSON UNKNOWN AT THIS ADDRESS. The story ends with the lawyer's heartfelt exclamation of pity for Bartleby and humankind.

## II

What did Melville think of Bartleby? The lawyer's notion that Bartleby was insane is of course not to be taken at face value. For when the scrivener says that he knows where he is we can only believe that he does, and the central irony is that there was scarcely a difference, so far

as the writer's freedom was concerned, between the prison and Wall
Street. In Wall Street Bartleby did not read or write or talk or go anywhere or eat any dinners (he refuses to eat them in prison too) or, for
that matter, do anything which normally would distinguish the free
man from the prisoner in solitary confinement. And, of course, the office in which he had worked was enclosed by walls. How was this to be
distinguished from the place where he died?

> The yard was entirely quiet. It was not accessible to the common
> prisoners. The surrounding walls, of amazing thickness, kept off all
> sounds behind them. The Egyptian character of the masonry weighed
> upon me with its gloom. But a soft imprisoned turf grew under foot.
> The heart of the eternal pyramids, it seemed, wherein, by some
> strange magic, through the clefts, grass-seed, dropped by the birds,
> had sprung.

At first glance the most striking difference between the Wall Street
office and the prison is that here in prison there are four walls, while
only three had been visible from the lawyer's windows. On reflection,
however, we recall that the side of the office containing the door, which
offered a kind of freedom to the others, was in effect a fourth wall for
Bartleby. He had refused to walk through it. The plain inference is that
he acknowledged no distinction between the lawyer's chambers and the
world outside; his problem was not to be solved by leaving the office,
or by leaving Wall Street; indeed, from Bartleby's point of view, Wall
Street *was* America. The difference between Wall Street and the Tombs
was an illusion of the lawyer's, not Bartleby's. In the prison yard, for
example, the lawyer is disturbed because he thinks he sees, through the
slits of the jail windows, the "eyes of murderers and thieves" peering
at the dying Bartleby. (He has all along been persuaded of the writer's
incorruptible honesty.) But the writer knows where he is, and he offers
no objection to being among thieves. Such minor distinctions do not interest him. For him the important thing is that he still fronts the same
dead-wall which has always impinged upon his consciousness, and upon
the mind of man since the beginning of time. (Notice the archaic Egyptian character of the prison wall.) Bartleby has come as close to the wall
as any man can hope to do. He finds that it is absolutely impassable,

and that it is not, as the Ahabs of the world would like to think, merely a pasteboard mask through which man can strike. The masonry is of "amazing thickness."

Then why has Bartleby allowed the wall to paralyze him? The others in the office are not disturbed by the walls; in spite of the poor light they are able to do their work. Is it possible that Bartleby's suffering is, to some extent, self-inflicted? that it is symptomatic of the perhaps morbid fear of annihilation manifested in his preoccupation with the dead-wall? Melville gives us reason to suspect as much. For Bartleby has come to regard the walls as permanent, immovable parts of the structure of things, comparable to man's inability to surmount the limitations of his sense perceptions, or comparable to death itself. He has forgotten to take account of the fact that these particular walls which surround the office are, after all, man-made. They are products of society, but he has imputed eternality to them. In his disturbed mind metaphysical problems which seem to be timeless concomitants of the condition of man and problems created by the social order are inextricably joined, joined in the symbol of the wall.

And yet, even if we grant that Bartleby's tortured imagination has had a part in creating his dead-wall, Melville has not ignored society's share of responsibility for the writer's fate. There is a sense in which Bartleby's state of mind may be understood as a response to the hostile world of Wall Street. Melville has given us a fact of the utmost importance: the window through which Bartleby had stared at the wall had "originally . . . afforded a lateral view of certain grimy backyards and bricks, but . . . owing to subsequent erections, commanded at present no view at all, though it gave some light." Melville's insinuation is that the wall, whatever its symbolic significance for Bartleby, actually served as an impediment to (or substitute for?) the writer's vision of the world around him. This is perhaps the most awesome moment in Melville's cold self-examination. The whole fable consists of a surgical probing of Bartleby's motives, and here he questions the value, for a novelist, of those metaphysical themes which dominate his later work. What made Bartleby turn to the wall? There is the unmistakable hint that such themes (fixing his attention on "subsequent erections") had had the effect of shielding from view the sordid social scene ("grimy backyards and bricks") with which Melville, for example, had been more directly concerned in earlier novels such as *Redburn* or *White-Jacket*. At this point we are apparently being asked to consider whether Bartleby's obsession was perhaps a palliative, a defense against social experience which had become more than he could stand. To this extent the nature of the Wall Street society has contributed to Bartleby's fate. What is important here, however, is that Melville does not exonerate the writer by placing all the onus upon society. Bartleby has made a fatal mistake.

Melville's analysis of Bartleby's predicament may be appallingly detached, but it is by no means unsympathetic. When he develops the contrast between a man like Bartleby and the typical American writers of his age there is no doubt where his sympathies lie. The other copyists in the office accept their status as wage earners. The relations between them are tinged by competitiveness—even their names, "Nippers" and "Turkey," suggest "nip and tuck." Nevertheless they are not completely satisfactory employees; they are "useful" to the lawyer only half of the time. During half of each day each writer is industrious and respectful and compliant; during the other half he tends to be recalcitrant and even mildly rebellious. But fortunately for their employer these half-men are never aggressive at the same time, and so he easily dominates them, he induces them to do the sort of writing he wants, and has them "verify the accuracy" of their work according to his standards. When Bartleby's resistance begins they characteristically waver between him and the lawyer. Half the time, in their "submissive" moods ("submission" is their favorite word as "prefer" is Bartleby's), they stand with the employer and are incensed against Bartleby, particularly when his resistance inconveniences *them;* the rest of the time they mildly approve of his behavior, since it expresses their own ineffectual impulses toward independence. Such are the writers the society selects and, though not too lavishly, rewards.

One of Melville's finest touches is the way he has these compliant and representative scriveners, though they never actually enlist in Bartleby's cause, begin to echo his "prefer" without being aware of its source. So does the lawyer. "Prefer" is the nucleus of Bartleby's refrain, "I prefer not to," and it embodies the very essence of his power. It simply means "choice," but it is backed up, as it clearly is not in the case of the other copyists, by will. And it is in the strength of his will that the crucial difference between Bartleby and other writers lies. When Nippers and Turkey use the word "prefer" it is only because they are unconsciously imitating the manner, the surface vocabulary of the truly independent writer; they say "prefer," but in the course of the parable they never make any real choices. In their mouths "prefer" actually is indistinguishable from "submission"; only in Bartleby's does it stand for a genuine act of will. In fact writers like Nippers and Turkey are incapable of action, a trait carefully reserved for Bartleby, the lawyer, and the social system itself (acting through various agencies, the lawyers' clients, the landlord, and the police). Bartleby represents the only real, if ultimately ineffective, threat to society; his experience gives some support to Henry Thoreau's view that one lone intransigent man can shake the foundations of our institutions.

But he can only shake them, and in the end the practical consequence of Bartleby's rebellion is that society has eliminated an enemy. The lawyer's premonition was true; he finally sees Bartleby in death. Again the story insinuates the most severe self-criticism. For the nearly lifeless Bartleby, attracted neither by the skyward-tending white wall, nor the cistern-like black wall, had fixed his eyes on the "dead" wall. This wall of death which surrounds us, and which Melville's heroes so desperately needed to pierce, has much in common with the deadly White Whale. Even Ahab, who first spoke of the whale as a "pasteboard mask" through which man might strike, sensed this, and he significantly shifted images in the middle of his celebrated quarter-deck reply to Starbuck:

> All visible objects, man, are but as pasteboard masks. . . . If man will strike, strike through the mask! How can the prisoner reach outside except by thrusting through the wall? To me, the white whale is that wall, shoved near to me.

Like the whale, the wall will destroy the man who tries too obstinately to penetrate it. Bartleby had become so obsessed by the problem of the dead-wall that his removal to prison hardly changed his condition, or, for that matter, his state of being; even in the walled street he had allowed his life to become suffused by death.

The detachment with which Melville views Bartleby's situation is perhaps the most striking thing about the fable. He gives us a power-

ful and unequivocal case against Wall Street society for its treatment
of the writer, yet he avoids the temptation of finding in social evil
a sentimental sanction for everything his hero thinks and does. True,
the society has been indifferent to Bartleby's needs and aspirations;
it has demanded of him a kind of writing he prefers not to do; and,
most serious of all, it has impaired his vision by forcing him to work
in the shadow of its walls. Certainly society shares the responsibility
for Bartleby's fate. But Melville will not go all the way with those who
find in the guilt of society an excuse for the writer's every hallucina-
tion. To understand what led to Bartleby's behavior is not to condone
it. Melville refuses to ignore the painful fact that even if society shares
the blame for Bartleby's delusion, it was neverthless a delusion. What
ultimately killed this writer was not the walls themselves, but the fact
that he confused the walls built by men with the wall of human mor-
tality.


III

Is this, then, as F. O. Matthiessen has written, "a tragedy of utter
negation"? If not it is because there is a clear if muted note of affirmation here which must not be ignored. In the end, in prison, we
are made to feel that the action has somehow taken us closer to the
mysterious source of positive values in Melville's universe. "And see,"
says the lawyer to Bartleby in the prison yard, "it is not so sad a place
as one might think. Look, there is the sky, and here is the grass." To
the lawyer the presence of the grass in the Tombs is as wonderful as
its presence in the heart of eternal pyramids where "by some strange
magic through the clefts, grass-seed, dropped by birds, had sprung."
The saving power attributed to the green grass is the clue to Melville's
affirmation.[3]

3. Recall that two years before, in the letter to Hawthorne which I quoted at
the beginning of this essay, Melville had contrasted the unhappy circumstances
under which he wrote *Moby-Dick* to "the silent grass-growing mood in which a
man *ought* always to compose." Later in the same letter he described his own
development in the identical image which comes to the mind of the lawyer in
"Bartleby":

I am like one of those seeds taken out of the Egyptian Pyramids, which,
after being three thousand years a seed and nothing but a seed, being

The green of the grass signifies everything that the walls, whether black or white or blank, do not. Most men who inhabit Wall Street merely accept the walls for what they are—man-made structures which compartmentalize experience. To Bartleby, however, they are abstract emblems of all the impediments to man's realization of his place in the universe. Only the lawyer sees that the oustanding characteristic of the walls, whether regarded as material objects or as symbols, is that they are "deficient in . . . 'life.'" Green, on the other hand, *is* life. The color green is the key to a cluster of images of fecundity which recurs in Melville's work beginning with *Typee.* It is the color which dominates that tropical primitive isle. It is the color of growth and of all pastoral experience. Indeed the imminent disappearance of our agrarian society is an important motive for Ishmael's signing on the *Pequod.* "Are the green fields gone?" he asks as *Moby-Dick* begins. And later he says, in describing the ecstasy of squeezing sperm: "I declare to you that for the time I lived as in a musky meadow." So he gives a green tint to his redeeming vision of "attainable felicity," a felicity which he says resides in the country, the wife, the heart, the bed—wherever, that is, men may know the magical life-giving force in the world. And *Pierre,* published the year before "Bartleby," also begins with a vision of a green paradise. There Melville makes his meaning explicit. He compares a certain green paint made of verdigris with the "democratic element [which] operates as subtile acid among us, forever producing new things by corroding the old. . . ."

> Now in general nothing can be more significant of decay than the idea of corrosion; yet on the other hand, nothing can more vividly suggest luxuriance of life than the idea of green as a color; for green is the peculiar signet of all-fertile Nature herself.

By some curious quirk of the human situation, Bartleby's uncompromising resistance, which takes him to prison, also takes him a step closer to the green of animal faith. Melville deftly introduces this

---

planted in English soil, it developed itself, grew to greenness, and then fell to the mould.

That this same constellation of images reappears in "Bartleby" in conjunction with the same theme (the contrast between two kinds of writing) seems to me conclusive evidence of the relation between the parable and the "dollars damn me" letter.

note of hope by having the lawyer compare the grass in the prison yard to the mystery of the grass within the pyramids. In time greenness, the lawyer suggests, may penetrate the most massive walls. Indeed green seems virtually inherent in time itself, a somehow eternal property of man's universe. And in a Wall Street society it is (paradoxically) most accessible to the scrivener when he finds himself in prison and at the verge of death. Why? If Bartleby's suicidal obsession has taken him closer to grass and sky, are we to understand that it has had consequences both heartening and meaningful? Is Melville implying, in spite of all the reasons he has given us for being skeptical of Bartleby's motives, that an understanding of his fate may show us the way to a genuine affirmation? Before attempting to answer these questions, it is appropriate to note here how remarkable a fusion of manner and content Melville has achieved. While the questions are never explicitly asked, they are most carefully insinuated. The unique quality of this tale, in fact, resides in its ability to say almost nothing on its placid and inscrutable surface, and yet so powerfully to suggest that a great deal is being said. This quality of style is a perfect embodiment of the theme itself: concealed beneath the apparently meaningless if not mad behavior of Bartleby is a message of utmost significance to all of us.

While the presence of the grass at Bartleby's death scene is the clue to Melville's affirmation, the affirmation can only exist outside the scrivener's mind. Green now means nothing to him. In the Wall Street world he had known, the green fields *were* gone; he was able to see neither grass nor sky from the walled-in windows. The only green that remained was the artificial green painted upon his flimsy screen, the screen behind which he did his diligent early work. But the screen proved a chimerical means of protection. Again Melville seems to be pointing the most accusing questions at himself. Had not his early novels contained a strong ingredient of primitivism? Had he not in effect relied upon the values implicit in the *Typee* experience (values which reappeared in the image of the inaccessible "insular Tahiti" in *Moby-Dick*) as his shelter from the new America? Was this pastoral commitment of any real worth as a defense against a Wall Street society? The story of Bartleby and his green screen, like the letter to Hawthorne (dollars damn me!), denies that it was. In this fable, artificial or man-made green, used as a shield in a Wall Street office, merely abets self-delusion. As for the other green, the natural green of the grass in the prison yard, it is clear that Bartleby never apprehended its meaning. For one thing, a color could hardly have meant anything to him at that stage. His skepticism had taken him beyond any trust in the evidence of his senses; there is no reason to believe that green was for him any less illusory a color than the black or white of the walls. We know, moreover, that when he died Bartleby was still searching: he died with his eyes open.

It is not the writer but the lawyer, the complacent representative American, who is aware of the grass and to whom, therefore, the meaning is finally granted. If there is any hope indicated, it is hope for his, not Bartleby's, salvation. Recall that everything we understand of the scrivener's fate has come to us by way of the lawyer's conscious-ness. From the first the situation of the writer has been working upon the narrator's latent sensibility, gradually drawing upon his capacity for sympathy, his recognition of the bond between his desperate em-ployee and the rest of mankind. And Bartleby's death elicits a cry of compassion from this man who had once grasped so little of the writer's problem. "Ah, Bartleby! Ah, humanity!" are his (and Melville's) last words. They contain the final revelation. Such deeply felt and spontane-ous sympathy is the nearest equivalent to the green of the grass within reach of man. It is an expression of human brotherhood as persistent, as magical as the leaves of grass. Charity is the force which may enable men to meet the challenge of death, whose many manifestations, real and imagined, annihilated the valiant Bartleby.

The final words of the fable are of a piece with Melville's undevi-ating aloofness from his hero: they at once acknowledge Bartleby's courage and repudiate his delusion. If such a man as the lawyer is ulti-mately capable of this discernment, then how wrong Bartleby was in permitting the wall to become the exclusive object of his concern! The lawyer can be saved. But the scrivener, like Ahab, or one of Haw-thorne's geniuses, has made the fatal error of turning his back on man-kind. He has failed to see that there were in fact no impenetrable walls between the lawyer and himself. The only walls which had separated them were the folding (manipulable) glass doors, and the green screen. Bartleby is wrong, but wrong or not, he is a hero; much as Ahab's mad quest was the necessary occasion for Ishmael's salvation, this writer's annihilation is the necessary occasion for Everyman's perception.

Among the countless imaginative statements of the artist's problems in modern literature, "Bartleby" is exceptional in its sympathy and hope for the average man, and in the severity of its treatment of the artist. This is particularly remarkable when we consider the seriousness of the rebuffs Melville had so recently been given by his contemporaries. But nothing, he is saying, may be allowed to relieve the writer of his obligations to mankind. If he forgets humanity, as Bartleby did, his art will die, and so will he. The lawyer, realizing this, at the last moment couples Bartleby's name with that of humanity itself. The fate of the artist is inseparable from that of all men. The eerie story of Bartleby is a compassionate rebuke to the self-absorption of the artist, and so a plea that he devote himself to keeping strong his bonds with the rest of mankind. Today, exactly a century after it was written, "Bartleby the Scrivener" is a counter-statement to the large and ever-growing canon of "ordealist" interpretations of the situation of the modern writer.

# Henry Thoreau

## Excursions

By the time Henry Thoreau returned to Concord from Minnesota, in July 1861, he must have known he was dying. During the winter his tuberculosis had become acute, and the prescribed Western excursion, begun in May, had only weakened him. He was forty-four years old, the author of two books (neither of them widely read or greatly admired), a number of poems, essays, and reviews, and a vast manuscript journal. Although he had drawn from the journal much of his finished writing, there was no telling how many more books it might still contain. (After his death various editors culled half a dozen more or less coherent volumes from it, yet even the fourteen-volume edition of 1906 is far from complete.) Now, in the summer of 1861, he did not have much time, and it cannot have been easy to decide how to use it.

Yet one thing was clear: an entirely new book, another integral work such as *A Week on the Concord and Merrimack Rivers* or *Walden,* was out of the question. The journal consisted of fragments, many of them brilliant to be sure, but fragments nonetheless. No one knew better than Thoreau what was required, in the way of time, energy, passion, and faith, to mold a book with a controlling theme out of these disjointed materials. Hence he wisely chose to put a few short essays in final form. Lying in the living room of the family home on

Main Street, often dictating to his sister Sophia, he kept on working. Roughly half of *Excursions,* the first posthumous book, a miscellaneous collection, is the product of this deathbed effort.

After Thoreau died in May 1862, Emerson helped Sophia prepare the manuscript for Ticknor and Fields. (The publisher, James T. Fields, also was the editor of the *Atlantic Monthly,* where the last four essays in *Excursions* appeared during 1862 and 1863.) The initial aim of the editors, apparently, was to publish these final pieces. But lacking enough material for a book, they added a recent paper on forest growth, four of Thoreau's earliest essays, and a revised version of the talk Emerson gave at the funeral, which also had appeared in the *Atlantic.* The book, which has a distinctly post-mortem air, was ready for the public in October 1863. The title page of the first edition reads: *Excursions,* "by Henry D. Thoreau," and cites no other names; however, page 7 is headed "Biographical Sketch. By R. W. Emerson."

Leaving aside Emerson's piece, the book neatly falls into two parts. The first part consists of work published in 1842 and 1843, before the decisive sojourn at Walden Pond, and before Thoreau's purpose or his style were fully formed. A sixteen-year break separates these four apprentice essays from the other five, all of which were written, or at least put together, after 1860, in the presence of death. Because the selection straddles the climactic period of integration when Thoreau did his truly memorable work, it has a curious "before and after" effect, as if the editors were saying, "Here is the beginning and the end of a writer's career; let us see where he entered his vocation and where he came out."

But we are not allowed to make up our minds unaided. By the time of the funeral Henry's friend Waldo was ready with an answer, and here it is, one of the most severe "eulogies" in literary history. No display of a writer's achievement could be more devastating—especially since it approaches the sad truth—than that collection of Thoreauvian sentences and odd bits ("The locust z-ing.") near the end of Emerson's speech. Paying no serious attention to *A Week* or *Walden* as whole books, ignoring "Civil Disobedience," a classic statement of anarchist political doctrine destined to make itself felt around the world, Emerson pictures Thoreau as an inept poet, the captain of a huckleberry party who died in the middle of his "broken task."

To this day the taint of failure, thus bestowed upon it at the grave-side, clings to Thoreau's name. Of course he had encouraged detractors of his work by seeming to care so much more for his life, or one might say his soul. Still, Emerson should not have been fooled; nor can his acerbity be accounted a preference for the man as against the art. As a human being, Thoreau does not come off much better. Emerson says he was "a protestant *à l'outrance,* and few lives contain so many renunciations"—a statement which seems right on the mark, and might even be thought to confer a certain heroism were it not for a canny, unobtrusive retraction later in the paragraph: "He had no temptations to fight against,—no appetites, no passions, no taste for elegant trifles." The more one considers this chilling sentence, the circumstances for which it was composed, the more astonishing it seems. Habitually a generous man, here Emerson sounds like a disappointed master, like Freud, for example, deliberately taking down an errant disciple. In closing Emerson firmly fixes the image of Thoreau as an outlandish Yankee seeker, a crank, a provincial Byronic egoist who expended himself on transcendental heights searching out the elusive Edelweiss, emblem of the "Noble Purity" which he fancied "belonged to him by right."

But it is not easy to get around Emerson's knowing criticism, so much of it is sound or, at any rate, plausible. The course of Thoreau's career, as plotted by *Excursions,* does tend to confirm Emerson's harsh judgment. (Can this have been a reason for the strange design of the volume?) It is saddening to read these essays in sequence. First we are shown the work of a self-assured, ambitious young writer. Then, without having seen his promise fulfilled, we become witnesses to his ineluctably failing powers. Several questions arise. What had happened to Thoreau? Why did he lose rather than gain control? Had there been a crucial weakness in his method from the beginning? That the young writer had begun with what he took, however mistakenly, to be Emersonian doctrine, merely adds an unusual ironic twist.

Nevertheless, quite apart from the many superb passages it contains, *Excursions* is a valuable book. Beginning with just the right selection, the "Natural History of Massachusetts," it throws a singularly clear light on Thoreau's cardinal theme. How fitting, indeed, that Emerson should have got his young admirer started by asking him to review these particular volumes—scientific reports on the flora and fauna of his native state. In a fine essay on "Thoreau in the Context of International Romanticism," Perry Miller has recently shown that this assignment confronted Thoreau with his major problem. Here was an up-to-date, precise, scientific way of describing that natural world from which he derived endless delight. But the reality to which these cool reports referred—how was it to be related to that other reality: the vital, abounding, tough-fibered, pure, immortal, orderly, disinterested, serene Nature of his own experience? Was it possible that the source of his elation lay hidden somewhere behind these uninspired collections of fact? Yes, said Thoreau, with the sublime assurance of a saint, "Let us not underrate the value of a fact; it will one day flower in a truth."

To realize this audacious prophecy (he says the fact *will*, not *may* become a truth) was Thoreau's obsessive purpose. (How could Emerson think that he lacked passion?) By 1842 his direction was set. He boldly put aside the scientific reports, treating them, he said, "with as much license as the preacher selects his text." Although this remark might have alerted readers to the devotional character of his work, and although he repeatedly distinguished between the aims of scientists and his own, Thoreau again and again has been mistaken for a naturalist. To be sure, he always wanted to get the facts absolutely straight, but that is not, as some people would have it, the exclusive concern of natural science. A rigorous fidelity to the facts was for Thoreau a religious commitment. For he assumed, having accepted Emerson's premises, that any natural fact, if properly perceived, becomes an equally reliable yet far more exhilarating moral-aesthetic fact. Just where the power to effect the conversion originates, he did not claim to know. But he had no doubt about his job as a writer. If he could only connect the right words to the right facts, he could then transmit feeling, hence ideas, beauty, meaning, and value, across the gap between minds.

With Thoreau, therefore, epistemology is the basis of style. To enable us to see what he saw watching a fox run across the snow on the pond, he concentrates all his powers upon the details:

When the ground is uneven, the course is a series of graceful curves, conforming to the shape of the surface. He runs as though there were not a bone in his back. Occasionally dropping his muzzle to the ground for a rod or two, and then tossing his head aloft, when satisfied with his course. When he comes to a declivity, he will put his forefeet together, and slide swiftly down it, shovelling the snow before him. He treads so softly that you would hardly hear it from any nearness, and yet with such expression that it would not be quite inaudible at any distance.

Obviously there is more than precise observation at work here. What engages Thoreau is the perfect adaptation of the fox to the terrain, and he would repeat that harmony in a chain that ultimately links the reader to the cosmological order thus: fox and terrain; writer's eye and scene; words and image; reader and written passage. At the end our attention is compelled by a miraculously apt sensuous paradox, much as if we were there trying to decide whether or not we had heard the footfall of the fox. Here, as everywhere, the hallmark of Thoreau's best prose is the thrust to get beyond the phenomenon without distorting it: the controlled elation of a tough, self-denying teleologist.

The radical renunciation which Emerson saw as the key to Thoreau's life was a primary condition for his art. Every concern that might possibly distract us from his ruling theme had to be put aside. In these essays we are invited to forget, or to dismiss as trivial, most of the everyday preoccupations of mankind: wealth, status, power, social institutions, politics, family relations, sex—the list is so comprehensive that we may well wonder what can possibly remain. A natural fact—it might be anything, the fox running, or the wild apple scrub that wins a twenty-year struggle with the cows in "Wild Apples"—is what remains. Thoreau's unique power resides in his ability, reminiscent of certain Chinese painters, to place an infinitely wide margin around the objects of his fierce attention. Finally the apple tree seems to hang these in absolute space, an embodiment of pure perseverance. Emerson's most appreciative sentence acknowledges the rare intensity of

Thoreau's perception: "Every fact lay in glory in his mind, a type of the order and beauty of the whole."

Although the pieces in *Excursions* often have been called "travel essays," only an unregenerate literalist could take them as such. Thoreau is a religious writer, and his special genre, the transcendental essay, is an odd nineteenth-century form of prose meditation. That he could scarcely write anything else is hinted by the failure of "The Landlord." Here he aimed at the marketplace, trying to turn out a relaxed, sophisticated, familiar essay after the manner of Irving or Lamb. But neither the subject nor the manner was right, and the result is vapor. This piece is an instructive testimony to his lifelong struggle to get beyond the facts and somehow find an organizing principle for his transcendental epiphanies.

In his entire career Thoreau hit upon only one satisfactory structural pattern, and it is named by the well-chosen title, *Excursions*. All his successful works are accounts of excursions. Adapting a conventional device of Christian writers, Thoreau uses the story of an excursion as a vehicle for a spiritual quest. To Dante or Bunyan, however, faith supplied a destination; a sure allegorical method coupled the levels of the metaphoric journey. But an excursion is by definition more tentative, less certain of its direction or its goal. What excitement Thoreau arouses has little or nothing to do with the outcome of the actual excursion. It depends entirely on the intensity of his perceptions *en route,* on his ability to maintain the evanescent feeling, as in the glimpse of the fox, that we are on the verge of a thrilling revelation. Yet given his respect for fact, he was forced to accept the achievement of form, the aesthetic unity he so desperately sought, as a surrogate for what the Puritans had called justification. Judged by this standard, the most successful of the *Excursions* are the two walks, each in its way a preparatory exercise for the longer excursions on the river and beside the pond.

After *Walden* he lost control of the method. "I see details," he confessed, "not wholes nor the shadow of the whole." Not one of the essays in the second half approaches the unity of "A Walk to Wachusett." Now particular facts and metaphysical ideas no longer cohere. In the wonderfully lucid paper on forest growth he veers toward matter-of-factness and rigor in generalizing. It is his closest approach to a genuinely scientific style, revealing how effective he might have been working in a less ambitious, naturalistic medium. But his need to reach out toward the absolute was too great. In "Walking," which begins firmly enough, he cuts ideas loose from observations, and form crumbles into page after page of tedious, homiletic assertion. Now he speaks as an extreme primitivist-anarchist. (Until *Walden* his point of view had been closer to the calm, harmonizing spirit of pastoral.) It is one thing to repudiate the workaday world, as he once had done, for aesthetic purposes: to clear the ground for concentrated perception; but it is quite another to propose this regressive attitude as an overall prescription for living. In the end Thoreau's doctrine of "wildness" becomes indistinguishable from the shadowy bliss of infantile mindlessness.

Two of the final pieces, "Autumnal Tints" and "Night and Moonlight," fail to come off. They lack spine. At points they sound like products of the more effusive, sentimental cult of nature. Of course the failure must be attributed in some measure to Thoreau's illness. But it is also true that increasingly, during the 1850s, he had been getting into a difficult situation. No longer able to fuse facts and ideas, he needed desperately to step back and reassess his problem. But, unfortunately, among the creations of man's collective behavior which he now renounced, along with virtually all social institutions, was the usual way of the intellect. He had little use for the ordinary, distinction-making, analytic method of thought itself.

Looking back at *Walden* from the perspective of *Excursions,* it is clear that much of Thoreau's success had been due to his willingness to exceed the strict limits of the original formula. The unity, power, and truth of the book did not result from the spontaneous flowering of fact. As J. Lyndon Stanley has shown, Thoreau owed far more than he would admit to the deliberate, organizing capacity of his intellect. But as he became more desperate, toward the end, he intensified his renunciation of reason. Avid of order, yet without confidence in mind, Thoreau now fell back on a doctrine of instinct or "wildness." But it manifestly was not enough. In the absence of a revelation, he had renounced too much.

# The Two Thoreaus

I

Until 1965, when Walter Harding's careful biography, *The Days of Henry Thoreau*, was published, we had nothing like a reliable, comprehensive record of Henry Thoreau's life. Richard Lebeaux is the first scholar to use that book as a basis for a fresh examination of the writer's inner life. The findings he sets forth in *Young Man Thoreau** point to a strikingly new, demythicized conception of the man. By carefully matching outward circumstances and events with the way Thoreau and others perceived them—down to minute details of their day-by-day responses as recorded in diaries, letters, poems, essays— Lebeaux is able to reconstruct the psychic struggle that culminated in the experiment at Walden Pond. For the first time, accordingly, we come away from a biography with a plausible way of thinking about the relationship between the two Thoreaus: the guilt-ridden young writer who resolves the crisis of vocation by taking up his solitary residence at the pond, and that self-assured character, the narrating "I" whose voice we first hear in the epigraph of *Walden* exuberantly announcing his intention not "to write an ode to dejection, but to brag as lustily as chanticleer in the morning."

The key to this fascinating book is Lebeaux's recognition of the peculiar relevance of Erik Erikson's psychohistorical method to his subject. Most of the factual evidence he deploys in *Young Man Thoreau* was previously available, and the book's originality derives almost entirely from Lebeaux's painstaking rereading and rearranging of the known facts in the light of Eriksonian psychology. In his pioneering studies, *Young Man Luther,* and *Gandhi's Truth,* Erikson demonstrated the illuminating power of his concept of a prolonged postadolescent "identity crisis" in charting the hazardous passage of a certain kind of great man, a worldly saint, from childhood to creative maturity. The pertinence of Erikson's model to Thoreau's life and personality is

* (Amherst: University of Massachusetts Press, 1977.)

obvious enough, and Lebeaux seized upon it in its entirety and without any significant reservations.

Lebeaux's aim in *Young Man Thoreau* is to show how brilliantly Erikson's ego psychology illuminates the emergence of this "great man" from his long, precarious struggle for independence from his timorous childhood self. And that it does. But one also must accept the fact that this biography is a work of apprentice scholarship, written with a sort of homely academic earnestness, and though Lebeaux's uncritical embrace of Erikson can be annoying, it is finally justified by the remarkable insights it allows.

The focus of *Young Man Thoreau* is upon the critical years of indecision between 1837, when the twenty-year-old Harvard graduate moved back into his parents' house in Concord, and 1845 when he moved a mile or so down the road to the cabin at Walden Pond. As Lebeaux retells the story, it turns on Thoreau's tangled relations with his family, especially his mother, Cynthia. She was an exceptionally vigorous and assertive woman, an activist and reformer; to supplement the family income she took in boarders and ran something of a ladies' village salon. Her friends referred to her as vivacious, proud, outspoken; to less admiring observers she was garrulous, harsh, sarcastic, status-seeking, intimidating. But most witnesses agree that her formidable presence overshadowed that of her quiet husband, John. He was a small, subdued man—some say "mousy"—chronically enervated by his efforts to bolster various shaky business enterprises. Times were particularly hard during the years following the panic of 1837 when young Thoreau was wrestling with the problem of vocation.

Cynthia Thoreau evidently was the one who had decided that Henry, rather than his older brother, John, should go to Harvard. (The four children were Helen, the oldest, then John, David Henry, and Sophia.) She was ambitious for her college-educated son, and assumed that he would enter a profession or at least find a lucrative job. Not long before his graduation, he asked for her advice about his future. She suggested that he might buckle on a knapsack and go abroad to seek his fortune, whereupon David Henry burst into tears. His sister Helen put her arm around him, saying, "No, Henry, you shall not go: you shall stay at home and live with us." And that is what he did. The

interlude of solitary householding described in *Walden* is the paramount exception to that sad truth.

Lebeaux interprets young Thoreau's behavior between 1837 and 1845
as being governed by a grim tug of war between almost evenly matched
psychic antagonists. On one side, anxiously pulling him back toward
home and mother, was a clinging, childlike self; on the other, trying to
break away, were the slowly forming elements of a new, presumably
more adult, independent, or—to use one of his own favorite terms of
praise—a "manly" identity. The first explicit symptom of the conflict
is agonizing self-doubt. One of his early poems begins,

> I am a parcel of vain strivings tied
> By a chance bond together,
> Dangling this way and that, their links
> Were made so loose and wide,
> Methinks,
> For milder weather.

This theme, or, in Eriksonian language, "identity confusion," per-
meates the early writing. Sometimes it seems explicit—Thoreau himself
often expresses a fear of "losing" his "identity"; and sometimes it is
indirectly figured in the vocabulary fashioned from his painstaking
observations of external nature. A passage on the coming of spring
("It never grows up, but . . . creeps on molelike under the snow,
showing its face nevertheless occasionally by fuming springs and water-
courses") could almost describe his slow, subterranean advance toward
manhood. Read in this way, the first volume of the *Journal* is an ab-
sorbing, almost self-contained account of a classic identity crisis. So
far as the underlying conflict is named, it turns upon the problem of
vocation ("What may a man do and not be ashamed of it?"), but it
also is apparent, in Lebeaux's close reading, that for men like Thoreau
"vocation" includes just about everything that matters.

Not long after he returned to Concord, he began to sign his name
"Henry David Thoreau." He stopped using his given name at this time,
although years later his mother was still referring to "my David
Henry." Resistance took many other forms. In letters to John, who

shared Henry's fascination with the spartan life of Indian braves, the sort of lean, ascetic male-bonding featured in adolescent fantasies, he railed against the domination of the "pale faces" who also tended to be "squaws"—gabby, bossy women. Why then didn't he leave home, as his mother had recommended? He did make many gestures in that direction. At one point, he and John announced their plan to go West together, but nothing came of it. He made a seemingly earnest effort to find jobs up and down the eastern seaboard, but Lebeaux demonstrates that the effort was somewhat less than wholehearted. He applied for a teaching post in Virginia, but since he lacked the stated qualifications he could have expected to be turned down—and he was.

His reluctance to leave home becomes even more apparent a few years later, after Emerson had persuaded him to serve as tutor to the child of his brother, William, who lived on Staten Island. The idea, among other things, was to give Henry's literary career a boost by putting him in touch with New York literary people. But he was miserably lonely and homesick, and after six months he resigned and returned to Concord.

Lebeaux assumes that the strongest ties holding Thoreau close to home and mother were psychological and, in large measure, unconscious. But they are by no means the only ones he recognizes. The fact that Emerson also lived in Concord is of immense importance for this Eriksonian and pointedly post-Freudian analysis, in which greater force than Freud would have allowed is imputed to conscious motives, hence to social and cultural circumstances and, above all, to the influence of ideology. For young Thoreau, Emerson, fourteen years his senior, was the exemplary "great man," a national spokesman for a dissident ideology to which he surely would have been attracted even if they never had met. But here was Emerson, living in Concord, and the self-appointed sponsor of the literary vocation to which Thoreau hardly dared aspire. Moreover, the nonconformist doctrine expounded by Emerson in this, his most radically individualistic phase, intensified Thoreau's disdain for most of the "particular callings" available to college graduates.

As a Harvard senior, even before he and Emerson had become friends, Thoreau had written a denunciation of the acquisitive ethos of capitalism called "The Commercial Spirit." He told his classmates that a "blind and unmanly love of wealth" was threatening to become "the ruling spirit" of the Republic, and he went on to recommend a reversal of the nation's work habits: six days of the week should be a sabbath of the affections and the soul, he said, and the seventh a day of toil. At the time, as it happens, release from toil had been made all too real for many thousands of New England workers by the financial panic of 1837 and the depression that followed. With so many out of work, however, the oddity of a Harvard graduate living at home with his mother and father in what looked like idleness cannot have seemed as great as in normal times. The economic crisis helped, along with the dissident Emersonian ideology, to provide a sanction—one might almost say a "cover"—for Thoreau's remaining at home and not working in a conventional job or profession.

Yet in Lebeaux's judgment the chief reason for young Thoreau's protracted indecision was the neurotic conflict surrounding his relations with his immediate family. Though he outwardly resisted his mother's powerful influence, he nevertheless embraced her conviction that he had been singled out for greatness. His journals for the years between 1837 and 1845 are filled with evidence of his yearning to be a great man.

> My fate is in some sense linked with that of the stars, and if they are to persevere to a great end, shall I die who could conjecture it? It surely is some encouragement to know that the stars are my fellow-creatures, for I do not suspect but they are reserved for a high destiny.

Emerson's generous encouragement of his literary talent lent plausibility to this belief. But his father's passivity, or "psychological absence," made the difficult choices of this critical period all the more difficult. Henry respected his father, but he could not avoid feeling pity and resentment when he also saw him, through the town's eyes, as weak and submissive—a failure. The result, according to Lebeaux, was a conflict from which he never wholly escaped: he was determined to achieve the distinction he and his mother envisaged, yet he could not bear the thought of seeming to triumph over his father. What he was searching for, in Lebeaux's words, was "a way to be a hero, a success, without provoking guilt feelings."

During the eight-year search, however, the bad conscience connected with his ambitions seemed to taint his relations with everyone, including his beloved brother John. Henry looked up to John, who was the more confident and personable of the two, as a kind of second father, and yet again and again he found himself vying with John for approval or love. On this topic, incidentally, Lebeaux makes his most important contribution to our knowledge of Thoreau's life. His sensitive reconstruction of the initially covert, finally traumatic, rivalry between the brothers is new and fascinating, and it yields insights comparable, for their revelatory power, to Leon Edel's uncovering of the tangled relations between the James brothers. The rivalry came to the surface during the brothers' partnersip in keeping a village school (Concord Academy) from 1839 to 1841. The pupils naturally compared the Thoreau brothers, their only teachers, and taciturn Henry had to face the fact that he was not nearly as well liked as his easygoing, affable, older brother.

But it was only when they both fell in love with Ellen Sewall, the seventeen-year-old daughter of a conservative Unitarian minister, that the rivalry became open. For more than a year, while he and John were contending for Ellen's favor, Henry oscillated between yielding and pursuit. John eventually took the initiative, proposed, and was accepted—but only briefly. When Ellen, who evidently preferred Henry, changed her mind, Henry barely was able to muster the resolve to visit her and perhaps—the evidence is unclear—to propose. At the last minute, in any event, Ellen's father intervened and stopped the whole affair. A year later, however, John cut his finger, contracted lockjaw, and after a brief, agonizing illness, died in his brother's arms. The shock was incapacitating, literally paralyzing: within three weeks Henry developed the precise symptoms of a fatal case of lockjaw, and it was months before he had fully recovered. (So far as we know, he made no other serious gestures toward intimacy with a woman.)

Lebeaux's analysis of Henry's psychosomatic grief reaction shows the superiority of *Young Man Thoreau,* for all its excessive reliance upon Erikson, to most psychobiographies. The abundant detailed evidence that Lebeaux brings to bear in demonstrating the presence of guilt behind Henry's case of sympathetic lockjaw is impressive. In the absence of that evidence, to be sure, Lebeaux's explanation may seem extrava-

gant and his prose florid, but in the context he creates it strikes me as
substantively persuasive:

> . . . somewhere deep in his being, Thoreau felt that it was he who
> was responsible for his brother's death. In many earlier instances, he
> had wished his brother out of the way, his "elder deceased." The
> most extreme instance had also been the most recent—during his
> pursuit of Ellen. . . .
>    Now, to his horror, his most secret and terrible wishes had come
> true. John had died, and the mortal wound had been inflicted by a
> blade which Henry, on some level, feared he had wielded. Because
> he loved his brother so much, Thoreau experienced unbearable guilt.
> His psychosomatic illness could be interpreted as a way of punishing
> himself and trying to share the fate of John, thereby relieving his
> guilt.

The severity of Thoreau's strange illness, a kind of hysteria, indicates
what he was up against by way of unconscious resistance in his struggle to create an adult identity. Erikson had singled out a similar episode
in Gandhi's life, involving his imagined neglect of his dying father, as
an instance of the sort of "curse" that often shows up in the lives of
spiritual innovators with relentless consciences. But the curse, from the
clinician's viewpoint, is a "cover memory," or concentration of a pervasive childhood conflict upon a particular dramatized scene. Thus
Thoreau's grief seems a more acute seizure of the self-punishment de-
spondence brought on when he tried, for example, to live away from
Concord. The alternation between initiative and guilt, between trials
of self-reliance and interludes of regression, describes a rhythm which,
were it not for his growing confidence in his literary powers, might
well have resulted in a barren, neurotic standoff.

It is a pity that Lebeaux does not have more to say about the emotional implications of Thoreau's developing ability to shape his experience in language; all this occurred while he was working diligently at
becoming a writer. Keeping his journal had become the really serious
business of his day, and with Emerson's help he had begun to publish
reviews, essays, and poems. The written word enabled him to assert
himself—in effect to create a self. A month before John's fatal accident,

early in 1842, he had enjoyed an access of self-confident vitality. "It is time that I begin to live," he wrote. But the tragedy further prolonged his adolescent moratorium, and it was not until the spring of 1845, a few months after Emerson had bought some land on the shore of Walden Pond, that he finally hit upon a psychologically tolerable way to declare his independence.

To live alone on the outskirts of Concord was an ideal solution. It is hard to imagine any other way that Thoreau could have met the impossibly stringent conditions he had set for himself. At Walden Pond he could be on his own, yet remain within easy walking distance of home and mother. His mother and sisters made special trips to Walden every Saturday with various culinary delicacies, and he took particular delight in raiding the family cookie jar on his frequent visits home. Under the circumstances, there is something comical about his reputation as one of the company of rugged American woodsmen and loners.

At Walden he had what he needed most, an opportunity to make a bid for greatness without being crippled by guilt. He could try to write, and yet, given the uncertain status of serious writers in America, he could do so with a negligible risk of achieving the worldly success he feared. At the same time he would comply with Emerson's prescription of nonconformity and self-reliance; while remaining securely within the Concord orbit of transcendentalism, in fact, he might outshine the master himself in heroic renunciation. His first task, the "unfinished business" he refers to early in *Walden*, would be to compose a memoir of the boat trip he and John had taken together. By writing *A Week on the Concord and Merrimack Rivers* he would pay his emotional debt to his dead brother and prepare himself for the main business of his pastoral retreat: the creation of a new, purified identity for himself. On Independence Day, July 4, 1845, he took up his residence at Walden.

II

*Young Man Thoreau* ends with the twenty-eight-year-old writer's move to the pond. It therefore contains no extended discussion of *Walden*, which did not appear until nine years later. But Lebeaux's modest study opens the way to a new understanding of the relationship between

Thoreau's life and his masterwork, its hero, and the myth surrounding that imaginary figure.

*Walden,* when read with the new biographical knowledge in mind, is an exultant account of David Henry's transformation into the "Henry Thoreau" he wanted to be. His governing motive, if we accept Lebeaux's analysis of his struggle over his identity and his guilt, is self-purification. On this view *Walden* is the autobiography of Thoreau's otherwise unappeasable desire for autonomy. In many respects, to be sure, this description accords with the received view of the book as a narrative of spiritual rebirth. It can be reconciled, for example, with many of the insights of Stanley Cavell, who in *The Senses of Walden* describes the book as a quest "for the recovery of self, as from an illness," arguing that *Walden,* by virtue not only of its manifest theme and structure, but of the "extremity and precariousness" of mood generated by its inwardly spiraling sentences, is a prophetic scripture in the mode of the Old Testament prophets Ezekiel and Jeremiah.

New England Puritans would have recognized in *Walden* an account of a conversion. But it is worth noting that Thoreau discloses remarkably little of his prior state of mind, of that despair, or sickness of soul, which characteristically precedes the climactic experience in accounts of spiritual regeneration. In an early, fragmentary inscription for the book, it is true, he had alluded to his previously dispirited condition. "I could tell a pitiful story about myself," he wrote, ". . . with a sufficient list of failures, and flow as humbly as the very gutters." In revising the manuscript, however, he substituted the self-assurance of the present epigraph, carelessly omitted in many reprints nowadays, and the one sentence in *Walden,* Cavell observes, that appears twice: "I do not propose to write an ode to dejection, but to brag as lustily as chanticleer in the morning, standing on his roost, if only to wake my neighbors up," And brag he does. One might say in fact that the "I" of *Walden* is the writer's extravagant idealization of himself. It is as though he had created this "Henry Thoreau" by reversing certain painful facts about his situation.

The hero of Walden is a model of self-sufficiency, untroubled by guilt or anxiety or worldly ambition. At the pond he lives out the fantasy of an indefinitely protracted adolescence: a way of living that entails no commitment to a particular calling, no job, no literary discipline, no obligations to family or children, no intimacy, no sexual relationship, nor, for that matter, any acknowledged need for other people. In view of Thoreau's apparent incapacity to leave home, the largest and most touching boast of *Walden*'s hero is that he depends on no one. Once, he admits, he did feel lonesome, but then only for an hour, and in the event that unpleasant mood—there was, he recalls, "a slight insanity" about it—proved to be the prelude to a Wordsworthian revelation:

> In the midst of a gentle rain while these thoughts prevailed, I was suddenly sensible of such sweet and beneficent society in Nature, in the very pattering of the drops, and in every sound and sight around my house, an infinite and unaccountable friendliness all at once like an atmosphere sustaining me, made the fancied adavntages of human neighborhood insignificant, and I have never thought of them since. Every little pine needle expanded and swelled with sympathy and befriended me. I was . . . distinctly made aware of the presence of something kindred to me. . . .

Here and throughout *Walden* the hero's regeneration is closely bound up with the displacement of his strongest feelings from people, or "society," to nature. Those tumescent pine needles are not easily ignored, for one thing, and besides, critics have long recognized the patently libidinized character of Thoreau's landscapes. (Thus Edmund Wilson in a vein of Princetonian naughtiness: "He dipped his wand / In Walden Pond— / He thought a sheet of water was a beautiful blond.") William James, in his discussion of "Saintliness" in *The Varieties of Religious Experience,* quotes this passage as an instance of the shining and transfigured look the world takes on for the recently converted.

Religious and sexual motives in fact appear to be inseparably interfused, both in the composition of *Walden* and in the writer's life. While young Thoreau lived with his family (or the Emersons) in Concord, his feelings about others often led him to feel unworthy, tainted, and incapable of decisive action on his own behalf. In writing *Walden,* however, he managed to project this deadness of spirit upon other people: it is the other nameless inhabitants of Concord—the mass of men—who lead lives of quiet desperation, whereas the "I" who addresses us speaks confidently of the sensuous delights he enjoys in the sweet and beneficent company of "Nature."

What Lebeaux's study brings into sharper view, then, is the "pitiful story" Thoreau decided not to tell, with its melancholy "list of failures" and the testimony to the unconscious guilt he transmuted, in composing *Walden,* into an inspiring rite of purification. By describing his ideal life beside Walden Pond, noted in the region for its uncommon depth and purity, Thoreau had vicariously if incompletely rid himself, like a snake shedding its skin, of his outworn, dependent self.

In his first enraptured glimpse of the pond he all but names the sources of its regenerative power:

> For the first week, whenever I looked out on the pond it impressed me like a tarn high up on the side of a mountain, its bottom far above the surface of the other lakes, and, as the sun arose, I saw it throwing off its nightly clothing of mist, and here and there, by degrees, its soft ripples or its smooth reflecting surface was revealed, while the mists, like ghosts, were stealthily withdrawing in every direction into the woods, as at the breaking up of some nocturnal conventicle. The very dew seemed to hang upon the trees later into the day than usual, as on the sides of mountains.

This passage anticipates Thoreau's many loving descriptions of the pond, with its heaving breast, its soft ripples, and its smooth, tremulous, undulating surface. But in the delicate image of the rising mist, it should be noted, the sense of an illicit passion is no less religious than erotic; the stealthily withdrawing, ghostly mist is likened to the breakup of "some nocturnal conventicle" as well as to a woman throwing off her clothes. A conventicle is a secret or illegal religious gathering. One thinks of a clandestine meeting of English Puritans, another reminder of the singular efficacy of *Walden,* among the many American books we owe to the legacy of Puritanism, in reviving the original sense of that movement's derisive name, the dangerous Protestant craving to be inwardly cleansed, or purified.

Sexual and religious (or metaphysical) motives are joined in Thoreau's very conception of the pond. He places it at the center of *Walden*—the center, that is, of both its literary structure (the chapter devoted to it, "The Ponds," is the ninth of eighteen) and of its symbolic

topography. In addition to his minute observations of the pond's changing physical state, like those of a naturalist, Thoreau calls it "God's
drop" and "earth's eye." Walden Pond is a kind of geological orifice
or vessel filled with translucent liquid, an evocative trope for the penetrability—by vision, thought, measurement, feeling, language—of the
hard material crust of reality.

But Lebeaux also casts new light on the unpleasant, irrational extremes of asceticism to which Thoreau was led by his fervent quest for
purity. Toward the end of the chapter on "Higher Laws" there is a
grim passage, seldom mentioned by *Walden*'s admirers, in which Thoreau recommends the renunciation of bodily pleasure in accents befitting
a 1920s' H. L. Mencken or pre-Perry Miller notion of a repressive
Puritan. Citing traditional Christian and Vedic teachings about the
spirit's need to curb the flesh, Thoreau reflects upon the shameful
"wildness" human beings display by their inclination to kill animals
(fishing and hunting), to drink stimulating or intoxicating beverages,
and to enjoy eating and copulating. He begins with the appetites he
considers easiest to eradicate or purify, but by the time he gets to eating,
an unmistakable note of revulsion has crept in. It is a wonder to him,
he admits, how we, "how you and I, can live this slimy beastly life,
eating and drinking."

> We are conscious of an animal in us, which awakens in proportion
> as our higher nature slumbers. It is reptile and sensual, and perhaps
> cannot be wholly expelled; like the worms which, even in life and
> health, occupy our bodies.

As for what he calls the "generative energy," it "dissipates and makes
us unclean" when we are "loose," but invigorates and inspires us
"when we are continent."

> All sensuality is one, though it takes many forms; all purity is one.
> It is the same whether a man eat, or drink, or cohabit, or sleep sen-
> sually. They are but one appetite, and we only need to see a person
> do any one of these things to know how great a sensualist he is. The
> impure can neither stand nor sit with purity. When the reptile is at-
> tacked at one mouth of his burrow, he shows himself at another. . . .
> Nature is hard to be overcome, but she must be overcome.

This distraught language is an aberration, even in a strictly literary sense, within the *Walden* text. The voice, for one thing, is not that of chanticleer or of the scrupulous writer who aims at an exact correspondence between ideas and observed facts. It is not merely the anxious tone that is anomalous, however; it is the whole demeanor of the speaker, this nature lover suddenly overwhelmed by mistrust of his instincts. What a picture he evokes—comic and sad—a solemn, Yankee countryman in a frenzy to keep those reptilian impulses down in their burrows, and with that final, exasperated, defeated injunction: nature must be overcome.

After having cast the abstract noun, Nature,* as the chief redemptive force in the life of man, and having repeatedly personified Nature as an essentially innocent, pure, motherly presence, kindred to ourselves—he implores us to overcome her. Whether we think of "nature" here in its external sense, as the biophysical environment, or in its psychological sense, as our instinctual endowment, the enjoinder remains a puzzle. It blunts the force of Thoreau's cultural radicalism. For the power of the feelings aroused by his affectionate attachment to physical nature derives partly from its tacit subversion of the unexamined faith in technological progress conceived, in the popular phrase of his day, as the "conquest of nature." Yet here Thoreau seems to join the conquerors.

No critic, to my knowledge, has satisfactorily elucidated this incongruous passage. But if we accept the idea that Thoreau's governing motive was the creation of a new, undefiled identity, and that his passionate attachment to the natural world—the painstaking, loving care he lavished upon his literary effort to possess that world—was in some measure an expression of feelings displaced by guilt from their original, human objects, an explanation comes into view. Thoreau had become,

---

* Since "nature" is the first word of Thoreau's sentence ("Nature is hard to be overcome . . .") we cannot be sure whether the word is "nature" or "Nature." But Thoreau more or less consistently follows the transcendentalist practice of using the humble, lower-case form, "nature," to refer to the surface of the environment: everything (including the human body) knowable by means of sensory perception; and of using the capitalized form, "Nature," to refer to the norm, or timeless essence, behind the apprehensible surface of things. In his essay, *Nature* (1836), Emerson had provided a formulaic version of the metaphysical presuppositions back of this usage by describing visible nature as "the present expositor of the divine mind."

in a literal sense seldom intended by users of this worn figure, a lover of nature. But it was a difficult role for him to sustain, not surprisingly, in writing about sensuality. The panicky voice we hear, for just a moment, from behind the persona of *Walden*'s self-possessed narrator, sounds like no one so much as Cynthia Thoreau's self-punishing son, David Henry.

The very conspicuousness of this lapse bears witness to the psychological, as well as literary, triumph presented by *Walden*. On this theme Lebeaux is particularly engaging. That Thoreau's "strengths were born partly out of struggle with weaknesses," he writes, "should increase, rather than diminish, our admiration for his accomplishments." What Lebeaux tends to ignore, however, is that Thoreau's skill as a writer of autobiography also began the myth-making process which has, until now, so effectively obscured the historical record.

If Thoreau created his own myth, then Emerson's famous eulogy at his friend's funeral should be credited (somewhat like Plato's *Apology* in the case of Socrates) with reinforcing it. Like the hero of *Walden*, Emerson's Thoreau was a free and self-contained spirit, uncorrupted by worldly ambition, a man who "lived for the day." Instead of "engineering for all America," Emerson said, "Thoreau was the captain of a huckleberry party."

What is misleading is the implication left by Emerson that Thoreau had had no true vocation, that he only casually and incidentally had been a writer, and many other people, including biographers and scholars, have continued to endorse this view. But it is proved false by the clear, readily accessible record of Thoreau's dedication and productivity as a writer. During a relatively brief literary career (he was after all only forty-four when he died), he wrote more than two million words. At times he evidently wrote between 10,000 and 15,000 words a day. The complete edition of his work in preparation at Princeton will comprise twenty-five volumes.

More than the quantity, however, it is the painstaking intensity of his method as a writer that testifies to this consuming passion. We know that his *Journal* consists in large measure of rewritten material, and that he composed his finished essays by taking disparate bits and pieces of the journal and fitting them together. In some cases a single paragraph is an amalgam of three or four entries, each from a different

year. In the case of *Walden,* this fussy "mosaic" method of composi-
sion (Margaret Fuller's apt term) entailed the writing of seven distinct drafts during seven or eight years, and the ironic fact is that
*Walden,* which so many readers take for an offhand, virtually unedited
transcription of immediate experience, may well be the most artfully,
deliberately, meticulously *composed* prose work in our classic American literature.

It also should be said, however, that Thoreau did his best to conceal
the intensity of his commitment to literature. Apart from a statement
in a letter to President Jared Sparks of Harvard, from whom he was
trying to get a special library privilege ("I have chosen letters for my
profession"), he rarely identified himself as a professional writer. It is
reasonable to suppose that the activity to which he devoted a large
part, perhaps most, of his waking hours, was writing, yet if you ask
readers of *Walden* what Thoreau's "life in the woods" was like, one
of the last answers you will get—a good reason being that he neglects
to mention the fact—is that he spent much of the time sitting at a
table putting words on paper.

III

Like several others among the revered American literary scriptures,
*Walden* begins with its hero-narrator in a mood of extreme disaffection with his society. At the heart of the powerful opening chapter,
"Economy," is his shocked discovery—remarkably similar in its animus
to that of young Karl Marx in the *Economic and Philosophic Manuscripts* (written in 1844, the year before Thoreau's retreat to the
pond)—of the alienating effects of the minority ownership of the
means of production on every sphere of life. "I cannot believe," Thoreau says, "that our factory system is the best mode by which men may
get their clothing," and if the lives of the workers are miserable, he
adds, that is not surprising, "since . . . the principal object is not that
mankind may be well and honestly clad, but, unquestionably, that the
corporations may be enriched." Like Marx, Thoreau seems to base his
criticism of bourgeois culture upon the radical distinction between production for profit and production for use, and it would be hard to find
in Marx's work any sharper criticism of the mindless operation of the

market economy than, say, Thoreau's offhand remark about men having become the tools of their tools, or his witty, still serviceable definition of our inventions as improved means to an unimproved end.

In spite of the radical anticapitalist implications of the beginning of *Walden,* however, Thoreau's criticism of the Concord way is not finally political. It is not the material or social conditions of life, it is not capitalism, that in his view accounts for the quiet desperation felt by the mass of men: it is their own spiritual inertia. So far from causing him to identify his interests with theirs, this awareness leads him to set himself apart from them, to see most of the typical adults among them as blind to his experiment.

> Girls and boys and young women generally seemed glad to be in the woods. They looked in the pond and at the flowers, and improved their time. Men of business, even farmers, thought only of solitude and employment, and of the great distance at which I dwelt from something or other.

The urgent message of *Walden,* like any Puritan sermon, is that we too could—if we but would—be redeemed. Although withdrawal into Nature is not the prescribed means of preparation for grace, Thoreau's account conveys, in secular language, the essential spirit of Augustinian piety. As he settles into his life at the pond, however, the problems of ordinary people recede from his consciousness. What politically minded admirers of *Walden* tend to ignore, I think, is the effect of the book's action as a whole in dissipating the radical social awareness it generates at the outset. Considered as a single structure of feeling, Thoreau's masterwork may be described as superbly effective in transmuting incipiently radical impulses into a celebration of what Emerson called "the infinitude of the private man." And when the hero matter-of-factly remarks, at the end of his stay at the pond, that he is returning to Concord, the point is that in his new, reborn state he is better able, psychologically, to deal with the corrupt way of life he initially had repudiated.

Thoreau had little use for politics, and he was anything but an activist. His only activities apart from writing that might be called political were a few speeches and one fleeting gesture of civil disobedience. In the essay he wrote on that subject, moreover, he forthrightly admits that the purpose of the nonviolent resistance he is recommending is self-exculpation, not social justice.

> It is not a man's duty, as a matter of course, to devote himself to the eradication of any, even the most enormous wrong; he may still properly have other concerns to engage him; but it is his duty, at least, to wash his hands of it, and, if he gives it no thought longer, not to give it practically his support.

The reason for his famous tax refusal, it seems evident, was for Thoreau to free himself of moral complicity in the criminal enslavement of black people; only incidentally was it to help free the slaves from bondage. It is a disturbingly self-involved approach to politics and the public life, and one cannot help wondering, in view of the new biographical evidence given us by Lebeaux, about the extent to which it was warped by unconscious motives.

*Young Man Thoreau*, far from denigrating the writer's genius, encourages new respect for his determined conversion of emotional limitations into literary power. This means, however, that we are compelled to enforce a sharper distinction that has hitherto been made between Thoreau the writer and his quasi-autobiographical self. On this view, the "Thoreau" most readers know has far less in common with David Henry than he does with all of those patently fictive embodiments of pastoral disengagement that play so conspicuous a role in our classic American literature. I am thinking of such characters and voices as Cooper's Natty Bumppo, Melville's Ishmael, and Hawthorne's Hester; of the "I" of Emerson's *Nature* and Whitman's "Song of Myself"; of Huck Finn, Nick Adams, and Ike McCaslin; of the speaker of Robert Frost's pastoral lyrics and of Wallace Stevens's cosmic poet and worldmaker—the list could be extended into the present, but the main point is that all of these figures, whatever their differences, tend to represent their deepest longings in gratifying visions of the natural landscape. In one way or another, they all express the urge, in the face of the growing power and complexity of organized society, to withdraw to a simpler environment, closer (as we say) to nature, in search of innocence or happiness.

The difference is, however, that many readers perceive Thoreau less as an artist than as a prophet of redemption from the devastations and deprivations peculiar to urban industrialism. What distinguishes his work from the rest, what leads people to take it as a guide to life, is in no small part his extraordinary skill in suspending disbelief in the authenticity of his fictive self. Beginning with the original subtitle of *Walden* (*or, Life in the Woods*), and the incomparably forthright tone with which he addresses his readers. ("In most books, the *I,* or first person, is omitted; in this it will be retained; that, in respect to egotism, is the main difference"), and including the tacit standard by which at the outset he asks to be judged ("I . . . require of every writer, first or last, a simple and sincere account of his own life . . .")—beginning with all this on the first page, *Walden* successfully induces many readers to accept it as a literal record of direct experience. Perhaps this is only to say that Thoreau is read as a prophet because he felt himself to be one, because he identified with that literary tradition and mastered its conventions. What would his fame have been if he had attributed the pastoral retreat enacted in *Walden* to an avowedly fictive narrator? Richard Lebeaux has given us a new understanding of the relations between Thoreau's life and his mythic self—a portrait of the young writer on his way to becoming a prophet.

# Robert Frost:
# A Literary Life

On the eve of the First World War, London still beckoned aspiring American poets. Ezra Pound arrived in 1908, Robert Frost in 1912, and T. S. Eliot in 1914. When Pound arrived he was only twenty-three, Eliot was twenty-six, but Frost was almost thirty-nine. He had been writing poetry, most of it unpublished, for some twenty years, and the difference in style was striking. Set beside the early work of Pound and Eliot (or of Wallace Stevens and William Carlos Williams, for that matter), Frost's "simple" lyrics might have seemed to be some sort of throwback—as if they belonged far down the back slope of the great Modernist watershed. But those same unassuming poems earned Pound's immediate praise, and though Frost remained stubbornly impervious to avant-garde poetics, his work was soon accorded high critical esteem. How shall we account for his success in the face of triumphant Modernism? One of the incidental merits of William Pritchard's readable and instructive "literary life" is that it implies a new way of answering this most puzzling question.[1]

Pritchard begins with an amusing account of Frost's rapid entry into

1. William Pritchard, *Frost: A Literary Life Reconsidered* (New York: Oxford University Press, 1985).

101

literary London. When he arrived with his wife, four children, and two or three manuscript collections of poems, he could not have been more of an outsider. He did not know a soul in England, nor is there reason to suppose that anyone in England had ever heard of him or his work. He had not yet published a book. Only a few of his poems had appeared in relatively unstylish American magazines. He carried no letters of introduction. Yet somehow, perhaps on the advice of a taxi-driver, he quickly located a publisher for his first book, *A Boy's Will*, which appeared early in 1913. He attended the opening of Harold Monro's Poetry Bookshop in Bloomsbury, where he met F. S. Flint, who sent him a book of his poems. The poetry was, in Pritchard's phrase, "rich in inexpressible yearnings"—the sort of writing Frost could not abide. He nonetheless found a way to praise it, Flint was delighted, and one thing quickly led to another.

Flint introduced him to the high-flying Pound, who by then had published six books and seemed to know every writer in England. Pound quickly took his unworldly compatriot in hand. When told that the first copy of *A Boy's Will* might be at the publisher's, Pound determinedly walked miles across London with Frost to pick it up, kept Frost waiting while he read through the poems, and then magisterially announced that Frost could leave (according to one version, without his only copy of the book), so that Pound could write a review. In the event he wrote two favorable reviews—one for a British, the other for an American magazine. Through Pound, Frost also met Yeats, who is said to have praised his new work ("the best poetry written in America for a long time"). Frost soon became friendly with the Georgian poets Lascelles Abercrombie, W. H. Davies, and Wilfrid Gibson, and formed a truly close friendship, probably the closest of his life, with Edward Thomas.

Frost and his family sailed for home early in 1915. The outbreak of war had cut short his foray into literary London, but from a crassly opportunistic standpoint it could hardly have been more successful. In two and a half years the unknown Frost had become a recognized writer, and his work had won the respect of many of the leading poets writing in English. By the time he left for home, two of his books were in print in England (*North of Boston* having appeared in 1914), and he had arranged to have them both published in the States. To prepare a favorable reception for his work at home, meanwhile, he had dispatched elaborate instructions about reviews and other forms of publicity to his American supporters. Now that he was shifting his sights to the American scene he took pains to dissociate himself from Pound, whose sponsorship had been invaluable, but whose condescension he resented. Besides, he was made nervous by Pound's aggressive rebuke of certain American editors for their alleged refusal to publish his work. This was no time to offend such people. As he explained to one admirer, "I expect to do something to the present state of literature in America."

It is typical of Pritchard's seemingly arbitrary method that he begins with his subject in middle age, and that he devotes such a disproportionate amount of attention to Frost's English sojourn. But his rationale is compelling. He is writing a *"literary* life" in the strict sense that here biography serves criticism. He focuses on those aspects of the life which bear most directly on—or help most to illuminate—Frost's theory and practice of his craft. By starting with the poet's shrewd London campaign, Pritchard quickly establishes his major theme: Frost's absolute confidence in his own genius, his singleminded pursuit of his career. True, this entails the scanting of many episodes in Frost's life, but if one is to deal with the art as well as the life within the compass of a single volume, ruthless selectivity is essential. After all, Pritchard argues, Frost lived for almost ninety years, and readers who want to follow the year-by-year course of the poet's life can always turn to Lawrance Thompson's two thousand-page official biography.

One of Pritchard's aims is to rescue Frost from what he regards as Thompson's insensitive, moralistic, all-but-defamatory characterization. Thompson's book left readers with the impression that Frost was a "monster," "a hateful human being," and a man of "demonic vileness." This characterization stems primarily from Thompson's account of Frost's alleged callousness toward other people, especially his wife and children, and it raises complicated issues which Pritchard can scarcely hope to unravel in the limited space he allows himself. To be sure, he does persuade us that Thompson, who had been close to Frost, and who had been chosen by Frost for the task, had developed an excessive antipathy to his subject in the course of writing his immense biography. What Pritchard offers us, in place of Thompson's overdrawn portrait of an irremediably self-involved man, is an impressionist sketch of a somewhat more human, intermittently affectionate, yet disconcertingly feckless, husband and father.

The behavior Thompson depicts as chilling careerism Pritchard treats as the charming insouciance of a truly poetic temperament. In Thompson's version of the London years, the cagey Yankee poet is a shameless flatterer and manipulator whose conscience more often than not was overborne by his enormous ambition. Acts that seemed duplicitous or self-seeking to the literal-minded Thompson, Pritchard regards as merely subtle or playful or *poetical*. So far from having us deplore them, Pritchard would have us admire them, as we do the poems, for their "ingenuity and expertness." Pritchard allows that Frost was, as he coyly said of himself, "not undesigning," but he takes at face value the poet's notion of living *poetically:* his designing merely testifies to the intensity of his aspiration toward a free, morally unconstrained, playful way of life. This idea is the key to Pritchard's understanding of the close interplay between Frost's life and work: "Here we touch on as deep a conviction as is to be found in the life or the poetry; for . . . this insistence on a "free" action, unmotivated by reasons of prudence or foresight or sentimental feeling, is . . . something Frost believed centrally about his own life."

The difference between "poetical" and ordinary behavior, it seems, is like the difference between the figurative and literal, poetic and prosaic, uses of language. But the moral limits to such behavior are obscure. Pritchard seems remarkably untroubled by the difficulty of reconciling this ideal of "poetic" freedom and disinterestedness with the poet's boundless egotism and opportunism. Frost's frequent misstatements of fact about himself are not easy to distinguish from lies, but here many of them are seen as harmless instances of a man acting playful and poetical. Pritchard is almost as tolerant of Frost's notoriously reactionary political attitudes: his chauvinism and racism, his anti-intellectualism and his unconcern with social justice. All in all, then, Pritchard's effort to rescue Frost's reputation from the damaging effect of Thompson's heavy-handed moralizing is only half-successful. He conclusively demonstrates that Thompson's portrait is misleading, but though his account of Frost's character and opinions is more believable, it perhaps is too indulgent to be a wholly acceptable substitute.

The most engaging passages derive their energy and lucidity from what Pritchard calls his "informed inwardness" with the poetry. A professor of English at Amherst College, where he had been an undergraduate, and where Frost taught for many years, Pritchard knew Frost slightly, and he wrote his Harvard doctoral dissertation, about Frost, under Reuben Brower; Brower, who also had been an undergraduate at Amherst, and a colleague of Frost's on the Amherst faculty before going to Harvard, was to write an excellent book about the poetry. An interesting essay might be written about this posthumous "Amherst-Frost connection" and the tacit doctrinal position it occupies in contemporary American criticism.[2] In any event, Pritchard writes about the poems with a confidence-inspiring, no-nonsense certitude that comes from having lived with them for a very long while. He is a fine reader, but because the poems are not reprinted in their entirety (to save on permission costs, one supposes), his commentary can be fully appreciated only by those who know Frost's work well, or who are willing, as Pritchard suggests, to stop and read the poems as he discusses them.

The real basis of Frost's London success, of course, was not his clever self-promotional activity, effective as it was, but the poetry—the achieved poetic style—he had brought from America. During his long solitary apprenticeship, while he had been earning a living as a poultry farmer and schoolteacher, Frost had developed a theory of poetry that distinguished his work, in Pritchard's view, from that of just about every poet then writing in English. The theory turns on the idea of making verbal music out of the cadence of whole sentences, or what Frost called "the sound of sense"—a concept Pritchard elucidates in this characteristically direct, helpful, teacherly summary: "The phrase may accommodate either an underlining of 'sound' or of 'sense,' thereby setting up a playful shuttling between the poem as communicating something, some grain of wisdom or truth about the world (the sound of *sense*), and the poem as wholly embodying that truth through its particular music, so that one is mainly aware of something heard (the *sound* of sense)."

2. Brower's book, *The Poetry of Robert Frost: Constellations of Intention* (1963), remains one of the best close readings of Frost's work. Pritchard also expresses his admiration for the more recent study by another Amherst graduate, Richard Poirier: *Robert Frost: The Work of Knowing* (1977). I should add that the present writer was a member of the Amherst College faculty for eighteen years.

Pritchard is at his best in showing how Frost succeeds in breaking the vernacular cadence of ordinary sentences with all their irregularity of accent across the meter's regular beat. His most telling illustrations of this stylistic accomplishment are from *North of Boston,* which featured such powerful, highly compressed blank-verse narrative poems as the well-known "Death of the Hired Man" and "Home Burial." But Pritchard makes a point of discussing the less familiar poems. Here, for example, is the narrative voice heard in the opening lines of "The Black Cottage":

> We chanced in passing by that afternoon
> To catch it in a sort of special picture
> Among tar-banded ancient cherry trees,
> Set well back from the road in rank lodged grass,
> The little cottage we were speaking of,
> A front with just a door between two windows,
> Fresh painted by the shower a velvet black.
> We paused, the minister and I, to look.
> He made as if to hold it at arm's length
> Or put the leaves aside that framed it in.
> "Pretty," he said. "Come in. No one will care."

The first seven lines spoken by this quiet, detached, coolly observant narrator, Pritchard observes, "have almost no tone," yet the sentence sound is there, and it is made all the more conspicuous by the overtly conversational lines that follow. "It is all a matter of pace; Frost's accomplishment is to make that pace expressive of the activity supposedly going on, so if 'We paused, the minister and I, to look,' 'we' do so in a line that is a complete sentence and whose commas create the pause." Pritchard underscores Frost's insistence that he was writing for the ear, not the eye; that his technique was as much the content as what we ordinarily think of as content or theme; and that, indeed, this poet had no burning desire to convey a "meaning." What matters most about a Frost poem is that it exists "just for itself" or, in other words, that it is " 'free' in the nature of its expressiveness."

An obvious advantage of this kind of radically selective "literary life" is sharpness of critical focus. Unlike a comprehensive, minutely documented biography, in which discussion of the writer's work often is swamped by a detailed chronicle of events, *Frost* never strays far from what matters most: the poet's theory and practice of art. The book is a model of critical forthrightness, but its corresponding defect is a relative thinness of context, a virtual absence of cultural history. Although Pritchard attaches central importance to Frost's success in bringing the cadences of American speech into poetry, he slights the prior history of that project: the tradition that goes back at least as far as Emerson's ideas about language, and includes Whitman's quite different practice. Nor does Pritchard relate the idea of a poetic grounded in sentence sounds to its prosaic counterpart: the distinctively American vernacular prose style developed by Mark Twain, Ernest Hemingway, and company.

The absence of historical depth is also evident where Pritchard is at his best: in his sensitive discussion of Frost's most admired and distinctive poems, the pastoral lyrics. (The working title for *North of Boston* was *New England Eclogues.*) In the "typical plot" of the early lyrics, Pritchard says, "the protagonist goes forth into nature, encounters somebody or something, is moved to consider its significance, and ends with a balanced reflection—a composed version of the 'wisdom' in which (he [Frost] says) the figure a poem makes should end." This is accurate enough, but it encourages the impression of a poet working more or less directly from his own casually selected, idiosyncratic experience. We get little sense of the extent to which this whole process—going forth into nature, encountering something, considering its significance, etc.—was a well-established, if subtly changing, cultural rite. We get little sense, to put it differently, of Frost's place in the record of romantic pastoralism in America.

The result is that Pritchard's unfailingly precise and perceptive discussion of these poems lacks the resonance it might easily have had. Speaking to the American Academy of Arts and Sciences in 1958, Frost talked about his mother's early fondness for Emerson, and about his being "brought up" in an Emersonian "religion." Emerson was not given to formulaic statements, but the chapter "Language" in his 1836 manifesto, *Nature,* contains the essential formula, at once literary and metaphysical, for the viewpoint from which a great many American works, including Frost's pastoral lyrics, depart: "1. Words are signs of natural facts. 2. Particular natural facts are symbols of particular spiritual facts. 3. Nature is the symbol of spirit."

From the beginning, these propositions constituted the hypothesis, or point of departure, for much of Frost's memorable work. "Mowing," a poem from *A Boy's Will* discussed by Pritchard, reads like a skeptical enactment of the notion that a writer might hope, by attaching the right words to the natural facts, to open a channel to a transcendent meaning. The speaker recalls that the only sound he heard while mowing a field was that of his scythe "whispering to the ground."

> What was it it whispered? I knew not well myself;
> Perhaps it was something about the heat of the sun,
> Something, perhaps, about the lack of sound—
> And that was why it whispered and did not speak.

In one sense, he has already answered his question: but the rest of the poem is about the way he comes to terms with his inability to translate the scythe's whisper (a natural fact) into words (which in turn convey a meaning or "spiritual fact"). In his yearning to get at the presumed meaning of the fact he had overreached the evidence, and he now reveals some of the illusory meanings he later had been forced to reject:

> It was no dream of the gift of idle hours,
> Or easy gold at the hand of fay or elf.

To have invested that whispery sound with such spurious significance would only have diminished the experience.

> Anything more than the truth would have seemed too weak
> To the earnest love that laid the swale in rows . . .

In the end, he had pulled back to the unadorned, irreducible fact with which he had begun.

> The fact is the sweetest dream that labor knows.
> My long scythe whispered and left the hay to make.

Like many of Frost's most moving lyrics, this is an inverted or failed
pastoral, a minimalist version of a design that figures prominently in
classic American literature. The action, a "going forth into nature," has
a distinctive New World aura, and it arouses expectations of achieving
a meaningful harmony with nature that it eventually disappoints. The
outcome is in effect a repudiation of the Emersonian notion that natural
facts, properly understood, can be made to figure forth value, meaning
or purpose. Yet the poem derives its essential power from the viewpoint it repudiates.

Frost continued to write such pastorals of failure throughout his career, and though the tone changed, the underlying pattern did not. In
"The Most of It" (1942), as in "Mowing" (1913), the pastoral impulse to locate meaning in otherness is thwarted, and the speaker or
protagonist is finally thrown back on the hard facts alone. What counts
for everything, then, is what the poet can make of the failed quest—
in the sense, not of fashioning a surrogate for nature's non-meaning,
but of demonstrating his technical skill.

Pritchard suggests the close if somewhat covert affinity between Frost's
work and the Modernist spirit. In a brilliant discussion of *A Witness
Tree* (1942), he notes the increasingly stylized, unreal, dislocated character of the situations Frost depicts in these poems. There is something
"perverse-looking," a "weird fairy tale cast," about poems like "The
Most of It," "The Subverted Flower" and "Never again would birds'
song be the same." The intrinsic strangeness of these poems is particularly revealing in the light of Frost's changing (or simply more candid)
self-conception. As he became increasingly absorbed in self-promotion
and in sheer publicity, he tended, in Pritchard's words, to present himself in the language of "prowess and performance and play."

The real subject of many Frost poems, with their "prevailing artificiality," is the poet's own performance. Although they display few of
the familiar marks of the experimental avant-garde, they are akin to
the work of certain Modernist poets in their studied avoidance of most
connections with actual social life and, above all, in their manifest aspiration toward becoming purely self-referential objects. Pritchard never
suggests that Frost was a Modernist in the received sense of the word,
but he enables us to see the underlying compatibility between some of

Frost's best work and the spirit of an aesthetic Modernism that is, in a peculiar, inadvertent way, more radical, that veers closer to a thorough-going moral nihilism, than anything in the work of Eliot, Stevens, or Williams.

# PART II

# The Machine in the Garden

> . . . the artist must employ the symbols in use in his day and
> nation to convey his enlarged sense to his fellow-men.
>
> RALPH WALDO EMERSON[1]

I

The response of American writers to industrialism has been a typical
and, in many respects, a distinguishing feature of our culture. The Industrial Revolution, of course, was international, but certain aspects of
the process were intensified in this country. Here, for one thing, the
Revolution was delayed, and when it began it was abrupt, thorough,
and dramatic. During a decisive phase of that transition, our first significant literary generation, that of Hawthorne and Emerson, came to
maturity.[2] Hence it may be said that our literature, virtually from the
beginning, has embodied the experience of a people crossing the line
which sets off the era of machine production from the rest of human
history. As Emerson said, speaking of the century as the "age of tools,"
so many inventions had been added in his time that life seemed "almost
made over new."[3] My aim here is to demonstrate one of the ways in
which a sense of the transformation of life by the machine has con-

1. "Art," *Complete Works* (Boston, 1904), II, 352.
2. The decisive character of technological change in this period has been set
forth in detail by George R. Taylor; see *The Transportation Revolution, 1815-
1860* (New York, 1951). Edward C. Kirkland, in a symposium on "The Flowering of New England," suggested the close relationship between the literary and
technological developments at this time. See *The Cultural Approach to History,*
edited by Caroline Ware (New York, 1940).
3. "Works and Days," *Works,* VII, 158.

tributed to the temper of our literature. The emphasis is upon the years before 1860, because the themes and images with which our major writers then responded to the onset of the Machine Age have provided us with a continuing source of meaning.

Some will justifiably object, however, that very little of the work of Emerson, Thoreau, Hawthorne, or Melville actually was *about* the Industrial Revolution. But this fact hardly disposes of the inquiry; indeed, one appeal of the subject is precisely the need to meet this objection. For among the many arid notions which have beset inquiries into the relations between literature and society, perhaps the most barren has been the assumption that artists respond to history chiefly by making history their manifest subject. As if one might adequately gauge the imaginative impact of atomic power by seeking out direct allusions to it in recent literature. Our historical scholars do not sufficiently distinguish between the setting of a literary work (it may be institutional, geographical, or historical) and its subject-matter or theme. A poem set in a factory need be no more about industrialism than *Hamlet* about living in castles. Not that the setting is without significance. But the first obligation of the scholar, like any other reader of literature, is to know what the work is about. Only then may he proceed to his special business of elucidating the relevance of the theme to the experience of the age.

But here a difficulty arises: the theme itself cannot be said to "belong" to the age. It is centuries old. The Promethean theme, for example, belongs to no single time or place; history periodically renews man's sense of the perils attendant upon the conquest of nature. This obvious fact lends force to the view, tacit postulate of much recent criticism, that what we value in art derives from (and resides in) a realm beyond time, or, for that matter, society. Yet because the scholar grants his inability to account for the genesis of themes, he need not entertain a denial of history. True, he should not speak, for example, of *the* literature of industrialism, as if there were serious works whose controlling insights originate in a single, specific historical setting. But he has every reason to assume that certain themes and conventions, though they derive from the remote past, may have had a peculiar relevance to an age suddenly aware that machines were making life over new. That, in any case, is what seems to have happened in the age of Emerson and Melville. Because our writers seldom employed industrial settings until late in the century we have thought that only then did the prospect of a mechanized America affect their vision of life.[4] My view is that an awareness of the Machine Revolution has been vital to our literature since the eighteen thirties.

But what of a man like Hawthorne, whom we still regard as the "pure" artist, and whose work apparently bears little relation to the Industrial Revolution of his age? In his case it is necessary to demonstrate the importance for his work of matters about which he wrote virtually nothing. Here is "Ethan Brand," a characteristic story developed from an idea Hawthorne recorded in 1843: "The search of an investigator for the Unpardonable Sin;—he at last finds it in his own heart and practice."[5] The theme manifestly has nothing to do with industrialization. On the contrary, it is traditional; we correctly associate it with the Faust myth.[6] Nevertheless, some facts about the genesis of the tale are suggestive. For its physical details, including characters and landscape, Hawthorne drew upon notes he had made during a Berkshire vacation in 1838. At that time several new factories were in operation along the mountain streams near North Adams.[7] He was struck by the sight of machinery in the green hills; he took elaborate notes, and conceived the idea of a malignant steam engine which attacked and killed its human attendants.[8] But he did nothing with that idea, or with any of his other observations upon the industrialization of the

4. Edmund Wilson, for example, criticized Maxwell Geismar for suggesting that the criticism of industrial society in the literature of the 1930s was "something quite new." Wilson contended that this was a point of view to be found in our literature in the period from 1870-1900. Most standard histories of American literature accept the same chronology. For Wilson's comment, see his review of Geismar's *The Last of the Provincials* in *The New Yorker*, XXIII (1947), 57.

5. Randall Stewart, ed., *The American Notebooks* (New Haven, 1932), 106.

6. This connection has been thoroughly explored by William Bysshe Stein, *Hawthorne's Faust* (Gainesville, Florida, 1953).

7. According to some accounts, the production of textiles in the North Adams area had increased by over 400 percent between 1829 and 1837, the year before Hawthorne's visit. See John W. Yeomans, "A History of the Town of Adams," in *A History of the County of Berkshire, Massachusetts,* . . . (Pittsfield, Mass., 1839), 422-42.

8. *American Notebooks,* 42. This idea follows Hawthorne's record of a visit to a shop for the manufacture of marble. The press at this time featured stories of such industrial accidents. And it is worth remarking that similar images later caught the attention of Emerson (*Works*, VI, 115) and Henry James (*The American* (London, 1921), 263).

Berkshires. And the fact remains that nowhere, in "Ethan Brand" or the notebooks, do we find any explicit evidence of a direct link between Hawthorne's awareness of the new power and this fable of the quest for knowledge of absolute evil.

II

Nevertheless this connection can, I believe, be established. What enables us to establish it is the discovery of a body of imagery through which the age repeatedly expressed its response to the Industrial Revolution. This "imagery of technology" is decisively present in "Ethan Brand."

Although the theme is traditional, some components of the tale take on their full significance only when we consider what was happening in America at the time. Between 1830 and 1860 the image of the machine, and the idea of a capitalist society founded upon machine power suddenly took hold of the public imagination. In the magazines, for example, images of industrialism, and particularly images associated with the power of steam, were widely employed as emblems of America's future.[9] They stood for progress, productivity, and, above all, man's new power over nature. And they invariably carried a sense of violent break with the past. Later, looking back at those years, Henry Adams compressed the essential feeling into his account of the way "he and his eighteenth century . . . were suddenly cut apart—separated forever . . ." by the railroad, steamship, and telegraph.[10] It is the suddenness and finality of change—the recent past all at once a green colonial memory—to which American writers have persistently called attention. The motif recurs in our literature from *Walden* to *The Bear*.

But at first our writers did not respond by writing *about* the Industrial Revolution. Long before they knew enough to find concepts for the experience, as Adams later could do, they had invested their work with ideas and emotions it provoked. To this end they drew upon images of technology already familiar to the public. Such collective representa-

9. A survey of this material has been made possible by a grant from the Research Fund of the Graduate School, University of Minnesota, and by the assistance of Mr. Donald Houghton.
10. *The Education of Henry Adams* (New York, 1931), 5.

tions, or "cultural images," allowed them to express what they could not yet fully understand. And at times they heightened these images to the intensity of symbols. The symbolism of Hawthorne and Melville was, after all, designed to get at circumstances which gave rise to conflicting emotions, and which exceeded, in their complexity, the capacities of understanding.[11] Indeed, there is reason to believe that the unprecedented changes then taking place may have provided a direct impetus to the use of symbolic techniques.[12] Hawthorne admitted as much in explaining why he required the image of the railroad to convey that sense of loneliness in the crowd he thought characteristic of the new America. This image, he said, enabled him to present the feeling of a "whole world, both morally and physically, . . . detached from its old standfasts and set in rapid motion."[13]

Now, as the statements of Emerson, Adams, and Hawthorne suggest, the evocative power of the imagery of industrialism is not to be attributed to any intrinsic feature of machines. What gives rise to the emotion is not the machine, but rather its presence against the felt back-

11. According to Carl Jung, the very essence of symbolism is that it "attempts to express a thing for which there exists *as yet* no adequate verbal concept." It conveys perceptions which can *"as yet,"* neither be apprehended better, nor expressed differently." The emphasis upon "as yet" is the present author's, and is intended to call attention to the temporal, or historic, factor in this conception of symbolism. The implication is that the elements of experience which most urgently demand symbolic expression are the novel elements. For Jung's formulation, see *Contributions to Analytical Psychology* (London, 1928), 225-49.

12. The common concern of our writers with symbolism, so far from indicating an essentially aesthetic (or technical) turn of mind, might profitably be reexamined as a response to needs presented by the age. This suggestion is made as a possible alternative to the views of Charles Feidelson. In *Symbolism and American Literature* (Chicago, 1953), Feidelson argues that the "really vital common denominator" among our writers of the age was their "devotion to the possibilities of symbolism." His account of their symbolic vision is convincing, but he suggests that the concern with technique on the part of these men is a measure of their "purely" literary bent. Here he is taking issue with such critics as F. O. Matthiessen, who have insisted upon the decisive significance of the cultural context. There is no need, however, for forcing a choice between a technical (aesthetic) and a cultural (historic) interpretation of our literature. We need an awareness of both.

13. "The Old Apple Dealer," *The Complete Works of Nathaniel Hawthorne* (Boston, 1883), II, 502. Hawthorne later used virtually the same image in *The House of the Seven Gables*. For Hawthorne's development of the railroad symbol, see Leo Marx, "Hawthorne and Emerson: Studies in the Impact of the Machine Technology Upon the American Writer," unpublished dissertation (Harvard, 1950).

ground of the older historic landscape. The American landscape, in fact, accounts for another singular feature of the response to our Industrial Revolution. In this country mechanization had been arrested, among other things, by space—the sheer extent of the land itself. Then, suddenly, with the application of mechanized motive power to transport, this obstacle had been overcome. Hence the dramatic decisiveness of the changes in Hawthorne's time, when steam power was suddenly joined to the forces already pressing to occupy the virgin land. In America machines were pre-eminently conquerors of nature—nature conceived as space. They blazed across a raw landscape of wilderness and farm.

Now it is hardly necessary to discuss the high value, aesthetic, moral, and even political, with which the landscape had so recently been invested. Henry Nash Smith has indicated how central a place images of the landscape occupied in the popular vision of America's future as new Garden of the World.[14] The sudden appearance of the Machine in the Garden deeply stirred an age already sensitive to the conflict between civilization and nature. This symbolic tableau recorded the tension between two opposed conceptions of man's relations with his universe. The society prefigured by the myth of the Garden would celebrate a passive accommodation to nature's law. There, survival would depend upon organic production or growth. But the machine foretold an economy designed by human intelligence, and it implied an active, indeed proud, assertion of humanity's dominion over nature. Hence the writers of the American "renaissance," not unlike Shakespeare's contemporaries, confronted one of the more rewarding situations history bestows upon art: the simultaneous attraction of two visions of a people's destiny, each embodying a discrete view of human experience, and each, moreover, accompanied by fresh and vivid symbols. The theme was as old as the story of Prometheus and Epimetheus, but its renewed vitality in Hawthorne's day may be attributed to the power with which fire was making life over new.[15]

14. *Virgin Land, The American West as Symbol and Myth* (Cambridge, 1950). Though he does not explicitly develop the idea, Smith's material suggests that the myth may have taken shape, or at least reached its fullest development, under pressure from industrialization.

15. The contrast between Epimetheus and Prometheus offers a particularly close analogue to the theme under discussion. Epimetheus, whose name may actually have connoted a concern with the past, was committed to tradition, to a passive, some would say "feminine," celebration of the organic. But Prometheus, who

III

In 1838, five years before Hawthorne had formulated the moral germ of "Ethan Brand," he had been struck by an actual sight of this change in American society. "And taking a turn in the road," he wrote, "behold these factories. . . . And perhaps the wild scenery is all around the very site of the factory and mingles its impression strangely with those opposite ones." Here was history made visible. What most impressed Hawthorne was a "sort of picturesqueness in finding these factories, supremely artificial establishments, in the midst of such wild scenery."[16] Nevertheless, ten years later, when Hawthorne so thoroughly mined this Berkshire notebook for "Ethan Brand," he passed over these impressions. The factories do not appear in the story. Nor is there any overt allusion to industrialization. To speculate about the reasons for this "omission" would take us far afield.[17] Whatever the

---

stole fire from the gods, was oriented toward the future, and a technology in the service of man. His attitude was aggressively man-centered; Epimetheus was reverent toward the gods. It is highly probable that the literary interest in this myth in modern times must be understood in relation to the development of technology in general, and to the use of fire in particular. The most exact parallel is the antithesis, suggested below, of Ahab and Ishmael. But with this difference: Ahab was concerned not with mankind, as in the case of Prometheus, but with himself. In this sense Ahab represents a perversion of the Promethean quest, as Richard Chase (*Herman Melville* (New York, 1949)) and M. O. Percival (*A Reading of Moby Dick* (Chicago, 1950)) have suggested.

16. *American Notebooks*, 34-35. Hawthorne's comment illustrates the close affinity between this characteristic experience of the age and the symbolic technique our writers developed at the time. (See note 11, above.) When confronted by this tableau of the Machine in the Garden, Hawthorne is most fascinated by the mingling of opposite impressions. Such polarizations of meaning within a single object of sense were precisely what called forth the symbolic method of the period. As Melville explained in expounding upon the symbolic power of the whiteness of the whale, the essential circumstance was the "bringing together [of] two . . . opposite emotions in our minds." The age dramatized such polarizations of meaning, and the symbolic technique was designed to encompass them.

17. One plausible explanation is suggested by Hawthorne's initial effort to describe the factories as aspects of the "picturesque." He was committed to the picturesque convention as a basis for selecting and treating the physical background of his fiction. However, this convention, with its stress upon the "natural" and the archaic, was hardly a congenial medium through which to present such radically new phenomena as the new technology. "In one way or another," he wrote in 1843, ". . . the inventions of mankind are fast blotting the picturesque, the poetic, and the beautiful out of human life." ("Fire Worship," *Works*, II, 160.) Hence we might conclude that Hawthorne's well-known difficulty in handling such characteristic aspects of the modern environment as the factories is to be accounted for by an unwillingness to step outside the bounds

reason, the important fact is not that "Ethan Brand" contains no mention of the factories themselves, but that the ideas and emotions they suggested to Hawthorne are central to the story.

A sense of loss, anxiety, and dislocation hangs over the world of "Ethan Brand." The mood is located in the landscape. At the outset we hear that the countryside is filled with "relics of antiquity."[18] What caused this melancholy situation becomes apparent when Hawthorne describes the people of the region. Brand has returned from his quest. Word is sent to the village, and a crowd climbs the mountain to hear his tale. From among them Hawthorne singles out several men: the stage-agent, recently deprived of his vocation; an old-fashioned country doctor, his useful days gone by; and a man who has lost a hand (emblem of craftsmanship?) in the "devilish grip of a steam-engine" (pp. 486-87). He is now a "fragment of a human being." Like the Wandering Jew and the forlorn old man who searches for his lost daughter (said to have been a victim of Ethan's experimental bent), all are derelicts. They are victims of the fires of change. Like the monomaniac hero himself, all suffer a sense of not belonging.

This intense feeling of "unrelatedness" to nature and society has often been ascribed to the very historical forces which Hawthorne had

---

set by a literary convention; that he saw the choice as one between the literary convention on the one hand and the new subject matter on the other. If so, it is clear that he habitually chose the convention, and that the ideas and emotions he did feel in the presence of the new factories had to be invested, if they were to be given any expression, in other subjects. Hence they were expressed "covertly," or, as it were, symbolically.

But this is not to say that Hawthorne's difficulty in writing about the new material world was therefore "merely" aesthetic. On the contrary, the decision to continue working inside the convention was itself an indirect response to the changing environment. Why did he choose to work inside the convention when he found it unsuitable for presenting such obviously fascinating material? His choice here, it would seem, is as revealing of his underlying emotions as more direct expressions of anxiety such as the fantasy of the malignant steam engine. (See page 115.) He was uneasy about the changes foretold by the new technology, as a study of the imagery of industrialism in his work would bear out. He invariably used such images to convey a sense of menace, brutality, and generalized hostility to the human and the beautiful. Thus his attachment to the picturesque convention, which implicitly rejected the new technology, was a manifestation of the same emotions, and merely a special aspect of his total response to reality.

18. *Works*, III, 478. Subsequent references to "Ethan Brand" appear in the text.

observed in 1838. Discussing the intellectual climate of that era, Emerson once remarked that young men then had been born with knives in their brains. This condition was a result, he said, of the pervasive "war between intellect and affection." He called it "detachment," and found it reflected everywhere in the age: in Kant, Goethe's *Faust*, and in the consequences of the new capitalist power. "Instead of the social existence which all shared," he wrote, "was now separation."[19] Whatever we choose to call it—"detachment" or "alienation" (Karl Marx), or "anomie" (Emile Durkheim) or "dissociation of sensibility" (T. S. Eliot)—this is the malaise from which Ethan suffered.[20] Though there are important differences of emphasis, each of these terms refers to the state of mind of an individual cut off from a realm of experience said to be an indispensable source of life's meaning. The source may vary, but it is significant that the responsible agent, or *separator*, so to speak, is invariably identified with science or industrial technology. In this sense Hawthorne's major theme was as vividly contemporary as it was traditional. He gave us the classic American account of the anguish of detachment.

The knife in Ethan's brain was a "cold philosophical curiosity" which led to a "separation of the intellect from the heart."[21] Now it is of the utmost significance that this scientific obsession is said to have literally emanated from the fire. There was a legend about Ethan's having been accustomed "to evoke a fiend from the hot furnace" (p. 483). Together they spent many nights by the fire evolving the idea of the quest. But the fiend always retreated through the "iron door" of the kiln with the first glimmer of sunlight. Here we discover how Hawthorne's earlier impressions of industrialization have been transmuted in the creative process. Here is the conduit through which thought and emotion flow to the work from the artist's experience of his age. In this

19. "Historic Notes of Life and Letters in New England," *Works*, X, 307-47. See especially 307-311.

20. For the Marxian concept of "alienation" see Karl Marx and Friedrich Engels, *The German Ideology,* Parts I and III, edited by R. Pascal (New York, 1939).

Durkheim develops the conception of "anomie" in *The Division of Labor in Society*, tr. George Simpson (Glencoe, Ill., 1947); see especially pages 353-74.

For Eliot's conception of "dissociation of sensibility" see T. S. Eliot, "The Metaphysical Poets," *Selected Essays* (New York, 1950), 241-50.

21. *American Notebooks*, 106.

case the symbolic contrast between fire and sun serves the purpose. It blends a traditional convention (we think of Milton's Hell)[22] and immediate experience; it provides the symbolic frame for the entire story. "Ethan Brand" begins at sundown and ends at dawn. During the long night the action centers upon the kiln or "furnace" which replaces the sun as source of warmth, light, and (indirectly) sustenance. The fire in the kiln is at once the symbolic source of evil and of the energy necessary to make nature's raw materials useful to man. Moreover, it can be shown that the very words and phrases used to describe this fire are used elsewhere, by Hawthorne, in direct reference to industrialization.[23]

22. Francis D. Klingender has indicated that industrial imagery was being used in illustrations of Milton's Hell in editions of *Paradise Lost* published early in the nineteenth century. See *Art and the Industrial Revolution* (London, 1947), 103-8, 192-96. As Klingender suggests, this tendency to identify Satan with industrialism is to be found in the poem. Blake saw this and made it explicit in his *Milton* (1804-1808). In addition to the factories in Hell, *Paradise Lost* is relevant here for the marked use Milton made of the traditional opposition of fire (associated with human technology) and sun (associated with the divine creation). The poem was one of Hawthorne's favorite works of literature. The connection is particularly apparent in Milton's view that before the fall of Adam and Eve there were in the garden only such tools "as art yet rude, | Guiltless of fire had formed." (IX, 391-92.) After the fall, however, Adam and Eve resorted, among other techniques of self-preservation, to fire. (X, 1060-93.) *The Poems of John Milton,* edited by James Holly Hanford (New York, 1953).

23. The associative continuity between Hawthorne's emotions about the Industrial Revolution and "Ethan Brand" can be established. Here are a few of several instances of images which appear both in "Ethan Brand" and elsewhere in explicit reference to the new technology. (For further details see Marx, "Hawthorne and Emerson.")

$A_1$ "Fire Worship" (see note 17, above) is an essay on the changes which result from certain new inventions. There the stove is referred to as an "iron prison."

$A_2$ "Ethan Brand": the kiln is called the "hollow prison-house of the fire."

$B_1$ In "The Celestial Railroad," a satire on America's commitment to salvation by (technological) works, the narrator sees fire and smoke issuing from a hillside. There is some doubt as to whether this is the "mouth of the infernal region" or a place where "forges" have been "set up for the manufacture of railroad iron." (*Works*, II, 221.) The Bunyan aspect is explicit.

$B_2$ "Ethan Brand": the smoke and flame of the lime kiln is said to resemble "nothing so much as the private entrance to the infernal regions" in Bunyan. (III, 478.)

Other words in this cluster of technological association are *furnace, forge, coal, smoke,* and *iron.* Most of them are important in "Ethan Brand." Of the entire group, however, the word which seems to carry these implications closest to the center of Hawthorne's work is *iron.* In *The Scarlet Letter* and wherever he dealt with Puritanism, Hawthorne repeatedly used the word *iron* to convey the cold

In the magazines of the day fire was repeatedly identified with the new machine power.[24] Hence fire, whatever its traditional connotations, is here an emblem, or fragment of an emblem, of the nascent industrial order. The new America was being forged by fire.

But if fire cripples men and devastates the landscape in "Ethan Brand," the sun finally dispels anxiety and evil, restoring man's solidarity with nature. When Ethan dies, his body burned to a brand by the satanic flames which had possessed his soul, the fire goes out and the ravaged landscape disappears. In its stead we see a golden vision of the self-contained New England village. The sun is just coming up. The hills swell gently about the town, as if resting "peacefully in the hollow of the great hand of Providence." In pointed contrast to the murky atmosphere of Ethan's Walpurgisnacht, there is no smoke anywhere. The sun allows perfect clarity of perception. Every house is "distinctly visible." At the center of this pastoral tableau the spires of the churches catch the first rays of the sun. Now the countryside is invested with all the order and serenity and permanence which the fire had banished. This harmony between man and nature is then projected beyond time in the vision of a stepladder of clouds on which it seemed that (from such a social order?) "mortal man might thus ascend into heavenly regions." Finally, though he had already hinted that stage coaches were obsolete, Hawthorne introduces one into this eighteenth-century New England version of the Garden of Eden.

---

strain of utilitarianism in the Puritan character. In *The House of the Seven Gables,* the connection between Puritanism and the new industrial power is made clear.

In the magazines in Hawthorne's day this association of *iron* with the new power of steam was widespread. "The age may . . . be called an age of iron . . . ," said one writer, "for it is the supreme agent in motive-power, which may be truly said at the present time to govern the world. It is the ponderous machinery, instinct with the life which steam gives it, that connects countries. . . ." *Hunt's Merchants Magazine,* XXIII (Oct. 1850), 463.

24. Writing on the "Effects of Machinery," a contributor to the *North American Review* praised the new technology, and characteristically stressed the rôle of fire in the Revolution: "Last, and most wonderful of all, by the application of fire we transform water into that most potent of all agents, steam. Man, as it were, yokes the hostile elements of fire and water, and subjects them to his bidding. It is hardly a metaphor, to call steam the vital principle, the living soul of modern machinery." XXXIV (Jan. 1832), 244.

It should also be noted that lime kilns figured prominently in early industrial landscapes. See, for example, J. M. W. Turner, "Colebrook Dale, View of the Lime Kilns," reproduced in Klingender, 176.

Beneath the surface of "Ethan Brand" we thus find many of the ideas and emotions aroused by the Machine's sudden entrance into the Garden. But this is not to say that the story is *about* industrialization. It is about the consequences of breaking the magic chain of humanity. That is the manifest theme and, like the symbols through which it is developed, the theme is traditional. His apprehension of the tradition permits Hawthorne to discover meanings in contemporary facts. On the other hand, the capacity of this theme and these images to excite the imagination must also be ascribed to their vivid relevance to life in modern America. This story, in short, is an amalgam of tradition, which supplies the theme, and experience, which presents the occasion, and imagery common to both.

IV

But it may be said that, after all, this is merely one short story. The fact remains, however, that the same, or related, images may be traced outward from this story to Hawthorne's other work, the work of his contemporaries, the work of many later writers, and the society at large.

It is revealing, for example, that Hawthorne so often described his villains as alchemists, thereby associating them with fire and smoke. We recall that Aylmer, the scientist in "The Birthmark," made a point of building his laboratory underground to avoid sunlight.[25] Or consider Rappaccini, whose experiments perverted the Garden itself. His flowers were evil because of their "artificialness indicating . . . the production . . . no longer of God's making, but the monstrous offspring of man's depraved fancy. . . ."[26] From Hamilton's "Report on Manufactures" in 1791 until today, American thinking about industrialism, in and out of literature, has been tangled in the invidious distinction between "artificial" and "natural" production.[27] These adjectives, like so

25. *Works,* II, 56.
26. *Works,* II, 128.
27. Although Hamilton, in his celebrated Report, was stating the case for industrial development, he could not avoid the distinction. It was virtually a part of the language. "Report on Manufactures," *Industrial and Commercial Correspondence of Alexander Hamilton,* edited by Arthur Harrison Cole (Chicago, 1928), 247-322. See especially 247-56.

much of American political rhetoric, along with Hawthorne's theme of isolation, are a characteristic legacy of pre-industrial experience. They are expressions of our native tradition of pastoral, with its glorification of the Garden and its consequent identification of science and technology with evil. To Hawthorne's contemporaries, Emerson, Thoreau, and Whitman, the sun also represented the primal source of redemption.[28] "The sun rose clear," Thoreau tells us at the beginning of *Walden;* though he notes that the smoke of the train momentarily obscures its rays, the book ends with a passionate affirmation of the possibility of renewed access, as in "Ethan Brand," to its redeeming light: "The sun is but a morning star."[29]

In *Moby-Dick,* published three years after "Ethan Brand," the identical motif emerges as a controlling element of tragedy. The "Try-Works," a crucial chapter in Ishmael's progressive renunciation of Ahab's quest, is quite literally constructed out of the symbols of "Ethan Brand."[30] Again it is night, and vision is limited to the lurid light of a "kiln" or "furnace." Fire again is a means of production, rendering the whale's fat, and again it is also the source of alienation. Ishmael, at the helm, controls the ship's fate. Like Ethan he momentarily succumbs to the enchantment of fire, and so nearly fulfills Ahab's destructive destiny. But he recovers his sanity in time, and tells us: "Look not too long in the face of the fire, O Man! . . . believe not the *artificial fire* when its redness makes all things look ghastly. Tomorrow, in the *natural sun,* the skies will be bright; those who glared like devils in the forking

28. Consider, for example, the "Introduction" to Emerson's *Nature:* "The sun shines to-day also." *Works,* I, 3. Or the second section of "Song of Myself," Whitman's lines: "Stop this day and night with me and you shall possess the origin of all poems, | You shall possess the good of the earth and sun (there are millions of suns left,)." In each case the sun is presented as a source of redemption peculiarly accessible to Americans. But when Whitman came to recognize that, due to urbanization, the myth of the Garden no longer was relevant to the experience of most Americans, he announced his own rejection of the myth with the refrain, "Keep your splendid silent sun." See "Give Me the Splendid Silent Sun."

29. Henry Thoreau, *Walden,* Modern Library Edition (New York, 1937), 8, 297.

30. "The Try-Works," Chapter XCVI. The parallel to "Ethan Brand" is discussed by Howard P. Vincent, *The Trying Out of Moby-Dick* (New York, 1949), 335. There is no doubt that Melville had read and was impressed by "Ethan Brand" before completing *Moby-Dick.* See his letter to Hawthorne in *The Portable Melville,* edited by Jay Leyda (New York, 1952), 429-34. Leyda estimates that the letter was written about June 1, 1851.

flames, the more will show in far other, at least gentler relief; the glorious, golden, glad sun, the only true lamp—all others but liars!"[31]

From this passage we may trace lines of iconological continuity to the heart of Melville's meaning.[32] When the *Pequod* sailed both Ahab and Ishmael suffered the pain of "detachment." But if the voyage merely reinforced Ahab's worship of the power of fire, it provoked in Ishmael a reaffirmation of the Garden. Ahab again and again expressed his aspiration in images of fire and iron, cogs and wheels, automata, and manufactured men. He had his "humanities," and at times was tempted by thoughts of "green land," but Ahab could not finally renounce the chase.[33] In *Moby-Dick* space is the sea—a sea repeatedly depicted in images of the American landscape. The conquest of the whale was a type of our fated conquest of nature itself. But in the end Ishmael in effect renounced the fiery quest. He was cured and saved. His rediscovery of that pastoral accommodation to the mystery of growth and fertility was as vital to his salvation as it had been to the myth of the Garden.[34] The close identity of the great democratic God and the God of the Garden was a central facet of Melville's apocalyptic insight.

His was also a tragic insight. Ahab and Ishmael, representing irreconcilable conceptions of America's destiny, as indeed of all human experience, were equally incapable of saving the *Pequod*. From Melville to Faulkner our writers have provided a desperate recognition of this truth: of the attributes necessary for survival, the Ahabs alone have been endowed with the power, and the Ishmaels with the perception. Ishmael was saved. But like one of Job's messengers, he was saved to warn us of greater disasters in store for worshippers of fire. In this way imagery associated with the Machine's entrance into the Garden has served to join native experience and inherited wisdom.

31. *Moby-Dick*, edited by Willard Thorp (New York, 1947), 398. My italics.
32. Here and throughout this essay I am indebted to Erwin Panofsky for the method of iconological analysis. See *Studies in Iconology* (New York, 1939).
33. See especially, "The Symphony," Chapter CXXXII.
34. In the first chapter Ishmael asks whether the green fields are gone, and in Chapter XCIV Ishmael identifies the "meadow" with a series of organic and domestic images of man's attainable felicity.

# Literature, Technology, and Covert Culture

(with Bernard Bowron and Arnold Rose)

By covert culture we refer to traits of culture rarely acknowledged by those who possess them. In any society men tend to ignore or repress certain commonly learned attitudes and behavior patterns, much as an individual may ignore or repress certain personal experiences or motives. In the case of covert culture, the repressed traits are more or less common to members of a society, and they probably are transmitted in the same informal ways that the basic elements of the overt culture are transmitted. The covert traits are not more "true" or "real" than the overt traits; they are equally representative of people's attitudes and behaviors. The distinction lies in the degree of acknowledgment (to self and to others) and the degree of repression. If one were to suggest to a representative member of a society that his behavior, or that of his community, exhibits a particular characteristic of covert culture, he might be expected to scoff at the idea, and even reject it heatedly. Public responses to the Kinsey Report are a case in point. Similarly, Americans might deny the evidence of their disguised hostility toward machine technology which we present in this essay.

How then is covert culture recognized? We may assume we are in the presence of covert culture when we note a recurrent pattern of inconsistent or seemingly illogical behavior.[1] When most people in a given society or sub-society adhere to inconsistencies in their actions, when they resist with emotion any attempts to reconcile their actions with their expressed beliefs, and when they persist in this behavior over an extended period of time, then presumably we are dealing with covert culture. For obvious reasons, however, it is difficult to study covert culture. And in a heterogeneous society like our own, where variations in behavior are relatively common, it is unlikely that much of our culture remains covert. On the other hand, the little that does may be of the greatest importance in certain emotionally charged areas of behavior, such as racial or sexual relations or religion.

At this point it might be well to indicate what covert culture is not. In the first place, it is not a whole, complete culture that exists beneath the surface of the overt culture and "really" directs people's attitudes and behavior. It consists, rather, of parts of culture that happen to be seriously inconsistent with other parts of culture and so get driven underground.

Second, behavior in conformity with covert culture is not the same as alienation from culture (or "anomie," to use Durkheim's term). Covert elements of culture are just as much part of culture as overt elements. While behavior in conformity with an element of covert culture is inconsistent with respect to an element of overt culture, such inconsistency might also result from conformity with two incompatible elements of overt culture, although this disharmony would not be so extreme. Logical incompatibility between two elements of culture is likely to manifest itself frequently in a society based on heterogeneous traditions or in a society that is changing rapidly.

Third, covert culture is not a subculture. We are all familiar with the different roles that one plays in the various groups to which he belongs: contrast the behavior of the adolescent in his family and in his peer group. But, while members of each group are shocked or scornfully amused by behavior in the other group, they recognize each other's existence and—in a sense—regard the discrepancies as natural and even

1. This technique for observing covert culture has been presented in Arnold M. Rose, *Theory and Method in the Social Sciences* (Minneapolis: University of Minnesota Press, 1954), chap. 21, "Popular Logic in the Study of Covert Culture." Some elements of covert culture in the United States are suggested in this chapter.

desirable. The adolescent himself is aware of the disparity in his roles, whether or not it creates a conflict for him. Even the subculture of a minority group (such as, for example, the Mennonites or Jews) is in no way to be equated with covert culture. This is a different culture from the dominant one, practiced by a small section of the society, and while it may be deliberately hidden from the majority, its deviations from the dominant culture are quite well known and apparent to those living in both the minority group and the larger society. Sociologists call those living in two societies "marginal men"; they are understood to be fairly rare in any society. Covert culture traits, on the contrary, are exhibited by the large majority of persons in a society if not by all of them.

But it may be asked how covert culture is learned, if it is unacknowledged and secret. The question, however, implies that the transmission of *overt* culture is deliberate and rational. Actually, only a small part of the education of the young in the overt culture of a society is deliberate. While the child learns through language or other symbols such as gestures, most of the process is very subtle. As Hickman and Kuhn point out:

> Few, if any, fathers or mothers take their children aside and say, in effect, "I will now tell you what I know," "I will now tell you what you ought to know and believe," or "I will now tell you about our society and our culture." Any conversations of this general nature could have relatively little over-all influence on the child's attitudes. "Attitudes are caught, not taught."[2]

This is true for both overt and covert culture. The difference lies not in manner of learning, but in the degree of the adult's awareness of the cues he is emitting, or in the degree of his willingness to acknowledge the cues when they are called to his attention. One characteristic of this learning process is that the child picks up the cues of the covert culture, but at first does not know that they are "secret." He proudly displays the just-learned trait openly in behavior or speech, and then the parent is shocked. This negative reaction—coming once or several times—now teaches the child that he must "forget" and "deny" this part of what he has recently learned from the parent. It should be pointed out, however,

2. C. Addison Hickman and Manford H. Kuhn, *Individuals, Groups, and Economic Behavior* (New York: Dryden Press, 1946), p. 30.

that the difference between covert and overt culture is a relative matter; some aspects of covert culture are talked over by intimate friends "over the back fence," as it were. Adults "teach" other adults some aspects of covert culture just as they teach children other aspects.

Those who are probably in the best position to study a society's covert traits are observers who come to it with the perspective of an alien culture. Hence anthropologists and perceptive foreign travelers have until now provided much of the evidence of covert culture. The anthropologists have most frequently analyzed the concept itself.[3] This would suggest that the concept is most useful when direct impressions of a living culture are available. The study of covert culture does not at first thought seem possible through the analysis of written documents; hence the concept seems irrelevant to the study of past societies about which we have few other sources of evidence. It is our purpose here to suggest a means of uncovering elements of covert culture through the analysis of written, and particularly literary, evidence.

Now, to be sure, there is nothing new about the idea of studying literature as a source of information about culture. Historians have been doing it for a long time. When allowances are made for shifts in style and taste, the manifest content of literature may be assumed to reflect important characteristics of culture. But what about covert culture? Since we assume, to begin with, that most members of a society do not care to be reminded that they exhibit traits of covert culture, it follows that the writer who seeks a sizable audience will not knowingly portray them. On the other hand, popular literature may be studied for what it betrays as well as what it depicts. In other words, it may be approached as a

3. The anthropologists have concerned themselves more with the tendency of culture to form patterns or systems covertly rather than with the relationship of covert culture to behavior. See, for example: Edward Sapir, "The Unconscious Patterning of Behavior in Society," in E. S. Dummer (ed.), *The Unconscious: A Symposium* (New York: Alfred A. Knopf, 1928), Clyde Kluckhohn, "Patterning as Exemplified in Navaho Culture," in L. Spier, A. I. Hallowell, and S. S. Newman (eds.), *Language, Culture and Personality: Essays in Memory of Edward Sapir* (Menasha, Wis.: Sapir Memorial Publication Fund, 1941), pp. 109-28; Laura Thompson, "Attitudes and Acculturation," *American Anthropologist,* 50 (1958), 200-215. A few sociologists also have worked with the concept of covert culture: F. Stuart Chapin, "Latent Culture Patterns of the Unseen World of Social Reality," *American Journal of Sociology,* XL (July, 1934), 61-68; Robert K. Merton, *Social Theory and Social Structure* (Glencoe, Ill.: The Free Press, 1949), pp. 21-81.

projection of covert culture. Such an approach to the arts is well established in several areas. Psychologists have for some time been using graphic and lingual expression to get at the unconscious associations of individuals. Of these projective tests, the Rorschach, TAT, and Word Association tests are perhaps the best known. Similarly, literature widely accepted by the public, or a significant segment of the public, may provide an avenue to the unstated ideas of a society. Of course the Freudians and Jungians have studied literature, but not precisely in the way we are suggesting. They have sought recurring popular themes in the classics as projections of what they consider to be universal instincts or complexes. They are concerned with the traits common to virtually all men. What we are concerned with, on the other hand, is a technique for dealing with certain characteristics of a particular culture located in time and place.[4]

The projective component of written documents is chiefly to be found in imagery and metaphor, using metaphor in the broadest sense to include all the more common figurative modes of expression. When a writer uses such analogizing devices, in which the analogy is either explicit or implicit, he is in effect revealing a pattern of association which can only be partly conscious. That is to say, no matter how many reasons he may acknowledge for selecting a particular figure of speech, the fact remains that he selects it from a virtually infinite range of possibilities. Therefore no degree of deliberate calculation can fully explain his choice. For example, why does an author choose a machine to express menace; why not a storm or an earthquake? We are of course not concerned here with idiosyncratic quirks of personality. Our interest is limited to images and metaphors which recur frequently in the written expression of a particular society. We do not have in mind the mere cliché or faddish expression, but rather the metaphor *repeatedly used in*

4. Although the Freudians have characteristically been most concerned with universal rather than particular cultural traits, Freud himself did suggest the possibility of inquiries along the line of this essay. "The analogy between the process of cultural evolution and the path of individual development may be carried further in an important respect. It can be maintained that the community, too, develops a super-ego, under whose influence cultural evolution proceeds. It would be an enticing task for an authority on human systems of culture to work out this analogy in specific cases." *Civilization and Its Discontents,* trans. Joan Riviere (3rd ed.; London: Hogarth Press, 1946), p. 136.

*varying language* to describe similar phenomena.[5] We shall provide an example below.

First, however, a word must be said about our apparent tendency to favor more stereotyped modes of expression. It is true that the more unreflective the creative process, the more useful the work may be as a projection of the psyche, so to speak, of the entire society. But this is not to say that we underestimate the value of less hackneyed literary modes. We conceive of written documents as distributed along a spectrum from the most stereotyped or conventional at one end to the most original and perceptive at the other. The great writer is a sensitive observer, and needless to say, he does not merely project his culture. On the contrary, often he consciously reveals covert elements that less perceptive artists ignore; moreover, he sometimes reveals them precisely by turning stereotypes inside out. Hence this distinction between overt and covert culture should not seem completely unfamiliar to students of literature. Indeed, it is in some respects akin to a recurrent literary motif, the paradoxical relation between "appearance and reality." Not that there is an exact equivalence between the two sets of terms. When a writer indicates the presence of a "reality" hidden beneath "appearances" he usually intends more than we do by covert culture. Nevertheless he often includes an awareness of covert traits. For example, Shakespeare has Lear become aware of covert traits of culture; Cervantes, on the other hand, deliberately makes Don Quixote oblivious of them. In *King Lear* the discrepancy generates a tragic view of life; in *Don Quixote* it is the essence of comedy. In both works, however, the reader's illumination comes at least in part from the author's revelation of the disparity between what we have called overt and covert culture. That disparity is, however, but one aspect of the paradox of appearance and reality.

For an illustration of the use of written documents to reveal covert patterns, consider American culture during the onset of industrialism before the Civil War. Here, as most historians testify, was a society

5. While popular clichés have some interest to the social scientist, they are to be thought of as habits of speech (e.g., "pretty as a picture") rather than as unconsciously selected projections of covert culture, so that mere recurrence of metaphor is not a sufficient criterion. What is to be sought is a metaphor or image that is expressed recurrently in *varying* language used to describe the same set of phenomena.

wholeheartedly committed to the idea of progress. This was an era of unprecedented expansion, social mobility, and optimism. In the newspapers, magazines, and orations of the time we find countless celebrations of the new technology as emblematic of man's increasing dominion over nature. Take, as an example, a minister's address to the New York Mechanic's Institute in 1841. In expounding his theme ("Improvement of the Mechanic Arts"), the Reverend Mr. Williamson employed many commonplaces of the hour. The mechanic arts, he said,

> . . . change the face of nature itself, and cause the desolate and solitary place to be glad and blossom as the rose—the mountains are leveled—the crooked is made strait [*sic*] and the rough places plain— the ascending vapor is arrested in its upward course and converted into a power that well nigh enables us to laugh at distance and space—the broad Atlantic has become, as it were, a narrow lake. . . . And still the course is onward, and we even threaten to seize upon the forked lightning, and pluck from the faithful magnet a power, that shall render useless the canvass [*sic*] of the mariner and achieve a yet mightier triumph over the obstacles that space has interposed to the intercourse of man with his fellow-man . . . much of human happiness depends upon the cultivation of these arts . . . without them, man is but a helpless child, exposed to ten thousand dangers and difficulties, that he cannot control; but with them, he is strong, and can rule in majesty over that mighty empire which God has given him.[6]

To say that this rhetoric embodies certain dominant values of the culture is not to deny that there also were outspoken critics of technological innovation. There were. But they constituted a relatively small minority. Some spoke for the slavery interest or the emergent labor movement, others for various religious sects or utopian reform groups. By and large, however, Americans at this time enthusiastically endorsed the new machine power, and even more enthusiastically applied it. Many of the respected leaders of society, men like Daniel Webster and Edward Everett, paid homage to technology in language indistinguishable from

6. Rev. Bro. I. D. Williamson, *The Covenant and Official Magazine of the Grand Lodge of the United States,* I (June, 1842), 275-81. The original lecture was delivered on Nov. 18, 1841. A survey of responses to industrialization was made possible by a grant from the Graduate School, University of Minnesota, and by the research assistance of Dr. Donald Houghton.

Mr. Williamson's. On the basis of the written evidence, therefore, one might conclude that American culture, leaving aside a few groups of partially alienated people, exhibited only approval of industrialization.

But that is not quite the whole story. To be sure, it describes the dominant overt response to mechanization, but it fails to account for a certain contrary undertone that any close student of the period recognizes. To be more specific, in examining a large sample of reactions to technological change in this period, we discover some which defy simple classification. Here, for example, is an article by James H. Lanman on "Railroads in the United States," which appeared in Hunt's *Merchants' Magazine* in 1840.[7] In accordance with the spirit of this journal of commerce, the writer presents an affirmative survey of the advance of steam power in America. He regards "productive enterprise" as the distinguishing feature of American culture, and he praises the new machines as "the triumphs of our own age, the laurels of mechanical philosophy, of untrammelled mind, and a liberal commerce!" He finds railroads particularly inspiring; so far as he is concerned "it is clear that all patriotic and right-minded men have concurred in the propriety of their construction." If we confine attention to Mr. Lanman's manifest opinions, we have no reason to distinguish him from such ebullient devotees of progress as the Rev. Mr. Williamson.

Nevertheless a more searching examination of this article uncovers a curious anomaly. In spite of the writer's evident effort to enlist support for the new power, he repeatedly invokes images which convey less than full confidence in the benign influence of machines. Steamships and railroads are "iron monsters," "dragons of mightier power, with iron muscles that never tire, breathing smoke and flame through their blackened lungs, feeding upon wood and water, outrunning the race horse. . . ." Elsewhere Mr. Lanman is eager to allay fear of railroad accidents. Therefore he carefully evaluates statistics on deaths and injuries. He finds the results clearly favorable to railroads as compared with travel on "common roads." At the same time, however, he describes a train "leaping forward like some black monster, upon its iron path, by the light of the fire and smoke which it vomits forth."

In contrast to the manifest theme of the piece, these images associate

7. III (October, 1840), 273-95.

machines with the destructive and the repulsive. They communicate an unmistakable sense of anxiety and menace. Without more evidence, of course, we cannot prove that the writer actually was uneasy about the new power. By themselves these images prove nothing. But the fact is that we can produce many other examples of the same kind. Moreover, and this seems to us a most telling point, when we turn to these alienated writers who consciously try to arouse fear of machines, we find them deliberately choosing the same images. Robert Owen, for example, describes the new technology as a power "which neither eats nor drinks, and faints not by over-exertion, brought into direct competition with flesh and blood." "Who is there," he asks, "to check this mighty monster that is now allowed to stalk the earth . . . ?"[8] It was in this period that a kind of machine created in a writer's imagination entered the language as the prototype of terror and the demoniacal—Frankenstein's monster. A final example of the simultaneous attraction and fearfulness of the locomotive, with distinct Oedipal overtones, is provided by this doggerel:

> Big iron horse with lifted head,
> Panting beneath the station shed,
> You are my dearest dream come true;—
> I love my Dad; I worship you!
>
> Your noble heart is filled with fire,
> For all your toil you never tire,
> And though you're saddled-up in steel,
> Somewhere, inside, I *know* you feel.
>
> All night in dreams when you pass by,
> You breathe out stars that fill the sky,
> And now, when all my dreams are true,
> I hardly dare come close to you.[9]

To sum up, we conclude that expressions of the overt culture do not provide an adequate conception of the American response to industrial-

---

8. *New Harmony Gazette,* 2 (August 8, 1827), 347. Owen's words are from an address delivered to the Franklin Institute on June 27, 1827.
9. Benjamin R. C. Low, "The Little Boy to the Locomotive," in David L. Cohn, *The Good Old Days* (New York: Simon and Schuster, 1940), p. 188.

ization. From them we get the familiar picture of a confident, optimistic public and a few small dissident groups. But the concept of covert culture makes possible a somewhat different hypothesis. When we analyze the imagery employed even by those who professed approval of technological change, we discover evidence of widespread if largely unacknowledged doubt, fear, and hostility.[10] It is not necessary to our present purpose to account in detail for this phenomenon. Suffice it to suggest that American culture at this time also embraced a set of values and meanings inherently antithetic to the new technological power. This was a time, as everyone knows, when Americans tended to celebrate the "natural" as against the "artificial." At all levels of culture, from the relatively abstruse speculations of Emerson to the popular gift books, from Cooper's novels to the paintings of the Hudson River School, Americans affirmed values and meanings said to reside in nature. Natural process, that is, was conceived as containing the key, barely concealed, to all human problems. Needless to say, this belief was not peculiar to America. But as a consequence of the unique American geography—the actual presence of the wilderness—it did seem particularly relevant to this country. As Perry Miller has pointed out, what the European romantic dreamed the American actually experienced.[11] Now the progress of technology hardly was reconcilable, at least in the long run, with the sanctity of the natural order. For the use of power machines implied that nature was a neutral if not hostile force that men needed to dominate. This view was in obvious contradiction with the idea that man's felicity depended upon the ordering of life in passive accommodation to spontaneous operations of nature.

We are suggesting, though here we can hardly demonstrate, that this unacknowledged conflict of values may have been an important source of the anxiety revealed by the imagery to which we have called attention.[12] This is not to identify approval of technological progress with

10. It is possible that people betrayed their fear of the machine in casual conversation. But this source of information usually is not available to sociologists, much less to historians. If the sociologist asks people directly about their attitudes toward machines, he is likely to get "rational" answers about how much labor they save, how they provide products and services previously not available, and so on.

11. The Romantic Dilemma in American Nationalism and the Concept of Nature," *Harvard Theological Review*, 48 (October, 1955), 239-53.

12. It is interesting that as early as 1881, Dr. George Miller Beard, an Ameri-

overt culture, and hostility with covert. What is covert here results from the impulse to adhere (simultaneously) to logically incompatible values. In other words, it is the awareness of the contradiction that is repressed and that gives rise to the covert traits (in this case *unacknowledged* fear and hostility) revealed in imagery. Thus it is worth noting that Lanman, the writer who praised locomotives even as he called them monsters, also praised the "steam screw" which, he said, "should tear up by the roots the present monarchs of the forest, and open the ample bosom of the soil to the genial beams of the fertilizing sun." Recall that the writer speaks for a culture passionately devoted to nature—to Bryant's lyric view that "the groves were God's first temples." Is it surprising that he felt impelled to compare machines to terrible monsters? In any event, the disparity between the feelings latent in his images and the manifest optimism of his theme is highly suggestive. It gives some clue to the correspondence between this writer's strangely mixed feelings and the recurrent, if largely unexpressed, pattern of inconsistency in the culture of nineteenth-century America.

This interpretation, finally, is borne out by the work of the more sensitive and perceptive writers of the age. When we turn, for example, to Cooper, Thoreau, Hawthorne, and Melville we find a reiterated expression of precisely those contradictory meanings the typical magazine writers did not acknowledge. What is more, the great writers in many cases employed the same or similar imagery to get at these conflicts. But with an important difference. When Lanman called a machine a monster he was scarcely aware of what he was doing. When Thoreau or Hawthorne did the same thing, he was often deliberately complicating the significance of America's favorite symbol of progress. He gave the railroad an ambiguous meaning, not out of any inherent passion for ambiguity, but rather because he worked to convey as much of the meaning of experience as possible.[13] In other words, he grasped the contradiction

can physician, related the anxiety of Americans to the new technology. His pioneering work, *American Nervousness, Its Causes and Consequences* (New York, 1881), was taken seriously by Freud. See Philip P. Wiener, "G. M. Beard and Freud on 'American Nervousness,'" *Journal of History of Ideas* (April, 1956), 269-74.

13. We agree with Henry G. Fairbanks who, in a recent article, disagrees with scholars who regard Hawthorne as a doctrinaire and romantic opponent of science and technology. But, like the writers he criticizes, Mr. Fairbanks tends to misconstrue Hawthorne's aim in mentioning machines at all. Hawthorne was not

that Lanman, like many other Americans, refused to recognize. It is no accident, therefore, that serious men of letters in this period so often employ machines in symbolic opposition to various emblems of nature. They thus confirm the presence of those covert traits of culture which unreflective writers merely betray.

Repressed traits and attitudes of former periods need not be a closed book. Dead men answer no poll-takers, but they have left an extensive written record of their underground cultures. This record may be deciphered. One indispensable key is the analysis of systems of imagery and metaphor in diverse popular writings and in works of formal literary art. The sociologist need not regard this method of study as an exclusive possession of the literary scholars who originally developed it. Used with care and discrimination, it is equally available to him.

Such collaboration between literary and sociological scholarship is, fortunately, a two-way street. At least it should be. For the concept of covert culture, in turn, offers a rewarding approach to literary studies. This point cannot be developed here. But it is surely implicit in what has been said about formal literature's significant confirmation of the existence of culture traits that are revealed only inadvertently in popular modes of expression. Critics concerned with the devious ways in which a society nurtures its men of letters cannot afford to neglect the existence of covert culture and the writer's responses to it. Here is a major source of those tensions that give a work of literary art its structure, its irony, and its stylistic signature.

---

concerned to convey his opinions about the new technology, but rather to express its meaning, often ambiguous, within the larger pattern of human experience. In doing so, as we have tried to indicate, he revealed contradictions characteristic of American culture generally. See "Hawthorne and the Machine Age," *American Literature*, 28 (May, 1956), 155-64. For a somewhat different method of interpreting the response of American writers to the onset of industrialism see, for example, Leo Marx, "The Machine in the Garden," *New England Quarterly*, 29 (March, 1956), 27-42; "The Pilot and the Passenger: Landscape Conventions and the Style of *Huckleberry Finn*," *American Literature*, 28 (May, 1956), 129-46.

# American Institutions and Ecological Ideals

Anyone familiar with the work of the classic nineteenth-century American writers (I am thinking above all of Cooper, Emerson, Thoreau, Melville, Whitman, and Mark Twain) is likely to have developed an interest in what we recently have learned to call ecology. One of the first things we associate with each of the writers just named is a distinctive, vividly particularized setting (or landscape) inseparable from the writer's conception of man. Partly because of the special geographic and political circumstances of American experience, and partly because they were influenced by the romantic vision of man's relations with nature, all of the writers mentioned possessed a heightened sense of place. Yet words like *place, landscape,* or *setting* scarcely can do justice to the significance these writers imparted to external nature in their work. They took for granted a thorough and delicate interpenetration of consciousness and environment. In fact it now seems evident that these gifted writers had begun, more than a century ago, to measure the quality of American life against something like an ecological ideal.

The ideal I have in mind, quite simply, is the maintenance of a healthy life-enhancing interaction between man and the environment. This is layman's language for the proposition that every organism, in order to avoid extinction or expulsion from its ecosystem, must conform to certain minimal requirements of that system. What makes the concept of the ecosystem difficult to grasp, admittedly, is the fact that the boundaries between systems are always somewhat indistinct, and our technology is making them less distinct all the time. Since an ecosystem includes not only all living organisms (plants and animals) but also the inorganic (physical and chemical) components of the environment, it has become extremely difficult, in the thermonuclear age, to verify even the relatively limited autonomy of local or regional systems. If a decision taken in Moscow or Washington can effect a catastrophic change in the chemical composition of the entire biosphere, then the idea of a San Francisco, or Bay Area, or California, or even North American ecosystem loses much of its clarity and force. Similar difficulties arise when we contemplate the global rate of human population growth. All this is only to say that, on ecological grounds, the case for world government is beyond argument. Meanwhile, we have no choice but to use the nation-states as political instruments for coping with the rapid deterioration of the physical world we inhabit.

The chief question before us, then, is this: What are the prospects, given the character of America's dominant institutions, for the fulfillment of this ecological ideal? But first, what is the significance of the current "environmental crusade"? Why should we be skeptical about its efficacy? How shall we account for the curious response of the scientific community? To answer these questions I will attempt to characterize certain of our key institutions from an ecological perspective. I want to suggest the striking convergence of the scientific and the literary criticism of our national life-style. In conclusion I will suggest a few responses to the ecological crisis indicated by that scientific-literary critique.

In this country, until recently, ecological thinking has been obscured by the more popular, if limited, conservationist viewpoint. Because our government seldom accorded protection of the environment a high priority, much of the responsibility for keeping that end in view fell upon a few voluntary organizations known as the "conservation movement." From the beginning the movement attracted people with enough time and money to enjoy the outdoor life: sportsmen, naturalists (both amateur and professional), and of course property owners anxious to protect the sanctity of their rural or wilderness retreats. As a result, the conservationist cause came to be identified with the special interests of a few private citizens. It seldom, if ever, has been made to seem pertinent to the welfare of the poor, the nonwhite population, or, for that matter, the great majority of urban Americans. The environment that mattered most to conservationists was the environment beyond the city limits. Witness the names of such leading organizations as the Sierra Club, the National Wildlife Federation, the Audubon Society, and the Izaak Walton League. In the view of many conservationists nature is a world that exists apart from, and for the benefit of, mankind.

The ecological perspective is quite different. Its philosophic root is the secular idea that man (including his works—the secondary, or man-made, environment) is wholly and ineluctably embedded in the tissue of natural process. The interconnections are delicate, infinitely complex, never to be severed. If this organic (or holistic) view of nature has not been popular, it is partly because it calls into question many presuppositions of our culture. Even today an excessive interest in this idea of nature carries, as it did in Emerson's and in Jefferson's time, a strong hint of irregularity and possible subversion. (Nowadays it is associated with the antibourgeois defense of the environment expounded by the long-haired "cop-outs" of the youth movement.) Partly in order to counteract these dangerously idealistic notions, American conservationists often have made a point of seeming hardheaded, which is to say, "realistic" or practical. When their aims have been incorporated in national political programs, notably during the administrations of the two Roosevelts, the emphasis has been upon the efficient use of resources under the supervision of well-trained technicians.[1] Whatever the achievements of such programs, as implemented by the admirable if narrowly defined work of such agencies as the National Park Service, the U.S. Forest Service, or the Soil Conservation Service, they did not raise the kinds of questions about our overall capacity for survival that are brought into view by ecology. In this sense, conservationist thought is pragmatic and meliorist in tenor, whereas ecology is, in the purest meaning of the word, radical.

The relative popularity of the conservation movement helps to explain why troubled scientists, many of whom foresaw the scope and

1. S. P. Hays, *Conservation and the Gospel of Efficiency* (Cambridge: Harvard University Press, 1959).

gravity of the environmental crisis a long while ago, have had such a difficult time arousing their countrymen. As early as 1864 George Perkins Marsh, sometimes said to be the father of American ecology, warned that the earth was "fast becoming an unfit home for its noblest inhabitant," and that unless men changed their ways it would be reduced "to such a condition of impoverished productiveness, of shattered surface, of climatic excess, as to threaten the depravation, barbarism, and perhaps even extinction of the species."[2] No one was listening to Marsh in 1864, and some eighty years later, according to a distinguished naturalist who tried to convey a similar warning, most Americans still were not listening. "It is amazing," wrote Fairfield Osborn in 1948, "how far one has to travel to find a person, even among the widely informed, who is aware of the processes of mounting destruction that we are inflicting upon our life sources."[3]

But that was 1948, and, as we all know, the situation now is wholly changed. Toward the end of the 1960s there was a sudden upsurge of public interest in the subject. The devastation of the environment and the threat of overpopulation became too obvious to be ignored. A sense of anxiety close to panic seized many people, including politicians and leaders of the communications industry. The mass media began to spread the alarm. Television gave prime coverage to a series of relatively minor yet visually sensational ecological disasters. Once again, as in the coverage of the Vietnam War, the close-up power of the medium was demonstrated. The sight of lovely beaches covered with crude oil, hundreds of dead and dying birds trapped in the viscous stuff, had an incalculable effect upon a mass audience. After years of indifference, the press suddenly decided that the jeremiads of naturalists might be important news, and a whole new vocabulary (*environment, ecology, balance of nature, population explosion,* and so on) entered common speech. Meanwhile, the language of reputable scientists was escalating to a pitch of excitement comparable with that of the most fervent young radicals. Barry Commoner, for example, gave a widely reported speech describing the deadly pollution of California water reserves as a result of the excessive use of nitrates as fertilizer. This method of increasing

2. *Man and Nature,* David Lowenthal, ed. (Cambridge: Harvard University Press, 1965), p. 43.
3. F. Osborn, *Our Plundered Planet* (Boston: Little, Brown, 1948), 194.

agricultural productivity, he said, is so disruptive of the chemical balance of soil and water that within a generation it could poison irreparably the water supply of the whole area. The *New York Times* ran the story under the headline: "Ecologist Sees U.S. on Suicidal Course."[4] But it was the demographers and population biologists, worried about behavior even less susceptible to regulatory action, who used the most portentous rhetoric. "We must realize that unless we are extremely lucky," Paul Ehrlich told an audience in the summer of 1969, "everybody will disappear in a cloud of blue steam in 20 years."[5]

To a layman who assumes that responsible scientists choose their words with care, this kind of talk is bewildering. How seriously should he take it? He realizes, of course, that he has no way, on his own, to evaluate the factual or scientific basis for these fearful predictions. But the scientific community, to which he naturally turns, is not much help. While most scientists calmly go about their business, activists like Commoner and Ehrlich dominate the headlines. (One could cite the almost equally gloomy forecasts of Harrison Brown, George Wald, René Dubos, and a dozen other distinguished scholars.) When Anthony Lewis asked a "leading European biologist" the same question—how seriously should one take this idea of the imminent extinction of the race?—the scholar smiled, Lewis reports, and said, "I suppose we have between 35 and 100 years before the end of life on earth."[6] No—what is bewildering is the disparity between words and action, between the all-too-credible prophecy of disaster and the response—or rather the nonresponse—of the organized scientific community. From a layman's viewpoint, the professional scientific organizations would seem to have an obligation here—where nothing less than human survival is in question—either to endorse or to correct the pronouncements of their distinguished colleagues. If a large number of scientists do indeed endorse the judgment of the more vociferous ecologists, then the inescapable question is: What are they doing about it? Why do they hesitate to use the concerted prestige and force of their profession to effect radical changes in national policy and behavior? How is it that most scientists, in the face of this awful knowledge, if indeed it is knowledge, are able to carry on

4. *New York Times* (19 Nov. 1969).
5. *Ibid.* (6 Aug. 1969).
6. *Ibid.* (15 Dec. 1969).

business more or less as usual? One might have expected them to raise their voices, activate their professional organizations, petition the Congress, send delegations to the President, and speak out to the people and the government. Why, in short, are they not mounting a campaign of education and political action?

The most plausible answer seems to be that many scientists, like many of their fellow citizens, are ready to believe that such a campaign already has begun. And if, indeed, one accepts the version of political reality disseminated by the communications industry, they are correct: the campaign *has* begun. By the summer of 1969 it had become evident that the media were preparing to give the ecological crisis the kind of saturation treatment accorded the civil rights movement in the early 1960s and the anti–Vietnam War protest after that. (Observers made this comparison from the beginning.) Much of the tone and substance of the campaign was set by the advertising business. Thus, a leading teenage magazine, *Seventeen,* took a full-page ad in the *New York Times* to announce, beneath a picture of a handsome collegiate couple strolling meditatively through autumn leaves, "The environment crusade emphasizes the fervent concerns of the young with our nation's 'quality of life.' Their voices impel us to act now on the mushrooming problems of conservation and ecology."[7] A more skeptical voice might impel us to think about the Madison Avenue strategists who had recognized a direct new path into the lucrative youth market. The "crusade," as they envisaged it, was to be a bland, well-mannered, clean-up campaign, conducted in the spirit of an adolescent love affair and nicely timed to deflect student attention from the disruptive political issues of the 1960s. A national survey of college students confirmed this hope. "Environment May Eclipse Vietnam as College Issue," the makers of the survey reported, and one young man's comment seemed to sum up their findings: "A lot of people are becoming disenchanted with the antiwar movement," he said. "People who are frustrated and disillusioned are starting to turn to ecology."[8] On New Year's Day 1970, the President of the United States joined the crusade. Adapting the doomsday rhetoric of the environmentalists to his own purposes, he announced that "the nineteen-seventies absolutely must be the years when America

7. *Ibid.* (5 Dec. 1969).
8. *Ibid.* (30 Nov. 1969).

pays its debt to the past by reclaiming the purity of its air, its waters and our living environment. It is literally now or never."[9]

Under the circumstances, it is understandable that most scientists, like most other people (except for the disaffected minority of college students), have been largely unresponsive to the alarmist rhetoric of the more panicky environmentalists. The campaign to save the environment no longer seems to need their help. Not only have the media been awakened, and with them a large segment of the population, but the President himself, along with many government officials, has been enlisted in the cause. On 10 February 1970, President Nixon sent a special message to the Congress outlining a comprehensive thirty-seven-point program of action against pollution. Is it any wonder that the mood at recent meetings of conservationists has become almost cheerful—as if the movement, at long last, really had begun to move? After all, the grim forecasts of the ecologists necessarily have been couched in conditional language, thus: *If* California farmers continue their excessive use of nitrates, *then* the water supply will be irreparably poisoned. But now that the facts have been revealed, and with so much government activity in prospect, may we not assume that disaster will be averted? There is no need, therefore, to take the alarmists seriously—which is only to say that most scientists still have confidence in the capacity of our political leaders, and of our institutions, to cope with the crisis.

But is that confidence warranted by the current "crusade"? Many observers have noted that the President's message was strong in visionary language and weak in substance. He recommended no significant increase in funds needed to implement the program. Coming from a politician with a well-known respect for strategies based on advertising and public relations, this high-sounding talk should make us wary. Is it designed to protect the environment or to assuage anxiety or to distract the antiwar movement or to provide the cohesive force necessary for national unity behind the Republican administration? How can we distinguish the illusion of activity fostered by the media—and the President—from auguries of genuine action? On this score, the frequently invoked parallel of the civil rights and the antiwar movements should

9. *Ibid.* (2 Jan. 1969).

give us pause. For, while each succeeded in focusing attention on a dangerous situation, it is doubtful whether either got us very far along toward the elimination of the danger. At first each movement won spectacular victories, but now, in retrospect, they too look more like ideological than substantive gains. In many ways the situation of blacks in America is more desperate in 1970 than it was in 1960. Similarly, the war in Southeast Asia, far from having been stopped by the peace movement, now threatens to encompass other countries and to continue indefinitely. This is not to imply that the strenuous efforts to end the war or to eradicate racism have been bootless. Some day the whole picture may well look quite different; we may look back on the 1960s as the time when a generation was prepared for a vital transformation of American society.

Nevertheless, scientists would do well to contemplate the example of these recent protest movements. They would be compelled to recognize, for one thing, that, while public awareness may be indispensable for effecting changes in national policy, it hardly guarantees results. In retrospect, indeed, the whole tenor of the civil rights and antiwar campaigns now seems much too optimistic. Neither program took sufficient account of the deeply entrenched, institutionalized character of the collective behavior it aimed to change. If leaders of the campaign to save the environment were to make the same kind of error, it would not be surprising. A certain innocent trust in the efficacy of words, propaganda, and rational persuasion always has characterized the conservation movement in this country. Besides, there is a popular notion that ecological problems are in essence technological, not political, and therefore easier to solve than the problems of racism, war, or imperialism. To indicate why this view is mistaken, why in fact it would be folly to discount the urgency of the environmental crisis on these grounds, I now want to consider the fitness of certain dominant American institutions for the fulfillment of the ecological ideal.

Seen from an ecological perspective, a salient characteristic of American society is its astonishing dynamism. Ever since the first European settlements were established on the Atlantic seaboard, our history has been one of virtually uninterrupted expansion. How many decades, if any, have there been since 1607 when this society failed to expand its population, territory, and economic power? When foreigners speak of

Americanization they invariably have in mind this dynamic, expansionary, unrestrained behavior. "No sooner do you set foot upon American ground," wrote Tocqueville, "than you are stunned by a kind of tumult; a confused clamor is heard on every side, and a thousand simultaneous voices demand the satisfaction of their social wants. Everything is in motion around you. . . ."[10] To be sure, a majority of these clamorous people were of European origin, and their most effective instrument for the transformation of the wilderness—their science and technology—was a product of Western culture. But the unspoiled terrain of North America gave European dynamism a peculiar effervescence. The seemingly unlimited natural resources and the relative absence of cultural or institutional restraints made possible what surely has been the fastest developing, most mobile, most relentlessly innovative society in world history. By now that dynamism inheres in every aspect of our lives, from the dominant national ethos to the structure of our economic institutions down to the deportment of individuals.

The ideological counterpart to the nation's physical expansion has been its celebration of quantity. What has been valued most in American popular culture is growth, development, size (bigness), and—by extension—change, novelty, innovation, wealth, and power. This tendency was noted a long while ago, especially by foreign travelers, but only recently have historians begun to appreciate the special contribution of Christianity to this quantitative, expansionary ethos. The crux here is the aggressive, man-centered attitude toward the environment fostered by Judeo-Christian thought: everything in nature, living or inorganic, exists to serve man. For only man can hope (by joining God) to transcend nature. According to one historian of science, Lynn White,[11] the dynamic thrust of Western science and technology derives in large measure from this Christian emphasis, unique among the great world religions, upon the separation of man from nature.

But one need not endorse White's entire argument to recognize that Americans, from the beginning, found in the Bible a divine sanction for their violent assault upon the physical environment. To the Puritans of New England, the New World landscape was Satan's territory, a

10. A. de Tocqueville, *Democracy in America,* Phillips Bradley, ed. (New York: Knopf, 1946), new ed., vol. 1, p. 249.
11. L. White, Jr., *Science* 155, 1203 (1967).

hideous wilderness inhabited by the unredeemed and fit chiefly for conquest. What moral precept could have served their purpose better than
the Lord's injunction to be fruitful and multiply and subdue the earth
and exercise dominion over every living creature? Then, too, the millennial cast of evangelical protestantism made even more dramatic the
notion that this earth, and everything upon it, is an expendable support
system for man's voyage to eternity. Later, as industrialization gained
momentum, the emphasis shifted from the idea of nature as the devil's
country to the idea of nature as commodity. When the millennial hope
was secularized, and salvation was replaced by the goal of economic and
social progress, it became possible to quantify the rate of human improvement. In our time this quantifying bent reached its logical end
with the enshrinement of the gross national product—one all-encompassing index of the state of the union itself.

Perhaps the most striking thing about this expansionary ethos, from
an ecological viewpoint, has been its capacity to supplant a whole range
of commonsense notions about man's relations with nature which are
recognized by some preliterate peoples and are implicit in the behavior
of certain animal species. These include the ideas that natural resources
are exhaustible, that the unchecked growth of a species will eventually
lead to its extinction, and that other organisms may have a claim to life
worthy of respect.

The record of American business, incomparably successful according to
quantitative economic measures like the gross national product, also looks
quite different when viewed from an ecological perspective. Whereas
the environmental ideal I have been discussing affirms the need for each
organism to observe limits set by its ecosystem, the whole thrust of industrial capitalism has been in the opposite direction: it has placed the
highest premium on ingenious methods for circumventing those limits.
After comparing the treatment that various nations have accorded their
respective portions of the earth, Fairfield Osborn said this of the United
States: "The story of our nation in  the last century as regards the use
of forests, grasslands, wildlife and water sources is the most violent and
the most destructive in the long history of civilization."[12] If that estimate is just, a large part of the credit must be given to an economic sys-

12. Osborn, 175.

tem unmatched in calling forth man's profit-making energies. By the same token, it is a system that does pitifully little to encourage or reward those constraints necessary for the long-term ecological well-being of society. Consider, for example, the fate of prime agricultural lands on the borders of our burgeoning cities. What happens when a landowner is offered a small fortune by a developer? What agency protects the public interest from the irretrievable loss of topsoil that requires centuries to produce? Who sees to it that housing, factories, highways, and shopping centers are situated on the far more plentiful sites where nothing edible ever will grow? The answer is that no such agencies exist, and the market principle is allowed to rule. Since World War II approximately one-fifth of California's invaluable farm land has been lost in this way. Here, as in many cases of air and water pollution, the dominant motive of our business system—private profit—leads to the violation of ecological standards.

Early in the industrial era one might reasonably have expected, as Thorstein Veblen did, that the scientific and technological professions, with their strong bent toward rationality and efficiency, would help to control the ravening economic appetites whetted by America's natural abundance. Veblen assumed that well-trained technicians, engineers, and scientists would be repelled by the wastefulness of the business system. He therefore looked to them for leadership in shaping alternatives to a culture obsessed with "conspicuous consumption." But, so far, that leadership has not appeared. On the contrary, this new technical elite, with its commitment to highly specialized, value-free research, has enthusiastically placed its skill in the service of business and military enterprise. This is one reason, incidentally, why today's rebellious young are unimpressed by the claim that the higher learning entails a commitment to rationality. They see our best-educated, most "rational" elite serving what strikes them as a higher irrationality. So far from providing a counterforce to the business system, the scientific and technological professions in fact have strengthened the ideology of American corporate capitalism, including its large armaments sector, by bringing to it their high-minded faith in the benign consequences of the most rapidly accelerating rate of technological innovation attainable.

But not only are we collectively committed, as a nation, to the idea of continuing growth; each subordinate unit of the society holds itself to a similar standard of success. Each state, city, village, and neighborhood; each corporation, independent merchant, and voluntary organization; each ethnic group, family, and child—each person—should, ideally speaking, strive for growth. Translated into ecological terms, this popular measure of success—becoming bigger, richer, more powerful—means gaining control over more and more of the available resources. When resources were thought to be inexhaustible, as they were thought to be throughout most of our national history, the release of these unbounded entrepreneurial energies was considered an aspect of individual liberation. And so it was, at least for large segments of the population. But today, when that assumption no longer makes sense, those energies are still being generated. It is as if a miniaturized version of the nation's expansionary ethos had been implanted in every citizen—not excluding the technicians and scientists. And when we consider the extremes to which the specialization of function has been carried in the sciences, each expert working his own minuscule sector of the knowledge industry, it is easier to account for the unresponsiveness of the scientific community to the urgent warnings of alarmed ecologists. If most scientists and engineers seem not to be listening, much less acting, it is because these highly skilled men are so busy doing what every good American is supposed to do.

On the other hand, it is not surprising that a clever novelist like Norman Mailer,[13] or a popular interpreter of science like Rachel Carson,[14] or an imaginative medical researcher like Alan Gregg[15] each found it illuminating in recent years to compare the unchecked growth of American society, with all the resulting disorder, to the haphazard spread of cancer cells in a living organism. There is nothing new, of course, about the analogy between the social order and the human body; the conceit has a long history in literature. Since the early 1960s, however, Mailer has been invoking the more specific idea of America as a carcinogenic environment. Like any good poetic figure, this one has a basis in fact. Not only does it call to mind the radioactive matter we have deposited in the earth and the sea, or the work of such allegedly

13. N. Mailer, *Cannibals and Christians* (New York: Dial, 1966).
14. R. Carson, *Silent Spring* (Boston: Houghton Mifflin, 1962).
15. A. Gregg, *Science* 121, 681 (1955).

cancer-producing enterprises as the tobacco and automobile industries, or the effects of some of the new drugs administered by doctors in recent years, but, even more subtly, it reminds us of the parallel between cancer and our expansionary national ethos, which, like a powerful ideological hormone, stimulates the reckless, uncontrolled growth of each cell in the social organism.

In the interests of historical accuracy and comprehensiveness, needless to say, all of these sweeping generalizations would have to be extensively qualified. The record is rich in accounts of determined, troubled Americans who have criticized and actively resisted the nation's expansionary abandon. A large part of our governmental apparatus was created in order to keep these acquisitive, self-aggrandizing energies within tolerable limits. And of course the full story would acknowledge the obvious benefits, especially the individual freedom and prosperity, many Americans owe to the very dynamism that now threatens our survival. But in this brief compass my aim is to emphasize that conception of man's relation to nature which, so far as we can trace its consequences, issued in the *dominant* forms of national behavior. And that is a largely one-sided story. It is a story, moreover, to which our classic American writers, to their inestimable credit, have borne eloquent witness. If there is a single native institution which has consistently criticized American life from a vantage like that of ecology, it is the institution of letters.

A notable fact about imaginative literature in America, when viewed from an ecological perspective, is the number of our most admired works written in obedience to a pastoral impulse.[16] By "pastoral impulse" I mean the urge, in the face of society's increasing power and complexity, to retreat in the direction of nature. The most obvious form taken by this withdrawal from the world of established institutions is a movement in space. The writer or narrator describes, or a character enacts, a move away from a relatively sophisticated to a simpler, more "natural" environment. Whether this new setting is an

16. L. Marx, *The Machine in the Garden; Technology and the Pastoral Ideal in America* (New York: Oxford University Press, 1964).

unspoiled wilderness, like Cooper's forests and plains, Melville's remote Pacific, Faulkner's Big Woods, or Hemingway's Africa, or whether
it is as tame as Emerson's New England village common, Thoreau's
Walden Pond, or Robert Frost's pasture, its significance derives from
the plain fact that it is "closer" to nature: it is a landscape that bears
fewer marks of human intervention.

This symbolic action, which reenacts the initial transit of Europeans
to North America, may be understood in several ways, and no one of
them can do it justice. To begin with, there is an undeniable element of
escapism about this familiar, perhaps universal, desire to get away from
the imperatives of a complicated social life. No one has conveyed this
feeling with greater economy or simplicity than Robert Frost in the first
line of his poem "Directive": "Back out of all this now too much for
us." Needless to say, if our literary pastoralism lent expression only to
this escapist impulse, we would be compelled to call it self-indulgent,
puerile, or regressive.

But fortunately this is not the case. In most American pastorals the
movement toward nature also may be understood as a serious criticism,
explicit or implied, of the established social order. It calls into question
a society dominated by a mechanistic system of value, keyed to perfect-
ing the routine means of existence, yet oblivious to its meaning and
purpose. We recall Thoreau's description, early in *Walden*, of the lives
of quiet desperation led by his Concord neighbors, or the first pages of
Melville's *Moby-Dick*, with Ishmael's account of his moods of suicidal
depression as he contemplates the meaningless work required of the
inhabitants of Manhattan Island. At one time this critical attitude toward the workaday life was commonly dismissed as aristocratic or
elitist. We said that it could speak only for a leisure class for whom
deprivation was no problem. But today, in a society with the technological capacity to supply everyone with an adequate standard of living,
that objection has lost most of its force. The necessary conditions for
giving a decent livelihood to every citizen no longer include harder
work, increased productivity, or endless technological innovation. But
of course such an egalitarian economic program would entail a more
equitable distribution of wealth, and the substitution of economic sufficiency for the goal of an endlessly "rising" standard of living. The
mere fact that such possibilities exist explains why our literary pastorals,

which blur distinctions between the economic, moral, and aesthetic flaws of society, now seem more cogent. In the nineteenth century, many pastoralists, like today's radical ecologists, saw the system as potentially destructive in its innermost essence. Their dominant figure for industrial society, with its patent confusion about ends and means, was the social machine. Our economy is the kind of system, said Thoreau, where men become the tools of their tools.

Of course, there is nothing particularly American about this pessimistic literary response to industrialism. Since the romantic movement it has been a dominant theme of all Western literature. Most gifted writers have expended a large share of their energy in an effort to discover—or, more precisely, to imagine—alternatives to the way of life that emerged with the industrial revolution. The difference is that in Europe there was a range of other possible life-styles which had no counterpart in this country. There were enclaves of preindustrial culture (provincial, aesthetic, religious, aristocratic) which retained their vitality long after the bourgeois revolutions, and there also was a new, revolutionary, urban working class. This difference, along with the presence in America of a vast, rich, unspoiled landscape, helps to explain the exceptionally strong hold of the pastoral motive upon the native imagination. If our writers conceived of life from something like an ecological perspective, it is largely because of their heightened sensitivity to the unspoiled environment, and man's relation to it, as the basis for an alternative to the established social order.

What, then, can we learn about possible alternatives from our pastoral literature? The difficulty here lies in the improbability which surrounds the affirmative content of the pastoral retreat. In the typical American fable the high point of the withdrawal toward nature is an idyllic interlude which gains a large measure of its significance from the sharp contrast with the everyday, "real," world. This is an evanescent moment of peace and contentment when the writer (or narrator, or protagonist) enjoys a sense of integration with the surrounding environment that approaches ecstatic fulfillment. It is often a kind of visionary experience, couched in a language of such intense, extreme, even mystical feeling that it is difficult for many readers (though not, significantly, for adherents of today's youth culture) to take it seriously. But it is important to keep in view some of the reasons for this literary extravagance. In a commercial, optimistic, self-satisfied culture, it was not easy for writers to make an alternate mode of experience credible. Their problem was to endow an ideal vision—some would call it utopian—with enough sensual authenticity to carry readers beyond the usual, conventionally accepted limits of commonsense reality. Nevertheless, the pastoral interlude, rightly understood, does have a bearing upon the choices open to a postindustrial society. It must be taken, not as representing a program to be copied, but as a symbolic action which embodies values, attitudes, modes of thought and feeling alternative to those which characterize the dynamic, expansionary life-style of modern America.

The focus of our literary pastoralism, accordingly, is upon a contrast between two environments representing virtually all aspects of man's relation to nature. In place of the aggressive thrust of nineteenth-century capitalism, the pastoral interlude exemplifies a far more restrained, accommodating kind of behavior. The chief goal is not, as Alexander Hamilton argued it was, to enhance the nation's corporate wealth and power; rather it is the Jeffersonian "pursuit of happiness." In economic terms, then, pastoralism entails a distinction between a commitment to unending growth and the concept of material sufficiency. The aim of the pastoral economy is *enough*—enough production and consumption to ensure a decent quality of life. Jefferson's dislike of industrialization was based on this standard; he was bent on the subordination of quantitative to qualitative "standards of living."

From a psychological viewpoint, the pastoral retreat affirmed the possibility of maintaining man's mental equilibrium by renewed emphasis upon his inner needs. The psychic equivalent of the balance of nature (in effect the balance of *human* nature) is a more or less equal capacity to cope with external and internal sources of anxiety. In a less developed landscape, according to these fables, behavior can be more free, spontaneous, authentic—in a word, more natural. The natural in psychic experience refers to activities of mind which are inborn or somehow primary. Whether we call them intuitive, unconscious, or preconscious, the significant fact is that they do not have to be learned or deliberately acquired. By contrast, then, the expansionary society is figured forth as dangerously imbalanced on the side of those rational faculties conducive to the manipulation of the physical environment. We think of Melville's Ahab, in whom the specialization of function induces a peculiar kind of power-obsessed, if technically competent, mentality. "My means are sane," he says, "my motive and my object mad."

This suspicion of the technical, highly trained intellect comports with the emphasis in our pastoral literature upon those aspects of life that are common to all men. Whereas the industrial society encourages and rewards the habit of mind which analyzes, separates, categorizes, and makes distinctions, the felicity enjoyed during the pastoral interlude is a tacit tribute to the opposite habit. This kind of pleasure derives from the connection-making, analogizing, poetic imagination—one that aspires to a unified conception of reality. At the highest or metaphysical level of abstraction, then, romantic pastoralism is holistic. During the more intense pastoral interludes, an awareness of the entire environment, extending to the outer reaches of the cosmos, affects the perception of each separate thing, idea, event. In place of the technologically efficient but limited concept of nature as a body of discrete manipulatable objects, our pastoral literature presents an organic conception of man's relation to his environment.

What I am trying to suggest is the striking convergence of the literary and the ecological views of America's dominant institutions. Our literature contains a deep intuition of the gathering environmental crisis and its causes. To be sure, the matter-of-fact idiom of scientific ecology may not be poetic or inspiring. Instead of conveying Wordsworthian impulses from the vernal wood, it reports the rate at which monoxide poisoning is killing the trees. Nevertheless, the findings of ecologists confirm the indictment of the self-aggrandizing way of life that our leading writers have been building up for almost two centuries. In essence it is an indictment of the destructive, power-oriented uses to which we put scientific and technological knowledge. The philosophic source of this dangerous behavior is an arrogant conception of man, and above all of human consciousness, as wholly unique—as an entity distinct from, and potentially independent of, the rest of nature.

As for the alternative implied by the pastoral retreat, it also anticipates certain insights of ecology. Throughout this body of imaginative writing, the turn toward nature is represented as a means of gaining access to governing values, meanings, and purposes. In the past, to be sure, many readers found the escapist, sentimental overtones of this motive embarrassing. As a teacher, I can testify that, until recently, many pragmatically inclined students were put off by the obscurely metaphysical, occultish notions surrounding the idea of harmony with nature. It lacked specificity. But now all that is changing. The current environmental crisis has in a sense put a literal, factual, often quantifiable base under this poetic idea. Nature as a transmitter of signals and a dictator of choices now is present to us in the quite literal sense that the imbalance of an ecosystem, when scientifically understood, defines certain precise limits to human behavior. We are told, for example, that if we continue contaminating Lake Michigan at the present rate, the lake will be "dead" in roughly ten years. Shall we save the lake or continue allowing the cities and industries which pollute it to reduce expenses and increase profits? As such choices become more frequent, man's relations with nature will in effect be seen to set the limits of various economic, social, and political practices. And the concept of harmonious relations between man and the physical environment, instead of seeming to be a vague projection of human wishes, must come to be respected as a necessary, realistic, limiting goal. This convergence of literary and scientific insight reinforces the naturalistic idea that man, to paraphrase Melville, must eventually lower his conceit of attainable felicity, locating it not in power or transcendence but in a prior need to sustain life itself.

Assuming that this sketch of America's dominant institutions as seen from a pastoral-ecological vantage is not grossly inaccurate, what inferences can we draw from it? What bearing does it have upon our current effort to cope with the deterioration of the environment? What special significance does it have for concerned scientists and technologists? I shall draw several conclusions, beginning with a specific recommendation for action by the American Association for the Advancement of Science.

First, then, let me propose that the Association establish a panel of the best-qualified scientists, representing as many as possible of the disciplines involved, to serve as a national review board for ecological information. This board would take the responsibility for locating and defining the crucial problems (presumably it would recruit special task forces for specific assignments) and make public recommendations whenever feasible. To be sure, some scientists will be doing a similar job for the government, but, if an informed electorate is to evaluate the government's program, it must have an independent source of knowledge. One probable objection is that scientists often disagree, and feel reluctant to disagree in public. But is this a healthy condition for a democracy? Perhaps the time has come to lift the dangerous veil of omniscience from the world of science and technology. If the experts cannot agree, let them issue minority reports. If our survival is at stake, we should be allowed to know what the problems and the choices are. The point here is not that we laymen look to scientists for *the* answer, or that we expect them to save us. But we do ask for their active involvement in solving problems about which they are the best-informed citizens. Not only should such a topflight panel of scientists be set up on a national basis, but—perhaps more important—similar committees should be set up to help make the best scientific judgment available to the citizens of every state, city, and local community.

But there will also be those who object on the ground that an organization as august as the American Association for the Advancement of Science must not be drawn into politics. The answer, of course, is that American scientists and technologists are now and have always been involved in politics. A profession whose members place their services at the disposal of the government, the military, and private corporations can hardly claim immunity now. Scientific and technological knowledge unavoidably is used for political purposes. But it also is a national resource. The real question in a democratic society, therefore, is whether that knowledge can be made as available to ordinary voters as it is to those, like the Department of Defense or General Electric, who can most easily buy it. If scientists are worried about becoming partisans, then their best defense is to speak with their own disinterested public voice. To allow the burden of alerting and educating the people to fall upon a few volunteers is a scandal. Scientists, as represented by their professional organizations, have a responsibility to make sure that their skills are used to fulfill as well as to violate the ecological ideal. And who knows? If things get bad enough, the scientific community may take steps to discourage its members from serving the violators.

There is another, perhaps more compelling, reason why scientists and technologists, as an organized professional group, must become more actively involved. It was scientists, after all, who first sounded the alarm. What action we take as a society *and how quickly we take it* depend in large measure on the credibility of the alarmists. Who is to say, if organized science does not, which alarms we should take seriously? What group has anything like the competence of scientists and technologists to evaluate the evidence? Or, to put it negatively, what group can do more, by mere complacency and inaction, to ensure an inadequate response to the environmental crisis? It is a well-known fact that Americans hold the scientific profession in the highest esteem. So long as most scientists go about their business as usual, so long as they seem unperturbed by the urgent appeals of their own colleagues, it is likely that most laymen, including our political representatives, will remain skeptical.

The arguments for the more active involvement of the scientific community in public debate illustrate the all-encompassing and essentially political character of the environmental crisis. If the literary-ecological perspective affords an accurate view, we must eventually take into account the deep-seated institutional causes of our distress. No cosmetic program, no clean-up-the-landscape activity, no degree of protection for the wilderness, no antipollution laws can be more than the merest beginning. Of course such measures are worthwhile, but in undertaking them we should acknowledge their superficiality. The devastation of the environment is at bottom a result of the kind of society we have built and the kind of people we are. It follows, therefore, that environmentalists should join forces, wherever common aims can be found, with other groups concerned to change basic institutions. To arrest the deterioration of the environment it will be necessary to control many of the same forces which have prevented us from ending the war in Indochina or giving justice to black Americans. In other words, it will be necessary for ecologists to determine where the destructive power of our society lies and how to cope with it. Knowledge of that kind, needless to say, is political. But then it seems obvious, on reflection, that the study of human ecology will be incomplete until it incorporates a sophisticated mode of political analysis.

Meanwhile, it would be folly, given the character of American institutions, to discount the urgency of our situation either on the ground that technology will provide the solutions or on the ground that countermeasures are proposed. We cannot rely on technology because the essential problem is not technological. It inheres in all of the ways in which this dynamic society generates and uses its power. It calls into question the controlling purposes of all the major institutions which actually determine the nation's impact upon the environment: the great business corporations, the military establishment, the universities, the scientific and technological elites, and the exhilarating expansionary ethos by which we all live. Throughout our brief history, a passion for personal and collective aggrandizement has been the American way. One can only guess at the extent to which forebodings of ecological doom have contributed to the revulsion that so many intelligent young people feel these days for the idea of "success" as a kind of limitless ingestion. In any case, most of the talk about the environmental crisis that turns on the word *pollution,* as if we face a cosmic-scale problem of sanitation, is grossly misleading. What confronts us is an extreme imbalance between society's hunger—the rapidly growing sum of human wants—and the limited capacities of the earth.

# The Neo-Romantic Critique of Science

> I have insisted that there is something radically and systematically wrong with our culture, a flaw that lies deeper than any class or race analysis probes and which frustrates our best efforts to achieve wholeness. I am convinced it is our ingrained commitment to the scientific picture of nature that hangs us up.
>
> The scientific style of mind has become the one form of experience our society is willing to dignify as knowledge. It is our reality principle, and as such the governing mystique of urban industrial culture.
>
> THEODORE ROSZAK[1]

I

Serious, widespread criticism of science is a relatively recent development in the United States. Until World War II the national faith in the identity of scientific and social progress remained largely unshaken. Most Americans, even after the Great Depression of the 1930s, continued to regard the life-enhancing value of scientific knowledge as self-evident. But since Hiroshima, public anxiety about the consequences of scientific discovery has risen steadily. The nuclear arms race; the polluting and carcinogenic effects of new petrochemicals and other products of science-based industry; the actual and possible uses of electronic devices as instruments of social control; the prominent part played by certain science-based technologies of a particularly revolting kind in the prosecution of the American war in Southeast Asia; the

1. "Some Thought on the Other Side of This Life," *New York Times* (Apr. 12, 1973): 45.

160

potentialities for genetic engineering created by advances in molecular biology—these are only the more conspicuous causes for the rising public alarm about the results of scientific research. It is now evident that the American belief in the inherently beneficial character of science no longer can be taken for granted.[2] Judging by current discussion of the subject, however, one might infer that the legitimacy of science—by which I do not mean its lawfulness in any narrow sense, but rather its compatibility with accepted standards and purposes—is now being called into question for the first time.

But in Western culture the legitimacy of modern science has been in question since its emergence in the seventeenth century. To be sure, certain major themes in the legacy from the earlier critique of science have since lost their credibility and all but disappeared. The learned clergy, for example, no longer attacks science as a threat to the churches or as a deflection from the primacy of theological knowledge. Today no responsible clergyman would think of opposing a scientific research project on the ground that the worship of God precludes the study of nature. But it is necessary to add that serious criticism of science based on religious values, though not expressly identified as such, retains an immense appeal. Some of the more effective of the currently popular arguments against science prove, on inspection, to be secularized versions of an essentially religious, or teleological, conception of knowledge.

Another ancient theme in the critique of science which has virtually disappeared is in effect a defense of the older, aristocratic, humanism. On this view, widely held in the age of Pope and Swift, the proper study of mankind is man, not nature. At stake then was the moral instruction of a small, privileged, ruling class for whom scientific education was deemed inappropriate—which is to say, vulgar, unedifying, merely useful. Like the antagonism toward science grounded in theological preconceptions, this avowedly patrician argument is no longer invoked, for obvious reasons, by critics of science.

But the same cannot be said about the general ideas embodied in

2. In 1974 a survey commissioned by the National Science Foundation showed that 39 percent of the American people expressing any opinion do not agree with the proposition that "Overall, science and technology do more good than harm." See Loren Graham, "Concerns about Science and Attempts to Regulate Inquiry," in *Daedalus* 107 (1978), 1-21.

imaginative literature beginning in the late eighteenth century. On the contrary, most of the themes which figure prominently in the current criticism of science were anticipated by the writers of the romantic era. They called into question the legitimacy of science both as a mode of cognition and as a social institution.[3] To question the legitimacy of science as a mode of cognition means, I assume, to ask whether the conception of reality implicit in the scientific method is adequate to our experience. Is it reliable, coherent, sufficient? Insofar as it is not sufficient, does it mesh with what we know by means of other modes of knowledge? To question the legitimacy of science as an institution is to ask whether the methods (and products) of scientific inquiry are compatible with the expressed and tacit goals of society. Can the technological consequences of scientific discovery be assimilated, for example, to a more just, healthful, and peaceful social order?

Both kinds of question, to repeat, were implicit in the literary response to scientific rationalism and the innovations, technological and social, associated with it. At the core of the romantic reaction, in the well-known formulation of Alfred North Whitehead, was "a protest on behalf of the organic view of nature, and also a protest against the exclusion of value from the essence of matter of fact".[4] Implicit in each of these "protests" is a negative, or potentially negative, answer to the questions about the legitimacy of science raised above. The protest on behalf of the organic view of nature is directed against the presumed epistemological insufficiency of science. Scientific method is thus held to be inadequate to the (unified) nature of nature, which is assumed to be a whole distinct from the sum of its parts, and hence not apprehensible by means of the piecemeal, or analytic, procedures which dominate (normal) scientific inquiry.

The second "protest" identified by Whitehead (against "the exclusion of value from the essence of matter of fact") is applicable to both the cognitive and institutional senses of "science." It means that as a

3. Although the writers I have in mind seldom formulated the distinction between the two referents of the word "science"—science as a mode of perception or inquiry, a way of knowing the world, and science as organized activity, a way of behaving in society—it is often implicit in their thought. By now, in any case, its importance cannot be overstated; my impression is that much of the confusion surrounding discussions of the "limitations of science" derives from the tendency to conflate these two meanings of "science."

4. *Science and the Modern World* (New York: Macmillan, 1947), p. 138.

method of knowledge science lends insufficient expression to the distinctively human attributes of reality, those which are properties of
mind rather than merely of natural objects. But "exclusion of value"
also may be taken as a reference to the negative social and political results of scientific neutrality. It anticipates the now familiar charge that
scientists do not assume adequate responsibility for the social consequences of their work. The substantive moral neutrality of natural science as a method of inquiry is not a warrant, in this view, for the
morally uncommitted posture of scientists outside their laboratories or
classrooms. My point, in any case, is that much of today's criticism of
science, including the antagonistic viewpoint widely disseminated by
spokesmen for the dissident movement, or counterculture, of the 1960s,
may be traced to the double-barreled romantic reaction of European intellectuals which began in the late eighteenth century.


II

The mainstream of the European critique of science entered American
literary thought under the auspices of Ralph Waldo Emerson. The English writers who chiefly influenced his thinking on the subject—Wordsworth, Coleridge, Carlyle—had in turn been influenced by the several
versions of post-Kantian idealism then being imported into England
from Germany. If we accept for the moment the standard, oversimplified
handbook view of the spectrum of English literary attitudes toward science as extending from the hostility of Blake at one extreme to the admiration of Shelley at the other, then the writers who were congenial to
Emerson must be accounted middle-of-the-roaders. In view of today's
assumptions about the antagonism between the "two cultures," in fact,
these English moderates would seem, like Goethe, to have been remarkably hospitable toward the claims and prospects of science. Although
in one way or another they all recognized the limitations of scientific
rationalism, they expressed no serious doubts about the inherent validity of the scientific method. Nor were they frightened by the prospect
of the revolution in the conditions of life soon to result from the application of the new science to the fulfillment of economic needs. Their
optimism was most directly expressed in repeated assertions about the
essential compatibility between scientific and other modes of percep-

tion, especially aesthetic or literary, like this well-known statement of
Wordsworth's in the *Lyrical Ballads* preface of 1800:

> If the labors of men of science should ever create any material revo-
> lution, direct or indirect, in our condition, and in the impressions
> which we habitually receive, the poet will sleep then no more than
> at present; he will be ready to follow the steps of the man of science,
> not only in those general indirect effects, but he will be at his side,
> carrying sensation into the midst of the objects of the science itself.
> The remotest discoveries of the chemist, the botanist, or mineralogist
> will be as proper objects of the poet's art as any upon which it can
> be employed. . . . If the time should ever come when what is now
> called science, thus familiarized to men, shall be ready to put on, as
> it were, a form of flesh and blood, the poet will lend his divine spirit
> to aid the transfiguration, and will welcome the being thus produced,
> as a dear and genuine inmate of the household of man.[5]

Behind such optimism about the future collaboration between science
and poetry ("poetry" usually taken to represent aesthetic and moral discourse generally) was the assumption that the two modes of perception
stand in a potentially complementary relation to each other. Thus at
least the majority of scientists were presumed to be operating at the
level of the "Understanding." This is the empirical mode of apprehending external reality, based on sense perception, as set forth in John
Locke's "sensational" theory of knowledge. This theory had proved, by
Wordsworth's time, to be ideally suited to negotiations, theoretical and
practical, with the world of material objects. As Emerson put it, in what
came to be recognized as the philosophic manifesto of American transcendentalism, *Nature* (1836), the Understanding is the capacity of
mind which "adds, divides, combines, and measures," whereas the Reason, a mythopoeic, analogizing, intuitive mode of perception, "transfers
all these lessons [of the empirical Understanding] into its own world
of thought, by perceiving the analogy that marries Matter and Mind."[6]
Assertions on the plane of the Understanding are in effect data-
bound, and require only literal language, whereas assertions on the
plane of Reason transcend the "natural facts," require figurative lan-

5. M. H. Abrams ed., *Norton Anthology of English Literature*, Vol. 2 (New
York: Norton, 1962), p. 89.
6. *Complete Works* (Boston: Houghton, Mifflin, 1884), Vol. 1, p. 42.

guage, and thus contribute to epochal rearrangements of thought and feeling. Emerson's favorite illustration of this point, following the analogous distinction between the Fancy and the Imagination, is the difference between the practice of a merely fanciful poet and that of a truly imaginative genius, a Virgil, Dante, or Milton, whose work effects a symbolic reconstruction of reality. But Emerson clearly meant the distinction to apply, by analogy, to the work of scientists as well. It is the difference between routine science, which merely elaborates, confirms, and refines an established theoretical structure, and the revolutionary syntheses of a Galileo or a Newton. So far as Emerson's theory of knowledge can be taken as tacit criticism of science, it is directed against inquiry confined to the plane of the empirical Understanding. Besides, he is only questioning the sufficiency, not the reliability, of such knowledge. But the distinction between the two modes opens the way for those critics who would charge science with encouraging a dangerous imbalance on the side of the instrumental, empirical Understanding.

Thomas Carlyle was one of the first writers to invoke a similar distinction between two modes of knowledge as a way of calling into question the legitimacy of modern science as a social institution. In "Signs of the Times" (1829), he locates the governing spirit of the "Age of Machinery" in the empirical philosophy of John Locke. Locke's "whole doctrine," he asserts, "is mechanical, in its aim and origin, its method and its results. It is not a philosophy of the mind; it is a mere discussion concerning the origins of our consciousness, or ideas . . . a genetic history of what we see *in* the mind." By "mechanical" Carlyle refers to Locke's emphasis upon the accumulation and sorting of external data (accomplished by the Understanding), and a minimizing of the active, synthetic, and transformational powers of mind (accomplished by Reason). Because he conceives of the contents of the mind as contingent upon sense experience, upon facts flowing in from the outside, Locke tends to reduce thought to a reflex of the environment. This way of knowing is extremely useful for manipulating physical reality, but it leads to a quietist abdication, or fatalism, with respect to the controlling purposes of man's newly acquired power over nature. "The science of the age . . . is physical, chemical, physiological; in all shapes mechanical," hence the image of a machine best characterizes the dawning era of instrumental reason.

But the "mechanical philosophy," as Carlyle describes it, need not be destructive. On the contrary, it could be advantageous to mankind, and in fact he admits that in certain respects the age is advancing. The trouble is, however, that the advance is grossly unbalanced: while the physical sciences are thriving, the moral and metaphysical sciences are falling into decay. Carlyle's complaint in effect belongs to a later stage in the response to the advance of science which Lynn White has discerned as early as the fourteenth century. As scientists tended "to narrow their research methods to the mathematical, and their topics to the physical," according to White, there was a decline in conviction of the cogency of "trivial" argument, that is an argument in the essentially rhetorical language of the "trivium" as against argument in the essentially mensurative language of the "quadrivium."[7] In Carlyle's view, in any case, scientific rationality is spreading far beyond its proper sphere, and the result is that the culture is permeated by "mechanical" or technological thinking. The age of machinery overvalues those asepcts of life which are congenial to the "quadrivial" mode of thought, to use the terminology of the earlier age, which is to say they are quantifiable, calculable, manipulatable. By the same token it downgrades the sphere of the moral, aesthetic, affective, and imaginative—all that springs from the inner resources of the psyche: "the primary, unmodified forces and energies of man, the mysterious springs of Love, and Fear, and Wonder, of Enthusiasm, Poetry, Religion, all which have a truly vital and *infinite* character . . ." This neglected province, the antithesis of the mechanical, Carlyle calls "dynamical." His entire criticism of science rests upon the conviction that we need to develop both of these "great departments of knowledge," and indeed "only in the right coordination of the two, and the vigorous forwarding of *both,* does our true line of action lie." Carlyle continues:

> Undue cultivation of the inward or Dynamical province leads to idle, visionary impracticable courses . . . to Superstition and Fanaticism, with their long train of baleful and well-known evils. Undue cultivation of the outward, again, though less immediately prejudicial, and even for the time productive of many palpable benefits, must, in the long-run, be destroying Moral Force, which is the parent of all other

7. "Science and the Sense of Self: The Medieval Background of a Modern Confrontation," *Daedalus* 107 (1978), 47-59.

Force, prove not less certainly, and perhaps still more hopelessly, pernicious. This, we take it, is the grand characteristic of our age.[8]

This "grand characteristic" takes the form both of a cognitive and of an institutional imbalance. Within science it manifests itself in a neglect of what once was called Natural Philosophy, and a preference for piecemeal analysis: breaking complex problems down into small, simple, particularized elements, thereby anticipating the tendency of scientific inquiry in our own time in which Gerald Holton recognizes "an asymmetry between analysis and synthesis."[9] Implicit here, too, is a homology between the analytic mode of scientific inquiry and the new principles of economic and social organization. The secular, fragmenting, particularizing tendency within science has its counterpart in the management of the market economy and the new political bureaucracies. All in all, therefore, the mechanical philosophy is producing "a mighty change in our whole manner of existence."

> By our skill in Mechanism, it has come to pass, that in the manage-
> ment of external things we excel all other ages; while in whatever
> respects the pure moral nature, in true dignity of soul and character,
> we are perhaps inferior to most civilized ages.[10]

### III

Among the misconceptions fostered by C. P. Snow's "two cultures" thesis is the notion that in the twentieth century the humanities have been the province of unqualified hostility to science. My impression is that a comprehensive survey of literary thought, at least, would reveal a spectrum not unlike that which emerged in the age of Emerson and Carlyle. At one extreme, exemplified by the early writings of I. A. Richards, we find what amounts to the emulation of scientific "objectivity" or positivism. In his influential *Principles of Literary Criticism* (1924), and in *Science and Poetry* (1926), Richards embraced a virtual dichotomy between two uses of language, one scientific, the other "emotive."

8. "Signs of the Times," *Critical and Miscellaneous Essays* (Chicago: Bedford, Clarke, n.d.), p. 21.
9. "Analysis and Synthesis as Methodological Themata," *Methodology and Science* 10 (Mar., 1977): 3-33.
10. Carlyle, p. 21.

In science, which he conceives as a largely autonomous activity ("the impulses developed in it are modified only by one another, with a view to the greatest possible completeness and systemization, and for the facilitation of further references"), statements are made only for the sake of the reference, true or false, which they allow. This austerely denotative use of language corresponds to that which Emerson and other post-Kantian idealists associated with the Understanding. And like them, Richards opposes it to a connotative or suprareferential use of language for the sake of the effects, both in feeling and in attitude, it occasions. This he calls the "emotive" use of language, a term eloquent in its apparent acceptance of an invidious distinction between the disinterested, "objective" character of scientific statements and the personal bias or "subjectivity" of all other kinds of statements.[11]

It is true of course that Richards later changed his mind and repudiated this early, positivistic phase in his thinking. But it had a long afterlife, particularly within the formalistic "new criticism" which played a leading role in Anglo-American literary thought between, roughly, 1930 and 1960. Whatever their express ideas about the natural sciences (they sometimes were markedly antagonistic), the proponents of this analytic critical method often tended to emulate the posture of the dispassionate, impersonal, scientific observer. Their primary concern was with the "how" as against the "what" or "why" of literature, and in their effort to arrive at precise, neutral, verifiable knowledge, they tended to treat the literary text as comparable, in its susceptibility to precise analysis and in its virtual autonomy, to the isolatable data studied by physicists. Certain academic exponents of the "new criticism" carried the doctrine to extremes never envisaged by theorists like I. A. Richards. They taught students to confine assertions about literary texts to "the words on the page" and to heed the Blakean motto (taken out of context): "To generalize is to be an idiot." (Humanists often seem to associate scientific rigor with an extreme nominalism and avoidance of generalization.) The tacit aim of this kind of literary study, moreover, was chiefly to enhance the methodological power of specialists in literary study. Instead of being thought of as a capacity of general culture, available to all educated people, the ability to read imaginative literature was

11. See esp. chap. 34, "The Two Uses of Language," *Principles of Literary Criticism* (New York: Harcourt Brace, 1950), pp. 261-71.

recast by the more extreme practitioners of this new formalism into an arcane skill, like the ability to do physics, accessible only to a tiny minority of expertly trained initiates.

The point about scientism within the humanities—a misplaced application of the assumptions and methods of the natural sciences—is that it can be misleading to gauge the attitudes of humanists toward science by their express opinions alone. It is important to examine what they do (their tacit aims and methods and principles of organization) as well as what they say about science. For they often manage to combine an overt hostility toward the activities of professional scientists, toward science as an institution, with an uncritical and sometimes unconscious emulation of scientific assumptions and procedures. In the realm of literary criticism and scholarship, in any event, the scientistic impulse has remained powerful. After the "new criticism" had lost its vitality, in the 1960s, the yearning of humanists for exact "objective" knowledge, which is to say for a "scientific" critical method, reappeared in such new and ambitious forms as semiotics and a variety of methodological adaptations of "structuralist" principles derived from the latest developments in linguistics.

But the scientistic bent of humanists within the academy was a relatively inconspicuous feature of the cultural history of the recent past. Far more prominent was the new wave of antiscientific thinking that arose in the same period. Following Hiroshima, to repeat, a whole series of problematic science-based innovations had aroused public anxiety about the consequences of scientific discovery. Then the civil crisis of the Vietnam era alienated a large segment of the best-educated American youth from any mental work, but especially scientific and technological work, performed in the service of the government or other basic institutions. By the late 1960s, therefore, a large audience was prepared to accept the neo-romantic critique of science at the core of the dissident counterculture.

I V

The viewpoint of Theodore Roszak belongs at the other end of the spectrum of humanist scholars' attitudes toward science from that represented by I. A. Richards and the scientistic literary critics. Taken together, Roszak's two influential books, *The Making of a Counter Culture: Reflections on the Technocratic Society* (1969) and *Where the Wasteland Ends: Politics and Transcendence in Post-industrial Society* (1972),[12] comprise the most systematic effort to formulate a reasoned, coherent ideology expressive of the diffuse antagonism toward science, technology, and scientific rationalism within the dissident "movement" or counterculture which arose during the 1960s.

At first sight Roszak's epistemology would seem to be diametrically opposed to that of those humanists who aspire to exact, "objective" knowledge like that of natural scientists. Yet the striking fact is that a literary theorist like Richards, who in his early writing had endorsed the superior truth value of scientific statements, and Roszak, who regards them as dangerously inadequate, share certain basic assumptions. They both take for granted the antithetical character of objective and subjective, and therefore of scientific and moral (or aesthetic), modes of thought. They both assume that scientific statements are, or come close to being, or provide a compelling illusion of being, "objective." Or, to put it even more subtly, if total objectivity is not finally attainable, Roszak asserts, the fact remains that scientists can still feel and behave as if it were. If, he says, "an epistemology of total objectivity is unattainable, a *psychology* of objectivity is not. There is a way to *feel* and *behave* objectively, even if one cannot *know* objectively."[13]

The apparent objectivity of scientific knowledge is crucial, it would seem, to both the emulation and the antagonism it elicits from humanists. Whereas Richards (in his positivist phase) implied that objectivity conferred a superior authority upon statements made by scientists, Roszak believes just the opposite. He concedes that in the eyes of the gullible public scientific knowledge has immense authority, but it is a misplaced authority. To insist upon the quantifiability and verifiability of knowledge is, on this view, to ensure its shallowness and triviality. The experimentally verifiable results of scientific inquiry comprise a body of information of undeniable utility for the mastery and manipulation of the biophysical world. But when such information is deferred

---

12. *The Making of a Counter Culture: Reflections on the Technocratic Society* (New York: Doubleday, 1969); *Where the Wasteland Ends: Politics and Transcendence in Postindustrial Society* (Garden City, N.Y.: Doubleday, 1972).
13. *Ibid.,* p. 167.

to as the exemplar of true knowledge the results can be disastrous. For the "scientific picture of nature" it provides effectively screens out all qualities of mind and nature, all modes of perception and of being, except those with instrumental value.

> Objective knowing gives a new assembly line system of knowledge, one which relieves us of the necessity to integrate what we study into a moral or metaphysical context which will contribute existential value. We need no longer waste valuable research time and energy seeking for wisdom or depth, since these are qualities of the person. We are free to become specialists.[14]

The scientific style of mind, devoted as it is to "objective knowing," is the radical flaw in the culture of urban industrialism. Roszak calls this style, after William Blake, "the single vision": a one-dimensional, technologically useful, but humanly impoverished world-view. Although it happens to be the one form of experience now dignifiable as knowledge, it should not in his view be called that. It would be more accurate, Roszak contends, to call what science reveals to us about nature "information," and to reserve the term "knowledge" for those holistic, often ecstatic syntheses of fact and value—or nature, spirit, and self—which are properly called "gnosis." His epistemology, therefore, must be distinguished from that held by the moderate romantics (Wordsworth, Coleridge, Emerson) who envisaged an accommodation between the two modes of perception, empirical and transcendental, which could effect a "marriage," in Emerson's figure, between matter and mind. Again, Roszak's version of the neo-romantic critique of science is like the positivism of a Richards in seeming to rule out the potential complementarity between the two kinds of knowing.

Although Roszak draws upon the romantic poets, especially Blake, and indeed upon the entire legacy of visionary and prophetic literature going back to the Old Testament, he presses the case against practical reason to a new extreme. Many other writers have insisted on the superiority of intuitive, nonrational ways of knowing; many have pointed out the severe limitations of scientific rationalism; but few before now have singled out the scientific world view as *the* root cause of what is most alarming about modern societies. According to Roszak, however,

14. *Ibid.*, p. 171.

it is the critical variable in an essentially destructive, perhaps suicidal, pattern of collective behavior.

> Undeniably, those who defend rationality speak for a valuable human quality. But they often seem not to realize that Reason as they honor it is the god-word of a specific and highly impassioned ideology handed down to us from our ancestors of the Enlightenment as part of a total cultural and political program. Tied to that ideology is an aggressive dedication to the urban-industrialization of the world and to the scientist's universe as the only sane reality. And tied to the global urban industrialism is an unavoidable technocratic elitism.[15]

The notion that rationality, or the quasireligious belief in Reason, is the motive force behind urban industrialism exemplifies Roszak's idealistic theory of history. Unlike most contemporary historians, he imputes to ideas an almost exclusive efficacy in social change. He therefore portrays the contemporary world as the scene of an all-encompassing Manichean struggle between opposed views of reality, each marked by an ideal type of knowing: scientific rationalism and gnosis. One is reductive, partial, analytic; the other augmentative, holistic, synthetic. The social forms accompanying each are, for his purposes, largely irrelevant. So far from being important determinants of human behavior, indeed, social structures and processes are for Roszak relatively inconsequential reflections of the dominant mental style. What chiefly accounts for differences in ways of life, accordingly, are differences in the ruling conceptions of reality. Roszak's theory of history might be called a form of metaphysical or, to be more specific, epistemological determinism.

Assuming that theories of knowledge are the prime movers of history, Roszak deals with them apart from the social groups which embraced them or the functions they served in actual historical situations. This enables him to discuss the ecstatic, visionary mode of cognition (gnosis) "found in the world's primitive and pagan societies" without reference to its uses as an instrument of minority rule or, in many instances, of tyranny. The political role of the shaman is, so far as he is concerned, largely irrelevant; what matters is the shaman's "unitary

15. "The Monster and the Titan: Science, Knowledge, and Gnosis," *Daedalus* (Summer 1974): 17-32.

vision bringing together art, religion, science, and technics."[16] Similarly, he discusses the emergence of the purposive-rational way of knowing in the Enlightenment without any reference to the larger vision of scientific progress as a corollary of political, social, and psychological liberation. My impression is that Roszak's apolitical sense of history as a battlefield of free-floating ideas is characteristic of the view held by many adherents of today's counterculture.

The inadequacy of this simple, single-factor mode of historical explanation is nowhere more apparent than in Roszak's attempt to account for the destructive uses to which our society puts scientific knowledge. Whereas Whitehead's description of the romantic protest against science had allowed for the distinction between science as a mode of cognition and science as it functions in a particular social setting, Roszak's protest does not. On the contrary, his fundamental charge against a science grounded in instrumental reason is that the evil uses to which it is put follow from its epistemological inadequacy. But it is not clear whether he considers those evils a necessity or merely a possible consequence. Although his generalizations imply that scientific knowledge leads inevitably to flagrant abuses of mankind and of nature, his specific examples are ambiguous.

> We should by now be well aware of the price we pay for regarding aesthetic quality as arbitrary and purely subjective rather than as a real property of the object. Such a view opens the way to that brutishness which feels licensed to devastate the environment on the grounds that beauty is only "a matter of taste." And since one person's taste is as good as another's, who is to say—as a matter of *fact*—that the hard cash of a strip mine counts for less than the grandeur of an untouched mountain?[17]

What does it mean to say that rationality "opens the way" for strip mining? Roszak's point is that the sharp instrumental focus of modern science ignores the aesthetic attributes of the object. To protect the environment, so give mountains and trees adequate "standing" in our culture, we need to restore a sense of the absolute value inherent in natural objects comparable to the divinity imputed to them by primitive (animistic) modes of thought. But Roszak does not give us much help

16. *Ibid.*, p. 27.
17. *Ibid.*, pp. 25-26.

in imagining a mode of knowledge capable of coordinating a geological understanding of a mountain with an apprehension of its allegedly inherent beauty. We have reason to believe, for one thing, that the beauty is not inherent. As Marjorie Hope Nicolson demonstrated years ago, most English travelers before the late sixteenth century regarded the Alps as ugly excrescences on the face of nature.[18] Had they been practitioners of gnosis they presumably would have advocated strip mining on the slopes of Mont Blanc. In one sense, admittedly, the example is absurd. Roszak's point is that gnosis, by definition, entails a world-view incompatible with either modern geology or strip mining. Yet the absurdity does serve to illustrate the all-or-nothing character of the choice we are being invited to make. No accommodation between science as we know it and Roszak's conception of an adequate epistemology is conceivable.

To say that rationality "opens the way" for strip mining is in any case far from saying that the resulting devastation is attributable to science. Let us suppose that advances in geology are among the factors that have contributed directly to the feasibility of strip mining. It is still necessary to consider the relative influence of geological knowledge and economic profitability (Roszak's "hard cash") as motive forces here. Granted that technical competence (equated with "rationality" hence "science" in this lexicon) makes strip mining possible, the fact remains that a business corporation conceives and organizes the operation and a juridical system legitimizes it. In what sense, therefore, is science accountable here?

Roszak's answer embodies the crux of the countercultural critique of science. It is worth noting, incidentally, that he did not address the question in the original draft of this passage. Following the conference in which it was criticized, however, he added this telling afterthought:

> Is such barbarism [i.e., strip mining] to be "blamed" on science? Obviously not in any direct way. But it is deeply rooted in a scientized reality principle that treats quantities as objective knowledge and qualities as a matter of subjective preference.[19]

18. *Mountain Gloom and Mountain Glory* (Ithaca: Cornell University Press, 1959).

19. The Monster and the Titan," *op. cit.*, p. 26. This passage did not appear in the first mimeographed draft of the paper which was discussed by the present writer at a conference sponsored by *Daedalus*.

In other words, the technique of the mining engineer and the economic calculations of the corporate management, like the scientific information of the geologist, may be thought of as products of the same "scientized reality principle." An old-fashioned historian's distinction between the enabling power of scientific knowledge and the motives generated and sanctioned by socioeconomic institutions is not meaningful to Roszak. According to his idealistic interpretation of history, *all* of these activities are traceable to the one root cause: a rationalistic world-view. Since the domination of that ideology is a result of the advances of scientific knowledge, Roszak is in fact putting the ultimate blame for the destructiveness of modern society upon science.

To sum up, then, the strip miner's brutish devastation of the landscape typifies this conception of the way our flawed metaphysic issues in social evil. The epistemological flaw, again, is the reductionism characteristic of science: the screening out of those qualities of mind and nature, in this case aesthetic qualities, not useful to the purpose at hand. If one accepts the major premise of Roszak's metaphysical determinism, his apocalyptic conclusion follows logically enough. The scientific view of man's relations to nature is conducive to a kind of institutionalized moral nihilism. Hence the destructiveness of urban industrial society is irremediable, and our only hope is to replace it and the conception of reality from which it derives.


v

Today's criticism of science has a long history in Western thought. To be sure, a series of shocking events following World War II aroused widespread public anxiety about the latest advances in research. In one sense, therefore, the counterculture's attack upon rationality may be interpreted as an extreme expression of a current mood. But it is necessary to recognize that this recent development also is a new phase of the "romantic reaction" that began some two centuries ago. Then, as now, the reliability of scientific knowledge within its own proper sphere was not in question. Many thinkers noted, however, that the scientific view of reality imputes excessive importance to the small part of life susceptible to experimental and logical methods of analysis. Even a writer like Emerson, who retained much of his Enlightenment faith in scientific progress, expressed a characteristic post-Kantian skepticism about the sufficiency of practical reason. He did not doubt the absolute validity of "natural facts," and since he regarded "Nature" as "the present expositor of the divine mind,"[20] he believed that knowledge grounded in empirical facticity could in theory yield the kind of certainty and authority hitherto claimed for religious truth. But in order to satisfy the full range of human needs, it would be necessary to "marry" the neutral data to value-laden concepts arrived at by the other (intuitive, mythopoeic, holistic) way of knowing.

By thus insisting upon a coordination of the two modes of cognition, even the more optimistic critics of empiricism helped prepare the way for today's neo-romantic attack upon science. For the anticipated marriage of fact and value, matter and mind, did not occur. So far from effecting a closer, more meaningful and harmonious relationship between man and nature, science in the context of Western industrialism is perceived by its latter-day critics as having divested nature of its ultimate, or teleological, significance. At bottom, then, this critique of science is rooted in an essentially religious, suprasensual conception of man's relations with nature. We must recover our capacity for gnosis, according to Roszak, because we desperately require access to the value, meaning, and purpose presumed to reside in "things as a whole."[21] The monster created by science is meaninglessness. Instead of providing the unconditioned meaning sought by mankind, science in the nineteenth century came to be identified with new, more acute forms of alienation from nature.

The dislocation attendant upon the rapidly accelerating rate of industrialization and urbanization was destined, in the long run, to undermine confidence in science. Whether science "caused" these changes, or whether specific technological innovations did in fact derive from scientific research, is largely beside the point. Scientists, inventors, and entrepreneurs, as they functioned within an expanding capitalist society, would appear to critics of that society as kindred embodiments of the same predominantly analytic, secular, matter-of-fact mentality. The emergence of entire industries manifestly based upon recently acquired scientific knowledge, the electrical and chemical industries in

20. *Complete Works, op. cit.,* p. 68.
21. "The Monster and the Titan," *op. cit.,* p. 21.

particular, subtly eroded the ideal of science as the disinterested pursuit of truth. Idolators of "progress" boasted about the complicity of scientists in changing the face of nature. By the end of the nineteenth century the partnership of science, engineering, and capitalism was acknowledged by its defenders and critics alike. The old distinction between pure and applied science had lost much of its force long before the neo-romantic critique of science had been formulated.

These developments also were to lend more and more credence, as time went on, to Carlyle's choice of the machine as the cardinal metaphor for the emergent industrial system. Scientific knowledge, according to that figure, is the intellectual fuel upon which an expanding machinelike society runs. In the iconography of anti-industrialism, therefore, machines represent the most conspicuous products, both physical and cultural, of modern science. They simultaneously represent several aspects of science-based technology: (1) a new kind of apparatus and technique; (2) the rational organization of work and of economic activity generally; (3) the principles underlying the first two senses of "technology," which is to say the analytic mode of thought and, by extension, the social order typified by a perfection of means and a diminished control over ends.

Beginning with Carlyle's generation, novelists and poets invoked the imagery of mechanization to convey a sense of dwindling human agency, or what may be called, in retrospect, the incipient totalitarianism of industrial society. By the 1960s adherents of the dissident movement throughout the West were invoking the terms "technology" and "the system" and "the machine" more or less interchangeably. All referred to the controlling network of large-scale institutions (government, business corporations, universities) in whose services most scientists do their work. The "machine," in other words, is coterminous with organized society. We are reminded of the inception of the Berkeley uprising in 1964 when one of the leaders, after describing "the operation of the machine" as intolerably odious, called upon his fellow students at the University of California to throw their bodies upon it, if necessary, to make it stop.[22] What is striking about the episode is

22. Seymour Martin Lipset and Sheldon Wolin, eds., *The Berkeley Student Revolt*, (New York: Anchor, 1965), p. 163. For the background of this iconographical tradition in American and English literature, see Leo Marx, *The Ma-*

the extent to which the audience, and the rebellious youth movement
in general, seems to have accepted the meaning tacitly imparted to "The
Machine."

The received iconographical convention by which "the machine" of
science-based high technology is equated with organized society bears
witness to the deep-rooted, historical basis for the antiscientific strain
in contemporary culture. As Whitehead noted years ago, the literary
reaction to the scientific revolution of the eighteenth century expressed
the "deep intuitions of mankind penetrating into what is universal in
concrete fact." He insisted, moreover, on the philosophic cogency of
the great body of imaginative literature which testifies to the discord between those intuitions—aesthetic, moral, metaphysical—and the
mechanism of science."[23] The discord reflects an increasingly obvious
discrepancy between what science provides in the way of certain, verifiable knowledge, and what mankind would have in the way of a meaningful existence. In view of the history of the half century since Whitehead made these observations, and of the ambiguous part that science
has played in that history, it is not surprising that the discord has
grown sharper. Nor is there any reason to doubt that it will continue
to do so. It would be a serious mistake, accordingly, for those concerned
about the future of science to underestimate the appeal, or the force,
of the neo-romantic critique of science as a mode of knowing built upon
an inadequate metaphysical foundation.

chine in the Garden: Technology and the Pastoral Ideal in America (New York:
Oxford University Press, 1964) and Herbert Sussman, Victorians and the Machine (Cambridge: Harvard University Press, 1968).
   23. Science and the Modern World, op. cit., pp. 126-27.

# American Literary Culture and the Fatalistic View of Technology

> Artists are the antennae of the race.
>
> EZRA POUND

I take this to mean that, among other things, artists vibrate to new stimuli—apprehend them—before most of us do. Those who have not been instructed by the arts of the recent past are more likely to be caught unaware by what appear to be sudden changes in prevailing attitudes. I am thinking of the way many observers, including scientists and engineers, are reacting to the current American disenchantment with the mechanic arts or, as we say nowadays, "technology." The shift in vocabulary is of course part of the problem, but for the moment my point is simply that the public's apparent change of heart has come to many people as a complete surprise: sudden, unheralded—difficult to explain. They find it hard to believe that Americans, of all people, should be losing confidence in the science-based apparatus and power of modern industrial society. What shall we make of this change? With Ezra Pound's maxim in view, I want to see what we can learn by looking at the subject through the prism of our classic American literature.

I

There is a memorable episode in *The Education of Henry Adams* which will serve as a quintessential expression of the pessimistic view in ques-

179

tion. The episode occurs toward the end of the book when the sixty-
two-year-old Adams, under the guidance of Samuel Langley, inspects
the Gallery of Machines at the Great Paris Exposition of 1900. An
artful writer with an exceptional gift for self-dramatization, Adams
had taken pains to prepare readers of his third-person autobiographical
memoir for this moment of dire revelation. In the opening pages he
had described how, in 1844, when he was six years old, he and his
distinguished family's ordered eighteenth-century world had been, as
he so emphatically puts it, "suddenly cut apart—separated forever—in
act if not in sentiment" by the more or less simultaneous appearance
of the railroad, the transatlantic steamship, and the telegraph. Adams
subsequently makes of the century's triumphant sequence of scientific
discoveries and mechanical inventions a leitmotif; it serves as a gauge
of the rapid expansion of mankind's knowledge and power and, above
all, of the rapidly accelerating rate of change. He thereby endows history itself with velocity, as if the pace of events constantly is being
geared up to the revolutions of the latest, most powerful mechanism
for generating energy. By 1900, when he follows his mentor, Langley,
into the hall of dynamos, Adams is thinking about the significance of
the newest mode of locomotion: the automobile. It had appeared only
seven years before, yet in his view it already "had become a nightmare
at one hundred kilometres an hour."

But now, in the presence of the new dynamos, Adams's foreboding
takes a quantum jump. To convey his intense feelings he casts himself
as a kind of religious novice, and he transforms the powerhouse into
a gloomy setting out of some latter-day medieval romance. The eerie
hush, the whir of the giant engines, the ecclesiastical associations, the
intimation of dark, occult forces at work—all the gloomy mysterious
trappings contribute to the portentousness of the passage. "As he
grew accustomed to the great gallery of machines," Adams writes, as
if he had entered a dimly lit chapel, "he began to feel the forty-foot
dynamos as a moral force, much as early Christians felt the Cross."
Close up, the "huge wheel, revolving within arm's length at vertiginous
speed, and barely murmuring," strikes him as more impressive than
the planet Earth. This bravura description, composed in the style of
machine-age Gothic, evokes a premonitory shudder at the thought of
what could be in store for those who tamper heedlessly with forces as

absolute and supersensual, as seemingly anarchical,[1] as electromagnetism and radioactivity. In the murmur of Langley's new generators Adams detects a blind will to outdo God and Nature, and that is the tacit premise behind his effort to make of them a new twentieth-century "symbol of infinity": The Dynamo. He regards the power this symbol represents as without precedent in human experience, yet because mankind's response to new stimuli—to change itself—necessarily is governed by precedent, his final, self-consciously mordant gesture is to reenact the presumed response of our ancestors when faced with unanticipated interventions of divine and supernatural power. "Before the end," he says of his encounter with the dynamo cum Dynamo, "one began to pray to it; inherited instinct taught the natural expression of man before silent and infinite force."

On rereading "The Dynamo and the Virgin" today, one cannot help being struck by the aura of prophecy it now has acquired. Writing in 1905, forty years before Hiroshima, Adams identified the newly discovered Xray as one of the more fateful innovations he would have The Dynamo represent. (In the seven years following that discovery, he observes, man in effect had "translated himself"—a wonderfully resonant figure—into an entirely new universe of power.) Such a quick, sure reaction to the revolution in physics then under way certainly deserves respect, but it would be a mistake to credit Adams with a unique oracular gift. The essential cast of mind to which The Dynamo lent expression—the apprehensive response to mankind's new power over nature, and especially to such power as might be conveyed by an image of a machine—had been a common property of high literary culture since the early nineteenth century.[2] If that once rarefied literary

1. The alleged lawlessness of natural phenomena is a major theme of *The Education;* it expresses Adams's understanding of the crisis in late-nineteenth century physics ("The kinetic theory of gas is an assertion of ultimate chaos. In plain words, Chaos was the law of Nature; Order was the dream of man."), and it provided a kind of metaphysical parallel, or sanction, for the idea that technological innovation was producing social chaos. See esp. Chapter 31, "The Grammar of Science."

2. If one had to name a single writer whose work was a fountainhead of this viewpoint, influencing many others both in England and America, it would be Thomas Carlyle. His interpretation of the epoch as the "Age of Machinery," first outlined in "Signs of the Times" (1829), made itself felt in the work of many other English writers, notably Dickens, Arnold, Ruskin, and Morris; and in America it had a direct influence on the work of Emerson, Thoreau, Melville, and Adams.

attitude now seems to have been confirmed by subsequent events, the
prophetic mantle belongs—as Ezra Pound's motto implies—to writers
and artists as a collectivity, or to art as a social process of symbol-
making.

The significant point here, in any case, is that since World War II
a pessimistic attitude like that symbolized by Adams's Dynamo has begun to win favor among the politically disaffected—especially intellectuals, professionals, writers, teachers, and students—in the United States.
This is not to say that Adams's symbol itself has caught on, but much
of the significance he had imparted to it is represented, for this dissident minority, by their very idea of "technology" and its iconological
embodiments, notably "The Machine." That idea evidently has been
formed by a collective method not unlike that used by Adams in devis-
ing his symbol. His procedure simply had been to invest a particular
machine, one of the whirring dynamos he had described as actually
present to his eyes and ears in Paris in 1900, with meanings so abstract,
so large, as to transform the particular image into a universal type of
science-based mechanical power and its possible consequences—its potential for evil. A somewhat similar process would seem to account
for the accretion of meaning around the word "technology," but an
important difference is that Adams goes about his symbol-making business out in the open, which is to say, on the page where readers can
watch exactly what is going on. We can observe the way he enlarges
the significance of that image, how, for example, he attaches a sense
of religious foreknowledge and fate to it, and that makes it relatively
easy for us to refuse assent.

But it is not so easy to defend ourselves against such an imperious
leap of metaphor when it occurs as part of the continuing, invisible
process of language formation by which the idea of "technology,"
in the more grandiose current sense of the word, has evolved. It is not
uncommon these days to see or hear that amorphous entity referred to
as if it, like The Dynamo, might be a "moral force," silent yet infinite
in potency: a disembodied, autonomous agent of contemporary history?[3] The agent, to be sure, may be thought of as a force for good

3. For a useful survey of the idea of technological determinism in modern
thought, see Langdon Winner, *Autonomous Technology: Technics-out-of-Control
as a Theme in Political Thought* (Cambridge, 1977).

or evil, but here we are concerned with its service to pessimists. Yet to call the negative attitude conveyed by this idea of technology "pessimistic" surely is inadequate; a better name for it, as Adams had implied when he finally resorted to prayer, might be "submissive" or "fatalistic." However we choose to describe it, this profoundly negative view forms the sharpest contrast imaginable with that wholehearted affirmation of the mechanic arts which always had been a prominent feature of the American conduct of life.

What are we to make of this change? In one limited sense, of course, the explanation is obvious enough. Beginning with the use of the atom bomb to destroy Hiroshima in 1945, a series of ominous events has aroused a widely expressed fear of new knowledge and its consequences. The nuclear arms race; the actual and potential uses of new electronic devices as instruments of social control; the deployment of new weapons of a peculiarly revolting kind in the Vietnam War; the potentialities for genetic engineering created by advances in molecular biology; the polluting and carcinogenic effects of the new petrochemicals and other products of science-based industry—these have been only the more conspicuous of causes for alarm. Some of the evils identified with technical innovations were the consequence of accident or inadvertence, others of calculated policy; some already have occurred, others merely are frightening possibilities;* taken together, however, they certainly furnish a plausible explanation for the recent change of outlook. Is it any wonder, under the circumstances, that a great many Americans have come to fear the "impact," as we say, of advances in science and engineering? What is perhaps most surprising, when we stop to think about this darkening view of applied science, is that anyone should consider it surprising.

And yet, having said this, I want to suggest that the current change of attitude involves a good deal more, both as cause and as consequence, than a reflexive reaction to shocking events. Those events may tell us why the change is occurring at this time, but they do not account for the powerful attraction the dark, fateful, well-nigh apocalyptic idea of "technology" now exercises upon the imagination. What is involved, in

---

* If I were writing today (in 1986), I probably would include acid rain, Three Mile Island, Chernobyl, and the Challenger explosion in this list of disasters contributing to our technological pessimism.

other words, is not merely a revision of attitude toward the particular compartment of human knowledge and activity formerly associated with the work of engineers—work variously known as "applied science," or the "practical," "useful," or "mechanic" arts; it is not merely a change of attitude toward those arts, but rather an enlarged, virtually distinct conception of their nature and influence in the era of advanced corporate capitalism. To appreciate what is involved it is first necessary to recall the special part played by the mechanic arts in the formation and dissemination of the dominant American belief system.

II

Before the Revolution the American colonists had won an international reputation as preeminent inventors and users of mechanical devices. Their material situation had contributed to a need for innovations in the practical arts. Labor was scarce, resources were abundant, and a vast continent invited development. The largely self-selected population of Anglo-European immigrants, a high proportion of whom were skilled, disciplined members of the middle class, was exceptionaly well-qualified to meet the demand. They brought to the pursuit of worldly success an unexampled puritanical zeal, as Max Weber was to acknowledge when he chose as *the* literary exemplar of the protestant spirit of capitalism one Benjamin Franklin of Boston and Philadelphia.[4] On this view, the American colonists were the ideological advance guard of world capitalism. Yet the social commitments of the colonial merchant class, as given expression by Franklin, bear little resemblance to the unremittingly acquisitive ethos that was to characterize later, industrial capitalist culture. The difference is made clear by Franklin's insistence, in the *Autobiography,* upon mechanical invention as a communal possession. Inventing a new stove, like performing a scientific experiment or organizing a Philosophical Society, was in his view a contribution to collective well-being, and whatever benefits might issue from such acts of civic virtue should be considered public, not private, property. Not only did he decline a patent for his ingenious fuel-saving stove, he published a pamphlet describing how to make and use it—all on the principle, as

4. *The Protestant Ethic and the Spirit of Capitalism,* first published as a two-part journal article in 1904-5.

he put it, "That as we enjoy great Advantages from the Inventions of others, we should be glad of an Opportunity to serve others by any Invention of ours, and this we should do freely and generously."[5]

But the significance of the mechanic arts for Americans was to extend far beyond their manifest practical utility. With the onset of industrialism, the new forces of production, transportation and communication provided the chief icons—steam engines, factories, steamboats, railroads, the telegraph—for the increasingly dominant progressive world-view. By "world-view" I mean the picture a people holds, as Clifford Geertz puts it, "of the way things in sheer actuality are"—a shared if largely unarticulated sense of the essential interactions among nature, self, and society.[6] Such a collective world picture is more inclusive, less specific and programmatic, than what is ordinarily meant by a consciously avowed ideology; in fact it embodies many of the tacit presuppositions held in common by adherents of the conflicting ideologies of an epoch. The progressive world-view, to be sure, had been a product of the European Enlightenment, and its chief impetus, its intellectual sanction, derived from the scientific revolution we associate with the work of men like Bruno, Galileo, and Newton. No one put it more succinctly than Alexander Pope: "Nature, and Nature's Laws lay hid in Night. / God said, *Let Newton Be!* and All was *Light*."[7] The essence of the progressive world-view, with its core belief in the perfectability of man, is all there, but Newton's momentous theory was far too abstruse to have a direct impact upon the minds of most people, and although the import of the new science did in some measure filter down to the general public in popularized form, it was not until the industrial revolution, with its tangible, visible, usable apparatus, that secular progressivism took a firm hold on the popular imagination.

The new mechanical inventions had the effect, as nothing else did, of certifying the reality of progress. The wordless message conveyed by their manifest utility—their mere presence—was incomparably more arresting, immediate, vivid, stirring, and compelling to most people than, say, the theory of Newtonian mechanics. No schooling in math or physics was needed to appreciate the extent of the transformation of

5. *Anthology of American Literature,* ed. George McMichael (New York, 1974), I, 381.
6. *The Interpretation of Cultures* (New York, 1973), p. 127.
7. *The Poems of Alexander Pope,* ed. John Butt (London), p. 808.

life heralded by the new machine-powered factories or railroads. Science was abstract and invisible; machines were sensuous and incontestably "real"; it was like the difference between a prophet's merely verbal claim of supernatural power and his performance of a miracle in the presence of witnesses. As invoked by politicians, publicists, writers, and artists, the imagery of mechanized power provided the most persuasive evidence for the notion that the emergent industrial civilization would be—if it was not already—superior to all previous civilizations. These images were so habitually invoked for this purpose in mid-nineteenth-century American popular culture that the lesson they embodied no longer had to be made explicit. The entire progressive world-view was implicit in the objects themselves or, as Walt Whitman said of a great locomotive careening across the landscape, the machine simply *was* the "Type of the modern—emblem of motion and power—pulse of the continent."[8] The story told by such images was that mankind, having seized the hidden laws of nature, was assured henceforth of the steady expansion of knowledge and power in every realm of experience—material, intellectual, and moral (or spiritual).

Although European in origin, the dominant progressive world-view embraced by Americans of the nineteenth century took on at least two distinctive national characteristics. One was the idea that the Republic had been providentially singled out among all the nations—as in the cult of Manifest Destiny—to exemplify the progress of mankind. This extravagant, not to say millenial optimism arose from—was justified by—the nation's unique geopolitical good fortune. By the 1830s, when Alexis de Tocqueville visited the country, it had become commonplace to speak of the match between the Old World arts—especially the practical arts—and New World nature as an absolutely unique occurrence in world history. Or as Tocqueville put it: "The Americans are a very old and a very enlightened people, who have fallen upon a new and unbounded country, where they may extend themselves at pleasure and which they may fertilize without difficulty. *This state of things is without a parallel in the history of the world.*"[9] The raw state of the boundless terrain made the material progress of civilization in North America

8. "To a Locomotive in Winter," *Leaves of Grass,* ed. S. Bradley and H. W. Blodgett, (New York, 1973), pp. 471-72.
9. Alexis de Tocqueville, *Democracy in America,* ed. Phillips Bradley, (New York, 1945), II, 36, my emphasis.

infinitely more palpable and dramatic than in Europe. It also meant—
and this is the second of the distinctive national characteristics of the
progressive world-view I have in mind—that Americans, unlike Europeans, thought they could blend the idea of history as progress with the
ancient pastoral dream of regaining the Golden Age state of harmony
with nature. Americans, in other words, could proceed to carry out the
expansionary project of Western capitalism, leveling forests, building
roads and factories and cities in the wilderness, and still, at the very
same time, they could with some justice see themselves as engaged in
the recovery of a simpler, more natural way of life—simpler and more
natural, at least, as compared with the prototypical advanced societies of
Western Europe. While the country remained largely underdeveloped,
it was not implausible for Americans to embrace—simultaneously and
as if reconcilable—the progressive and the pastoral world-views.

To be clear about the significance of pastoralism in the American
context, let me say at once that it should not be thought of as the logical
antithesis of the modern belief in progress. That hypothetical role belongs to primitivism, the doctrine which holds that the environment
most conducive to human well-being is the purest, least developed state
of nature. The ideal situation that a true primitivist may be supposed to
cherish is located as far away as possible, in space or time or both, from
the urban centers of advanced civilization. The pastoral world-view, on
the other hand, comes into focus somewhere between the logical extremes of the primitivist and the progressivist views of change—of history. (In these modern, largely secular world-views, it seems, attitudes
toward history occupy a place of comparable centrality to that of
creation myths in the Weltanschauungen of non-Western, pre-industrial
peoples.) The pastoralist's viewpoint entails neither an uncritical embrace of material progress nor its total repudiation. What matters most
in the pastoral dispensation is the proper subordination of all material
concerns to the satisfactions of the inner life, whether they be defined in
moral, aesthetic, political, or religious terms. The pastoralist therefore
may be said to accept innovation or progress-up-to-a-point, the point
being the achievement of an economy of "contained self-sufficiency,"[10]

10. Renato Poggioli discusses the economic implications of the pastoral as a
mode in *The Oaten Flute, Essays on Pastoral Poetry and the Pastoral Ideal*,
(Cambridge, 1975), pp. 4-7.

or what our latter-day pastoralists might refer to as a "stable state economy." To put it much too simply for the moment: if we think of the advance of civilization as the progressivist's highest value, and the preservation of nature—the natural—as the primitivist's, then the pastoralist's characteristic posture is reconciliatory, as expressed by such contemporary slogans as "small is beautiful," or "alternative technology," or "voluntary simplicity"; the evident aim is to recover at least some of the harmony between man and nature that obtained, it is said, in the Golden Age.

As defined in this abstract way, the difference between the primitivist and the pastoralist world-views may seem to be less significant than the literary record indicates. Although they each embody strong feelings of alienation, and a powerful initial recoil from organized society, the primitivist creed calls for such an inhuman extreme of renunciation that in fact it has attracted few intelligent exponents and even fewer practitioners. One might almost describe it as a class without members, chiefly useful for purposes of analysis. Pastoralism, on the other hand, has won the favor—or the serious consideration—of many of Western culture's most gifted artists, writers, and intellectuals. The pastoral mode, as a body of aesthetic conventions, surely is our oldest, most supple and evocative means of expressing the ineradicable ambiguity, or what a contemporary economist would call the relative costs and benefits, of social change. Only in recent years, thanks to the students of early man, have we begun to appreciate the special bearing of the pastoral mode on those changes initiated by innovations in the practical arts. The original devices of the pastoral, after all, figure forth a retrospective idealization of the unconstrained ways of herdsmen, a fact which suggests that during the early phases of its history, in the days of the Homeric poets or the authors of the Old Testament, it probably lent expression to a degree of nostalgia generated by the first great technological revolution: the invention and subsequent triumph of settled agriculture and cities.[11] The continuing feature of pastoralism which may be said to connect the fable of Cain and Abel with Tho-

11. A useful summary of the relevant anthropological research on early man may be found in *Man the Hunter*, ed. Richard Lee and I. De Vore (Chicago, (1968). For a provocative rejoinder to my argument here, see David Halperin, *Beyond Pastoral, Theocritus and the Ancient Tradition of Bucolic Poetry* (New Haven: Yale University Press, 1983, pp. 86-7.

reau's *Walden* or the *Adventures of Huckleberry Finn,* is its animating motive: the desire, in the face of the increasing power and complexity of organized society, to recover some part of a simpler, more "natural" way of life.

During the formative years of the Republic, the exemplar of native pastoralism was Thomas Jefferson, the President whose enemies charged him with being less a statesman than a poet, and whose fond vision of the nation's future was a society of the middle landscape, midway between the overcivilization of Europe and the "savagery" of the Western frontier: an optimal blend of art and nature. His initial, highly charged revulsion at the prospect of building large cities and factories in postrevolutionary America often has been mistaken for an espousal of the essentially economic doctrine of agrarianism, but in fact it was a characteristic pastoral repudiation of the primacy of any economic criterion for the good society. It was the superior quality of life, public and private, made possible by the pre-industrial economy, not its presumed material superiority, that Jefferson was affirming with his famous plea to "let our work-shops remain in Europe." In his judgment, the intellectual, moral, and political independence of individual citizens was much more important than any economic index of national well-being, and to achieve such autonomy he was perfectly willing to sacrifice a considerable part of the nation's collective wealth and power.

At the same time, however, Jefferson was a knowledgeable man of affairs, and he recognized that his visionary conception of American society allowed far too little scope for the fulfillment of the soaring material aspirations of the citizenry—or at least of certain dominant groups within it. He appreciated the vigor and resourcefulness of Yankee merchant-capitalists, and he knew something about the attractive power of their Franklinian ideology of self-help, upward status mobility, and unbounded economic growth. Even as he enunciated his pastoral response to the factory system in the 1780s, with all that it implied about the need to curb economic appetites, Jefferson acknowledged that it was in fact a political will-o'-the-wisp. At some level he had grasped the untenability of the emergent national belief system, with its unqualified commitment to progress and its sentimental overlay of pastoral idealism. What he had recognized, to put it differently, was the instability—the inherent contradictoriness—of the national effort to combine the progressive and pastoral world-views. But in his political realism, Jefferson was far in advance of most of his countrymen, who for many years would have little difficulty believing that as Americans they could have it both ways: they could continue to believe that limitless material progress, as represented by images of machine power, was the appointed means by which their Republic would arrive at a unique state of harmony with nature.

By the 1840s, with the increasingly rapid onset of industrialization, the discordance of which Jefferson had been aware was becoming apparent to a larger minority of perceptive Americans. In retrospect, of course, the reason for that new awareness is far more apparent than it was at the time. We now can invoke an array of elaborate theories (Marxian, Weberian, Durkheimian, etc.), and a veritable lexicon of omnipotent terms like industrialization (capitalist development, urbanization, rationalization, secularization, modernization, etc.), all invented to describe and, with varying claims of completeness, to explain the transformation of society then beginning to make itself felt. We know now that it was indeed the *great* transformation (in Karl Polanyi's untendentious phrase), and that before the end of the century the relatively unstratified, decentralized, agricultural society of small property-holders would have disappeared forever. At the time, however, many ramifications of this process of change, including its astonishing magnitude and its unfathomable essence, were—perhaps still are—hidden from view. One intensely visible aspect of what was happening, on the other hand, was the exhilarating spectacle of a people marching across the land, subduing nature (including the Indians), and building a new society. No image conveyed the exultation associated with the nineteenth-century American belief in progress as well as that of a locomotive hurtling across the prairies and plains, over rivers, and through the heart of mountains on its westward course. What most Americans perceived as triumphant progress, however, looked to some others as the ravage of the continent. It was in the middle decades of the century, as I tried to demonstrate in *The Machine in the Garden,* that some of our most gifted writers seized and, so to speak, inverted that favorite progressive icon. In their work the image of the machine's sudden appearance in the landscape generates ideas and feelings irreconcilable with the progressive world-view.

The indirect power of this device to undermine the optimistic progressivism of the dominant culture is exemplified by a brief episode in the *Adventures of Huckleberry Finn*. It occurs at the end of Chapter XVI, where Clemens has Huck and Jim floating downstream on a foggy night. "It got to be very late and still," says Huck, "and then along comes a steamboat up the river."

> . . . She was a big one, and she was coming in a hurry, too, looking like a black cloud with rows of glow-worms around it; but all of a sudden she bulged out, big and scary, with a long row of wide-open furnace doors shining like red-hot teeth, and her monstrous bows and guards hanging right over us. There was a yell at us, and a jingling of bells to stop the engines, and a pow-wow of cussing, and a whistling of steam—and as Jim went overboard on one side and I on the other, she come smashing straight through the raft.

My chief point about this episode, leaving aside for the moment its immediate significance in the novel, is its typicality. Similar passages, all embodying variants of the thematic image of the machine power's sudden intrusion upon the native landscape, recur endlessly in the work of our best writers. It is no exaggeration, indeed, to describe the image as a great central figurative conception in our classic American literature. But we have arrived at the era when images of the mechanic arts, as in the case of Adams's Dynamo, were made to represent the determining, virtually autonomous "forces" of history, and this is a good place to sum up the argument.

So far my chief contention has been that responses to innovation in the mechanic arts cannot be understood apart from their cultural significance. It is wholly misleading to think of them as registering the "impact" of new, merely physical-utilitarian objects; the very use of that term often implies a shallow physicalist, or stimulus-response, conception of change. Our responses to discrete events like Hiroshima, or lesser catastrophes involving science-based inventions, inevitably occur within a context shaped by inherited patterns of belief. In America images drawn from the new industrial arts had served chiefly to validate an extravagantly hopeful amalgam of the progressive and pastoral world-views. Even at the time the unusual, not to say anomalous yoking of those inherently antithetical ideals was perceived to be a cultural by-product of the truly exceptional conditions of life enjoyed by European migrants to North America.

If any single bifurcation of experience may be said to have had an enduring vitality in Western culture since Plato, it is the presumed antagonism between material aspirations and the life of the mind. Yet here in the United States, in the unfolding of the benign drama of progress, that ancient antagonism was to be resolved. This was what Emerson meant when, in his most hopeful mood, he could say that "Machinery and Transcendentalism agree well."[12] But the peaceable kingdom did not materialize. As the unfulfilled promises of industrial capitalism became increasingly apparent to American writers, the social purpose of Franklin having been replaced by the greed of the robber barons, the latent contradictions within the prevailing belief system also became apparent. Images of the discordance created by mechanization afforded an evocative means of connecting feelings of disenchantment, loss, and fear to changes in society. Because the iconology of industrial power was so popular with the hierophants of progress it afforded a special opportunity to artists or writers disaffected with the dominant culture. To depict a machine as a threat to the promise of life was to invert the way most Americans had been accustomed to seeing their society and its future.

### III

Returning now to the passage from *Huckleberry Finn,* I want to suggest that the central figurative conception it examplifies prepared the cultural ground for the fatalistic attitude toward the mechanic arts—the idea of omnipotent technology—so prevalent today. To do so it is necessary to take note of the well-established body of literary conventions with which Clemens was working. Here, as always, we must consider modifications in form as well as subject matter, or thematic content, if we are to understand the interactive process by which changes in the actual conduct of life are transmuted into art or expression and back again. The narrative structure of *Huckleberry Finn,* like that of many American fables, might be described as that of a pastoral romance.

12. *Journals of Ralph Waldo Emerson,* ed. E. W. Emerson and W. E. Forbes (Boston, 1909-14), VI (1843), 397.

The action begins, as in the pastoral mode, with Huck's retreat from a relatively complex social environment to a relatively simple one, "closer" to nature. What follows, as in the typical romance, is a quest— the white boy and the black man enacting a distinctively American version of the perilous journey—down the Mississippi River on a raft.

So much has been written on the subject that we need not dwell upon the function of the raft as the vehicle, literal and metaphorical, of this quest for freedom. Somewhat less obvious, however, is the extent to which the raft makes possible the fulfillment of the pastoral ideal. On their floating island Huck and Jim enjoy a life that typifies, with remarkable completeness, that ancient and enduring dream of natural felicity. The absence of social constraint; the recovery of an easy, flowing tempo of life; the pleasures afforded by the sensory experience of nature, and especially the beauty of the landscape; the creation of a virtually self-contained economy whose purpose is not to achieve wealth or power, but material sufficiency; the relative independence of mind exhibited by an escaped slave and a white boy in defiance of an oppressive society—all of these are made possible—represented—by the raft, and it is of course that idyllic fantasy of freedom, above all else, of which the steamboat is the destroyer. What the episode implicitly conveys, then, is an ineluctable conflict between the pastoral and the progressive ideals. In one sense Clemens is replaying, in the local imagery of nineteenth-century America, the contrast between complex and simple ways of life, the one identified with advances in the arts, and the other with natural enjoyments, which always had been at the center of the pastoral mode in literature. But with this difference: the conception of the new order suggested by this image of machine power would seem to banish all hope of recovering the natural, and to presage the bleakest determinism.

But it may seem that I am exaggerating the significance of what is after all a brief episode in a single novel.[13] The dubiety of such an

13. At least two critics have argued against my reading on this ground. See, for example, Winfried Fluck, *Aesthetische Theorie und literaturwissenschaftliche Methode* (Stuttgart, 1975), pp. 224ff, and also "Aesthetic Premises in American Studies," in *Other Voices, Other Views, An International Collection of Essays from the Bicentennial,* ed. Robin W. Winks (Westport, Connecticut, 1978), pp. 21-30; Kenneth S. Lynn, "The Regressive Historians," *The American Scholar* (Autumn, 1978), 480-89.

interpretation also may seem to be reinforced by the knowledge that Clemens had been an enthusiastic patron of mechanical invention. The fact is that from an early age he had been an ardent believer in the idea of history as a record of continuous, perhaps inevitable, improvement in the human estate. On the other hand, we also know that for some time he had been having qualms about the direction of American society, and during his long struggle to finish *Huckleberry Finn* those qualms had become more serious. On his return visit to the Mississippi Valley in 1882, a journey which formed the basis for the troubled second volume of *Life on the Mississippi,* he had been appalled to see the virtual obliteration of the world he once had known or, as he referred to it, "that departed America." ("It will be dust and ashes when I come again," he had written to his wife during the journey.) But this is not to imply that he then was prepared to give up his belief in the humane benefits to be had from advances in scientific knowledge and ways of applying it. He almost certainly was not, but this fact hardly diminishes the significance of the episode in which the raft is destroyed.

The fact is that Clemens was having great difficulty in reconciling his commitment to the ideal of progress with the painful sense of loss and nostalgia he felt in contemplating the disappearance of the simple village world of his youth. This profound contrariety at the center of his response to change was a source of imaginative energy for his best work, but in large part it lay below the level of his express opinions, and it is not surprising that it made itself felt in the paralyzing crisis he experienced during the composition of *Huckleberry Finn*—a crisis that coincided with the writing of this very passage.[14] It would not be difficult to demonstrate that many attributes of the steamboat-smashing-the-raft episode correspond with the pattern of contrariety inherent in the work as a whole—its thematic and narrative structures, and in much of Clemens's other work; and when, in addition, we consider that this thematic image already had acquired the status of a cultural symbol, with widely accepted meanings in the general culture, and that variants appear in the work of many other major writers, it would be difficult to exaggerate its significance.

14. For a more detailed interpretation of the crisis in the composition of *Huckleberry Finn* see my intro. to the Library of Literature ed. (Bobbs-Merrill), Indianapolis, 1967.

What requires emphasis here is that Clemens had invested his darkening view of American society in the image of a machine as destroyer. In the novel as we have it, to be sure, the raft is merely damaged, but it is revealing that he originally had intended it to be irrevocably destroyed. "Back a little, CHANGE," he later had told himself in one of the working notes that finally got him started again, "—raft only crippled by steamer." The resurrection of the raft was part of the solution of the dilemma that had kept him from finishing the book; one hardly could ask for a more pointed demonstration of the intersection of a specific problem of literary composition and the painful ambivalence aroused by a writer's response to change associated with technology. In *Huckleberry Finn*, the steamboat is an alien intruder from a world felt to be wholly external to that of the raft and its occupants. Its sudden, traumatic appearance out of the fog "looking like a black cloud with rows of glow-worms around it; . . . with a long row of wide-open furnace doors shining like red-hot teeth, and her monstrous bows hanging right over us"—is that of some floating steel mill, a kind of huge mechanical dragon, as omnipotent and uncontrollable, as much like an "infinite force" as the Dynamo. A few years later, in the gory conclusion of *The Connecticut Yankee*, Clemens was to make this identification of mechanical innovations with the destructive element in modern society far more explicit. But though he was able to convey his feelings of alienation from the dominant culture, he only had half-escaped it, as George Santayana so cogently would phrase it, because he had had "nothing solid" to put in its place.[15]

Santayana's well-known insight is persuasive, at least until we try to imagine what that something "solid" might have been. At this point I find it useful to introduce Raymond Williams's distinction between dominant, residual, and emergent aspects of modern culture.[16] Like virtually every writer in the received canon of our literature, Clemens and Adams were highly critical of the dominant culture. (We have had no major writer, to my knowledge, who truly affirmed the characteristically unquestioning nineteenth-century belief in progress.) Like most of the others, moreover, Clemens and Adams expressed their disaffec-

15. "The Genteel Tradition in American Philosophy" (1911), in *The Genteel Tradition, Nine Essays by George Santayana*, ed. Douglas L. Wilson (Cambridge, 1967), p. 51.
16. *Marxism and Literature*, (Oxford, 1977), pp. 121-27.

tion by efforts to mobilize the energies of the residual culture. If in Clemens's case that effort took the form of recreating the life of the departed America he had known as a boy, in Adams's it meant a life-long enactment of his family's estimable, if obsolete, code of Cicero-nian service to society. (It also took the form of his idealized medieval-ism, as embodied in the image of the Virgin he set in symbolic opposition to the Dynamo.) But neither was capable, finally, of the capacity for illusion necessary to believe that those residual formations offered an efficacious alternative. Why, then, didn't they turn to the emergent culture? This question certainly occurred to Adams. No radical Marxist could have felt greater scorn for the business class and the financiers of State Street and Wall Street; he called them "gold bugs," and the patrician contempt he felt for the mean-spirited, shallow culture they represented was boundless. "By rights," he said of himself, "he should have been . . . a Marxist, but some narrow trait of the New England nature seemed to blight socialism, and he tried in vain to make himself a convert."[17] Whatever it was that "blighted" socialism for him—the sheer improbability of Henry Adams as a participant in a revolutionary mass movement of the working class perhaps suggests a sufficient explanation—the fact is that neither he nor Clemens was able to derive hope from any significant element of the emergent culture. It was as if the extravagantly optimistic ideology of industrial progress had pre-empted the future as a ground for hope.

To ascribe centrality to the figurative conception exemplified by the episode in *Huckleberry Finn* is to suggest that it prefigures in small the larger contours of the fictive world created by many of our best twentieth-century writers. It is the characteristic world of an inverted, or postindustrial, form of the pastoral. There, as in the old pastoral, we follow the movement of an alienated protagonist from a complex to a simpler environment (it may be symbolic rather than literal), but the machine power invariably serves to dramatize the unexampled and irresistible dynamism of the new industrial order. Not only is it made to seem antagonistic to the integrity and concerns of the self, it is the embodiment of social forces which, if unimpeded, may be expected to defile and desecrate the natural environment, the very ground on which

17. *The Education of Henry Adams,* Chapter 15.

the pastoral hope of recovery always had rested. The expectation aroused by any pastoral romance is of course that the protagonist's disengagement from organized society will lead, eventually, to some degree of redemption or recuperation—some "fruits for life" as William James might have put it—and although the classic American writers did not produce any fables which can be described as pastorals of unqualified "success," they have tended with increasing frequency to write "pastorals of failure." Consider, for example, the changing tenor of the outcome as we move from Thoreau's *Walden* to *Huckleberry Finn*, Hemingway's *In Our Time*, Fitzgerald's *The Great Gatsby*, Faulkner's "The Bear," West's *Miss Lonelyhearts*, and Mailer's *Why Are We in Vietnam?* To call works of this sort "inverted," "tragic," or "anti-" pastorals—"pastorals of failure"—is to say that they enact the old hope of recovering "the natural" only in order to deny it.[18] It is a formal embodiment of the fatalistic view of contemporary history which writers like Clemens and Adams had attached to images of machine power.

IV

Much of what I have said thus far is an attempt, in the light of our present concern, to recast the argument I had set forth in *The Machine in the Garden* (1964). One shortcoming of that book, soon made evident by events, had been my failure to recognize adequately the political basis for the continuing appeal of the pastoral world-view to Americans. Nothing in my discussion of the subject could have prepared readers for the resurgence of native pastoralism, or the widespread dissemination of the fatalistic view of technology it fostered, during the explosion of protest incited by the Vietnam War. On the contrary, I had meant to leave the impression that our national susceptibility to pastoral idealism had been the product of largely transient circumstances, and that it therefore could have been expected to wane in the era of high technology. A few weeks after the book was published, however, Mario Savio, a graduate student at the University of California at Berkeley, told a mass sit-in of students, faculty, and others that

18. For the distinction between pastorals of "success" and of "failure," see Harold E. Toliver, *Marvell's Pastoral Vision* (New Haven, 1960), p. 88ff.; Poggioli invokes the idea of the inverted pastoral in *The Oaten Flute*, pp. 33-34.

the time had come for them to throw their bodies on "the machine," if need be, in order to stop it. That demonstration marked a critical point in the emergence of the radical student movement, and Savio's speech helped to popularize a metaphor that epitomizes much of the radical thinking of the 1960s. This is what Savio said:

> There is a time when the operation of the machine becomes so odious, makes you so sick at heart, that you can't take part; you can't even tacitly take part, and you've got to put your bodies upon the gears and upon the wheels, upon the levers, upon all the apparatus and you've got to make it stop. And you've got to indicate to the people who run it, to the people who own it, that unless you're free, the machines [*sic*] will be prevented from working at all.[19]

In this exhortation Savio effectively translates the central figurative conception in our literature into a program of political action. At the outset he takes for granted the familiarity of his audience with his metaphoric reference to "the operation of the machine." Given the local situation, his meaning was absolutely clear. After all, this protest meeting was part of the conflict between the student Free Speech Movement and the university administration; only the year before, the President of the university, Clark Kerr, had propounded his technocratic theory of the new "multiversity," stressing its close affiliation with the large industrial corporations and the government, and the students had picked up that theme in the official ideology with their celebrated placard: "I AM A HUMAN BEING—PLEASE DO NOT FOLD, SPINDLE OR MUTILATE." To refer to a bureaucratic network of this sort as a "machine" is merely to invoke a venerable preindustrial metaphor. It is not substantially different from the way it had been used, say, by Hobbes in *The Leviathan* (1651) to refer to the nation-state, or by many other writers to refer to a wide range of manmade contrivances. But Savio obviously was not satisfied with that halfdead metaphor, and to energize it—this is what makes the passage so revealing—he introduces a recent version of the stock pastoral antinomy: the natural opposed to the new industrial technology. Hence

19. This version is taken from *The Berkeley Student Revolt; Facts and Interpretations,* ed. Seymour Martin Lipset and Sheldon S. Wolin (New York, 1965), p. 163. As I indicate below, the word in the last sentence should be "machine," not "machines."

the shift of reference from bureaucratic machinery to literal machines (industrial apparatus?) effected by bringing in those gears, wheels, and levers or, as he says, "all that apparatus" on which he invites the students to put their bodies.* But the chief source of imaginative power here is the idea, in the popular slogan of the day, of "putting your body where your mind is." To call upon the students to stop "the machine" with their bodies was to say, in effect, that only a final, desperate mobilization of the organic—the human body conceived as the ultimate repository of the natural—could overcome the forms of political organization and domination associated with industrial technology.

To trace the literary sources of Savio's speech one would have to go back at least as far as Thoreau's lecture on "Civil Disobedience" ("Let your life be a counter-friction to stop the machine"), and come down through Whitman, William Carlos Williams, and the Beat movement of the 1950s. It would not be difficult to demonstrate the presence of the same figurative conception in the work of Gary Snyder, Jack Kerouac, Allen Ginsberg, or Ken Kesey. It is particularly prominent in the two most popular works of that group, Kerouac's *On the Road* (1955) and Kesey's *One Flew over the Cuckoo's Nest* (1962). Late in the 1960s, Bruce Cook asked Allen Ginsberg to specify the elements of continuity he claimed to see between the Beat ethos and the radical counterculture of the Vietnam era. Which features, Cook asked, did the young dissidents pick up from the Beats? Ginsberg: "Drugs." Cook: "What else?" Ginsberg: "You could say we had a preoccupation with the Thoreauvian and Whitmanic tradition, and so we were very responsive to the whole rediscovery of the Body and the Land. . . ." At that point, says Cook, "I asked him how he might sum up the Beat movement as an idea. What was at the heart of it intellectually?" Ginsberg: "Well, there was the return to nature and the revolt against the

---

* That these mechanical images were interpreted as a reference to industrial technology is suggested by the mistaken form in which this passage was transcribed and subsequently reprinted. The tape made on the spot clearly indicates that in the final sentence Savio said that "the machine," not "the machines," will be "prevented from working at all." The point is noteworthy because it exemplifies the ambiguity surrounding the linked concepts of "the machine" and "technology" in current usage; they are used as umbrella references to real machines, i.e., physical apparatus and, at the same time, to virtually anything susceptible to such an analogy between mechanical apparatus and other things, especially the entire social structure or "the system."

machine, and I think this is very important, for you can see all this in the reduplication of the cycle today."[20]

During the 1960s the concept of technology implicit in this notion of a cyclical recurrence to the theme of a "return to nature *and* . . . revolt against the machine" [my emphasis] was reinforced by the work of theorists like Jacques Ellul and Lewis Mumford. It is significant that the English translation of Ellul's influential book, *The Technological Society* (1954), was not published in the United States until 1964, just as the escalation of the Vietnam War was beginning. Ellul's persuasive argument turns on a profound truism, namely that the attribute common to all modern technologies is something called *technique*. (In his foreword to the American edition, Robert Merton defined Ellul's key term as "any complex of standardized means for attaining a predetermined result.") By locating the essential destructiveness of advanced industrial societies in an abstraction of such undeniable universality, Ellul helped to reinforce and disseminate the potentially fatalistic notion of "technology" or "The Machine" as the prime mover of contemporary history. (That "technique" is omnipresent in our kind of society is irrefutable, but the notion that it is inherently destructive of higher ends neither can be confirmed nor disproven.) Although he later attacked Ellul precisely for his incipient fatalism,[21] Mumford helped to popularize a similar reified and potentially fatalistic conception. Here is the way he defined "The Machine" in 1965:

> Most of the creative forces in our time have been canalized into the Machine, a systematic organization of scientific discovery and technical invention that, under the pressure of excessive pecuniary gains and exorbitant political powers, has transformed the entire existence of the Western World. The insensate dynamism of this mechanical organization with no goals but its own ceaseless expansion and inflation, has broken down the continuities of history.[22]

Whether called "technology" or "technique" or "The Machine" or the "megamachine" (the term used by Mumford in the first, 1966, volume of his *The Myth of the Machine*), this putative entity invariably is invested with a kind of life, or self-contained power, that makes it in

---

20. Bruce Cook, *The Beat Generation* (New York, 1971), p. 104.
21. *The Pentagon of Power* (New York, 1970), pp. 290-91.
22. "Constancy and Change," *The New Yorker,* March 6, 1965, p. 162.

effect the chief agent of change in our world. To call that agent a "machine" is of course to make explicit the metaphoric power behind all of these abstractions; the image effects a two-way transfer of thought and feeling between the attributes of the metaphor's vehicle, or secondary subject, some self-powered, metallic mechanism, and its tenor, or primary subject, a mode of social organization. What matters most, I think, is the capacity of this metaphor to endow a production of mind with an independent, determinative existence.

This fatalistic view of technology, and the urgency of resistance to it, dominates the influential work of Norman Mailer during the 1960s (especially *Why Are We in Vietnam?*, 1967, and *The Armies of the Night*, 1968), and indeed helps to explain the astonishing belief, held by an influential minority of Americans between (roughly) 1968 and 1971, that a revolution was imminent in the United States. The instrument of the revolution was to be The Movement, a phantom coalition of all the protesting groups of dissident Americans which had come to the surface during the Vietnam upheaval. Although this Movement did include two genuine political forces, the civil rights movement and the antiwar movement, it was not, like them, an actual coalition of existing organizations with members, leaders, and more or less explicit objectives. One can get a sense of the amorphousness of the Movement idea, and of the pastoral ethos informing it, from Mitchell Goodman's huge, invaluable compendium of documents, *The Movement Toward a New America, The Beginnings of a Long Revolution* (1971). To understand the cast of mind of its intellectual adherents, it also is helpful to look at the more popular of the radical political ideas in circulation at the time, especially those of Herbert Marcuse (*An Essay on Liberation*, 1969), Theodore Roszak (*The Making of a Counter Culture: Reflections on the Technocratic Society and its Youthful Opposition*, 1969), Charles Reich (*The Greening of America*, 1970), and Jean-François Revel (*Without Marx or Jesus: The New American Revolution Has Begun*, 1971).

For all the differences in viewpoint represented by these books, each in its own way lends credence to the idea of "technology" as the effective principle of authority, domination, or oppression in the United States, and to the notion that a revolution against it is about to occur. It is not to be the old-fashioned, Old Left kind of revolution, effected by a self-assertive self-interested working class, but rather by an uprising of the alienated middle class, especially the young, bent upon some version of recovering the natural or—in Reich's inspired phrase—a *greening* of America. The kind of political action to which these books lend expression is likely to be another enactment of the pastoral impulse, an impulse to resist the accelerating power and complexity of advanced industrial society by mobilizing residual elements of the culture. A characteristic political act of the young radicals of the 1960s took the form of disengagement, or dropping out, or (a psychedelic variant) "taking a trip," all of which involved another sort of "return to nature." As applied to the incipient (relatively formless) ideology of 1960s radicalism, therefore, such a return may be understood as a movement toward a way of life identified with either or both (1) external nature (it may be seen as the tamed countryside or the wilderness, but in any case it is nature located in an environment marked by fewer signs of human intervention than the city), and (2) inner (human) nature (the integral self—some presumed precognitive, presocialized core of mind). By taking drugs or practicing a rigorous spiritual discipline, one can cut through the upper layers of conforming consciousness to the authentic, natural realm of being underneath. But here the significant point is that both kinds of disengagement involve the yoking together, as Ginsberg recognized, of the revolt against the machine and the recovery of the natural; as always, in expressions of the pastoral worldview, each of the opposed ways of life, the oppressive complexity of organized society and the relative simplicity sought by the move toward nature, derives a large part of its force from the felt presence of its opposite.

Although it would be a gross oversimplification to think of the cultural and political radicalism of the 1960s in its entirety as a chapter in the history of American pastoralism, the continuing grip of that world-view upon the imagination helps to explain many things about it. It is especially useful in accounting for the false expectations, like the belief in the existence of a potentially successful revolutionary Movement, aroused by the politics of disengagement. If the essential feature of the dominant system is perceived to be an entity as abstract as "technology" or "The Machine," it is not entirely unreasonable to believe that it could be toppled by a widespread alteration of consciousness. Those who (like Charles Reich) believed that a revolution was in prospect in 1968-70 were undeterred by the fact that the predominantly white, middle-class antiwar movement had had little or no success in making an effective alliance with the black militants of the civil rights movement or, for that matter, with any elements of organized labor and the working class. A central impulse of The Movement, in short, was resistance to the dominant culture through the reaffirmation and recovery of certain residual (or "green") aspects of American life, and the extravagance of the hope it had raised was made manifest by the speed with which it was dispelled. With the end of the military draft in 1972 and the Nixon administration's announced intention (whatever the tactical delays) to withdraw military forces from Vietnam, the illusory concept of a revolutionary Movement quickly vanished. In its aftermath, the resurgence of native pastoralism as a quasi-political ideology left among its adherents a widespread sense of failure, resignation, and apathy.

Nothing written at the time exhibits that mood of political enervation, or its ideological origins, as well as Sheldon Wolin's summary statement, contributed to a symposium on "The Meaning of Vietnam" just as the last American troops were escaping from Saigon in 1975.[23] It should be said that Wolin, a distinguished political scientist, had been closely involved in the dissident politics of the 1960s from the beginning; he wrote a book about the student uprising at Berkeley (he had been a member of that faculty at the time), and as a participant-observer in the antiwar movement he wrote some of the most trenchant political journalism of the period. But here he is summing up the significance of the entire political upheaval of the Vietnam era, not only the disastrous war in Southeast Asia, but also Watergate, racial violence, bankrupt cities, economic distress, and ecological warnings, and behind it all he sees one "new and awesome fact." That fact is exemplified by the narrowing options available to the American politician. "Wherever he turns," says Wolin, "he is hemmed in: by previous commitments, programs hardened into structures, once hopeful directions which now serve only as demanding grooves down which the present must run." If American politicians feel hemmed in, Wolin argues, it is because we, as

23. *New York Review of Books,* June 12, 1975.

a people, have paid a high price for the benefits of a large, centralized organization society. Immigrants have "effaced their origins, workers surrendered their skills and bodies to the tempo of machines, and localities traded history for the benefits of centralized control."

> All the fruits of progress, increase, and expansion have been purchased by the dependence of each of us on structures—governmental, economic, and educational—whose steady expansion has increased that dependence to the point where, as a society, we are literally enslaved, that is, our daily existence requires the expansion, let alone the perpetuation, of governmental bureaucracies, huge corporations, and international networks in which government and business are intricately interwoven.

This vast interlocking organizational structure is of course what is often meant in the popular rhetoric of our time by "technology" or The Machine. (Scholars like Mumford, activists like Savio, novelists like Mailer called it that.) Although Wolin includes the submission of workers to the "tempo of machines" as one element in the emergence of this complex structure, he does not resort to the misleadingly reductive metaphor or, to be more specific, the popular synecdoche, by which the whole (the institutional system) is equated with one of its subordinate parts, in this case machines or, in the old-fashioned narrow sense of the word, technology. This is the linguistic root of the larger issue here: the rhetorical device exemplifies the way in which essentially political feelings of discontent—feelings aroused by the socio-economic structure—so often are displaced upon a highly abstract, disembodied entity: a symbolic representation of what used to be called the mechanic arts. To think of this huge institutional structure as at bottom technological in nature, or The Machine, is in effect to assent to the notion that it is a direct and in all likelihood unavoidable product of advances in science-based technical knowledge, hence beyond the reach of most, perhaps all but the most extreme, not so say apocalyptic, forms of political action. The point is that this way of responding to change, so like that embodied in the figurative conception with which many of our best American writers recorded their responses to the onset of industrialism, is conducive to a deterministic idea of contemporary history. And though Wolin is too sophisticated a political thinker to invoke

the machine metaphor, the essential structure of his thought and feeling comports with the thematic images employed by Henry Adams and
Mark Twain. Here is the way he finally formulates the significance of
the political turmoil of 1964-72:

> What all of this means, Vietnam included, is a dramatic and
> qualitative break in American history. We have moved from a society
> of free choice and opportunity to a society shaped by necessity. In-
> stead of being the showcase refutation of Marxian determinism, we
> have become an instance of it.

Here once again, the steamboat has smashed the raft. Before Vietnam, we had enjoyed a society of "free choice and opportunity," but a
dramatic break[24] has occurred, and freedom has been replaced by necessity. The highly idealized conception of the recent past; the alien, abstract, largely external character of the intervening force; the sense of
tyrannous circumstances closing in all at once upon a landscape of infinite possibilities—all of this belongs to the familiar pattern. It is a
characteristic literary response to change that threatens the credibility
of the dominant belief system. But here Wolin goes further than the
1960s dissidents who merely expressed feelings of discouragement after
the collapse of the radical movements of the Vietnam era. If we feel as
if our freedom had been supplanted by necessity, he is saying, it is
because that is in fact the case. Wolin's notion that "Vietnam" actually
marked such a dramatic "break" in our history might be said to have
been borne out by the subsequent spread of that dark mood to large
segments of the population. In 1978 for the first time, according to one
professional student of public attitudes, most Americans had come to
believe that "the present, however bad it may be, is more likely to be
better than the future. . . . Traditionally a nation optimistic about the
future, America had turned pessimistic."[25]

24. For a witty essay about the tendency of Americans, and especially of
American historians, to discover crucial "watersheds" or "breaks" in almost every
period of our national history—breaks which usually entail the replacement of
freedom by necessity—see Marcus Cunliffe, "American Watersheds," *American
Quarterly,* 12 (Winter, 1961).
25. Daniel Yankelovich and Larry Kaagan, *Social Policy* (May/June, 1979),
p. 21. Yankelovich bases his assertion on the results of the studies of public
attitudes toward past, present, and future conducted by the firm, Yankelovich,
Skelly, and White, of which he is the president.

V

Nothing I have said is meant to imply that our writers were responsible, in the sense of having "caused," the recent change in American attitudes toward science-based technology. The major precipitants of that change were more immediate and more obvious. Since World War II the most fervent progressivists have been compelled to recognize at least some of the calamitous (or near calamitous) uses to which our society already has put its technology, as well as the far more terrifying military uses to which we are ready to put it at a moment's notice. By now, indeed, it is no longer possible to ignore the discrepancy between our technological power as a fearful aspect of social reality and the machine as it has figured in our progressive belief system. Our writers did not create the widespread awareness of that discrepancy, it is true, but they surely did anticipate it. In their reaction to the onset of industrialism, more than a century ago, they had prefigured the fatalistic idea of technology as a controlling and most dangerous agent of change.

If the testimony of our literature is reliable, moreover, there are good reasons for thinking that Americans may be peculiarly susceptible to this distinctive form of secular fatalism. There it is shown to be a propensity closely bound up with the disappointment of overoptimistic social expectations created, in part, by the very success of technological innovation. The severity of that disappointment, as exemplified by Henry Adams and Mark Twain, is implicit in the great central metaphoric conception of the machine as the destroyer of the hopes lent credence by an unspoiled landscape. On this view the fatalistic idea of technology is an aspect of today's pastoralism, and it may be understood in large measure as a displaced expression of social and political discontent. The pastoral world-view is particularly appealing to disaffected members of the professional middle class and intelligentsia who, for several reasons, are better able to identify with residual than emergent elements of the culture. If the experience of the Vietnam era is any indication, their political protest against the dominant culture is likely to be eruptive, unstable, and transient in character. The much sought after alliance with the civil rights or labor movements proved to be unattainable, and without such an alliance the politics of pastoralism might well become reactionary or, as in the late 1960s, simply evaporate. The idea of technology as the controlling agent of our destiny lends itself to such retreats from politics. To invest a disembodied entity like "The Machine" or "technology" with the power to determine events is a useful way to justify disengagement from the public realm and a reversion to inaction and privacy. In the world of power as in the world of art, the pastoral response to change makes possible a consoling absolution from the painful complexity of political choice. Whether it possibly could be channeled into a larger, forward-looking program of social transformation remains to be seen.

# The Puzzle of Anti-Urbanism
# in Classic American Literature

Whenever American attitudes toward the city are under discussion, we are likely to hear a familiar note of puzzlement. We hear it, for instance, near the end of the influential study by Morton and Lucia White, *The Intellectual Versus the City: From Thomas Jefferson to Frank Lloyd Wright* (1962). After making their case for the centrality of anti-urban motives in American thought and expression, the Whites invite us to share their perplexity. "How shall we expain this persistent distrust of the American city?" they ask. "Surely it is puzzling, or should be."[1]

But should it be? My aim here is to reconsider the bias against the city that allegedly makes itself felt in our classic American literature. At the outset it must be admitted that many of our greatest writers have not displayed anything like a fondness for or even, for that matter, much interest in the actualities of urban experience in America— far from it. To recognize just how far, we need only try to recall the way city life is depicted in the work of the poets in the main line that leads from Emerson to Whitman, Frost, and Stevens, or in the central tradition in prose that includes Cooper, Emerson, Thoreau, Hawthorne,

1. *The Intellectual Versus the City: From Thomas Jefferson to Frank Lloyd Wright* (Cambridge: Harvard University Press, 1962), p. 221.

Melville, James, Mark Twain, Fitzgerald, Hemingway, and Faulkner. Which of these writers may be said to have given us an adequate specification of city life in this country? Which is not vulnerable to the charge of neglect, whether benign or malign, of urban reality? The two who on first thought may seem most deserving of exemption from that charge are Whitman and James. But only at first. For though it is true that New York is the setting for much of Whitman's poetry, his New York is less like a city anyone ever inhabited than it is, in Richard Chase's apt words, "a paradoxically urban-pastoral world of primeval novelty."[2]

As for James, it is true that he also set his most important work in cities, but he made a sharp point of the fact that they were not American cities. His explanation hardly could be more pertinent to my argument. Invoking a musical analogy, James observed that the major key of urban life in the United States is, "absolutely, exclusively," the key of "down-town." Only by writing in that key, he admitted, could a novelist hope to attune himself to what really mattered in the American city, but to the key of "down-town" he nonetheless confessed to being incurably deaf.[3] A further inference of James's remark is that in London, Paris, and Rome—the sites he chose for his most ambitious novels—the key of "up-town" still had resonance enough to yield novelistic significance. On second thought, then, neither James nor Whitman is an exception. Their work manifests no more concern than that of the other writers mentioned for the exact rendering of urban reality in America.

Should we be puzzled by this fact? I think not, but even if I am correct in suggesting that much of the puzzle can be dispelled by ridding ourselves of the false assumptions which underlie it, the puzzle's very existence is an interesting, perhaps even significant datum of our cultural history, and it calls for some explanation. Why is it that our writers, artists, and intellectuals are *expected* to convey a fond approval of the modern city? If we can account for this largely misguided expectation, we will be in a better position, I think, to address the more im-

2. Richard Chase, *Walt Whitman Reconsidered* (London: Victor Gollancz, 1955), p. 95.

3. Henry James, "Preface" to *Daisy Miller*, in *The Art of the Novel: Critical Prefaces*, ed. Richard P. Blackmur (New York: Charles Scribner's Sons, 1955), pp. 272-274.

portant issue: how to understand the implicit attitude to the city in the work of so many of our most gifted writers. Let me say at once that I do not think it makes sense to interpret their neglect of urban reality as evidence of a deep bias against "the city" as such. In imaginative literature, indeed, the concept of "the city" must be understood as in large measure an abstract receptacle for displaced feelings about other things. I shall be arguing that the attitude the Whites and others have mistaken for anti-urbanism is better understood as an expression of something else: a far more inclusive, if indirect and often equivocal, attitude toward the transformation of society and of culture of which the emerging industrial city is but one manifestation.

First, however, let us consider a few of the more compelling reasons for expecting American writers to convey an affirmative attitude toward city life. Behind this expectation there is a view of history, and its starting point is the ineluctable fact that we have been a city-building people. From the very beginning, indeed, the European occupation of North America has been a process of relentless urbanization. During the Atlantic crossing in 1630, John Winthrop envisaged the colony the Puritans were about to establish as "a city upon a hill." The trope was conventional, to be sure, but it nonetheless expressed an important attribute of the Calvinist mentality. Though many of these migrating Englishmen were of rural origin, they were carriers of an essentially bourgeois culture, or what Max Weber was to call "the Protestant ethic." They were burghers in spirit, and like most other European settlers, they conceived of the colonizing enterprise as an affair of organized communities. Their aim was to set up villages, towns, and potential cities in the wilderness. During the colonial period, settlement by the unaffiliated was discouraged, and historians long since have discarded the beguiling notion of a westward-moving frontier comprised of individual "pioneers" like Daniel Boone or Natty Bumppo. The effective cutting edge of population until the end of the nineteenth century was a chain of small communities which often, as in the dramatic instance of Chicago, became cities overnight. Demographers have shown us that for many people the movement of population from east to west was a movement from one city to another, and it was accompanied by a simultaneous movement throughout the nation from country to city. When the Republic was founded, roughly nine out of ten Americans lived in a rural environment; by now that fraction is less than three out of ten. On this view of the past we are a city-building, city-dwelling people, and so it would seem reasonable to expect our high culture to "reflect" that ostensible preference for an urban way of life.

To this conception of the American past it is necessary to add the received wisdom concerning the ancient and virtually timeless affinity between city life and the life of the mind. Cities, after all, are the places where scholars, artists, and writers naturally congregate. They do so because, for one thing, most of the vital institutions of mental production—universities, libraries, theaters, museums, galleries, publishers, printers—almost invariably have been located in cities. (Monasteries probably are the outstanding exception.) Cities are the places where ideas travel most quickly, where one can most readily become knowing or, so to say, urbane. The origins of civilization itself are thought to have been closely bound up with the invention of settled agriculture and cities, and historians of early man often cite the relative size and prosperity of a people's cities as a more or less reliable index of the level of culture to which it has attained.

The long history of cities as the environment most conducive to thought lends credence to the claim that city life has been held in special favor by most intellectuals in the West. More often than not, they have chosen urban settings for their literary accounts of utopia, and by the same token many influential thinkers from Socrates to Karl Marx have looked upon the countryside as a region of mindlessness, not to say idiocy. All of which would seem to justify the notion that the anti-urban motives that make themselves felt in American literature, if that indeed is what they are, constitute a puzzle in need of explanation.

Now the first thing to be said about this argument is that it posits a banal and finally misleading conception of the relations between that urbanizing America out there in reality and the imagined world we encounter in literature. It assumes that a national literature invariably should "lend expression to" or "reflect" (as in a sort of copy image) the dominant features of national experience. But that is to universalize the specific aesthetic program of certain writers, especially the modern realistic novelists, whose chief aim indeed has been to create a fictive illusion of social actuality.

Think of all those important American writers, not yet mentioned, who in fact did make an effort to render the concrete particulars of urban experience in the United States. I have in mind, for example, Howells, Wharton, Norris, Crane, Dreiser, Dos Passos, Wright, Farrell, Baldwin, Ellison, and Bellow. It is significant that these names, often assigned to the categories of "realism" or "naturalism," seldom appear in the roster of "classic" American writers. When we stop to think about the tacit criteria for membership in that amorphous literary society,* as roughly defined in the work of several modern critics and scholars, notably D. H. Lawrence, Van Wyck Brooks, F. O. Matthiessen, and Charles Feidelson, Jr., we soon realize that a chief criterion has been a commitment to an essentially nonrepresentational and often expressly *anti*-realistic method of composition.[4] Nathaniel Hawthorne might have been speaking for most of the other classic American writers when he explicitly repudiated realism or, as he described it, that "form of composition . . . presumed to aim at a very minute fidelity, not merely to the possible, but to the probable and ordinary course of man's experience." Instead, he claimed for himself the artist's privilege of rearranging everyday experience and presenting it, as he put it, "under circumstances, to a great extent, of the writer's own choosing or creation."[5]

This is an absolutely vital distinction for anyone concerned to discriminate among the various literary treatments of urban life. Granted that no verbal composition actually can provide a mirror image of anything, much less a whole city, there still is an immense difference between a realistic novel aimed at creating some such illusion and an avowed "romance" of the sort Hawthorne defines. As he surely realized, the line between those two compositional types can become ter-

---

* The privileged status accorded to the "classic" writers by this honorific label is of course open to question. That the label carries with it a burden of class, gender ethnic, regional, and other unacknowledged assumptions seems obvious enough. For present purposes, however, the existence of this subcategory within the prevailing conception of American literature may be taken for granted. A certain academic legitimacy has been conferred upon it by the standard anthologies and course syllabi of our schools and universities, and by the mutually supporting judgments of writers, critics, teachers, and audiences which created the entire canon. However skewed, in other words, it is in a sense an authentic product of the dominant culture.

4. Consider, esp., Lawrence's *Studies in Classic American Literature* (1923); Brooks's *Emerson and Others* (1927) and *The Flowering of New England* (1936); Matthiessen's *American Renaissance* (1941); and Feidelson's *Symbolism and American Literature* (1953).

5. Nathaniel Hawthorne, "Preface," *The House of the Seven Gables* (1851).

ribly fuzzy or disappear entirely, and yet the usefulness of the distinction, where it is discernible, cannot be exaggerated.

In *Sister Carrie,* for example, Dreiser immediately reveals his documentary purpose. It is apparent in the opening pages that he wants his readers to respond by saying, in effect, "Yes, of course, this is a perfect picture of Chicago, just the way it must have been when Carrie Meeber got off the train on that day in August, 1889." When a writer manifestly sets out to present us with an exact, detailed, seemingly comprehensive imitation of urban reality, then it certainly makes sense to ask whether he has selected truly significant details and has got them right. But such a test is beside the point in reading the work of a writer like Hawthorne, who immediately signals his unconcern with any such accurate, solidly specified rendering of the environment.

Hawthorne's practice in *The Scarlet Letter* exemplifies the way a writer's concept of form—in this case an explicitly nonrepresentational form—governs his treatment of the city. Since this romance is set in seventeenth-century New England, moreover, we can assume that it will not provide us with any *direct* evidence (the sort we might expect to derive, for instance, from descriptive imagery) of Hawthorne's attitude to American cities of his own time. The nearest thing to a city here is Boston, and though it is only a small outpost of civilization on the edge of a vast continental wilderness, we may think of it as a city because we know it is going to become one, and also because it already is the Puritan capital, the center of power and authority as well as the most densely populated place in Massachusetts Bay.

At the outset, Hawthorne exercises his romancer's privilege by singling out three visible features of the town—the prison, the cemetery, the scaffold—and by casting a high light upon them. He is not in the least interested in conveying a literal image of the way Boston looked at the time, a fact whose significance was lost, unfortunately, on the makers of the recent television production who went to such disconcertingly great lengths to create an historically accurate and detailed naturalistic set. On the contrary, Hawthorne deliberately focuses all of our attention upon three tangible manifestations of the hard, reality-oriented, authoritarian spirit of the Calvinists whose power is concentrated there.

As decreed by the characteristically American moral geography, the original source of that iron-hearted spirit lies to the east, in Europe, and

it is only natural that the deepest yearnings of someone like Hester
Prynne, a victim of Puritan repression, are identified with the untrammeled forest that stretches out to the west. On the quotidian plane of
the action, of course, the forest is the only place where she and Dimmesdale can risk any gestures of intimacy. Nature, the wild territory beyond
the confines of Boston, is Hester's true orbit, the locus of the freedom
and self-fulfillment of which she dreams. The moment she is released
from prison, accordingly, she moves out of Boston to a comparatively
remote cottage facing the forest toward the west.

> On the outskirts of the town, within the verge of the peninsula, but
> not in close vicinity to any other habitation, there was a small
> thatched cottage. It had been built by an earlier settler, and aban-
> doned because the soil about it was too sterile for cultivation, while
> its comparative remoteness put it out of the sphere of that social
> activity which already marked the habits of the emigrants. It stood
> on the shore, looking across a basin of the sea at the forest covered
> hills towards the west. . . . In this little, lonesome dwelling, . . .
> Hester established herself, with her infant child.[6]

To live on the outskirts of Boston proper is important to Hester. Her
choice of this half-in, half-out relation to the town is one of the first
signs we get of her concealed but obdurate resistance to the dominant
culture. As it turns out, of course, she is anything but your typical
have-it-both-ways suburbanite, and her peninsula home proves to be
only a way station on the spiritual route to the great climactic forest
episode. There in the moral wilderness, she finally discloses to Dimmesdale the heretical extremism of her ruminations, and her bold plan
to gain freedom for them both. It entails nothing less than his willingness to join with her in a public repudiation of everything for which
Boston stands. " 'Doth the universe lie within the compass of yonder
town?' " she asks him. " 'And what hast thou to do with all these iron
men, and their opinions? They have kept thy better part in bondage too
long already.' "[7]

On its face, admittedly, this is an unlikely choice of a text to exemplify the way the city is represented in our classic American literature.
The animus Hester directs against the Puritan town obviously is not

6. Hawthorne, chap. 5, "Hester at Her Needle," *The Scarlet Letter.*
7. Hawthorne, chap. 7, "The Pastor and His Parishioner," *The Scarlet Letter.*

evoked by its comparatively urban character. Boston is made to seem grim and repressive, it is true, but we are given no reason to suspect that Hawthorne (or Hester) considers those qualities intrinsic to urban life. It is not Boston's cityness, realized or potential, that she would repudiate; it is the kind of society whose power is concentrated there. Express attitudes toward the city qua city, in short, have little or nothing to do with the matter, and that is just the point I am trying to make. To Hawthorne the significant attributes of this place—its essential qualities as a human habitat—are part of something else: the Puritan way of life. His judgment of that culture, not his personal feelings about cities as places to live, is what governs the way he writes about Boston in *The Scarlet Letter*.

The point would be too obvious to mention if it were not so often ignored. It is chiefly ignored by academicians who regard the literary treatment of cities as a question, at bottom, of representational accuracy. I have in mind the kind of investigation of "the image of the city" in art or literature which is conducted in American studies these days. The investigator proceeds on the assumption that literature "reflects" reality. In spite of frequent denunciations by critics, incidentally, the metaphor of "reflection" still seems to be the most popular figure available for conveying a sense of the relationship between art and life. In any case, a corollary of the representational theory of literature is the assumption that passages dealing with a particular subject, such as the city, have inherent significance when detached, more or less arbitrarily, from their immediate literary context and compared with each other and with what we know about those real cities out there in the writer's society.

But of course no work of art, including the work of the most literal-minded, programmatic, realistic novelist, bears any such direct, unmediated relation with raw experience. There are significant differences, however, between the planes of abstraction on which the relationship—that mediation of form—may be established. Hence the first problem for a critic is to identify that plane or, to put it differently, to grasp the principles, explicit or implied, governing the way literary form mediates the transmutation of experience in a particular piece of writing. It makes no sense to approach the work of the classic American writers in search of "responses" to the city on the plane of direct sensory experi-

ence, as if the writers were attempting to convey exact images of the
real thing.

Hawthorne's conception of Boston is formed on that relatively high
plane of abstraction where his most general ideas about art converge
with his most general understanding of society and its history. That
conjunction is apparent, for example, in his choice of the scaffold as a
focal point of Boston life in *The Scarlet Letter*. It is at once an expression of his theory of fiction, or romance, as a symbolic reconstruction
of reality, and of his recognition of the centrality, in our collective experience, of those large organizing symbol systems we now refer to,
in the anthropological sense, as "cultures." His ambivalent attitude toward Puritan culture, rather than an effort to imitate the character of
daily life in seventeenth-century Boston, is what governs his treatment
of that town in *The Scarlet Letter*.

In opting for a nonrepresentational method, Hawthorne had no intention of cutting all ties between his kind of fiction and social reality.
He did not want to create a free-floating world of pure imagination,
but rather a "neutral territory," as he put it, "somewhere between the
real world and fairyland, where the Actual and the Imaginary may
meet, and each imbue itself with the nature of the other."[8] Hawthorne
believed that in fiction, to cite Melville's cogent formulation of their
shared understanding, we should look for "even more reality" than in
"real life." Like religion, Melville said, fiction "should present another
world, and yet one to which we feel the tie."[9] As Melville understood,
I believe, Hawthorne had dismissed the too literal program of the
realistic novel—dismissed it in favor of what Dostoevski would call a
higher realism. That is the meaning of Hawthorne's famous stricture
to the effect that a "romance" must "rigidly subject itself to laws,
and . . . sins unpardonably so far as it may swerve from the truth
of the human heart."[10] This statement usually has been taken as a
brief for "psychological realism," but its implications reach far beyond
the sphere of individual motives. Judging by his best work, the "laws"
of mental life to which he refers apply to collective as well as individual, public as well as private, experience. Indeed, Hawthorne is pro-

8. Hawthorne, "The Custom House," Intro. to *The Scarlet Letter*.
9. Herman Melville, chap. 33, *The Confidence Man* (1857).
10. Hawthorne, "Preface," *The House of the Seven Gables*.

pounding a more ample method of literary representation designed with a view to the particularly complex conception of reality it aims to convey. Because this reality includes the mental set of those who experience and, in a measure, create it, it cannot be apprehended by any merely pictorial "reflection" of the external world, or by any rendering, however detailed, of individual sense experience. To represent the shared mentalities through which the experience of Hawthorn's characters have been screened, only a symbolic rearrangement of "real life" will suffice.

All of this enables us to account for the seeming anti-urbanism in Hawthorne's work. The tacit key to any one of his characters' attitudes to the city is the degree of that person's identification with the dominant culture. The Puritans in *The Scarlet Letter* presided over the building of Boston. It is their town; hence the ruling elect and those who most nearly identify with them understandably exhibit the most affirmative attitude toward the place. At the other extreme, comporting with her embrace of a radical antinomian, or separatist, viewpoint, is Hester's alienation and her scheme for getting away. Between these polar viewpoints, presumably, a hypothetical spectrum of attitudes may be imagined, and a vital aspect of this dialectical concept of culture— dialectical in the sense that Hawthorne posits a conflict of value as its essence—is continuity over time. Thus each of the opposed attitudes toward Puritan life (including the Puritan city) has its nineteenth-century equivalent, and much of the power of *The Scarlet Letter* derives from Hawthorne's skill in suggesting how the conflict it dramatizes is being replayed in his own day.

T. S. Eliot once observed that Hawthorne had "a very acute historical sense,"[11] and in truth he had recognized, long before Max Weber or Perry Miller, that the first settlers had brought with them, embedded in their theology, the seeds of the narrowly utilitarian, acquisitive ethos which had burst into full secular bloom two centuries later. In the self-righteous saints who had persecuted Hester Prynne, Hawthorne would have us recognize the ideological forebears of Judge Pyncheon of *The House of the Seven Gables*. He is the kind of successful man of affairs who dominates the nineteenth-century New England city,

11. T. S. Eliot, "Henry James," in *The Shock of Recognition*, ed. Edmund Wilson (New York: The Modern Library, 1955), p. 861.

and who is described at one point as "subtle, worldly, selfish, iron-hearted, and hypocritical."[12]

The epithet "iron-hearted" here helps to convey Hawthorne's sense of the historical continuity of culture. Indeed, the image of iron is the nucleus of a recurrent cluster of images in his work which includes rust, fire, smoke, and blackness, and it serves to make graphic the connection between the hell-fired mentality of the first generation and the prevailing belief system in that society in the era of emerging industrial capitalism. Iron connotes the practical and specifically technological bent that was to become a distinguishing feature of the new industrial order, and it accords with the Puritan view of nature and the natural as the sphere of the satanic: a fallen world redeemable only by the elect. In a deft satirical sketch, "The Celestial Railroad," Hawthorne depicts Calvinism as the incubator of that belief in material and technological progress which had replaced Christianity as the dominant American faith; it was an ideological transformation closely bound up with the metamorphosis of the Puritan town into the modern Vanity Fair or capitalist city.

But it would be wrong to imply that the critical attitude to the American city implicit in Hawthorne's work derives only—or even chiefly—from a negative view of the dominant culture. In the forest, when Hester disdainfully refers to "yonder town" as a place she and her lover ought to leave forever, she is not merely impelled by her contempt for its iron-hearted ruling class. As important in hardening her will is her impassioned belief in the attainability of an alternative way of life. In imploring Dimmesdale to forget the past and begin a new life elsewhere, she repeatedly refers to the presence of nature—represented, initially and most tangibly at least, by the forest that surrounds them—as evidence that the necessary conditions for a new beginning are accessible to them. She perceives untrammeled nature as the embodiment of a moral and metaphysical as well as a literal (physical) sanction for her extravagant conception of the freedom and happiness she and Dimmesdale might gain by leaving Boston. " 'Doth the universe lie within the compass of yonder town,' " she asks,

12. Hawthorne, chap. 18, "Governor Pyncheon," *The House of the Seven Gables.*

which only a little time ago was but a leaf-strewn desert, as lonely as this around us? Whither leads yon forest track? Backwards to the settlement, thou sayest! Yes; but onward, too! Deeper it goes, and deeper into the wilderness, less plainly to be seen at every step! until, some few miles hence, the yellow leaves will show no vestige of the white man's tread. There thou art free! So brief a journey would bring thee from a world where thou hast been most wretched, to one where thou mayest still be happy!

Hester's language, like the natural setting, conveys the continuing ideological force of her visionary individualism two centuries later—in Hawthorne's own time. At the outset, to be sure, he had taken pains to associate her with "the sainted Ann Hutchinson," the antinomian heretic banned by the Puritan orthodoxy. The honorific epithet indicates that Hawthorne's narrator is sympathetic with this native strain of radical nonconformism, and the doctrine Hester espouses in her effort to strengthen Dimmesdale's will (" 'What we did had a consecration of its own. We felt it so!' "), closely approximates the root theological assumptions of antinomianism. But Hawthorne also describes Hester's secret reflections in a way calculated to evoke the largely secularized radicalism of his dissenting contemporaries, the transcendentalists. When he says, in chapter XIII, that Hester's repudiation of authority had reached the extremity at which "the world's law was no law for her mind," he manifestly is echoing Emerson (in "Self-Reliance"): "No law can be sacred to me but that of my nature." A constant feature of this Protestant viewpoint is that degree of assurance, or self-trust, consonant with a protesting or nondeferential attitude to received modes of thought and behavior. But whereas Ann Hutchinson would have attributed a "consecration" like that claimed by Hester to the intervention of a transcendent deity, Hester's language places her closer to Emerson and his belief in nature as "the present expositor of the divine mind."[13]

Hester's susceptibility to an Emersonian feeling for Nature is what lends her views a seeming anti-urban bias. In pleading with Dimmesdale to leave Boston she does sound, it must be admitted, as if she were asking him to reject all forms of social habitation—whether village, town, or city—in favor of some other sort of life "closer to na-

---

13. Ralph Waldo Emerson, chap. 7, "Spirit," *Nature* (1836).

ture." She urges him to contemplate the happiness that awaits them in the trackless forest (" 'There thou art free' "), as if she took literally the metaphor of a journey into the deep heart of Nature. Given the tone of the duplicitous narrator, moreover, a careless or gullible reader might be led to suppose that Hawthorne was ratifying Hester's belief. But as the subsequent action reveals, she had been carried away by the rapture of the moment, and it seems evident that the entire forest episode is meant to expose what Hawthorne regards as the large element of projection, or wish-fulfillment fantasy, in transcendental pastoralism.

Much of this becomes clear in the chapter of virtual parody in which Hawthorne "so manages his atmospherical medium" as to have the clouds reciprocate the lovers' mood.[14] When they are completely intoxicated by the prospect of their imminent liberation, the gloomy forest ("Such was the sympathy of Nature . . . with the bliss of these two spirits!") suddenly is lit by a burst of sunshine. But of course this is not much more ridiculous than Hester's notion that she and Dimmesdale have only to plunge off into the forest to be free and happy. That idea is of a piece with the rest of Hester's extravagantly utopian expectations. It has nothing whatever to do with a bias against "the city" as such, a fact which becomes evident when we learn that the lovers actually had decided not to escape into nature after all. "It had been determined," Hawthorne casually reveals in chapter XX, after the aura of the forest idyll has been dispelled, "that the Old World, with its crowds and cities, offered them a more eligible shelter and concealment than the wilds of New England, or all America."

I want to suggest that Hawthorne's theory and practice will serve as an almost paradigmatic example of the way the classic American writers treat the environment. Their work in nonrealistic in the sense that they represent place not chiefly for what it is, but for what it means. The meanings they attach to forests, oceans, mountains, prairies, villages, towns, cities, and so forth, are dialectical, not univocal: they derive from a play of conflicting ideas and feelings represented in the narra-

14. Hawthorne, chap. 18, "A Flood of Sunshine," *The Scarlet Letter.*

tive. (The town and the forest in *The Scarlet Letter* have diametrically opposed significance for the orthodox and for Hester.) This enacted conflict of values and meanings within the text usually can be aligned with a similar conflict in that extra-literary realm we call, for shorthand purposes, American society or culture.

A distinguishing feature of this body of writing is its domination by protagonists, like Hester, whose deepest yearnings are expressed in numinous visions of the natural landscape. She might be speaking for any one of them when she urges Dimmesdale, in the forest, to " 'Begin all anew! Hast thou exhausted possibility in the failure of this one trial?' " I am thinking of that familiar roster of pastoral figures: Natty Bumppo, the "I" of Emerson's *Nature* and Thoreau's *Walden*, Ishmael, Christopher Newman,* Huckleberry Finn, Jay Gatsby, Nick Adams, and Ike McCaslin. All of these characters enact the ideal life of the American self journeying away from the established order of things into an unexplored territory we tend to think of as Nature. The object of the journey, implied or avowed, is the nearest possible approximation to the situation of the autonomous unencumbered self.

The entire canon might be described, in other words, as a continuous replaying or testing of the Emersonian doctrine of self-reliance as the epitome of "the natural." (It is interesting that Lawrence, who evidently was fascinated by Emerson but for some reason ended up not writing about him, initially had called his *Studies in Classic American Literature*, "The Transcendental Element in American Literature."[15]) To realize that ideal condition of the self is to disengage from ordinary social reality, but to describe this omnipresent pastoral motive as an expression of a bias against cities is grossly reductive and misleading. The topography here—place in a literal sense—is a vitally important but nonetheless secondary subject, or vehicle, of the great central figurative conception whose primary subject, or tenor, is the search for inner freedom and fulfillment. As Thoreau said about

---

* Although Newman, like the protagonists of James's later international theme novels, finally goes to Europe, his idea of disengagement from his business vocation initially comes to him when he impulsively leaves Wall Street and drives out to Long Island to contemplate the rustic landscape.

15. D. H. Lawrence, *The Symbolic Meaning, The Uncollected Versions of "Studies in Classic American Literature,"* ed. Armin Arnold (New York: Centaur Press, 1962).

his ardent cultivation of the bean-field, these repeated moves away from society—or the city—are undertaken chiefly for the sake of tropes and expression. To call *Walden* "a bible of anti-urbanism," as the Whites do, is a grand impertinence.[16]

That anti-urbanism is largely beside the point is further indicated by the fact that the pastoral impulse enacted in these typical American fictions seldom is rewarded with success. The outcome of the action in *The Scarlet Letter* reinforces Hawthorne's judgment of Hester's vision, implicit in the ironic rigging of the forest episode, as magnificently extravagant and infeasible. The truth is that not one of the works in question finally can be described as an unqualified "pastoral of success."[17] *Walden* comes as close as any to being that, but the more carefully one reads the book, the more narrowly personal and limited Thoreau's triumph seems. Since Thoreau's time, in any event, our best writers working in this mode increasingly have tended to compose pastoral romances of manifest failure. They continue to enact the retreat/quest, but it would seem that they do so chiefly in order to deny it, and the resulting state of mind is one of structured ambivalence.

Perhaps the most revealing twentieth-century instance of this mode of rendering the modern industrial city by an American writer is *The Great Gatsby*. Fitzgerald's fable is particularly useful for our purposes because he has Gatsby (and, to a lesser extent, Nick Carraway) assimilate their conceptions of New York to an illusionary pastoral viewpoint. That that is Gatsby's mode of perception becomes evident to Nick, in his role as narrator, in the famous ending when he finally discovers the clue to Gatsby's character. Lying on the beach, looking across the Long Island Sound at dusk, Nick suddenly recognizes that all of the incongruities of Gatsby's behavior can be explained by his characteristically American propensity to credit the pastoral hope. It is a view of life which initially had been fostered in Europeans by the image of the beautiful, rich, vast, seemingly unclaimed continent. The physical reality of the place, all that it promised in the way of material satisfaction, also was assumed to have made available an

16. *The Intellectual Versus the City*, p. 30.
17. For the concept of pastorals of "success" and "failure," see Harold E. Toliver, *Marvell's Pastoral Vision* (New Haven: Yale University Press, 1960), pp. 88-89.

inner freedom and fulfillment such as Gatsby seeks. In the beginning of the European settlement of America, at least, there had been reason to believe that the actualizing of the ancient pastoral dream really might be feasible in such a "new" world. A palpable sense of that possibility is another distinctive quality of American pastoralism. As Nick puts it, Gatsby's dream of Daisy, represented by the green light, "must have seemed so close that he could hardly fail to grasp it"—another way of saying what Hester had tried to convey to her self-hating lover by pointing to the unbounded forest: " 'There thou art free! So brief a journey would bring thee from a world where thou hast been most wretched, to one where thou mayest still be happy!' " But that possibility had existed a long while ago, Nick realizes, and what Gatsby did not know is that it "was already behind him, somewhere back in that vast obscurity beyond the city [before America had become an urban industrial society], where the dark fields of the republic rolled on under the night."

Gatsby's failure to grasp this historical truth is of a piece with his distorted view of certain realities before his eyes, and Nick's view of the world is only somewhat less skewed by a similar susceptibility to illusion. Nowhere is this more obvious than in Nick's account of New York itself. He sees the city from the vantage of an ambitious young man, like Gatsby, just in from the western provinces. To him it is a ceaselessly beckoning fairyland.

> Over the great bridge, with the sunlight through the girders making a constant flicker upon the moving cars, with the city rising up across the river in white heaps and sugar lumps all built with a wish out of non-olfactory money. The city seen from the Queensboro Bridge is always the city seen for the first time, in its first wild promise of all the mystery and the beauty of the world.[18]

Nick pastoralizes the streets of Manhattan as naturally as Thoreau does the landscape at Walden Pond. "We drove over to Fifth Avenue," he says, "so warm and soft, almost pastoral, on the summer Sunday afternoon that I wouldn't have been surprised to see a great flock of white sheep turn the corner." This image occurs to Nick shortly after

---

18. F. Scott Fitzgerald, chap. 4, *The Great Gatsby* (New York: Charles Scribner's Sons, 1925).

he has described an appalling urban wasteland—a passage which in fact gives us our first sight of the city proper in *The Great Gatsby*. It is the opening paragraph of chapter II. Before that Nick has described the white palaces and spectacular green lawns of Long Island suburbia where his main characters live. But this is quite another New York.

> About half way between West Egg and New York the motor road hastily joins the railroad and runs beside it for a quarter of a mile, so as to shrink away from a certain desolate area of land. This is a valley of ashes—a fantastic farm where ashes grow like wheat into ridges and hills and grotesque gardens; where ashes take the forms of houses and chimneys and rising smoke and, finally, with a transcendent effort, of men who move dimly and already crumbling through the powdery air. Occasionally a long line of gray cars crawls along an invisible track, gives out a ghastly creak, and comes to rest, and immediately the ash-gray men swarm up with leaden spades and stir up an impenetrable cloud, which screens their operations from your sight.

This is a modern city at its ugliest, and it has no place in a green vision of America like Gatsby's. His inability to recognize the discrepancy between the underside of urban industrial society, as embodied in the valley of ashes, and the idealized world of his aspirations is the direct cause of his death and his failure. Every significant element of the tale, indeed—the characters and landscape and action—has discrepant meanings in accord with this duality. As Nick describes it, this other city is utterly remote and unreal. Its ashen inhabitants, who dimly go about their obscure operations, already are crumbling in that polluted air. These are people, like the auto mechanic, Wilson, whose lives are largely circumscribed by material conditions, and who share none of Gatsby's gratifying sense of a felicitous dream about to be consummated. Glimpses of this other New York, composed of the material and human detritus of industrial society, are fleeting but crucial in *The Great Gatsby*. They provide the measure by which we know that the main characters inhabit a realm shaped by myth as well as wealth. Near the end, when Nick tries to imagine how the world might have looked to Gatsby when divested of its mythic veil, he describes it hauntingly as "A new world, material without being real, where poor ghosts, breathing dreams like air, drifted fortuitously about . . . like that ashen, fantastic figure gliding toward him through the amorphous trees." The ashen figure is Wilson on his way to kill Gatsby. He kills him because of Gatsby's unwillingness—or inability—to let go of his patently false conception of Daisy and, by extension, of the world.

In *The Great Gatsby* and *The Scarlet Letter,* human habitations derive their meanings from essentially the same conflict of views. At one extreme we are shown a town or city as it exemplifies a highly critical conception of the dominant culture. It also is represented in each case by a crowd: the people who attend Gatsby's parties and the nameless witnesses to Hester's release from jail. These cities are real places typified at their worst by emblems of oppression and suffering like the valley of ashes or the scaffold. At the other ideological extreme, we are given the perception of that place by a pastoral figure like Hester or Gatsby. It is true, of course, that Hester is alienated from Puritan Boston—is eager to get away—whereas Gatsby and Nick are more or less enthralled by the glamour and excitement of New York. But this difference is not as significant, finally, as the similarity: the fact that in each work a pastoral figure with a vision of an alluring alternative is set against the grim image of urban pain, oppression, and ugliness. Gatsby and Nick (until the very end) see New York from an idealized perspective very much like the one to which Hester lends expression in the forest. (" 'I'm going to fix everything just the way it was before,' " Gatsby says of his relations with Daisy.) But Fitzgerald points to Europe as the truly significant place from which the symbolic disengagement has been made, and for Gatsby all America—urban, rural, wild—retains the attributes of that fresh green breast of the New World envisaged by arriving Europeans. This is the illusion that ashen-faced Wilson finally destroys. Thus the outcome of the action in both works may be understood as exposing the glorious impracticality of the alternative each has posed to urban reality.

What we have then, in our classic American literature, is not a single, fixed attitude to the city, but rather a kind of semantic, or ideological, field in which a range of attitudes, some of them diametrically opposed, is generated. The field is bounded on one side by representations of the status quo, which is to say, by various embodiments of the dominant culture of industrial capitalism. (These are likely to be negative images like the scaffold or the valley of ashes.) On the other side, however, the field is bounded by the distinctively intense demands and expectations of a restless, journeying American self impelled by pastoral visions of possibility. Pastoralism seems to be the alternative program to the established order most attractive to Americans. It proposes not to change or resist the system as it is, but simply to withdraw in the direction of Nature in search of alternatives. (Nature, as we have seen, refers to the presocialized resources of the self, as well as to relatively undeveloped social and political areas of the environment.) Although the illusory character of the alternative is insisted upon, and often made to have tragic consequences, it retains a remarkably powerful hold on the imagination. As the closing sentences of *The Great Gatsby* imply, we are prisoners of this dead dream: "So we beat on, boats against the current." And in their continuing fascination with it, our greatest writers attest to its vitality even as they expose its falsity.

This fictional charting of American attitudes is far more persuasive, I submit—it captures more of historical actuality—than the notion that Americans harbor some special bias against cities as such. Indeed, it casts a reasonable doubt upon the validity of the abstract conception, *the city,* for it stresses the difference, rather than the similarity, between American cities and the classic preindustrial cities of Europe. Most American cities, after all, have been built since the onset of industrialization, and unlike London, Paris, or Rome, they embody relatively few features of any social order other than that of industrial capitalism. If the American city is perceived chiefly as the locus of a particular socio-economic order, that view accords with the historical fact that millions of Americans have moved to cities, not necessarily because they preferred urban to rural life, but rather because of the inescapable coercion of a market economy.

The idea that the distinguishing features of the American city do not reside in its cityness becomes more evident when we consider, for example, the mass exodus of the white middle class from our cities in the recent past. Why did they leave? The usual explanation has to do with poverty and race and violence and the decline of services. Our cities are close to bankruptcy because, for one thing, the social resources of the nation have had to be deflected from the satisfaction of immediate human needs to meet the ostensible imperatives of "national defense" and the overall "health" of the economy. In other words, the reason for the exodus from the city, like the reason for the influx of rural white and black southerners after World War II, has little or nothing to do with the intrinsic character of cities. Nor does it have much to do with the personal preferences of the people involved for the inherent attributes of rural or suburban as against urban life. It is a consequence, like so many of our "urban problems," of the larger socioeconomic system and its accompanying culture. All of which suggests that the bias of American intellectuals against "the city" is more apparent than real, and not a cause for puzzlement so much as it is a misconception of the relationship between art and life.

# PART III

# F. O. Matthiessen

## The Teacher

The last time I was in Matty's classroom he was talking about Theodore Dreiser. It was in the spring of 1948. A friend who had never heard him asked me to go, and we sat in the back row of the big room in Emerson Hall where he met the elementary course in American literature. There were several hundred students in the class.

Matty was not an impressive figure on the platform. Short, almost bald, his voice impersonal and a little metallic, he had none of the verbal grace one might expect of a Harvard professor of literature. Nor did he indulge in the lecture-room histrionics which win popularity polls. He began talking about Dreiser's career in a matter-of-fact, somewhat halting conversational style. At first his manner seemed austere. Standing behind the desk, intermittently glancing down at his notes, he described Dreiser's youth, the poverty, the struggle for and against the family, and most important, the omnipresent sense of being far off on the periphery of the promised American life. Dreiser never forgot what it was to be an immigrant's son, an outsider eagerly looking in upon the easy-living men and women who got here first. From this core of his experience stemmed two qualities which Matty was able to describe with particularly strong feeling: Dreiser's unfailing sympathy for the dispossessed, and his awe of those on the inside.

As he spoke of Dreiser the "outsider," Matty's manner changed perceptibly. He abandoned his notes, edged around the desk, and planting his feet at the forward rim of the platform talked directly to the students. Some of the nervous quality seemed to go out of his voice, or at least his earnestness made it less noticeable. The measure of Dreiser's greatness, he said, was his ability to cut beneath the smug idealizations of American life fostered by the genteel tradition. This he had been able to do partly because he knew so well how the plush world of luxurious hotels and financiers' mansions looked when you came to it through service entrances. Finding ideas which excited him, Matty stepped up his pace and accented his sentences with sharp, ejaculatory slices of his right hand. He gave the unmistakable impression of a man thinking.

On reflection now it is possible to see not only what excited him in Dreiser but also what must have been unbearably saddening during this last lonely year of work on his study of Dreiser. That day in Emerson Hall he spoke of Dreiser's instinctive rejection of Howells's prescription that our novelists confine themselves to the happy, smiling aspects of life. He seemed to share Dreiser's feeling that inside the cozy American home, cushioned with sentiment, there dwelled a cold acquisitiveness, an anesthetic indifference to the central fact that in our system a few enjoyed the labors of the many. Thinking now about Matty's suicide, it is clear to me that his final depression must have been deepened not only by current tensions between the great powers, but also by a painful recognition that the world of righteous respectability, the tough official downtown America which Dreiser re-created, was every day more firmly in power, and would demand an ever more absolute conformity. Dreiser's financiers are too clear-headed and competent, his average Americans too unaware and helpless to have offered much hope to a socialist in 1950.

In the lecture, however, Dreiser was a symbol of the vitality of the new immigrants, of their will to claim a place in our culture. His was one of the first non-Anglo-Saxon names of importance in American literature. When Matty said this, one could actually observe that strange amalgam of eagerness and hostility which was in everything he did. His was the aggressiveness of the small man. Holding his compact body as taut as a boxer's, he turned to Dreiser's later radicalism.

Occasional sharp forward thrusts of his jaw were signs that he knew what some of the Republican sons of Harvard in the room were thinking. He was extremely sensitive to the faintest intimation of disapproval, and it always led to more rather than less emphatic statement. Though he very seldom injected his own politics into teaching, there was for him no divorce between the professor's job in class and his activities as a citizen. Whenever it seemed pertinent he told his students that he was a socialist and that it was up to them to discount whatever bias they discovered. This was part of his deliberate effort to avoid the tendency of the academic mind to compartmentalize thought and to keep ideas immaculately shorn of emotion. The teacher's duty was to provide a demonstration of the whole man thinking. Matty, in his maturity, disagreed with virtually everything Irving Babbit had represented, but he often acknowledged that that unblushing classroom proselytizer was the most valuable teacher he had had.

Matty treated this class of undergraduates as he would any audience of mature people capable of coming to grips with controversial ideas. In the course of the hour he referred, with what seemed to my friend a humility rare in college lecture halls, to something he had learned from "an authority in this class"—a student who had written an essay on Dreiser. He might have cited a dozen professional critics, but he knew the encouragement and confidence such a passing remark could create. He was always able to give his best students the feeling that their own ideas were important and that he was anxious to learn from them. To many of his colleagues this seemed a means of courting favor, and they were annoyed by his ability to surround himself with a group of bright admiring undergraduates. It is certainly true that he had a greater need than most professors for a close relation with his students, though it is also true that he was transparently impatient with those who were slow, lazy, or indifferent.

When he was at his best, the class caught his enthusiasm as if by contagion. In describing what he found in Dreiser, he wanted to suggest what the experience of reading the novels might be for the students. Listening to the comments as we left the room afterwards, we could tell that many found this method exciting and would return to the novels with heightened interest, but the inveterate note-scribblers who wanted the material carefully packaged and delivered with neat epigrams were dissatisfied. Too much was left up in the air. He had, for instance, confessed his wonder at Dreiser's ability to sympathize with the fate of a Hurstwood at the same time that he obviously gloried in Cowperwood's will to power. Matty refused to explain away such contradictions with pat formulas. Himself a loyal member of Yale's Skull and Bones and a trustee of the Sam Adams Labor School, he knew that Dreiser probably could not have given a rational account of his divided sympathies.

But Matty was not at his best teaching large classes. His methods were too personal, and he conceived of the University as a communal institution in which teaching should be a cooperative activity. Like Henry Adams he thought most lectures ineffectual. Accordingly his first allegiance was to Harvard's tutorial system, particularly as it operated in the study of History and Literature. The existence of this combined field of concentration, or "major," attracted Matty to Harvard because he believed that the study of literature is most rewarding when placed in its full historical context. Students in this field concentrate upon a national culture or an historic epoch, taking as many courses in the history, literature, political theory, or the arts of that society as they can. The tutor's function is to help integrate the material the student gets from his courses. To be effective here the tutor must properly be a "cultural historian," a phrase Matty used to describe his own calling. Although he recognized how crude had been the work of the sociological and political literary critics of the twenties and thirties, and in spite of his deep interest in the close analysis of formal aspects of art, he never followed the swing of literary fashion to an oblivious absorption with matters of form. He insisted that it was possible and in fact necessary to treat each piece of literature as a work of art *and* as a social organism, to heed what was being said as well as how it was said. This attitude toward literature was of course related to his determination to combine the life of the scholar with an active part in politics. If he printed essays in literary quarterlies where politics are regarded as nasty and vulgar, and went to meetings of devoted leftists who think literature an indulgence, he was able to convey to many of his students the realization that art and political action are indispensable means of expression, each enriching the meaning of the other.

Since students in History and Literature at Harvard must take their courses from the conventional departments, the tutorial conference provides the best chance to explore fully the relations between art and society which most interested Matty. He considered such conferences the last bulwark against standardization in a large university. Once a week he met each of his students for a discussion of the work he had previously assigned. Usually he asked the student to come in with a brief essay on the book he had read, and so his own ideas were the basis for discussion. There was every reason to expect that either the student or his tutor might be forced beyond his depth during the conference. Matty regarded this prospect, so frightening to many teachers, as a desirable stimulus to creative thinking.

During his tutorial conferences Matty turned all his rather awesome powers of concentration upon the student and his ideas. His eyes seldom betrayed that preoccupation with more pressing matters so familiar to most students. He silently listened to the entire essay and then, in a calm though sometimes menacing way, began to ask questions. This could be unnerving. He had a devastating way of going to work on the glib masters of the generalization and pinning them down to the facts. Without quite knowing how it had happened the student might find himself supplying the ammunition which blew up his own neat, schematic formulation. But Matty seldom spent the hour without discovering at least the germ of a fresh idea which he encouraged the student to reflect upon and perhaps to develop for the following meeting. To have the next assignment spontaneously suggested by the discussion was his purpose. He thought the tutor's main function was to make the student alive to the possibilities for converting the most complex experience into conscious thought. To do this, Matty did not feel that the tutor had to be an expert in all the areas in which he taught. The teacher truly in command of himself should be able to range far beyond his special field and yet perform the essential job of helping the student to find his own way. Matty's own range of subjects was impressive. Though best known as a teacher of American literature, he taught such diverse courses as the criticism of poetry, Shakespeare, and the forms of the drama from Aeschylus to Shaw; he considered it his responsibility to keep up with historical scholarship as well as the latest developments in anthropology, political theory, and philosophy.

The years between the outbreak of the Spanish Civil War and Pearl

Harbor probably were the high point of Matty's Harvard career. They satisfied his need for action as well as contemplation. When the generation which had come to adolescence during the Depression reached the colleges an era of intense student politics began. It is difficult today to recapture the electric mood of that time, but what happened at Harvard was happening throughout the country. Perhaps the outstanding characteristic of those New Deal years when Madrid was being heroically defended, and later when it still seemed possible to defeat fascism without war, was the feeling that what we said and did really mattered. Every turn of international events had its repercussions in the Yard. Students of all persuasions formed their organizations and had their allies on the faculty, and the left-wing Student Union came to rely on Matty as its most steadfast faculty friend. The Student Union, which had several hundred members at is peak in 1939 and 1940, published its own magazine, *The Harvard Progressive,* sponsored a lively drama group, and nurtured a college generation of indefatigable petitioners, pickets, and pamphleteers.

Those were tense and exciting days: rival torchlight processions clashed in the Yard at night; any strike in Harvard Square enlisted a corps of student pickets; the Brattle Street ladies came with earphones and sealskin capes to see Leonard Bernstein's superb production of *The Cradle Will Rock;* Leadbelly sang on behalf of the Spanish Loyalists; and Matty spoke to hundreds of students at the annual Peace Strike. One of the few faculty members wholeheartedly sympathetic to the Student Union, he generously gave time, money, and advice. As President of the Harvard Teacher's Union he urged its members to take the students seriously, and as a matter of fact the fatal split in the Teacher's Union came on a debate about a $5 donation to a Student Union peace fund. In the spring of 1941, just after *American Renaissance* was published, student and faculty friends gave Matty a testimonial dinner which not only expressed their thanks and affection but, as some then suspected, appropriately marked the end of that tumultuous era.

After Pearl Harbor it was all over. The university became largely a center of technical and scientific training, and Matty, rejected by the Marine Corps for being too short, decided that his chief responsibility was to keep alive a sense of the importance of the humanities in wartime. As he said in the preface to his book on Henry James in 1944, a leading aim in total war should be the preservation of art and thought. He characteristically dedicated the book to three "instigators" who, in the anxious winters of 1942 and 1943, had insisted on getting the best possible education until the Army needed them. It is common enough academic practice for young scholars to dedicate their work to influential teachers, but this was an unusual instance of a book inscribed by a teacher to his students.

Matty was never again to experience quite that sense of rapport with a section of the student body which he had known before the war. Though his own political thinking continued to be colored by the emotions of the late thirties, the students had changed and so had his relations with them. Many of the returning veterans were far more mature and serious than any students he had known before, but the bond of a common political purpose was gone. There was none of that somewhat innocent and cavalier headiness of Popular Front days. More important, of course, was the fact that undergraduate attitudes themselves reflected a profound change in the world situation. It was no longer quite so easy to identify the forces of good and evil. Now the big political issues seemed to many of the veterans to remain in the category of military strategy, and they tended to think that they had little more to say about American relations with the Soviet Union than they had had about the timing of the Normandy invasion.

More than ever before Matty was now isolated from his colleagues. Though still recognized as one of Harvard's outstanding teachers, he no longer commanded the same student following. At the weekly luncheons of the tutors in History and Literature he often seemed strained and irritable. Students said his teaching suffered, and someone coughing during a lecture once provoked an embarrassing outburst of temper. The failure of Henry Wallace's third-party movement, which Matty had enthusiastically supported, was a hard blow. Then the critics of the Left joined those on the Right in attacking his journal of his 1947 trip abroad, *From the Heart of Europe*. *Partisan Review* and *Life* treated him as a dupe of the Communists, while the *Masses* thought him a soft idealist. His sense of loneliness became more intense. He received threatening letters. All these things strengthened his determination to speak out, as if he were mindful of Emerson's warn-

ing to the American Scholar not to defer to the popular cry. Cut off
from many former friends, Matty was now actually more dependent
than ever upon teaching as a means of communication, and it is to be
noted that his death came toward the end of an academic year during
which he had had no teaching duties. This was the year he had devoted
to his book on Dreiser.

Anyone who knows the temper of our universities today must recognize, if only from the suicide note, how rare a teacher he was. At a
time when commitments of any kind are unfashionable he was a
Christian and a socialist. One hundred years ago in New England, he
might well have been a minister, and it is significant that when he
contributed his "credo" to the *Harvard Progressive* in 1940 he spoke
of taking a job at Harvard as "accepting a call." Today most professors,
and particularly professors of literature, regard political involvement as
a sign of immaturity or naiveté; they have so admirably catholic a spirit
that they can entertain all ideas without endorsing any. To be at once
a Christian and as close to Marxism as Matty was would seem absurdly
inconsistent. Yet perhaps the most profound and elusive lesson he
taught was that a smooth and absolutely logical structure of ideas is not
necessarily a sign of the greatest intellectual maturity. It was here that
he was closest to the tradition which runs from Emerson to the open
universe of William James. He knew, though he could not always put
what he knew into practice, that the mind, with its categories and abstractions, always trails behind life. And he felt that the value of a
teacher, to borrow Henry James's criterion for the novel, depended
upon the amount of life he contained.

He was a great teacher because he unstintingly taught out of himself.
In the classroom, in tutorial conferences, and in politics he steeled himself to speak from as deep in his heart as he knew how to reach. Ideas
and literature were never things apart, they were always felt experience.
If he was able to avoid the obvious dangers of so personal a method it
was through the rigorous use of a cool and incisive mind. And yet he
never allowed his students to ignore for a minute the severe limitations
of the human intellect. He had read too deeply in Hawthorne and
Melville to forget the inevitable doom of the solitary thinker. Though
himself wholeheartedly committed to the life of the mind, he had an

unusually vivid and unrelenting awareness of the desolation that awaits
an intellect unsustained by affection, a life not bound to other lives.
This he need not have taught those who knew him well. It was his own
tragedy.

## "Double Consciousness" and the
## Cultural Politics of F. O. Matthiessen

> The bulk of mankind believe in two gods. They are under
> one dominion here in the house, as friend and parent, in social
> circles, in letters, in art, in love, in religion; but in mechanics,
> in dealing with steam and climate, in trade, in politics, they
> think they come under another; and that it would be a prac-
> tical blunder to transfer the method and way of working of one
> sphere into the other. What good, honest, generous men at
> home, will be wolves and foxes on 'Change. What pious men
> in the parlor will vote for what reprobates at the polls! To a
> certain point, they believe themselves in the care of a Provi-
> dence. But in a steamboat, in an epidemic, in war, they believe
> a malignant energy rules.
>
> RALPH WALDO EMERSON

His given names were Francis Otto, his friends called him Matty—and
still do—but on the title pages of his books and to his readers generally
he is F. O. Matthiessen (1902-1950). No writer in the last half-century
has had a greater influence on the prevailing conception of American
literature and its relation to our history. He was a prolific, accomplished
literary scholar and cultural historian whose masterwork, *American Renaissance* (1941), remains an indispensable text in American studies; a
Harvard teacher whose principles and passion won him a devoted student following; a committed trade unionist, member and sometime
president of the Harvard Teachers' Union; a socialist, lifelong partisan
of the left and, of special pertinence here, an early benefactor of the
independent socialist journal, *Monthly Review*. "It was owing to . . .

[his] interest and generosity," wrote the editors, Paul Sweezy and Leo Huberman, soon after his death, "that we were able to found *Monthly Review.*"[1]

But Matthiessen's desire for an explicit affiliation with a socialist movement was frustrated. For a short time in the early 1930s he was a member of the Socialist Party, but he soon lost patience with its lack of militancy and its inability to enlist working-class support. Much as he wanted to belong to an organized socialist party, he never seriously considered joining the Communist Party because, among other things (as he repeatedly explained), he was a Christian, not a Marxist.

To aid a Marxist journal while declaring his differences with Marxism was characteristic of Matthiessen and his resolute heterodoxy. Doctrinal consistency was of little concern to him. What mattered most in politics were social justice, peace, and civil liberty, and like many left-tending intellectuals whose allegiances were formed in the era of the Great Depression and the Spanish Civil War, he came to believe as a matter of principle in a united front, or coalition, of all left-wing parties. Before the defeat of the fascist powers that policy had been a manifest necessity; it was the only policy, indeed, that made sense in the presence of Hitler, Mussolini, and their potential allies within the capitalist democracies. After 1945, however, collaboration with Communists took on a very different meaning, and the fact that Matthiessen was not a Marxist did not spare him, along with many on the left, from becoming entangled in the historical trap created by Stalinism.

In the fear-ridden aftermath of the Second World War he was, more than ever, convinced of the need for a united front. The Cold War was beginning, nuclear weapons were a terrifying novelty, and the effective purge of Communists from the American labor movement looked to be the first stage in a far-reaching repression of all dissent. During the autumn of 1947, after having taught with immense satisfaction at the first session of the Salzburg Seminar, Matthiessen was a visiting professor at Charles University in Prague. At that time a Czech regime led by Eduard Benes was attempting to work out a compromise, or middle

---

1. Paul M. Sweezy and Leo Huberman, eds., *F. O. Matthiessen: A Collective Portrait* (New York: Henry Schuman, 1950), p. vii. This book originally appeared as a special issue of *Monthly Review* in Oct. 1950. A list of the books about Matthiessen mentioned in this essay appears on p. 260.

way, between East and West. After returning home, Matthiessen quickly wrote a book, *From the Heart of Europe*, based on the journal he had kept while abroad. There he admiringly describes the Benes regime as an exemplary effort to mediate between Soviet collectivism and capitalist democracy.

While the book was still in press, however—in February 1948—the Czech Communists seized power. Jan Masaryk, the foreign minister whom Matthiessen had met and liked, died under mysterious circumstances (he either jumped or was pushed from a window). These events came as a real blow to Matthiessen. Although he was invited to make last-minute revisions in his account of the situation in Czechoslovakia, he decided instead to add, as a long footnote, most of a letter from a Czech friend explaining—and very nearly condoning—the coup. The letter suggests that Masaryk, a man "more sensitive than rational," probably had killed himself. It also argues that most Czech workers did not care about "freedom of mind," only about "economic freedom," hence their unhesitating support of the new pro-Soviet regime. His correspondent's conclusion is that this Czech "revolution" was aimed at "limiting freedom and democracy for some, only to give it back, revived and strengthened, to all." (pp. 187-89) Although Matthiessen did not explicitly endorse this viewpoint, it is a good example of the kind of rationalization to which he, like many of us at the time, lent respectful attention.

In domestic politics Matthiessen also remained faithful to the waning ideal of a united, suprasectarian left. During the election of 1948 he was an active supporter of the Progressive Party, and at its national convention he gave one of the speeches seconding the nomination of Henry Wallace for President. The Wallace candidacy was widely attacked as another cynical Stalinist stratagem, and Matthiessen's involvement in it, along with the publication of *From the Heart of Europe*, made him a conspicuous target for red-baiting. By now the persecutory fever, soon to be known as McCarthyism, was rising. People on the right and the left accused Matthiessen of being a "fellow traveler" or "dupe" of Communists. The House Un-American Activities Committee interrogated him, *Life* magazine went after him, and Irving Howe wrote what he himself called a "very harsh and polemical" piece about him in *Partisan Review*.

These political attacks surely contributed to Matthiessen's growing sense of isolation in the period leading up to his premature and violent death. Early in the morning of April 1, 1950, he jumped to his death from a Boston hotel window. In the last of several postscripts to his suicide note he wrote: "How much the state of the world has to do with my state of mind I do not know. But as a Christian and a socialist believing in international peace, I find myself terribly oppressed by the present tensions."[2] This widely publicized statement, along with the other political circumstances surrounding his death, helps explain the legendary character of Matthiessen's reputation. In the press, especially outside the United States, his suicide was depicted as a political act, and he was perceived by many as having been a casualty of the Cold War.

But Matthiessen knew better. However much the oppressive political atmosphere had deepened his melancholia, he knew very well that it was not the major source. In the body of his final note, with a certainty sharply contrasting with his conjectural postscript, he emphasized his state of exhaustion and the "many severe depressions" to which he recently had been subject. By now we know a lot more about his mental condition during the winter of 1949-50 than anyone knew, or cared to discuss, at the time. By his own account his state of mind then resembled the acute, suicidal depression from which he had recovered, after a brief hospitalization, twelve years earlier. (In 1938 he also had had an impulse to jump to his death from a high place.) But a vital difference between the two episodes, as Louis Hyde suggested not long ago,[3] is that in 1938 Matthiessen's closest friend and lover, the painter Russell Cheney, was standing by, ready to help him re-enter the world. They had lived together for some twenty years before Cheney's death in 1945, and all of us who knew Matty well in his own last years were aware of his desperate loneliness. What most people could not have known much about before the publication of the Matthiessen-Cheney letters in 1978 was the nature—the closeness, depth, and centrality—of the relationship between the two.

It comes as something of a shock, if also as an encouraging index of

---

2. The complete text of the note appears in *A Collective Portrait*, pp. 91-2.
3. *Rat & the Devil: Journal Letters of F. O. Matthiessen and Russell Cheney*, Louis Hyde, ed., Introduction (Hamden, Connecticut: Archon Books, 1978), pp. 3-4.

cultural change, to realize that as recently as 1950 Matthiessen's friends considered his homosexuality unmentionable—at least in print. Nowhere in the *Collective Portrait,* including John Rackliffe's otherwise astute "Notes for a Character Study," is there any forthright reference to the subject. Nor does it figure in the life of Edward Cavan, the fictive Harvard professor whose suicide, more or less undisguisedly based on Matthiessen's, is the catalytic event in May Sarton's 1955 novel, *Faithful Are the Wounds.* Perhaps this is more surprising, since homosexuality was to be a prominent theme in Sarton's later novels. The distorting effect of this inhibition is discernible in just about everything that has been written about Matthiessen, but it presumably will be corrected by George Abbott White. A Boston teacher and psychotherapist who never knew Matthiessen, White already has devoted several years to gathering material for a thoroughly documented biography.[4]

The fascination that Matthiessen continues to exercise upon new generations of scholars is unusual. Most scholarly writing is quickly superseded and most scholars are quickly forgotten—perhaps never more quickly (or deservedly) than in the United States in these days of enforced academic publication. One reason that Matthiessen is an exception, of course, is that his work occupies a unique place in the development of modern American studies. When he was a Rhodes scholar at Oxford in the early 1920s, the study of literature was still dominated by Germanic philology and a bland, documentary form of literary history. But Matthiessen responded sympathetically to two fresh, seemingly antithetical approaches to literature, and in bringing them together he developed his own critical method.

One of the new approaches was the analytic formalism identified with the early work of I. A. Richards and the essays of T. S. Eliot, soon to be known as the New Criticism. To Matthiessen this meant a liberating concern with the text itself and a belief that form, or the "how" of literary practice, is as important as the content or the "what." Close attention to the power of individual texts became an essential principle

4. White expresses his interest in the problem in his review of *Rat & the Devil:* " 'Have I Any Right in a Community That Would So Utterly Disapprove of Me If It Knew the Facts?' " in *Harvard Magazine* (September-October, 1978), pp. 58-62. Harry Levin also discusses the problem of Matthiessen's homosexuality in a trenchant review of *Rat & the Devil,* "The Private Life of F. O. Matthiessen," *New York Review of Books* (July 20, 1978), pp. 42-46.

of his criticism. Almost everything he wrote was directed at the understanding and evaluation of particular works; he disliked the idea of using literature as raw material for the construction of some other kind of scholarly edifice. The critic's ultimate aim should be to redirect the reader to the text with heightened understanding. In teaching and writing he found the analytic methods developed by the New Critics immensely useful, and he was confident that they could be detached from the reactionary mandarinism that so often accompanied their application.

Besides, the other new approach embraced by Matthiessen was, in the broadest sense of the word, political; it entailed an appreciation of the indirect ways in which the greatest American writers had lent expression to distinctive aspects of national experience. From the beginning he recognized that the significant interactions between literature and society occur well below the level of a writer's express political ideas, opinions, and institutional affiliations. Politics in this sense begins with assumptions about human nature, society, and even, for that matter, literary form and practice. In *The Rediscovery of American Literature* (1967), an examination of six scholar-critics who helped recast the way we think about our literature, Richard Ruland credits Matthiessen with having contributed the decisive, culminating work. Following Van Wyck Brooks, Irving Babbitt, Paul Elmer More, Stuart Sherman, Lewis Mumford and H. L. Mencken, Matthiessen completed the job of liberating America's cultural past from the deadly grip of WASP Victorianism.

It is hard to remember how provincial, belletristic, and unremittingly genteel the reigning conception of our literature was before the publication of *American Renaissance*. To be sure, the authority of that official canon had been undermined by the work of D. H. Lawrence, V. L. Parrington, and Yvor Winters (as well as by those discussed by Richard Ruland). The fact remains, however, that Holmes, Longfellow, Lowell, and Whittier still occupied prominent positions in the canon, and American literature in its entirety was condescendingly regarded by American as well as British professors of English as a minor offshoot of British high culture. Rather than attack the dominion of the Brahmins, Matthiessen simply applied the method of close reading to demonstrate the clarifying power and pleasure available to readers of his five major writers: Emerson, Thoreau, Whitman, Hawthorne, and Melville. By carefully elucidating particular texts and the concepts of form behind them, he revealed for the first time just how inventive, bold, and intellectually robust the classic American writers had been. All of these writers lent expression to the egalitarian, self-assertive, well-nigh anarchic energy released by the American system, although two of them (Hawthorne and Melville) also recognized the destructive form that energy could take in our ruthless economic individualism. All of them illuminated the deep conflicts, or contradictions, in the life around them. From a classical Marxist viewpoint, to be sure, Matthiessen's conception of these conflicts—the central theme, for example, of the "individual" in conflict with "society"—is too abstract, too obscurely related, if at all, to the opposition between social classes. But of course the character and extent of class conflict in the northern American states before the Civil War remains a subject of serious historical controversy. In any case, Matthiessen's emphasis upon the contradictions rather than the harmonies of meaning, value, and purpose, marks an important turning point in American studies. It signaled the virtual disappearance of the older, complacent idea of our national culture as an essentially homogeneous, unified whole.

Another reason for the continuing fascination with Matthiessen is that his work embodies a rare combination of scholarly dispassion and personal engagement. It did not occur to him that his strong convictions might skew his perceptions, partly because he tended to think of the critic's job as divided into two distinct stages. In the first stage he or she is a disinterested reader, holding off judgment, open to every possible implication of the text, with the aim of seeing the work whole, including the most serious flaws in the best-liked works. Matthiessen was impatient with ideologically bound students who tried to tailor the evidence to fit a priori schemes. In the second stage, however, the critic is permitted—indeed obligated—to bring in all his or her pertinent convictions. True criticism, like all scholarship in the humanities, is finally an act of the critic's whole being. Everything that Matthiessen wrote was part of his lifelong project of discovering what he himself believed. Unlike most academic writing, therefore, his work conveys a strong sense of passionate involvement.

It is not surprising that interest in Matthiessen and his work was renewed during the resurgence of radicalism in the Vietnam era. To many young teachers and activist intellectuals he provided an example of the engaged scholar. The editors of a volume of essays on literature and radical politics (including one on the role of ideology in Matthiessen's *American Renaissance*) dedicated the book to his memory.[5] More recently, Giles Gunn and Frederick Stern, neither of whom knew Matthiessen, have written books about him as a critic. Both focus upon the relationships among his critical principles, his practice, and his extraliterary ideas. Gunn is chiefly concerned about the bearing of his religious ideas upon his criticism, whereas Stern is more interested in his politics.[6]

Frederick Stern's book is a sympathetic, searching examination of Matthiessen's work by a literary scholar with avowedly "radical leftwing concerns." At the outset Stern describes his excited discovery of *American Renaissance* when he was an undergraduate in the late 1940s. What impressed him was the fact that a book could be passionately devoted to a political ideal (literature for a democratic culture) yet still be a work of rigorous scholarship, "not a piece of propaganda." Later Stern wrote a doctoral dissertation, an early version of the present book, called "The Lost Cause: F. O. Matthiessen, Christian Socialist as Critic." As the title suggests, Stern interpreted Matthiessen's career as a finally unsuccessful if admirable effort to fuse his various commitments (literary, religious, political) into a logically coherent, workable whole. My impression is that Stern's earlier analysis had a sharper critical edge—a fact that presumably explains why he dropped the phrase "The Lost Cause" from the original title. What most interests Stern is Matthiessen's effort to reconcile "views of life as disparate as Christianity, socialism, and 'the tragic.' " (He rightly stresses Matthiessen's belief that tragedy, as a literary kind, and the tragic view of life, are touchstones of aesthetic and intellectual profundity—of ultimate wisdom.) But Stern recognizes that Matthiessen was no system-builder, and that abstract theorizing was uncongenial to him, and he therefore touches lightly

5. George Abbott White and Charles Newman, eds., *Literature in Revolution* (New York: Holt, Rinehart and Winston, 1972). White's contribution is "Ideology and Literature: *American Renaissance* and F. O. Matthiessen," pp. 430-500.

6. Giles B. Gunn, *F. O. Matthiessen: The Critical Achievement* (Seattle: University of Washington Press, 1975); Frederick C. Stern, *F. O. Matthiessen: Christian Socialist as Critic* (Chapel Hill: University of North Carolina Press, 1981).

upon the alleged irreconcilability of his subject's basic commitments. In view of the "seemingly incompatible elements" in Matthiessen's thought, Stern concludes that he succeeded in developing "a remarkably unified critical structure."

But the quest for unity in Matthiessen's thought may be misleading. Even the use of "Christian Socialist" to describe him implies a greater cohesion and certitude than he ordinarily claimed for his own beliefs. "I would call myself a Christian Socialist," he wrote, "except for the stale and reactionary connotations that the term acquired through its current use by European parties."[7] Although he occasionally invoked the term, he also knew that to American ears it sounds bloodless, feeble, and foreign. The phrasing he more often used, "a Christian and a socialist," suggests the yoking together of separate, not easily combined, religious and political beliefs. The point is not merely that Matthiessen, like Emerson and Whitman, set little store by logical consistency. (He liked to quote Whitman's witty lines: "Do I contradict myself? / Very well then, I contradict myself, / (I am large, I contain multitudes.)") The more important point is that he recognized a positive, generative value in the embrace of opposed ideas. Unlike conventional academic empiricists, the disengaged "experts" who unify their thought by narrowing its scope, he habitually tested his mental reach by widening the boundaries of his sympathies. This habit of mind is in my view a key to Matthiessen's creativity and to the close affinity he felt with the five writers who are the subjects of his most important book.

Their heroic effort to cope with powerful contrarieties of thought and feeling is a central if largely tacit theme of *American Renaissance*. In the opening sentence Matthiessen warns us that he is starting with the book's hardest problem: Emerson's habit, like Plato's, of stating things in opposites. In rejecting the formal or "linear" logic he associated with Lockean empiricism, Emerson opted for a compelling but risky way of thinking he called "double consciousness." Its worst feature, he confessed, is that we lead two lives which "really show very little relation to each other." One is a life of immediate, daily, practical experience, closely bound up with our physical existence, "all buzz and din"; the

7. *From the Heart of Europe*, p. 72.

other is largely inward, less implicated in the present than in the past and the future, in memory and desire, "all infinitude and paradise." This divergence, as Matthiessen noted, is traceable to the familiar Kantian distinction between two modes of perception, understanding and reason, but he was less interested in the European sources of the idea than in its characteristically American applications. In shifting the Kantian notion from the realm of learned metaphysical discourse to discourse about ordinary experience, Emerson had subtly changed it; what had been an idea chiefly concerned with two ways of knowing the world reappeared as an idea about two ways of living in the world.

Each of the writers Matthiessen focuses on in *American Renaissance* tended, like Emerson, to construe experience as a pattern of antinomies. Even Hawthorne, who was the least sympathetic to Emersonian idealism, was obsessed by the gap between the two worlds he inhabited: the solid, beef-and-ale, mercantile world of Salem, and the disembodied, free-floating, evanescent world he created out of his ideas and imaginings. A scholar less exacting about evidence, more prone to generalization than Matthiessen, might have tried to correlate this pervasive sense of doubleness, or inner conflict, with some general theory of conflict in society. But Matthiessen characteristically held back. He had been sharply critical of earlier attempts by liberal and Marxist critics to impose a political template on literature, and he recognized the pertinence to American literature of the New Critics' emphasis upon the inner tensions—the irony, paradox, and ambiguity—embodied in literary texts. In his measured criticism of Granville Hicks, whose Marxist interpretation of American writing had elicited Matthiessen's creedal "counterstatement," he explained what he did not like about the work of most politically oriented critics. In drawing close analogies between literature and politics, he said, they invariably succeeded in blurring the essential distinctions between them. Marxist critics, like Hicks and V. F. Calverton, often invoked "fatally easy simplifications of society," and their work was marred by the crude notion that writers only can have an adequate knowledge of their age "by coming to grips with its dominant economic forces." As for a liberal critic like V. L. Parrington, Matthiessen was most put off by his dismissive attitude toward the distinctively aesthetic aspects of literature—his tendency to derogate writers like Hawthorne or James because their work was deficient in explicit political meaning.[8]

His own method of placing writers in their historical context was to recreate the network of ideas and images relating them to earlier or contemporary writers and artists working in other, often more popular modes of thought and expression. In *American Renaissance* he ranges from folklore to ship design to political oratory to genre painting to architectural theory. One of the admirable things about the book is that Matthiessen manages to set forth this remarkably rich body of material without resorting to any general claim, or overarching thesis, about the character of the bonds between literature and the encompassing collective life we call "society." But such a thesis is latent in *American Renaissance;* it is embodied in the many correspondences that each writer's version of the double consciousness[9] enabled him to establish with the conflicting forces at work—economic, racial, political, regional, ethnic, religious—in a nation veering toward Civil War. The idea of depicting reality as a clash of opposites, whatever its ultimate validity, was immensely useful to writers attempting to see through the turbulent, opaque surface of nineteenth-century American life.

Two of their most important literary inventions may be interpreted, in Matthiessen's account, as devices for coping with the debilitating sense of disunity engendered by the double consciousness. Emerson's theory of organic form, borrowed from Coleridge and put into practice by Thoreau and Whitman, was in essence a program for achieving in

8. "*The Great Tradition:* A Counterstatement," a review of Granville Hicks, *The Great Tradition,* in *The Responsibilities of the Critic, Essays and Reviews by F. O. Matthiessen,* John Rackliffe, ed. (New York: Oxford University Press, 1952), p. 198. Matthiessen's scathing review of V. F. Calverton's earlier effort to interpret American literature from a Marxist vantage, *The Liberation of American Literature,* is reprinted in the same collection (pp. 184-89). For Matthiessen's reservations about Parrington, see the Preface to *American Renaissance.*

9. An obvious problem, too complex to be resolved here, is whether "double consciousness" refers to one or several states of mind. Among the distinctions with which it is associated in *American Renaissance* are (1) Kant's "understanding" versus "reason"; (2) Emerson's "natural facts" versus "symbols"; (3) Thoreau's acting versus self-observing selves; (4) Whitman's "soul" versus "other I am"; (5) Hawthorne's daylight recording of material reality versus his moonlit vision of an imagined world; and (6) Melville's upper air of benign appearances versus an undersea realm of murderous realities.

art the still unachieved but ostensibly emergent coherence of American life. The three American writers were, in the philosophic sense, idealists, and they tended to regard the ability of a nation's artists to transcend conflicts or divisions in thought (or art) as evidence—a kind of optimistic forecast—of the nation's ability to resolve analogous conflicts in reality. If they were the yea-sayers of the American renaissance, Hawthorne and Melville were the skeptical nay-sayers. Hawthorne's method of bipolar symbolism, later adapted to his own uses by Melville, was designed to figure forth the essentially ambiguous, illusory character of the relationship between ideas and things. *The Scarlet Letter* and *Moby-Dick* call into question the transcendentalist belief in a close correspondence, an "organic" relatedness, between nature and culture. Hawthorne's letter "A," officially designated to stand for "adultery," is subverted by Hester to mean "art" or "angel." And whiteness, in the world of *Moby-Dick,* may be taken to represent all things pure and virtuous or, simultaneously, the most hideous morbidity and evil. Ambiguity is inherent in the nature of things. As apprehended by the aesthetically unified but tragic vision of Hawthorne and Melville, the divided consciousness Emerson had posited is an expression of an unresolvable contradiction.

To appreciate why the double consciousness had a special resonance for Matthiessen, one has only to read the Matthiessen-Cheney letters. There we get some sense of what it was like, before the Second World War, to be a Harvard professor and a homosexual: the double life that he and Cheney felt compelled to live, and the many humiliating concealments and dissimulations it entailed. It is not surprising, then, that Matthiessen had a heightened sensitivity to the many variations in our literature on the theme of the disparity between appearance and reality. His own experience also made him particularly responsive to the inability of many of our most gifted writers to sustain a unified vision long enough to compose—fully compose—more than one book. (It is a striking fact that if we put aside the single masterpieces of Thoreau, Hawthorne, Melville, Mark Twain, or F. Scott Fitzgerald, the status of these men as "major" writers immediately comes into question.) Matthiessen was acutely aware of the insights the double consciousness allows and the precarious situation it creates—a situation that Emerson likens, in his essay on "Fate," to that of a circus rider with one foot planted on the back of one horse and the other foot planted on the back of another. To many of our artists and intellectuals, the creative life has meant just such a risk of being pulled apart by the very conflicts, conscious and unconscious, private and public, that energized their work.

It is revealing, in the light of Matthiessen's receptivity to dialectical modes of thought, to reconsider his ambivalent attitude toward Marxism. He made his final, most cogent statement of his views on that subject in his 1949 Hopwood Lecture, "The Responsibilities of the Critic." After his usual disclaimer ("I am not a Marxist myself but a Christian"), he went on to explain his belief that the principles of Marxism "can have an immense value in helping us to see and comprehend our literature."

> Marx and Engels were revolutionary in many senses of that word. They were pioneers in grasping the fact that the industrial revolution had brought about—and would continue to bring about—revolutionary changes in the whole structure of society. By cutting through political assumptions to economic realities, they revolutionized the way in which thinking men regarded the modern state. By their rigorous insistence upon the economic foundations underlying any cultural superstructure, they drove, and still drive, home the fact that unless the problems arising from the economic inequalities in our own modern industrialized society are better solved, we cannot continue to build democracy. Thus the principles of Marxism remain at the base of much of the best social and cultural thought of our century. No educated American can afford to be ignorant of them, or to be delinquent in realizing that there is much common ground between these principles and any healthily dynamic America.[10]

But he quickly followed this affirmation with a denial that Marxism contains "an adequate view of the nature of man," or that it "or any other economic theory" could provide a "substitute" for a critic's primary obligation to elucidate the interplay of form and content in specific works of art.

In 1949 Matthiessen's conception of Marxism as "an economic the-

10. *The Responsibilities of the Critic,* p. 11.

ory" was by no means idiosyncratic. On the contrary, it more or less accurately identified a version of Marxism in high favor during the Stalin era: a self-consciously hard, economistic, and essentially positivistic view of the world. It was positivistic in that it embraced a dichotomy between "scientific" thinking (including Marxism) and all other kinds of thinking. The scientific kind allegedly provides access, as physics does, to the underlying laws governing surface phenomena, whereas other non-scientific kinds inevitably tend to be superficial, sentimental, utopian, idealistic—in a word, unreliable. They do not yield true knowledge. From the retrospective viewpoint of the cultural historian, this Marxist-Leninist invocation of "science" belongs in part to a much wider tendency of thinkers to borrow, on behalf of any social or political theory, the impressive authority of the natural sciences as vehicles for arriving at hard, preferably quantitative, verifiable, exact knowledge.[11] This dichotomy between Marxist science and bourgeois apologetics comported with the absolutist, authoritarian political doctrines emanating from Moscow. But it would be wrong to attribute the dominion of this positivistic style of Marxism only to the power and influence of the Third International. For one thing, as Paul Sweezy reminds me, this tendency already was present in less dogmatic form in the work of such earlier followers of Marx as Kautsky and Plekhanov. For another, we should remember the incomplete state of the Marxist canon in Matthiessen's time. Even at the end of the Stalinist era such a conception of Marxism was made more plausible by the fact that several important countervailing texts, notably the *Economic-Philosophical Manuscripts of 1844* (the "Paris Manuscripts") and the *Grundrisse,* were not yet available.

What made this mid-century version of Marxism particularly objectionable to Matthiessen was the rank, seemingly ineradicable philistinism it fostered. Many Marxists of the era were Zhdanov types who tended, as Leon Trotsky put it, to "think as revolutionaries and feel as philistines."[12] They regarded religion, philosophy, art, all ideas and ac-

11. But this is not to suggest that all assertions of the "scientific" character of Marxism are tainted by vulgar "scientism." To resolve this complex problem it would be necessary, in each case, to consider the particular sense of "science" being invoked.

12. Quoted by Terry Eagleton, *Marxism and Literary Criticism* (Berkeley: University of California Press, 1976), p. 1.

tivities not bearing directly on the hard material facts of life, as mere derivations from those facts, and so they consigned literature to the flimsy "superstructure" that allegedly rests on society's material (economic and technological) "base." It is impossible to exaggerate the importance of this compelling architectural metaphor in disseminating the simple-minded reductionist ideas that passed for a Marxist theory of culture in that period. Even as originally invoked by Marx, the metaphor had been unfortunate—it is static and it lends itself to the mechanistic idea of a one-way, from the bottom up, interaction between the "real foundation" of society, the economic base, and the entire political, legal, and ideological superstructure. In recent years the metaphor has been the subject of extended discussion by Marxist theorists,[13] and the complicated question of its validity cannot be settled here. What remains clear, however, is that during the 1930s doctrinaire Marxists often removed the metaphor from its theoretical context and applied it so literally that it could be said to validate the undialectical notion of a direct economic determination of all ideas and, indeed, of all human behavior.

What might have given pause to Marxist critics of literature is the close resemblance between this philistine attitude and the characteristic utilitarian attitudes of bourgeois Victorians. Thus, Thomas Gradgrind, Dickens's archetypal nineteenth-century business philosopher, was a vehement exponent of a mechanistic base-and-superstructure model of reality. This was the aspect of "Marxism" that Matthiessen found most repugnant. In trying to explain himself to his Marxist friends and associates, he often recurred to their evident inability to take religious ex-

13. Perry Anderson, *Arguments Within English Marxism* (London: Verso, 1980), pp. 71-72; G. A. Cohen, *Karl Marx's Theory of History: A Defense* (Princeton: Princeton University Press, 1978), pp. 217-48; Terry Eagleton, *Marxism and Literary Criticism,* pp. 3-16; Paul M. Sweezy, *Four Lectures on Marxism* (New York: Monthly Review Press, 1981) pp. 20-25; E. P. Thompson, *The Poverty of Theory and Other Essays* (New York: Monthly Review Press, 1978, pp. 157-62; Raymond Williams, "Base and Superstructure in Marxist Cultural Theory," *New Left Review* 82, Nov./Dec., 1973, and *Marxism and Literature* (London: Oxford University Press, 1977), pp. 75-82. If a consensus can be said to be emerging from this discussion, it is the need to preserve the indispensable premise of the Marxist theory of history, namely, the primacy of the forces of production as ultimate determinants of the limits within which any society and culture can develop and, at the same time, the need to rid the theory of the static, unidirectional implications of the base and superstructure model.

perience, even the religious experience of the past, seriously. "If any of you really believe that religion is only 'the opiate of the people,' " he said at the dinner given in his honor when *American Renaissance* was published in 1941, "you cannot hope to understand the five figures I have tried to write about in *American Renaissance.*"[14]

In retrospect Matthiessen's rejection of what he took to be Marxism is doubly ironic. For one thing, some of today's practicing Marxist critics, Raymond Williams for example, would consider Matthiessen's literary theory (either as exemplified by his practice or as expressly set forth in the Hopwood Lecture) to be more acceptable—closer to their own theories—than the rigid economistic version of Marxism that Matthiessen found repugnant. This is not the place to review the remarkable development of Marxist thought since 1950, but its correlative literary theory has become a much more supple mode of analysis, far more responsive to the formal, aesthetic dimension of literature than it was in Matthiessen's time. That is partly a result of the fact that Marxists have recovered and in some measure reinstated the work of the young (Hegelian) Marx that had been dismissed by the 1930s commissars of culture as hopelessly utopian and idealistic.[15] To recover the work of the young Marx, incidentally, is not necessarily to belittle the importance of the passage Marx had effected during the 1840s from a Hegelian to a historical materialist viewpoint. But the overall tendency of Marxist thought during the last twenty years has been to allow much greater historical efficacy to ideas and non-material culture than was al-

---

14. *A Collective Portrait,* p. 142. Here Joseph H. Summers is quoting Matthiessen's impromptu remarks from memory.

15. A particularly compelling testimonial to the intimidating effect of such an anti-utopian bias, or what he calls "the scientific/utopian antinomy," is E. P. Thompson's reconsideration of his own 1955 study of William Morris. In a "Postscript: 1976" to the reissue of the book, Thompson vividly describes how his earlier treatment of Morris had been skewed by his adherence to what he later came to reject as an excessively rigid, mechanical materialism. At issue, he believes, is the place of "moral self-consciousness" and "a vocabulary of desire" within Marxism, and its tendency, in lieu of these, to fall back on the old utilitarian ideal of "the maximization of economic growth" (p. 792). See *William Morris, Romantic to Revolutionary* (New York: Pantheon Books, 1977), pp. 763-816. For other formulations of a less rigid Marxist literary theory, see Frederic Jameson, *Marxism and Form: Twentieth-Century Dialectical Theories of Literature* (Princeton: Princeton University Press, 1971), and *The Political Unconscious* (Ithaca: Cornell University Press, 1981); Raymond Williams, *Marxism and Literature* (London: Oxford University Press, 1977).

lowed by the mainstream Marxism of the Stalin era. It is this development which now makes Matthiessen's thought seem less distant from
Marxism than he himself believed it to be.

The striking fact is, moreover, that the ideas of the young Marx had
emerged from the same body of thought that Matthiessen wrote about
with so much sympathy in *American Renaissance*. In Hegel and in post-
Kantian idealism generally, Marx and the American writers who were
his contemporaries—especially Emerson—shared a common philosophic
legacy. In Marx's essay "On the Jewish Question," written in 1843,
roughly a year after Emerson's initial published formulation of the
"double consciousness," the young Marx had set forth a similar distinction. Adopting terms used by Feuerbach, he distinguished between a
person's awareness as an individual, activated by the self-serving imperatives of material life in a capitalist society, and a person's awareness
of being a member of the human species—or "species-consciousness." In
Western culture the sense of partaking in "species-life," formerly embodied in Christianity, had been displaced to the political state. The result of this divided consciousness, for Marx as for Emerson, is that people find themselves leading two almost completely unrelated lives.

> The perfected political state is, by its nature, the *species-life* of
> man as *opposed* to his material life. All the presuppositions of this
> egoistic life continue to exist in *civil society outside* the political
> sphere, as qualities of civil society. Where the political state has
> attained to its full development, man leads, not only in thought, in
> consciousness, but in *reality*, in *life*, a double existence—celestial and
> terrestrial. He lives in the *political community*, where he regards
> himself as a *communal being*, and in *civil society*, where he acts
> simply as a *private individual*, treats other men as means, degrades
> himself to the role of a mere means, and becomes the plaything of
> alien powers.[16]

Although Matthiessen's own work exhibits some aspects of this post-
Kantian legacy (one writer has referred to his "profound grasp of hu-

16. Karl Marx, "On the Jewish Question," in Robert C. Tucker, ed., *The
Marx-Engels Reader* (New York: W. W. Norton, 1978), pp. 26-52. The quota-
tion is from pp. 34-35. Emerson's concept of the double consciousness, cited by
Matthiessen in *American Renaissance*, p. 3, is from "The Transcendentalist"
(1842).

manist dialectics"[17]), he did not recognize the significance of the close affinity between the ideas of the young Marx and those of Emerson. This is surprising because Matthiessen had been a publicly avowed socialist for some ten years before the appearance of *American Renaissance,* and during that time he often had deplored the absence of a working-class socialist movement in the United States. Under the circumstances, he might have been expected to seize upon the initial conjunction and subsequent divergence of proto-Marxism and American literary thought (exemplified above all by Emerson) as a way of illuminating the vexed issue of "American exceptionalism." (Among the advanced capitalist countries of the world the United States is "exceptional" in the failure of its intelligentsia to take Marxism seriously, in the failure of socialism to gain a mass following, and in the absence of a working-class socialist party.) Unfortunately Matthiessen ignored the entire subject. This lacuna, along with his conspicuous inattention to Marx and Marxist thought in a book notable for its wide-ranging allusiveness and its highly individualized perspective, is in large measure attributable, I believe, to Matthiessen's overreaction to the shallow, mechanistic Marxism that prevailed during the 1930s.[18] Yet the lack of explicit attention to Marxism in *American Renaissance* is somewhat misleading. In his subtle treatment of the interplay between literature and society, Matthiessen in a sense anticipated the development of a more supple Marxist cultural and literary theory since its liberation from the rigid doctrinal cast of the Stalin era.

The second irony in Matthiessen's rejection of what he took to be Marxism is that he nevertheless allowed that doctrine to skew his own

17. Maynard Solomon, *Marxism and Art: Essays Classical and Contemporary* (New York: Alfred A. Knopf, 1973), p. 275; quoted in Stern, *F. O. Matthiessen,* p. 223.

18. "Over-reaction" because Matthiessen, with his aversion to theory in general, and his failure to devote himself to extra-literary problems with anything like the seriousness he devoted to literature, simply ignored the available work of Marxist or quasi-Marxist theoreticians from which he might well have profited. Among them were T. W. Adorno, Walter Benjamin, Kenneth Burke, Lucien Goldmann, Antonio Gramsci, George Lukacs, and Hans Meyer. (The fact that all but Burke were Europeans also suggests the distorting effect of Matthiessen's preoccupation with American thought.) Stern discusses the reasons for Matthiessen's failure to come to grips with Marxist cultural theory in *F. O. Matthiessen,* pp. 221-31.

political thinking.[19] Some of the very formulas he repudiated within the context of literary theory informed his response to the political "line" emanating from the Soviet Union. This is not to suggest that he condoned the Stalinist repression, but rather that his opposition to it was softened by the received justification for that authoritarian regime. Like many other non-Marxists, Matthiessen was impressed by the anti-fascist policies of the USSR during the early 1930s, and his thinking about the long-term prospects in Russia followed the standard first-things-first logic inherent in the base-and-superstructure model of social reality. (Notice, incidentally, the uncritical way in which he invoked that treacherous metaphor in the passage from the Hopwood Lecture cited above.) He assumed that the aim of the Communist Party of the Soviet Union was to build the indispensable economic base for social-ism, and that during the period of primitive socialist accumulation a degree of authoritarianism was a more or less unavoidable necessity. The fact that Russia had not had a bourgeois revolution, and that it was a peasant society without democratic institutions, gave added credence to this viewpoint. At bottom the cogency of the argument rests on a fun-damental assumption of historical materialism—one that Matthiessen, for all his protestations about not being a Marxist, was intermittently prepared to accept: the ultimate, long-term, or "in the final analysis" primacy of a society's economic structure. Hence the need for the non-Communist left to reserve judgment or, in effect, to tolerate a hiatus be-tween the building of the economic base and the raising of a truly socialist (hence truly democratic) superstructure.

This widely accepted latitudinarian argument was behind Matthies-sen's adherence, even after 1945, to the "united front" strategy. He had long since abandoned the liberal reformism typical of American academics; he thought of himself as a radical, and did not require in-

19. On this subject I am relying on first-hand experience as much as on Mat-thiessen's published writings. Between 1945 and 1950 I spent a great deal of time with Matty in my capacity as a graduate student, a fellow tutor in the His-tory and Literature department at Harvard, and as a friend. We had many long conversations on these issues. For corroboration I have relied on Jane Marx, my wife, who participated in many of those conversations, especially during the summer months we spent with Matty in Kittery, Maine. I also have had the benefit of criticism of this essay by former friends of Matthiessen's: Richard Schlatter, Paul Sweezy, J. C. Levenson, and G. R. Stange.

struction on the systemic character of our society's problems. Then, too, he was actuely aware of the reactionary use to which anti-Communism was being put in the early years of the Cold War. "One of the most insistent clichés of the right and even of the liberal press," he wrote shortly before his death, "is that there can be no cooperation on any level between Communists and non-Communists."[20] But of course the insoluble problem was to define the extent of that cooperation. At the local level it involved the elusive issue of "Leninist" tactical duplicity, and on the global level it involved the question of limits (in duration and severity) to the allegedly temporary "dictatorship of the proletariat." But in the rush of events there was no time for Matthiessen (or anyone else) to clarify, much less resolve, these questions. Commenting on the support that Matthiessen and other non-Communists gave to Henry Wallace's presidential candidacy in 1948, Professor Stern simply notes that they were "mistaken about the possibilities and realities of Soviet life after World War II." They were listening, he says, to "their own wishes rather than to evidence and reason."[21] He might have added that Matthiessen, trapped between Stalinism and reformism, was accepting a kind of casuistry that he had identified and pointedly rejected in the interpretation of literature.

But it is doubtful, finally, whether Matthiessen's objections to Marxism would have been satisfied by the work of today's revisionists. To be sure, he would have been far more sympathetic with the "humanist" Marxism of Adorno, Fromm, and Marcuse, or the literary methods of Williams, than he was with the orthodoxy of his time. In his arguments against that doctrine, indeed, Matthiessen anticipated many of the current arguments *within* Marxism—especially those leveled by E. P. Thompson against the ideas of Louis Althusser.[22] Matthiessen charged Marxists generally, as Thompson does Althusser, with constructing their

20. "Needed: Organic Connection of Theory and Practice," *Monthly Review* (May 1950), p. 11. This was one of two posthumously published fragments bearing on the problems of the left. The other, "Marxism and Literature," was a brief that Matthiessen had prepared for the defense in the trial of the leaders of the Communist Party (U.S.A.) under the Smith Act. *Monthly Review* (Mar. 1953), pp. 398-400.
21. *F. O. Matthiessen*, p. 27.
22. Thompson's attack on Althusser is contained in "The Poverty of Theory—or an Orrery of Errors," *The Poverty of Theory and Other Essays* (New York: Monthly Review Press, 1978); for a useful interpretation of the argument, see Perry Anderson, *Arguments Within English Marxism, op. cit.*

theories at too great a distance from the hard evidence—the concrete particularities—of political life. And like Thompson, Matthiessen felt that mainstream Marxism, with its bias toward economic reductionism, tends to neglect that half of culture which derives from the affective and moral consciousness. For Matthiessen, as for Thompson, a crucial shortcoming of the work of twentieth-century Marxists has been their neglect of the imaginative and utopian faculties of humanity. Unlike Thompson, however, Matthiessen did not believe that those faculties could be adequately accommodated within any form of historical materialism.

Hence Matthiessen's continuing adherence to his unfashionable, demanding, explicitly political version of Christianity. He took the commandment to love thy neighbor as thyself as "an imperative to social action." Indeed, it was "as a Christian," he said, that he found his "strongest propulsion to being a socialist." He acknowledged that this distinguished his religious views from those of "most orthodox Christians of today." It also distinguished his conception of human nature from the one he imputed to Marxism: a simplistic, psychologically shallow notion of human perfectibility; by asserting its rational, economic interests, the working class might be relied on to achieve liberation for—eventually—all humankind. In contrast to this sanguine view, and under the influence of Freudian psychology and Niebuhrian theology, Matthiessen endorsed the doctrine of original sin—the idea that human beings inescapably are "fallible and limited, no matter what . . . [the] social system."[23] At this point his belief in the tragic character of human experience impinged upon, and in a sense joined, his commitment to Christianity and to revolutionary socialism. The essence of tragedy, in his view, is the ultimate inseparability of the human capacity for destructiveness, or evil, and the capacity for nurturance, or good. In effect Matthiessen was disavowing the millennial strain that runs through Marxism and indeed the entire left tradition of political thought. This optimistic tendency of mind underestimates the psychological or, more broadly, behavioral constraints upon social amelioration. "Evil is not merely external," he wrote in distinguishing his views from both the

---

23. His clearest statement of his creed appears in the autobiographical section of *From the Heart of Europe,* pp. 71-91, reprinted in *A Collective Portrait,* pp. 3-20.

shallow Marxism and the complacent Christianity of his time, "but external evils are many, and some societies are far more productive of
them than others."

Today the political import of Matthiessen's religious belief, with its
attendant critique of Marxism, is more obvious and more telling than it
was during his life. At that time, when only one nation professed a
commitment to revolutionary Marxism, the shortcomings of Soviet society were relatively easy to explain away. But the coming to power of
revolutionary socialist movements around the world has made it more
difficult to ignore the discrepancy between political realities and the
millennial expectations of Marxism. Today many of the arguments
within Marxism turn upon fundamental issues raised by F. O. Matthiessen forty years ago.

# "Noble Shit": The Uncivil Response of American Writers to Civil Religion in America

Let me begin by acknowledging a debt to Norman Mailer for the scatological title. The phrase "noble shit" occurs in *The Armies of the Night* (1968) where Mailer is reflecting on the uses of obscenity in saving what is worth saving in our democratic ethos. It is important to add, however, that Mailer also denies having invented this vigorous poetic epithet. He gives all the credit to an anonymous G.I. in World War II. I take pleasure in this fact because anonymity is a distinguishing mark of my subject here: the vigor, poetry, and truth so many writers have found in that anonymous work of the collective imagination called the American vernacular. Obscene language, to be sure, is a special kind of vernacular, a distinctive and especially potent kind. Here is the way Mailer describes its power and its virtues:

> There was no villainy in obscenity for him, just—paradoxically, char-
> acteristically—his love for America: he had first come to love Amer-
> ica when he served in the U.S. Army, not the America of course of
> the flag, the patriotic unendurable fix of the television programs and
> the newspapers, no, long before he was ever aware of the insti-
> tutional oleo of the most suffocating American ideas he had come
> to love what editorial writers were fond of calling the democratic
> principle with its faith in the common man. He found that principle

and that man in the Army, but what none of the editorial writers ever mentioned was that that noble common man was obscene as an old goat, and his obscenity was what saved him. The sanity of said common democratic man was in his humor, his humor was in his obscenity. And his philosophy as well—a reductive philosophy which looked to restore the hard edge of proportion to the overblown values overhanging each small military existence—viz: being forced to salute an overconscientious officer with your back stiffened into an exaggerated posture. "That Lieutenant is chickenshit," would be the platoon verdict, and a blow had somehow been struck for democracy and the sanity of good temper.[1]

For all his playfulness, Mailer is making a serious claim for obscenity here. He regards it as a weapon in a continuing struggle for egalitarian rights and principles—a kind of class struggle, enlisted men against officers, dirty words against the pretentious vocabulary of domination. When confronted with the "institutional oleo of the most suffocating American ideas," obscene language can be extremely effective. It is an appropriate and salutary response to expressions of what we lately have been instructed to call "civil religion"—that is, the effort to invest the highest political authority with religious legitimacy. In what follows, I propose to endorse—or at least partially endorse—Mailer's claim by demonstrating that it has the tacit support of a long line of gifted American writers. Beginning at least as far back as Emerson's time, they prepared the way, both in theory and practice, for the use of *un*civil language as a natural and proper means of coping with the rhetoric of a spurious civil religion.

But, first, a word about the concept of civil religion. The term initially was introduced by Rousseau, in *Du Contrat social* (1762) and so far as I know it never had been applied to American thought until Robert Bellah's controversial essay, "Civil Religion in America" (1966).[2] There Bellah argues that in the United States we have had, alongside of and rather clearly differentiated from the churches, an elaborate and

1. New York, 1968, p. 47.
2. Bellah's paper was first delivered at a *Daedalus* conference on American Religion in May, 1966, and it was published in that journal (Winter, 1967, pp. 1-21). It was reprinted with critical comments and a rejoinder in *The Religious Situation: 1968*, edited by Donald R. Cutler, Boston, 1968, and in Bellah's collected essays, *Beyond Belief, Essays on Religion in a Post-Traditional World*, New York, 1970.

well-institutionalized civil religion—one that possesses "its own serious-ness and integrity." It is a body of beliefs, symbols, and rituals which provides a religious dimension for the whole fabric of American life, including the political realm. In defining the actual content of this na-tional religion, Bellah relies heavily upon the rhetoric of American pres-idents, and particularly their inaugural addresses—all but one of which, he notes, mentions or refers to God.

But unfortunately Bellah does not explain why we should take the sentiments contained in inaugural addresses as a genuine expression of collective religious motives. Although he admits that what people say on solemn occasions need not be taken at face value, he proceeds to use John F. Kennedy's inaugural address as a major exhibit of America's deep-seated religious values and commitments. After citing the begin-ning and the end of Kennedy's speech, both of which invoke the name of God, he quotes the following sentence as having a "distinctly biblical ring" and as being indicative of a national commitment to a "transcen-dent goal for the political process."

> Now the trumpet summons us again—not as a call to bear arms, though arms we need—not as a call to battle, though embattled we are—but a call to bear the burden of a long twilight struggle year in and year out, "rejoicing in hope, patient in tribulation"—a struggle against the common enemies of man: tyranny, poverty, disease and war itself.

In context it is evident that Bellah would have us believe that President Kennedy and his supporters really were committed, above all else, to a global struggle against tyranny, poverty, disease, and war. For it is on the basis of this sort of rhetoric that he invites us to concur in his as-tonishingly credulous endorsement of the seriousness and integrity of American civil religion. However, my chief purpose is not to quarrel with Bellah's argument or the evidence he brings to its support, but rather to indicate how differently certain of our most distinguished writers have reacted to this strain of nationalistic religiosity.

Returning now to Norman Mailer, I must add that his claim for ob-scenity is not confined to the efficacy of dirty words in deflating over-blown official pieties It also serves, he says, as a therapeutic and regen-erative medium. It helps to restore a sense of proportion, self-regard, even sanity. To speak religiously, Mailer imputes to the use of obscenity a kind of redemptive power, and not merely for individuals. It is capable of redeeming basic cultural resources. Obscenity, he seems to be saying, may be the key to another, more authentic, truly democratic, if as yet inchoate and unrealized form of civil religion. A close look at the way obscene words actually come into ordinary speech suggests to Mailer a possible method of salvaging certain traditional, lofty, if now moribund democratic ideals.

> . . . Mailer never felt more like an American than when he was naturally obscene—all the gifts of the American language came out in the happy play of obscenity upon concept, which enabled one to go back to concept again. What was magnificent about the word shit is that it enabled you to use the word noble: a skinny Southern cracker with a beatific smile on his face saying in the dawn in a Filipino rice paddy, "Man, I just managed to take me a noble shit." Yeah, that was Mailer's America. If he was going to love something in the country, he would love that.[3]

Quirky and faddish though it may sound, this notion of the saving power of obscenity has a long background in American literary history. In 1911, for example, George Santayana also had called attention to the discrepancy in America between an earthy native viewpoint, grounded in particulars, and another mode of thought characterized by abstract, largely imported ideals. "America," he said in his influential lecture on the genteel tradition, "is a young country with an old mentality."[4] It had inherited a traditional, essentially religious outlook from Europe, but while that genteel mode of thought was becoming increasingly attenuated, Americans also were developing a fresh and, as it were, underground mentality of their own out of their distinctive first-hand experiences. In fact, Santayana says, correcting himself, America really is "a country with two mentalities, one a survival of the beliefs and standards of the fathers, the other an expression of the instincts, practice and discoveries of the younger generations." In all the "higher things of the mind," meaning religious, literary, and moral activity, the heredi-

3. Page 48. For an interesting discussion of this passage, in somewhat different terms, see Richard Poirier, *Norman Mailer* (New York, 1972), p. 92ff.
4. "The Genteel Tradition in American Philosophy," *The Genteel Tradition, Nine Essays by George Santayana*, Douglas L. Wilson, ed. (Cambridge, Massachusetts), 1967, pp. 37-64.

tary spirit prevails, but in the realm of practical affairs—inventions, industry, social organization—the new mentality, grounded in the observations and instincts of the mass of people, has taken over. Had Santayana ventured to give this fresh, native outlook a name, it might well have been "vernacular." For the great divide he had discovered in American culture was exemplified by the obvious gulf between two languages. One was polite, upper-class, bookish, conventional, churchly, and associated with what now would be called the Eastern establishment. The other was cruder, more colloquial, closer to the raw, often profane particularities of everyday life in the West. This was the linguistic contrast Mark Twain had discovered in the discourse of the pilots and the passengers on Mississippi River steamboats.

Whether Santayana was correct about the continuing dominion of the genteel tradition in American writing as late as 1911 need not concern us here. (He seems not to have been aware of the radical innovations of writers like Crane, Norris, and Dreiser.) Later in the lecture, when he asks whether there had been any successful efforts to escape from the genteel culture, efforts to express something worth expressing behind its back, he feels obliged to mention Walt Whitman and Mark Twain, to whom I will return.

But the theoretical basis for Norman Mailer's defense of obscenity, its usefulness for cultural therapy, had been laid even earlier—by Ralph Waldo Emerson. It should be said that Santayana does discuss Emerson, but he neglects to mention Emerson's cogent ideas about the way a language—and by implication an entire culture—can lose its efficacy. It becomes corrupt at the same time, and for the same reasons, that civil life becomes corrupt. It is striking, incidentally, to see how much of the argument of George Orwell's influential essay, "Politics and the English Language," Emerson had anticipated in 1836.

> A man's power to connect his thought with its proper symbol, and so to utter it, depends on the simplicity of his character, that is, upon his love of truth and his desire to communicate it without loss. The corruption of man is followed by the corruption of language. When simplicity of character and the sovereignty of ideas is broken up by the prevalence of secondary desires—the desire of riches, of pleasure, of power, and of praise—and duplicity and falsehood take place of simplicity and truth, the power over nature as an interpreter of the

will is in a degree lost; new imagery ceases to be created, and old words are perverted to stand for things which are not; a paper currency is employed, when there is no bullion in the vaults. In due time the fraud is manifest, and words lose all power to stimulate the understanding or the affections. Hundreds of writers may be found in every long-civilized nation who for a short time believe and make others believe that they see and utter truths, who do not of themselves clothe one thought in its natural garment, but who feed unconsciously on the language created by the primary writers of the country, those, namely who hold primarily on nature.[5]

Emerson is describing a psychological process by which words are drained of evocative power and meaning. The crux of the matter is the conflict between the forthright expression of motives and what he calls "secondary desires." When a concern for wealth, power, pleasure or praise intervenes, the language becomes corrupt. Right here, according to Emerson, we are at a precise point of intersection between literature and politics. As Orwell would put it a century later, "The great enemy of clear language is insincerity. When there is a gap between one's real and one's declared aims, one turns as it were instinctively to long words and exhausted idioms, like a cuttlefish squirting out ink."[6] But the problem, for Emerson, was how a language, once corrupted, could be purified. How was a serious writer to do his work when the medium had been expropriated for fraudulent purposes? The cure, he said, would come from those wise writers who abandoned the moribund language and renewed the living relation between words and nature[7]—

5. "Nature," 1836, in *The Complete Essays . . . of Ralph Waldo Emerson,* ed. Brooks Atkinson (Modern Library Edition, New York, 1940), p. 17.

6. *The Collected Essays . . . of George Orwell,* 4 vols. (New York, 1968), IV, 137.

7. The distinction between a corrupt language used by writers who are under the sway of "secondary desires" and a vital language used by writers who "hold primarily on nature" is grounded in a more basic distinction between two modes of perception that Emerson drew from a variety of sources including the ideas of Wordsworth, Carlyle, Coleridge (all probably traceable to Kantian philosophy), but also (by a kind of osmotic process) from his New England theological forebears. Jonathan Edwards, for example, held that God had made man capable of a "twofold understanding or knowledge of the good," one that was "merely speculative and notional," the other that consisted of "the sense of the heart." The former was an abstract kind of knowledge, whereas the latter was grounded in sense experience and therefore engaged "the will, or inclination, or heart." "There is a difference," Edwards wrote, "between having a rational judgment that honey is sweet, and having a sense of its sweetness. A man may have the

and by "nature" here, it should be said, he meant something much closer to what we nowadays would mean by "experience."

> But wise men pierce this rotten diction and fasten words again to visible things; so that picturesque language is at once a commanding certificate that he who employs it is a man in alliance with truth and God. The moment our discourse rises above the ground line of familiar facts and is inflamed with passion or exalted with thought, it clothes itself in images. A man conversing in earnest, if he watch his intellectual processes, will find that a material image more or less luminous arises in the mind, contemporaneous with every thought, which furnishes the vestment of the thought. Hence, good writing and brilliant discourse are perpetual allegories. This imagery is spontaneous. It is the blending of experience with the present action of the mind. It is proper creation.[8]

In "The American Scholar," the following year (1837), Emerson urged the close affinity between radical egalitarianism and the purification of language. In a democratic era, he argued, truth-telling writers would supplant a polite literary language with one that is common, low, even vulgar. Speaking of the "auspicious signs" of an Age of Revolution, he said:

> One of these signs is the fact that the same movement which effected the elevation of what is called the lowest class in the state, assumed in literature a very marked and as benign an aspect. Instead of the sublime and the beautiful, the near, the low, the common was explored and poetized.

By now, I realize, it is extremely difficult to attend to the meaning of these too-familiar propositions. But they embody a conception of language and of literature in relation to the politics of democracy which points directly toward Mailer's defense, in our time, of obscenity. Whatever we may say about Emerson's failure to practice what he preached, his commitment *in theory* was unequivocal. He was endorsing a litera-

---

former, that knows not how honey tastes; but a man cannot have the latter unless he has an idea of the taste of honey in his mind." For Edwards, like Emerson, the language of redemption had to be a language nurtured by a bond with physical nature, that is, by actual sensory experience. See his 1734 sermon, "A Divine and Supernatural Light," in *Jonathan Edwards, Representative Selections,* Clarence H. Faust and Thomas A. Johnson, eds. (New York, 1935), pp. 106-7.
   8. Emerson, p. 17.

ture rooted in the common life, and in a language closer to American speech than to the idiom of Augustan gentility still associated with Literature by his educated contemporaries.

> The literature of the poor, the feelings of the child, the philosophy of the street, the meaning of household life, are the topics of the time. It is a great stride. It is a sign—is it not?—of new vigor when the extremities are made active, when currents of warm life run into the hands and the feet. I ask not for the great, the remote, the romantic; . . . I embrace the common, I explore and sit at the feet of the familiar, the low . . . This perception of the worth of the vulgar is fruitful in discoveries.[9]

Later, during the slavery crisis of the 1850s, Emerson had the melancholy opportunity to apply his theory of the homologous corruption of language and of politics to the notorious case of Daniel Webster. For Emerson as for many other New Englanders, the senator was a political hero—a great American statesman whose eloquence was thought to have derived from profound integrity of mind and spirit. No small part of Webster's reputation rested upon an elaborate, Ciceronian oratorical style—the kind of public rhetoric echoed in the periodic sentences of the Kennedy inaugural address, with its trumpeting summons: "not as a call to bear arms, though arms we need—not as a call to battle, though embattled we are." Here is a sentence from the peroration of Webster's famous reply to Hayne (1830), a favorite set piece for declamation by school children:

> I have not accustomed myself to hang over the precipice of disunion, to see whether, with my short sight, I can fathom the depth of the abyss below; nor could I regard him as a safe counsellor in the affairs of this government, whose thoughts should be mainly bent on considering, not how the Union may best be preserved, but how tolerable might be the condition of the people when it should be broken up and destroyed.[10]

A few sentences later Webster concluded with an apostrophe to the flag, a cardinal symbol of our official civil religion, that remains one of

9. Emerson, "The American Scholar," pp. 60-61.
10. *Speeches and Documents in American History,* ed., Robert Birley, 4 vols. (London, n.d.), II, 77.

the purplest passages in the annals of American oratory. "When my eyes shall be turned to behold for the last time the sun in heaven," he says, "may I not see him shining on the broken and dishonored fragments of a once glorious Union. . . ."

> Let their last feeble and lingering glance rather behold the glorious ensign of the republic, now known and honored throughout the earth, still full high advanced, its arms and trophies streaming in their original lustre, not a stripe erased or polluted, nor a single star obscured, bearing for its motto . . .

And so on and on, rising in the end to the ringing "Liberty *and* Union, now and for ever, one and inseparable!" Many of Emerson's contemporaries equated this orotund style with eloquence, signifying that the speaker had won access to a plane of higher truth.

But then, in 1850, Webster had thrown his whole weight (as Emerson saw it) on the side of Slavery, and had helped to ease the passage of the odious Fugitive Slave Law. Emerson's reaction is particularly pertinent here because Webster, one of the high priests of American civil religion, in effect had sacralized the very idea of the republic. In order to justify his support of compromise with the slave power he made preservation of the Union his primary commitment, and in the show-piece speech of the Seventh of March, 1850, he mobilized all of his rhetorical ingenuity in its behalf. But Emerson did not share the general admiration for Webster's performance, as he explained in his own speech on "The Fugitive Slave Law" in 1854. In Webster's earlier speeches, Emerson said, the senator had earned the nation's gratitude as one "who speaks well for the right—who translates truth into language entirely plain and clear!" But on the Seventh of March Webster evidently had abandoned that standard. As always, he had displayed literary skill, clear logic, even eloquence, but these were relatively unimportant as compared with the fact that he ended up on the wrong side.

> Nobody doubts that Daniel Webster could make a good speech. Nobody doubts that there were good and plausible things to be said on the part of the South. But this is not a question of ingenuity, not a question of syllogisms, but of sides. *How came he there?*[11]

11. "The Fugitive Slave Law," pp. 861-76.

The answer, Emerson suggests, is that he came there because of a defect in character. Webster lacked "what is better than intellect, and the source of its health," namely, the quality of thought which derives from the heart. In his rousing peroration Webster had found it possible to make statements like this: "We have a great, popular, constitutional government, guarded by law and by judicature, and defended by the affections of the whole people. . . . In all its history it has been beneficent; it has trodden down no man's liberty; it has crushed no State. Its daily respiration is liberty and patriotism. . . ."[12] With this sort of passage in view, Emerson argued that Webster had exhibited a lack of "moral sensibility."

> There are always texts and thoughts and arguments. But it is the genius and temper of the man which decides whether he will stand for right or for might. Who doubts the power of any fluent debater to defend either of our political parties, or any client in our courts? . . . But the question which History will ask is broader. In the final hour, when he was forced by the peremptory necessity of the closing armies to take a side—did he take the part of great principles, the side of humanity and justice, or the side of abuse and oppression and chaos?

Although Emerson's charge against Webster may strike us as well founded, it is not at all clear that the senator had betrayed the principles of civil religion as Professor Bellah defines them. Emerson held Webster to the test of "humanity and justice," but according to Bellah these are not among the first principles of the dominant American form of civil religion. "The God of the civil religion . . . ," he writes, "is . . . much more related to order, law, and right than to salvation and love." Appropriately enough, the God of this nation state "is actively interested in history, with a special concern for America."[13] The point is that worship of such a God is easily reconciled with a shallow kind of political instrumentalism entailing a commitment to law and order, to the imperatives of "history," whatever that means, and to the corporate well-being of the republic. The question of the "right" for which this God allegedly stands, however, is more ambiguous. The

12. *Speeches and Documents,* p. 182.
13. Bellah, p. 175.

slavery crisis had split the concept of right in America down the middle, separating the right of property from those other rights—life, liberty, and the pursuit of happiness—to which the revolution also had been committed. It seemed to Emerson that Webster had come down on the side of the right to own slaves.

But Emerson did not see Webster's defection as a special case. On the contrary, his want of moral sensibility struck Emerson as symptomatic of the condition of many thinking Americans. Webster, in effect, was a representative man, and what he represented is that "prevalence of secondary desires" (for riches, pleasure, power, and praise) over "simplicity of character and the sovereignty of ideas" which marks the simultaneous corruption of language and of politics. Why was this happening to American democracy? Why did educated men so easily relinquish their moral judgment? Emerson's answer is stunningly relevant—and poignant—in the era of the Vietnam war, Watergate, and the Iran/Contra scandal.

> The way in which the country was dragged to consent to this, and the disastrous defection (on the miserable cry of Union) of the men of letters, of the colleges, of educated men, nay, of some preachers of religion—was the darkest passage in the history. It showed that our prosperity had hurt us, and that we could not be shocked by crime. It showed that the old religion and the sense of right had faded and gone out; that while we reckoned ourselves a highly cultivated nation, our bellies had run away with our brains, and the principles of culture and progress did not exist.[14]

II

But the following year Emerson was compelled to admit that the principles of a native culture had not entirely disappeared into the great American belly. One day in July, 1855, he received an unsolicited package containing the work of an unknown poet who spoke a language as different from Webster's as could be imagined. Here are some of the lines Emerson read in the first edition of Walt Whitman's *Leaves of Grass:*

14. Emerson, "The Fugitive Slave Law," p. 867.

Walt Whitman, an American, one of the roughs, a kosmos,
Disorderly fleshy and sensual . . . eating drinking and breeding,
No sentimentalist . . . no stander above men and women or
   apart from them . . . no more modest than immodest.

Unscrew the locks from the doors!
Unscrew the doors themselves from their jambs!

Whoever degrades another degrades me . . . and whatever is
   done or said returns at last to me,
And whatever I do or say I also return.

. . . . . . . . . .

Through me forbidden voices,
Voices of sexes and lusts . . . voices veiled, and I remove the
   veil,
Voices indecent by me clarified and transfigured.

I do not press my finger across my mouth,
I keep as delicate around the bowels as around the head and heart,
Copulation is no more rank to me than death is.

I believe in the flesh and the appetites,
Seeing hearing and feeling are miracles, and each part and tag
   of me is a miracle.

Divine I am inside and out, and I make holy whatever I touch
   or am touched from;
The scent of these arm-pits is aroma finer than prayer,
This head is more than churches or bibles or creeds.[15]

Whitman, as we know, had been inspired by Emerson's conception
of the poet and of poetic language. "Thought," Emerson had said,
"makes everything fit for use. The vocabulary of an omniscient man
would embrace words and images excluded from polite conversation.
What would be base, or even obscene, to the obscene, becomes illustri-
ous, spoken in a new connection of thought."[16] But Whitman had
carried this principle much further than Emerson had imagined a poet

15. *Leaves of Grass, The First* (*1855*) *Edition,* Malcolm Cowley, ed. (New
York, 1959), pp. 48-49.
16. "The Poet," p. 327.

should or could. He had taken a long step toward exemplifying what Mailer was to call the "reductive philosophy" of the common man, a defiant use of forbidden, indecent language which "looked," as Mailer put it, to restore the hard edge of proportion to overblown values.

Yet it cannot be said that Whitman was rejecting the idea of an American civil religion. Rather he was attempting to relocate it, to identify the vitality and uniqueness in our national life—perhaps even the possibility of trancendence—with the "disorderly fleshy and sensual" as against the refined, polite and conventional. This symbolic relocation of the sacred is very much like the process Mailer was to employ in our time; its goal was the emergence of a vernacular civil religion capable of supplanting the official creed. Although Whitman celebrated American democracy, his democratic God is not the God usually invoked by our Presidents on inauguration day. Whitman's is a populist deity unsympathetic with a hierarchical social order; if he can be said to have a "special concern for America" it is because he perceives America as the embodiment of a universal, international spirit of egalitarian fraternity. So far as the Brooklyn "rough" who speaks for Whitman believes in a civil religion, it has about it a flavor of undiscriminating, irreverent, sans-culottish narcissism:

Who goes there! hankering, gross, mystical, nude?
How is it I extract strength from the beef I eat?

What is a man anyhow? What am I? and what are you?
All I mark as my own you shall offset it with your own,
Else it were time lost listening to me.

I do not snivel that snivel the world over,
That months are vacuums and the ground but wallow and filth,
That life is a suck and a sell, and nothing remains at the end but
    threadbare crepe and tears.

Whimpering and truckling fold with powers for invalids . . .
    conformity goes to the fourth-removed,
I cock my hat as I please indoors or out.

Shall I pray? Shall I venerate and be ceremonious?
I have pried through the strata and analyzed to a hair,

> And counselled with doctors and calculated close and found no
> sweeter fat than sticks to my own bones.[17]

In 1855 it would have been difficult to imagine a viewpoint (or a
tone) better calculated to make Americans think of Walt Whitman,
in Santayana's phrase, as "an unpalatable person." Only foreigners
seemed to accept the notion, said Santayana, that Whitman's undiscriminating poetry might be lending expression to the spirit and the
inarticulate principles really animating American society.[18] But in retrospect it seems more likely that the foreigners, like Whitman himself,
had misjudged the majority of Americans. The poet had hoped that
his countrymen would absorb him as affectionately as he had absorbed
his country, but in fact they preferred the genteel and far more conventional verses of Henry Wadsworth Longfellow. By the same token,
they preferred the idea of joining the polite middle class to the
Whitmanian notion of remaining permanently among the uncouth,
free-spirited, unacquisitive "roughs." Perhaps this is only to say that
Whitman had ignored, or underestimated, the attractiveness of upward
social mobility in an expanding capitalist society.

After the Civil War Whitman experienced a disillusion with the
moral sensibility of the nation not unlike Emerson's during the slavery
crisis. Whitman's tortured essay, "Democratic Vistas" (1871), surely
is one of the most searching examinations of civil religion by an
American writer. That a "religious element" necessarily lies at the
core of democracy, Whitman had no doubt; but in America, he was
forced to admit, that capacity for belief in the potential virtue and
good sense of the mass of men had somehow failed to develop. What
he found, instead of a democratic faith, comports with Emerson's
earlier image of a nation whose bellies had run away with its brains:

> I say we had best look our times and lands searchingly in the face,
> like a physician diagnosing some deep disease. Never was there, per-
> haps, more hollowness at heart than at present, and here in the
> United States. Genuine belief seems to have left us. The underlying
> principles of the States are not honestly believed in (for all this
> hectic glow, and these melo-dramatic screamings), nor is humanity

17. Page 43.
18. *The Genteel Tradition*, pp. 52-53.

itself believ'd in. What penetrating eye does not everywhere see through the mask? The spectacle is appalling. We live in an atmosphere of hypocrisy throughout. The men believe not in the women, nor the women in the men. A scornful superciliousness rules in literature. . . . A lot of churches, sects, etc., the most dismal phantoms I know, usurp the name of religion. . . . The depravity of the business classes of our country is not less than has been supposed, but infinitely greater.[19]

The ultimate standard of national well-being invoked by Whitman in "Democratic Vistas" is not the standard implied by the genteel, or presidential civil religion. It is not the degree of "order, law, and right" achieved by the republic; nor is it the nation's corporate power or prosperity—though Whitman assumes that a certain modest level of affluence is a prerequisite for civic health. No, for Whitman the real test is the kind of men and women, hence the quality of thought and feeling, the society nurtures. "Are there, indeed," he asks, "*men* here worthy the name? . . . Are there perfect women, to match the generous material luxuriance? . . . Are there arts worthy freedom and a rich people?" And then, with a clear implication that he is asking the crucial question: "Is there a great moral and religious civilization—the only justification of a great material one?" The question merits special emphasis because it so often is present if unexpressed—veiled behind the contemptuous attitude held by American writers toward the officially sanctioned civil religion. It is a question, moreover, to which the rhetoric of most presidential addresses hardly provides an adequate answer. Whitman's own answer, in the very next sentence, anticipates T. S. Eliot's powerful twentieth-century image of urban-industrial culture as an arid wasteland. "Confess," says Whitman, "that to severe eyes, using the moral microscope upon humanity, a sort of dry and flat Sahara appears, these cities, crowded with petty grotesques, malformations, phantoms, playing meaningless antics. Confess that everywhere, in shop, street, church, theatre, bar-room, official chair, are pervading flippancy and vulgarity, low cunning, infidelity . . ."[20]

In canvassing possible alternatives to this profane spirit, Whitman

19. *Leaves of Grass and Selected Prose* (Modern Library Edition, New York, 1950), p. 467.
20. Page 469.

did not look to the upper stratum of culture. In the judgment of a poet who had begun his career by boasting, "I too am not a bit tamed . . . / I sound my barbaric yawp over the roofs of the world," the American literary scene in 1870 was contemptible. "Do you call those genteel little creatures American poets?" he asked. At least this much seemed clear: what was needed was not more polish, more cultivation, or more preachment from on high. In our times, he said,

> . . . refinement and delicatesse are not only attended to sufficiently, but threaten to eat us up, like a cancer. Already, the democratic genius watches, ill-pleased, these tendencies. Provision for a little healthy rudeness, savage virtue, justification of what one has in one's self, whatever it is, is demanded.

So far from attributing vulgarity to an excess of democracy, Whitman felt that it derived from too little. "I should demand a program of culture," he said, ". . . not for a single class alone, or for the parlors or lecture-rooms, but with an eye to the practical life, the west, the working-men, the facts of farms and jack-planes and engineers, and of the broad range of women also of the middle and working strata. . . ." Here Whitman seems to recognize that the vernacular, as a medium of expression, can only be effective as part of a larger "program of culture." Literature alone cannot do the job. This is a fact that many of our writers, including Mailer, often have tended to forget. Whitman affirms the need for a "little healthy rudeness," not as an end in itself, but as part of the effort to achieve an essentially classless culture. In effect he is looking for a manifestation of the vernacular spirit that arises from an egalitarian way of life, and he has a pretty good hunch about where it might be found.[21]

> Today, doubtless, the infant genius of American poetic expression, (eluding those highly-refined imported and gilt-edged themes . . .), lies sleeping far away, happily unrecognized and uninjur'd by the coteries, the art-writers, the talkers and critics of the saloons, or the lecturers in the colleges—lies sleeping, aside, unrecking itself, in some western idiom, or native Michigan or Tennessee repartee, or stump-speech . . . , or in some slang or local song or allusion of the Manhattan, Boston, Philadelphia or Baltimore mechanic. . . . Rude and

21. Page 75; p. 483; p. 487; p. 489.

coarse nursing-beds, these; but only from such beginnings and stocks, indigenous here, may haply arrive, be grafted, and sprout, in time, flowers of genuine American aroma, and fruits truly and fully our own.[22]


I I

In retrospect anyone familiar with American literature may be expected to identify this rude genius of the native idiom. By now Mark Twain's preeminence in shaping the basic colloquial style of modern American writing has been universally acknowledged. But what is less fully appreciated is the extent to which he seized upon the vernacular, and the viewpoint it embodied, as (to use Mailer's term once again) the medium of a "reductive philosophy." What delighted Mark Twain was the opportunity afforded by Huck Finn's speech, like the obscene talk of Mailer's G.I.'s, to deflate overblown values. The very essence of Mark Twain's humor derived from the contrast between the boy's rude idiom and the kind of piety and pretension associated with polite civil religion. Consider an example from a decisive episode (chapter thirty-one) in *Huckleberry Finn*. The boy is having one of his periodic spells of anxiety about what might happen when the word got around that he had "helped a nigger to get his freedom." "The more I studied about this," he says, "the more my conscience went to grinding me, and the more wicked and low-down and ornery I got to feeling." Henry Nash Smith has explained what happens next.[23] As the inner dialogue continues, what we hear sounds less and less like the boy's usual voice and more and more like the stock cadence and diction of a preacher. It is as if the dominant religious culture had quite literally invaded his consciousness, supplanting his own sensibility, and transforming the very structure and rhythm of his sentences.

> And at last, when it hit me all of a sudden that here was the plain hand of Providence slapping me in the face and letting me know my wickedness was being watched all the time from up there in heaven, whilst I was stealing a poor old woman's nigger that hadn't ever done me no harm, and now was showing me there's One that's al-

22. Page 504.
23. *Mark Twain, The Development of a Writer* (Cambridge, 1962), p. 121.

ways on the lookout, and ain't agoing to allow no such miserable do-
ings to go only just so fur and no further, I most dropped in my
tracks I was so scared.[24]

Of course it may be objected that the voice we are hearing is not,
strictly speaking, that of the *civil* religion but of the organized church.
In a sense that is true, but the two are not so easily separated. As Robert
Bellah says, civil religion in America "borrowed selectively from the
religious tradition in such a way that the average American saw no
conflict between the two."[25] In this case, moreover, the guilt Huck feels
is stirred in part by his violation of the civil law. In his rudimentary
sense of things, obeying the law and observing the rituals of the church
are equally important prerequisites for social respectability. To be accepted by those he calls the "quality" one should pray and one should
respect the sanctity of property in slaves.

But Huck's surrender to this conformist impulse is only temporary.
No sooner has he written the note to Miss Watson betraying Jim than
he gets to thinking about their trip down the river, reliving it in his
mind, recalling specific images of their shared life on the raft, so that
he *sees* Jim before him "all the time, in the day, and in the night-time,
sometimes moonlight, sometimes storms, and we a floating along, talking, singing, and laughing." Here, Mark Twain brings the reductive
power of the vernacular into play, recording the boy's mental process
as he discovers the disparity between the learned abstractions of the
genteel culture (there's One that's always on the lookout" etc.) and
the sensory details of the downstream journey with his black compan-
ion. As his feeling of loyalty to Jim revives, he reverts to his native
idiom. What is happening, in Emerson's language, is that Huck now
"pierces" the "rotten diction" of pro-slavery law and order he had
adopted in a spasm of guilt, and he does so in precisely the way Emerson had recommended: *by fastening words again to visible things.* The
process by which he reverses himself can be described in psychological
or linguistic terms, but in the dramatic unfolding of the episode the
crux of the matter is political. At the critical moment everything depends on Huck's choice of sides. Which side is he on? "I was a trem-

---

24. *Adventures of Huckleberry Finn* (Library of Literature, Indianapolis,
1967), p. 242.
25. *Beyond Belief,* pp. 180-81.

bling," he says, "because I'd got to decide, forever, betwixt two things, and I knowed it." The famous decision ("All right, then, I'll *go* to hell") is a pointed repudiation of the civil religion of the old South, with its racist God and its continuing hold on people long after the Civil War.

Like Mark Twain, whose seminal influence he acknowledged, Ernest Hemingway delighted in the specificity and the deflationary power of the vernacular. In a sense his treatment of the theme stands midway between Mark Twain's and Mailer's. By the time he began writing, after the First World War, American civil religion was becoming closely identified with the kind of bellicose nationalism so familiar today. In *A Farewell to Arms* (1929) the narrator, Lieutenant Henry, is provoked to a long rumination on the subject by the passing remark of Gino, his patriotic Italian comrade. "What has been done this summer," Gino says, "cannot have been done in vain."

> I did not say anything. I was always embarrassed by the words sacred, glorious, and sacrifice and the expression in vain. We had heard them, sometimes standing in the rain almost out of earshot, so that only the shouted words came through, and had read them, on proclamations that were slapped up by bill-posters over other proclamations, now for a long time, and I had seen nothing sacred, and the things that were glorious had no glory and the sacrifices were like the stockyards at Chicago if nothing was done with the meat except to bury it. There were many words that you could not stand to hear and finally only the names of places had dignity. Certain numbers were the same way and certain dates and these with the names of the places were all you could say and have them mean anything. *Abstract words such as glory, honor, courage or hallow were obscene beside the concrete names of villages, the numbers of roads, the names of rivers, the numbers of regiments and the dates.*[26]

Thus Hemingway points directly toward Mailer's argument on behalf of obscenity. To his Lieutenant Henry the sacralizing abstractions of the civil religion—*glory, hallow, sacrifice,* and *sacred*—are themselves "obscene." In view of his commitment to realistic dialogue, Hemingway obviously would have liked to record the characteristic response of soldiers to such indecent pieties. What makes them indecent, of course,

---

26. *A Farewell to Arms* (Scribners, New York, 1954), p. 191, my emphasis.

is that they bear so little relation to the facts. Or, put more bluntly, they are used to tell lies. They exemplify the simultaneous corruption of language and of politics, hence they call forth the combat soldier's talent for obscenity. But in 1929 it was not yet possible for a writer to get dirty words in print. In theory, to be sure, the vernacular style always had aimed at linguistic verisimilitude, but in practice it never had reached that goal. Only recently John Seelye has demonstrated, by rewriting *Huckleberry Finn,* how much damage the conventional nineteenth-century standards of propriety had done to that great book. By endowing the fourteen-year-old boy with a natural interest in sex, and with an adequately indecent vocabulary, Seelye shows that Mark Twain's narrator is simply too nice to be wholly credible.[27] Yet we know that Mark Twain, according to the standards of his day, was something of a bold innovator. We should not forget that as recently as 1940 Ernest Hemingway had to resort to outlandish contrivances (" 'Oh, obscenity them,' Primitivo said with an absolute devoutness of blasphemy . . . 'Oh, God and the Virgin, obscenity them in the milk of their filth.' ") to render the speech of combatants in the Spanish Civil War.[28]

### I V

But this is not the place to survey the erosion of restraints upon the printing of hitherto unprintable words since World War II. We need only recall that in the United States the virtual disappearance of restrictions, at least with respect to imaginative writing in book form, coincided with the civil crises of the 1960s. The new radical politics and its affiliate, the cultural underground, gave a strong push to the old campaign for linguistic freedom. This minority of the disaffected included, along with many young people and blacks, a large segment of the academic and literary communities. Like Hemingway's Lieutenant Henry, moreover, adherents of the civil rights and the anti-Vietnam War movements were repelled by the mendacious language used to justify national policies. (This of course included the rhetoric used

27. *The true adventures of Huckleberry Finn,* as told by John Seelye (Evanston, 1970).
28. *For Whom the Bell Tolls* (Penguin Books, London, 1955), p. 275.

by Presidents of the United States.) They felt that it was obscene, and they responded with the strident vulgarity of their own language. A close study of linguistic patterns in this period would supply abundant evidence, I believe, for the symbiotic relation between the sanctimonious rhetoric of national celebration and obscenity. It is worth recalling that the Berkeley Free Speech movement, which marked an important stage in the emergence of student radicalism, came to an end as a somewhat feckless campaign to legitimate the use of dirty words. According to sociolinguists, every society seems to have at least three linguistic style levels: (1) formal or polite; (2) colloquial; and (3) slang or vulgar.[29] During the 1960s the radicals used an increasingly vulgar language to counter what they regarded as an increasingly meretricious (root meaning: whorish) polite language. In the underground press, in slogans displayed on placards carried in demonstrations, and in their everyday speech, many of the militants felt obliged to use words like "shit" and "fuck" as often as possible.

But their promiscuous use of these once-forbidden words points to several difficulties with the argument on behalf of obscenity. It seems obvious that in many instances this verbal reflex is of a piece with such other expressions of adolescent rage as trashing, ripping off, and vandalism. It is truly characteristic, though not in the exact sense in which he used it, of what Lenin called "infantile leftism." But then some would say that the use of obscenity is never anything more than a childish, trivial, and ineffectual gesture of defiance. To make a habit of linguistic stridency is always self-defeating. After a barrier of convention has been crossed often enough, the excluded idiom quickly loses its power to shock, as decreed by the law of diminishing returns. The stale, repetitious "pig language" of some sixties radicals is a good illustration. But, even more serious, this criticism of the use of obscenity is akin to the one that Santayana leveled against other vernacular modes of resistance to the genteel culture. Referring to humorists like Mark Twain, he noted that they were unable to abandon the tradition they mocked. Although they were skillful in pointing to what contra-

---

29. Susan Ervin-Tripp, "On Sociolinguistic Rules: Alternation and Co-occurrence," in John J. Gumperz and Dell Hymes, eds., *Directions in Sociolinguistics* (New York, 1972), pp. 213-50. For the sociolinguistic implications of obscenity I also am indebted to my colleague, Elizabeth W. Bruss.

dicted the genteel ethos in the facts, he said, they had "nothing solid to put in its place."[30] Cannot the same charge be brought against writers like Mailer, who rely upon obscenity to oppose the vapid idiom of the official American civil religion? Do they have anything more solid than a few dirty words to put in its place?

My answer is a qualified yes, they do. They do have something more than a vocabulary to offer, though whether that something can be called "solid" is another question. The point, in any case, is that no serious claim on behalf of the vernacular (or the obscene) can rest solely upon the power of the words in and of themselves. It is not a particular language in itself that matters, but rather the ethos or system of value it embodies; the vernacular is prized because it embodies a tacit alternative to the ethos inherent in the language used by celebrants of the genteel civil religion. The vernacular, in other words, derives a large part of its power from the felt presence of its opposite. As Mailer says in the anecdote about the Southern cracker in the rice paddy, the common man's use of obscenity is a feature of his humor, and his humor in turn is an expression of his "reductive philosophy." What the G.I. in the story reduces when he exclaims, "Man, I just managed to take me a noble shit," is everything the word "noble" implies about a hierarchy of status based on arbitrary rank. (Once the target had been the feudal hierarchy, here it is the military hierarchy of the United States.) In the old sense "noble" referred to exalted, lofty ideals detached from the earthy facts of the common life. The humor here consists in the G.I.'s casual, economical transfer of such grandeur as nobility connotes to a physical act as commonplace yet universal as a bowel movement. Incidentally, the idea of making nobility a modifier of excrement is a variant of a device often favored by Mark Twain as, for example, when he has the two scoundrels in *Huckleberry Finn* call themselves the King and the Duke.

In each case reduction is merely the first stage in a complicated process. "What was magnificent about the word shit," Mailer says, "is that it enabled you to use the word noble again . . ." Similarly, the vernacular perspective from which *Huckleberry Finn* is written has the effect of relocating the positive attributes of nobility. It removes the

30. *The Genteel Tradition*, p. 50.

qualities of magnanimity and greatness from people upon whom the titles king or duke formerly had been conferred, and it bestows them upon social riffraff like the illiterate son of the town drunk. It is worth recalling that when *Huckleberry Finn* was published conservative critics were alarmed by its potentially subversive power; they saw it as a threat to values "cherished by accredited spokesmen for American society," and they attacked it for "irreverence" as well as for "coarseness."[31] In spite of such attacks, however, the vernacular style was to become a dominant—probably *the* dominant—style of modern American literature.[32] Far from being idiosyncratic, in fact, Mailer's high estimate of the American vulgate as a literary medium has been endorsed, in practice if not in theory, by many of our most admired twentieth-century writers. It would not be difficult to illustrate this fact by citing passages from the work of, say, Faulkner, Salinger, Ellison, Williams (both Tennessee and William Carlos), O'Connor, or Burroughs. It seems obvious, moreover, that all of them turned to the vernacular partly in an effort to locate an alternative to the dominant genteel culture.

The linguistic process exemplified by Mailer's story about "noble shit" has for its aim regeneration as well as reduction. Obscenity is not merely a linguistic solvent for the old, threadbare national religion, it is a means of generating a new religion. In *The Armies of the Night* Mailer manifestly hoped, by using this method, to renew a feeling for

31. Henry Nash Smith, *Mark Twain,* p. vii. This hostile reaction to the use of the vernacular in the 1880s is not unlike the current hostility to the use of obscenity. Linguists, particularly sociolinguists and psycholinguists, help to account for this fact. To some extent words are considered "obscene" because of their association with a particular group—often one that has a low social status. (Thus "fornication" is acceptable but "fuck" is obscene.) Words also may fall into this category when they are used to violate a putatively sacred "domain of use." Presumably the meeting ground of religion and government represented by "civil religion" constitutes such a domain. Joshua A. Fishman, "Domains and the Relationship between Micro- and Macrosociolinguistics," in Gumperz and Hymes, eds., *Directions in Sociolinguistics,* pp. 435-53; Stanley Newman, "Vocabulary Levels: Zuni Sacred and Slang Usage," in Dell Hymes, ed., *Language in Culture and Society* (New York, 1964), pp. 397-406; E. Sagarin, *The Anatomy of Dirty Words* (New York, 1962); Harold J. Vetter, "Language and Taboo," *Language Behavior and Communication* (Itasca, Illinois, 1969), pp. 169-87.

32. Richard Bridgman, *The Colloquial Style in America* (New York, 1966); Leo Marx, "The Vernacular Tradition in American Literature," *Studies in American Culture,* Joseph J. Kwiat and Mary C. Turpie, eds. (Minneapolis, 1960), pp. 109-22.

his country akin to what we usually call patriotism. It is surprising to discover that a number of other disaffected or radical writers of the 1960s shared this motive. In the work of Paul Goodman, for example, one can hear (along with the outrage he directed against the "organized system") a lament for old-fashioned patriotic feelings.

> Our case is astounding. For the first time in recorded history, the mention of country, community, place has lost its power to animate. Nobody but a scoundrel even tries it. Our rejection of false patriotism is, of course, itself a badge of honor. But the positive loss is tragic and I cannot resign myself to it. A man has only one life and if during it he has no great environment, no community, he has been irreparably robbed of a human right. This loss is especially damaging in growing up . . .[33]

Susan Sontag was provoked to similar reflections by her discovery, during a trip to Hanoi, of the "essential purity" of Vietnamese patriotism. The contrast with her country was discouraging.

> Ever since World War II, the rhetoric of patriotism in the United States has been in the hands of reactionaries and yahoos; by monopolizing it, they have succeeded in rendering the idea of loving America synonymous with bigotry, provincialism, and selfishness. But perhaps one shouldn't give up so easily. . . . Probably no serious radical movement has any future in America unless it can revalidate the tarnished idea of patriotism.[34]

And most recently John Schaar, a political theorist who would like to see a revitalization of radical politics in America, took up the same theme.[35] His elaborately wrought "case for patriotism" is particularly relevant here because, in developing his argument, he finds it necessary to draw a sharp line between an acceptable form of national affirmation and the Rousseauian mode of civil religion. The kind of patriotism Schaar advocates derives from Lincoln's idea of America as a covenanted republic. We are a nation formed by a covenant, that is, by

33. *Growing Up Absurd, Problems of Youth in the Organized Society* (New York, Vintage Edition, 1962), p. 97.
34. *Trip to Hanoi* (New York, 1968), pp. 81-82.
35. "The Case for Patriotism," *American Review* (May, 1973), pp. 59-99.

dedication to the libertarian and egalitarian principles of the Declaration of Independence, and those principles comprise the standard by
which we must judge ourselves. Lincoln would consider the nation to
be righteous and to deserve being honored "only insofar as it honors
the covenant." This conception is markedly different from Rousseau's
civil religion. It provides a moral standard for judging national behavior, whereas Rousseau designed his religion chiefly in order to in-
duce the citizen to venerate the nation and, in his own words, to make
him "love his duties."[36] In America, Schaar believes, the Rousseau-like
conception "drove out" Lincoln's, an observation that helps to account
for the antipatriotic tone adopted by so many of the writers I have been
discussing.[37] What they wanted, it seems evident, was a view of their
country which would enable them to judge it as well as to venerate it.

The desire of writers for a renewal of some form of patriotism is
a significant feature of the ambiguous political context in which Mailer
formulated his rationale for obscenity. Like Goodman, Sontag, and
Schaar, he wanted to "love something in the country," and the most
likely thing he could find was the vernacular of the common man—
a language as far removed as possible from the language of national
celebration. Up to a point, it must be admitted, American politics of
the 1960s lent credence to such an identification of uncivil language
with radical protest. The conservative backlash at the end of the decade
was marked by a new and more stringent effort to stop the outpouring
of obscenity associated with long hair, black militants, Whitmanesque
life styles, unorthodox sexual behavior, and radicalism. The 1973 de-

36. *Rousseau, Political Writings,* Frederick Watkins, ed., trans. (Edinburgh,
1953), p. 152. Compared with the moral complexity of Lincoln's covenant,
Rousseau's civil religion rests upon a blandly reassuring, simple-minded creed.
"The dogmas of the civil religion," he writes, "ought to be simple, few, and
precisely formulated, without explanations or commentaries. The existence of
a powerful, intelligent, benevolent, foreseeing and providential God, the con-
tinuance of life after death, the happiness of the just, the punishment of the
wicked, the sanctity of the social contract and the laws, these are the positive
dogmas." (p. 153)
37. Schaar's observation also may help to account for the confusion surrounding Robert Bellah's controversial essay. For Bellah had tried to formulate a theory
of civil religion embracing the ideas of both Rousseau and Lincoln. If Schaar is
correct, the two are mutually exclusive, and the task Bellah had set for himself
was unachievable.

cision of the Supreme Court, with its provision for a lax form of "local option" in the control of indecent works of art and literature, would seem to belong to this reaction against the radical counterculture. In rejecting the possibility of any hypothetical definition of obscenity for the nation as a whole, the court urged juries to apply "contemporary community standards"—a phrase that carries more than a hint of deference toward a "middle American" viewpoint. From the vantage of both the articulate radicals and conservatives of the period, then, the political significance of indecent language would seem to be fairly clear.

When we try to extend this line of reflection beyond organized politics to Mailer's "common man," however, the presumed affinity between users of the vernacular and political radicalism quickly evaporates. During the 1960s men like the "skinny Southern cracker" of *The Armies of the Night* were more than likely to be followers of Richard Nixon, if not George Wallace. Cannot the same be said of most of the male peer groups, the men in gyms, locker rooms, and barracks whose rhetorical virtuosity Mailer admires? Their speech may exhibit the vitality of the American vernacular, but it is unlikely that their political attitudes bear any resemblance to those of Emerson, Whitman, Lincoln, or Mailer. On the contrary, they may be expected to assume, along with today's conservatives, that obscene language is for men only, and that to use it in public (where "ladies" are present) is a badge of political disreputability. Their egalitarianism is vitiated by, among other things, the sexist prejudices that usually accompany the use of obscenity as a language of male bonding. They are a long way from the viewpoint one would associate with a truly democratic culture. To say this is only to repeat the point made earlier about Whitman's failure to win a mass audience. The readers he hoped to reach, so far as they read any poet, preferred Longfellow's work. They had no desire to identify with Whitman's crude working-class heroes; they were willing, if not eager, to adopt genteel values (including polite language) as a necessary condition of upward social and economic mobility. To pretend that today most Americans are free (or ever have been) to espouse a view of language like Mailer's is to ignore the extent to which language behavior, like all other cultural activity, is constrained by social structure.

V

And yet, having said all this, it is still possible to discern the tacit alternative to the reigning culture, including polite civil religion, embodied in the vernacular strain in American writing. It may not be a "solid" alternative, as Santayana suggested, in the sense that "solid" implies a firm basis in social and political reality, but it is philosophically coherent nevertheless. The first principle of the vernacular ethos is radical egalitarianism. It takes seriously the basic proposition to which the nation, as Lincoln phrased it, had dedicated itself in 1776. What is more (a second principle), the vernacular style tends to associate egalitarian ideals of justice and of governmental authority with a forthright recognition of all the physical aspects of human existence. As Whitman said, the person who is "no stander above men and women or apart from them" does not press his fingers across his mouth. He does not deny, he does not avert his attention from, any bodily function, including sexuality and death. Writers have a duty to liberate culture from all the pruderies: "voices indecent *by me* clarified and transfigured." And, finally, the third basic principle, naturalism, may be the most important in distinguishing the vernacular ethos from genteel civil religion and from the dominant tradition in Western theology—the religion of the churches. So far as it lends credence to spiritual experience, to any possibility of transcendence, the vernacular locates that experience in the natural realm, in this life, here and now. It recognizes no separate realm of the spirit, either here or beyond this world.

Whether we regard such an ethos as secular or religious is finally, I suspect, a semantic question. The significant fact, in any case, is that many of our most gifted writers have been committed to it, and in varying degrees they all have been compelled to recognize America's failure to develop a vernacular culture. Their increasingly strident use of colloquial language, including obscenity, is in large measure attributable to that failure. As the gap between the rhetoric of our democratic civil religion and our collective behavior has widened, they have resorted to the forbidden language as a kind of verbal shock therapy. Like many features of American life these days, however, there is something of a desperate, apocalyptic quality about the resort to dirty words.

Once the obscenities have made their way into polite letters, what then? What is to be the next phase in the development of this vernacular strain in American writing? To ask these questions is to evoke what Frank Kermode calls a "sense of an ending." It is as if our writers are rushing, along with the republic itself, toward that act of judgment which Lincoln held forth as an indispensable feature of a genuine civil religion. In conclusion, therefore, I want to recall what is probably the most affecting, and the most explicitly religious, evocation of this egalitarian commitment in our literature—one that forms the basis of a prophetic judgment.

The passage is from chapter twenty-six of *Moby-Dick*. Ishmael, the narrator, has been commenting upon the fortitude of Starbuck, the first mate, and about a certain "immaculate manliness" he associates with him. But he is quick to dissociate that quality from any conception of rank, hierarchy, or socially defined nobility. "This august dignity I treat of," he says, "is not the dignity of kings and robes, but that abounding dignity which has no robed investiture." The source of this dignity is at once religious and political. It radiates from God: "The great God absolute! The centre and circumference of all democracy! His omnipresence, our divine equality!" Here again a kind of "reductive philosophy" is at work; divinity is an attribute of equality and not the other way around. Divine equality! It is an ultimate moral principle, and although Melville does not write in the vernacular here, he includes a rationale for what can only be called the vernacular perspective in his appeal to the idea of equality as a sanction for writing a special kind of book—one that imputes high qualities, hitherto reserved for the nobility, to ordinary seamen.

> If, then, to meanest mariners, and renegades and castaways, I shall hereafter ascribe high qualities, though dark; weave round them tragic graces; if even the most mournful, perchance the most abased, among them all, shall at times lift himself to the exalted mounts; if I shall touch that workman's arm with some ethereal light; if I shall spread a rainbow over his disastrous set of sun; then against all mortal critics bear me out in it, thou just Spirit of Equality, which has spread one royal mantle of humanity over all my kind! Bear me out in it, thou great democratic God! who didst not refuse to

the swart convict, Bunyan, the pale, poetic pearl; Thou who didst
clothe with doubly hammered leaves of finest gold, the stumped
and paupered arm of old Cervantes; Thou who didst pick up
Andrew Jackson from the pebbles; who didst hurl him upon a war-
horse; who didst thunder him higher than a throne! Thou who, in
all Thy earthly marchings, ever cullest Thy selectest champions from
the kingly commons; bear me out in it, O God!

Melville's fervent apostrophe to the God of equality lends force to
both his hope and his fear for American democracy. It justifies him in
attributing noble qualities, even a capacity to evoke tragic emotions, to
low characters, and it also sustains his conception of the terrible end of
their journey. The idea of a democratic God informs the prophetic judgment implicit in the final destruction of the Pequod. So far from re-
specting the principles of divine equality, Captain Ahab is an arrogant,
contemptuous manipulator of his crew. He is driven by irrational motives which stem from a lifetime of repression. In *Moby-Dick* the defeat of democratic hopes is related directly to the psychic and bodily
disharmonies resulting from a way of life compulsively devoted to aggressive, competitive achievement, in this case killing whales for profit.
Arrant, absolute individualism is the underside of this democratic culture. The psychopathology of the Ahabian quest is pertinent here because it comports with the association of egalitarian values and the liberation from sexual taboos that had been implicit in the vernacular perspective since Emerson's time. It therefore helps to place the argument
on behalf of obscenity in historical perspective. As Mailer has said, "the
obsession of many of us with scatology is attached to a disrupted communication within us, within our bodies."[38]

For all of these reasons, therefore, it is not wholly fanciful to think of
Melville's apostrophe to the great democratic God as having been delivered on behalf of a long line of American writers from Emerson to
Whitman, from Mark Twain to Hemingway to Norman Mailer. Their
work does offer us something to put in the place of a genteel culture and
a complaisant civil religion. It is an unsteady, intermittent apprehension

38. *Cannibals and Christians* (New York, 1966), p. 281. Cited by Poirier,
*Norman Mailer*, p. 55.

of social equality as an ultimate good. Of course Santayana was correct, this alternative is not very solid. How could it be? It is a mere principle, or a vision of an ideal condition, and the job of incorporating it in our institutions, first undertaken in 1776, has scarcely begun.

# Susan Sontag's "New Left" Pastoral: Notes on Revolutionary Pastoralism in America

On another occasion, he [Lenin] and Gorky were listening to Beethoven's *Appassionata:* "I know nothing [Lenin said] that is greater than the *Appassionata:* I'd like to listen to it every day. It is marvelous superhuman music. I always think with pride—perhaps it is naive of me—what marvelous things human beings can do!" Then screwing up his eyes and smiling, he added, rather sadly: "But I can't listen to music too often. It affects your nerves, makes you want to say stupid nice things and stroke the heads of people who could create such beauty while living in this vile hell. And now you mustn't stroke anyone's head—you might get your hand bitten off. You have to hit them on the head, use force against anyone. Hm, hm, our duty is infernally hard."

I

A puzzling feature of recent American radicalism has been the promiscuous mingling of pastoral and revolutionary motives. According to received definitions the two are irreconcilable. The psychic root of pastoralism is the seemingly universal impulse, in the face of society's increasing complexity and oppressiveness, to withdraw to a simpler environment "closer to nature." For most men in most times and places, needless to say, the pastoral retreat has not been a live option. There seldom has been any place for them to go, and even if there had been, they lacked the means of getting there and starting a new life. In the West in the modern era, the notable exception was the colonization and continuing resettlement of the American continent. This recurrent "event" no doubt accounts for the peculiarly strong hold of the pastoral ethos upon the native imagination. Still, the fact remains that most of the pleasure derived from the pastoral ideal has been a vicarious pleasure mediated by the work of artists and writers. The concern of pastoralism, moreover, has been to change the individual consciousness, not the structure of society. It has been an aesthetic ethos for the privileged, not a political program for the masses.

Since the emergence of the New Left, however, this distinction has been obscured. One of the first rallying cries of the protest against the Vietnam war—*Make love not war!*—is a nice example. To older radicals it seemed a curiously apolitical slogan. But to initiates familiar with the esoteric pastoral idiom it was another invitation to retreat from a brutal society and be like shepherds: simple and caring and poor, and contemptuous of The World. *Make love not war!* is a variant of a call the disaffected young have been hearing through every medium of the counterculture, and during the sixties, as we all know, many heeded the call. They became hippies, flower people, psychedelic tripsters, transcendental meditators, organic food cultists, ecology activists, rural communards, etc. To sympathizers like Charles Reich they all had enlisted in the ranks of a "revolution": "There is a revolution coming," he writes. "It will not be like revolutions of the past. It will originate with the individual and with culture, and it will change the political structure only as its final act. It will not require violence . . ." How appropriate that he prefigures this unique revolution as a *greening* of America!

In view of what has been happening to our society, the strength and ubiquity of these pastoral impulses is understandable enough. What remains puzzling, however, is the effortless way they have been combined with seemingly disparate revolutionary impulses—not all of them by any means as bland and dreamy as the Reichian greening. Many of those who responded to the pastoral invitation thought of themselves, and were thought of by others, as political revolutionaries in the Marxist tradition. Often they joined, or lent support to, SDS, Progressive Labor, Black Panthers, Weathermen, Trotskyists, Maoists, and old-fashioned Communists. Anyone who has marched for civil rights or peace knows something about the easy fellowship that is possible between what might be called the pastoral and political groups within the movement. Many adherents of the counterculture move back and forth between the two. Yet the reasons for skepticism are compelling. It is not easy to imagine how an aesthetic ethos of disengagement and renunciation could be lastingly incorporated in an authentic revolutionary movement—one that aims to transform the system of wealth and power.

Respected authorities on pastoralism and revolution support this skeptical view. The most influential study of the pastoral mode written in this century, William Empson's *Some Versions of Pastoral* (1935), begins with an attack on the very concept of "proletarian literature," the reigning doctrine of revolutionary writing in the thirties. Empson argues that it is a bogus concept. It pretends to be written by, for, and about the people, but it is neither by nor for them, and in most cases it is not really about them either. Which is to say that it is not about the industrial working class. On inspection the hero "worker" often proves to be the courtier-shepherd in disguise, an unbelievably self-contained, sensitive, contemplative man who has few material needs or worldly ambitions. Your typical proletarian novel, says Empson, is an example of covert pastoral. Whether or not he is correct about that need not concern us here. What does matter is the presupposition (which he treats as axiomatic) that pastoralism—so far as it has political significance—tends to be counterrevolutionary. One of its chief functions, he says, is to assuage the anxiety and guilt of the dominant classes by figuring a "beautiful relation between the rich and the poor." (Who writes and reads "proletarian" novels anyway? Surely not the proletariat.) By masking an upper-class sensibility in the garb of a shepherd or a working man the pastoralist tells us that differences between the classes don't matter. It would be ironic, but not inconceivable, if today's Ivy League radicals in blue denim were performing a similar service for the Establishment. In any case, the political effect of pastoralism, as Empson describes it, is to reinforce illusions of class harmony.

If Empson is correct, the revolutionary pretensions of contemporary pastoralists are just that—specious. And it is striking, it must be admitted, how often the spirit of the old pastoral, with its patrician, quietistic bias, makes itself felt in Mitchell Goodman's fascinating compendium of New Left writing, *The Movement Toward a New America, The Beginning of a Long Revolution*.[1] For example, Goodman includes an excerpt from Gary Snyder's *Earth House Hold* in which Snyder explains why "Tribe" is the proper name for the radical counterculture. Like gypsies or American Indians, he says, the disaffected young believe that "man's natural being is to be trusted and followed." The signal by which they recognize each other all over the world is "a bright and tender look, calmness and gentleness, freshness and ease of manner." They belong to a Great Subculture which has had many earlier outcroppings in history, though fewer in the West than the East; it has always been inherently subversive of any society based on hierarchy and specialization, and now that our urban industrial system is proving to be obsolete, the Tribe is prepared to lead mankind into its next great phase: the exploration of consciousness itself. For Snyder, like Virgil or Spenser or Frost, the withdrawal to a rural or wild setting is primarily a means of arriving at the pastoralist's true destination: a Platonic landscape of the mind.[2] What chiefly interests him is the creation of an environment favorable to the contemplative life. If there is something of an anomaly about the idea it is partly because it appears in a volume dedicated to the prospect of a left-wing revolution. Just how anomalous that combination is is made evident by Snyder's description of the kind of man he regards as an ideal recruit for his Tribe:

> . . . a man of wide international reputation, much learning and leisure—luxurious product of our long and sophisticated history—[who] may with good reason wish to live simply, with few tools and minimal clothes, close to nature.

Perhaps we should not be surprised to discover that this lordly figure, an embodiment of the orthodox aesthetic theology of Renaissance pastoralism, survives in the United States in 1970. No doubt Snyder could produce a few real-life examples. But the question remains: how can his withdrawal from society conceivably help to effect a revolution?

Empson's view of the pastoral ethos as in essence counterrevolu-

---

1. (New York: Alfred Knopf, 1970.)

2. Let me here acknowledge a large debt to Richard Cody's fine study, *The Landscape of the Mind: Pastoralism and Platonic Theory in Tasso's 'Aminta' and Shakespeare's Early Comedies* (Oxford: Oxford University Press, 1969).

tionary would be supported, I think, by most modern advocates of political revolution. It is not difficult to guess what Lenin for one would say about the pastoralism of today's American radicals. As the anecdote cited at the outset suggests, he was highly sensitive to the incompatibility between aesthetic pleasure and political commitment.[3] One of the chief lessons of history for him is that power seldom if ever has been relinquished without the application of counterpower. To make a revolution, Lenin would argue, it is imperative to win the support of the working class. And that in turn requires the existence of a well-organized, ideologically sound, disciplined, combative vanguard party.

But of course a distinguishing mark of the New Left has been a deliberate repudiation of party organization and ideological rigor as prerequisites for revolution. As if obeying the old pastoral injunction to reject the aspiring mind, the new radicals have adopted a lifestyle which features gentle, other-worldly virtues: openness, spontaneity, tolerance, eroticism, nonviolence. *Make love not war!* Surely Lenin would have regarded this slogan as symptomatic of that anarchic, all-or-nothing romanticism which undermines the serious work of a revolutionary party. Those whose sympathies are engaged by the New Left might find it disconcerting to reread Lenin's *"Left-Wing" Communism, An Infantile Disorder* (1920) with the recent history of American radicalism in view:

> The petty bourgeois, "driven to frenzy" by the horrors of capitalism, is a social phenomenon which, like anarchism, is characteristic of all capitalist countries. The instability of such revolutionariness, its barrenness, its liability to become swiftly transformed into submission, apathy, fantasy, and even "frenzied" infatuation with one or another bourgeois "fad"—all this is a matter of common knowledge.

From a Leninist viewpoint the pastoralism of today's radical movement is a typical petty bourgeois fantasy, a self-serving aesthetic response to the ugliness and horror of the Vietnam era. Its appeal is thus largely restricted to the white affluent middle class. Although it pretends to offer an alternative to the military-industrial empire, this ethos of disengagement actually may be relied upon to leave the institutional structure of society

---

3. Gorky's story about Lenin's response to Beethoven's work is retold by Edmund Wilson in *To the Finland Station* (New York, 1940), p. 386.

intact. So far from being a revolutionary program, indeed, it is a symptom of a widespread "infantile disorder."

In the light of all this, how much sense does it make to speak about "revolutionary pastoralism"? If we cling to the received definitions of Empson and Lenin, we obviously must conclude that there can be no such thing. The term is self-contradictory, an oxymoron in a class with, say, "violent pacifism." The very emergence of the concept might be said to indicate the confusion of aesthetic and political motives at the core of contemporary radical behavior. On the other hand, there are reasons for thinking that the definitions themselves may in some measure be obsolete. The fact is that a large and steadily increasing number of people are committed to some version of the pastoral ethos as a means of transforming American society. Not only do they believe in it but, what is more important, many are trying to live by it. Who can predict the long term political consequences of their withdrawal from the dominant culture? After all, there is no precedent—certainly not Russia in Lenin's time—for the development of a revolutionary situation in an advanced industrial society like our own, with an immense, morally confused yet materially sated middle class. The technical possibility of economic sufficiency for the entire population makes an incalculable difference. If there was one fact of collective life which always had made pastoralism seem politically fanciful, unrealistic—a mere Arcadian dream—it was the seemingly unalterable fact of economic scarcity. Circumvent that barrier and it becomes plausible, at least, to imagine a revolutionary vanguard activated by those extraeconomic (moral and aesthetic) motives given expression by the pastoral ethos.

Notice, also, that certain New Left intellectuals have begun the job—almost without intending it—of reconciling this classic aesthetic philosophy with the more practical, militant, and egalitarian strain of revolutionary thought inherited from Marx and Lenin. Although the term rarely is invoked, pastoralism is a major theme in most discussions of "cultural revolution." I have already mentioned Mitchell Goodman's collection and Charles Reich's *The Greening of America* (1970). Even more significant is Herbert Marcuse's *An Essay on Liberation* (1969), for there he argues (as an avowed Marxist) that an *aesthetic ethos* may well provide "the common denominator of the aesthetic and the political," the possible form of a free society. To Marcuse even the psychedelic withdrawal may be seen as creating "artificial paradises within the society from which it withdrew," for it may contain a kernel of the new social form he seeks to define.

But in my view no recent work has brought this subject into clearer focus than Susan Sontag's brief essay (it appeared originally as a magazine article), *Trip to Hanoi* (1968). This is not to say that Sontag answers the question I have been discussing, "Can pastoralism be a revolutionary ethos?" In a literal sense, after all, the question is unanswerable right now. Only in the event itself can the revolutionary potential of this or any other ethos finally be confirmed. Besides, *Trip to Hanoi* does not deal expressly with this question. It is not a book *about* pastoralism so much as it is an effort to resolve the conflict between aesthetic and political motives as that conflict is experienced by a writer directly confronting the appalling consequences of our global politics. What concerns Sontag is how to live in good conscience if one is an artist, a radical, and a highly rewarded citizen of the American empire. She answers the question in the time-honored manner of the American writer, as an account of her temporary disengagement from this complex society, and of an exemplary journey—a brief encounter with another, simpler, more virtuous way of life. The result—somewhat inadvertent to be sure—is a pastoral—a political meditation in the pastoral mode. Although *Trip to Hanoi* does not answer my question, it does sharpen the issues, and it helps to explain why we are now witnessing the appearance in America of that strange new form of political behavior, revolutionary pastoralism.

II

When Susan Sontag accepted the invitation to visit North Vietnam in the spring of 1968 it was "with a pretty firm idea" of not writing about her experience. At the time she could not imagine what her subject would be. Although a committed opponent of the American invasion, she doubted that she could add anything worthwhile to the already eloquent opposition to the war. Nor did she have any illusions about contributing to the immense store of knowledge about the situation in Vietnam. For that she had few qualifications and several handicaps. She was not an Asian specialist; she did not know the language; she would only be in

North Vietnam for two weeks, and during that time she and her two companions almost certainly would see little other than what their guides wanted them to see. These were excellent reasons for her reluctance to write about her experience, but being an unregenerate writer she succeeded in overcoming that reluctance. She gives the reasons to her readers nonetheless, presumably so that they can defend themselves against her fallibility.

Before the trip, moreover, she had another, less obvious reason, at once psychological and literary, for thinking that she would keep silent. She confesses to having had a block against expressing her political views in print. Before going to Vietnam, she explains, "[I] had been largely unable to incorporate into either novels or essays my evolving radical political convictions and sense of moral dilemma at being a citizen of the American empire." In part that is because she had been introduced to radical politics during the Stalinist era. Her later disillusionment with the "philistine fraud" of the American Communist Party had made it difficult for her, as it had for other radicals of her generation, to tolerate the standard jargon of the (Old) Left. Even such respectable words as "capitalism" and "imperialism" had given her trouble until the late sixties. By sharing all of these qualms with her readers early on, Sontag manages to invest *Trip to Hanoi* with a literary self-consciousness characteristic of writing in the pastoral mode. She makes her literary problems themselves—her inhibitions, her difficulties in shaping her responses, her dubious authority and credibility as an observer—one of her overt themes. As a result, the reader is invited to question everything. Why did she abandon such compelling scruples against publication? What was there about the Vietnam experience which freed her from the inhibiting results of her disenchanting political childhood? Why should we credit her judgments? Having been warned against her unreliable observations, why should we believe what she tells us about the Vietnamese and their country?

Much of the bite can be taken out of these questions when we recognize that the chief subject of this odd book is an interior journey. *Trip to Hanoi* describes what happens inside the mind of an American writer who briefly undergoes that extreme political, psychic, and moral stress we Americans call "Vietnam." The word refers not only to a place on

the map—a country, a culture, a people—but to a conflict within the
American consciousness. From our government's official viewpoint North
Vietnam was the Enemy, but for radicals like Sontag it had come to be
the ideal Other. At least that is how she had felt while she was still in
the United States. Once she gets to North Vietnam, however, she is
compelled to recognize how much of warring America she has internal-
ized. She also finds the conflict in herself. Hence the structure of *Trip
to Hanoi* is largely determined by two sharp turns of feeling which
separate the book into three parts. The first section records Sontag's
initial "culture shock," her dismay at coming up against a seemingly
impassable barrier between herself and the real, living embodiments of
the ideal Other. To convey the immediacy of this reaction she relies on
the journal form, a selection of notes she had made during the first five
days of her visit. This is a time of disappointment, exasperation, confusion, and gloom. She suffers from a kind of sophisticated homesickness.
But about the fifth day, just when she is ready to give up on the Vietnamese—give up hope of understanding and liking them—the first turn
occurs:

> And then, suddenly, my experiences started changing. The psychic
> cramp with which I was afflicted in the early part of my stay began
> to ease and the Vietnamese as real people, and North Vietnam as a
> real place, came into view.

At this point, beginning the central section of the book, Sontag aban-
dons the journal. Now we get a discursive, essayistic tribute to the moral
beauty of the Vietnamese. It is in fact such an extravagant, uncritical
apostrophe to the grace and simplicity and virtue of these embattled
people that the reader's credulity is likely to be strained—especially because Sontag seems to have forgotten her own strictures against trusting
her impressions.

But then, just when a normally skeptical reader might be ready to
give up on *her,* she confronts what she calls her "crisis of credulity." In
effect she says, "If you are having trouble accepting what I have written,
I confess that I was having trouble believing the evidence of my senses."
This second turn is for me one of the more illuminating passages in
recent American writing. It marks the meeting of our sophisticated,

skeptical Western culture, grounded in notions of human imperfection or original sin, and certain brutally simple facts of contemporary political life:

> The moment one begins to be affected by the moral beauty of the Vietnamese, not to mention their physical grace, a derisive inner voice starts calling it phony sentimentality. Understandably, one fears succumbing to that cut-rate sympathy for places like Vietnam which, lacking any real historical or psychological understanding, becomes another instance of the ideology of primitivism. The revolutionary politics of many people in capitalist countries is only a new guise for the old conservative culture-criticism: posing against overcomplex, hypocritical, devitalized urban society choking on affluence the idea of simple people living the simple life in a decentralized, uncoercive, passionate society with modest material means. As eighteenth-century *philosophes* pictured such a pastoral ideal in the Pacific Islands or among the American Indians, and German romantic poets supposed it to have existed in ancient Greece, late twentieth century intellectuals in New York and Paris are likely to locate it in the exotic revolutionary societies of the Third World. If some of what I've written evokes the very cliché of the Western left-wing intellectual idealizing an agrarian revolution that I was so set on not being, I must reply . . .

I break off the excerpt here in order to direct attention to the range and significance of the issues Sontag has raised and must resolve in completing that crucial sentence. But first let me emphasize what may seem to be a merely formal, literary aspect of the dilemma. Sontag is writing a report about her experience in North Vietnam when she evidently realizes, partway through, that she has fallen into a stock literary attitude. Or is it *merely* a literary attitude? That is a large part of her dilemma, and one that American writers have been caught in for at least two centuries. In any case, it is not only an attitude she has assumed, but an entire conventional mode—a more or less complete way of organizing pieces of writing. Just how conventional it is may not be immediately apparent, for in a sense the topicality of her subject serves as a disguise. But the truth is that she is writing a pastoral, yes another romantic pastoral fable of a well-established American design. At the

risk of oversimplifying and schematizing a supple mode, let me describe
an ideal type or model of the design. It is a hybrid joining traditional
pastoralism and the nineteenth-century travel romance, a distinctive
American mode exemplified by such classic works as Melville's *Typee*
and *Moby-Dick*, Thoreau's *Walden*, Mark Twain's *Huckleberry Finn*,
Hemingway's *In Our Time*, Faulkner's *Go Down, Moses*, and many
others.

### III

The design is formed by a symbolic landscape, a narrative structure,
and a related series of mental states. A central figure, often a first-person
narrator, takes us through the tripartite scheme. We first meet him in a
relatively complex environment,[4] dominated by organized social institutions he perceives as oppressive, alienating, antihuman. It is a technologically oriented culture which tends to perfect the means of life and
neglect the ends. He suffers from a dissociation of his inner and outer
experience. The first stage of the action therefore is a retreat in the
direction of nature—nature as represented by a sector of the landscape,
either rural or wild, marked by fewer signs of human intervention. The
retreat may be described as an escape, to be sure, but it also is a quest.

The second and central stage, accordingly, entails an exploration of
this new setting in search of an alternative to the repressive culture. The
protagonist's aim is a recovery of innocence, nothing less than a simpler,
happier, more harmonious way of life. At some point, as if to confirm
the wisdom of the initial retreat, he enjoys an interlude of joyous, even
ecstatic fulfillment. Anxiety and guilt are supplanted by a sense of be-

4. The distinction between the complex and the simple in the pastoral mode
is a sociological, not an ecological, distinction. The key to complexity is differen-
tiation of function, or the division of labor, and this does not necessarily entail
intellectual or emotional complexity. According to this criterion, the United
States is a complex society, Vietnam is a simple one, regardless of the inner
complexities of Vietnamese culture. Interestingly enough, this distinction between
the complex and the simple is the exact reverse of the ecological distinction. A
Brazilian rain forest is an infinitely more complex, hence more stable, environment
than Manhattan Island, where most biological niches are unfilled and there are
few organisms besides human beings and microbes. But "closeness to nature" in
literary pastorals refers to a simpler way of life, and only indirectly to the ecosystem.

longing and virtue. Often this idyllic moment, which has distinct erotic and religious overtones, involves an encounter between the white hero and a person of non-Western origin—a Native American or a black or an Oriental. But the fulfillment of the pastoral impulse proves to be ephemeral. Certain other recurrent episodes heighten the sense of transcience. One is the "interrupted idyll," when a machine (or some token of advanced industrial society) suddenly bursts into the relative peace and quiet of this simple world, thereby reminding the central figure of the implacable advance of history and of his own place in it— or, more subtly, its place in him. Often, too, there is a chastening, even frightening encounter with the idealized or natural other, reminding the protagonist that Nature and the simpler way of life close to nature can be wild, foreign, threatening, and that he severs his cultural bonds only at the risk of a total loss of self. In short, the retreat makes possible some consciousness-expanding moments, but no basis for a lasting alternative to the repressive culture from which it emanated.

The third and final stage of the action, therefore, entails some kind of return. But the endings of these pastoral fables tend to be inconclusive if not deliberately equivocal. It is seldom clear just what the retreat has accomplished. The most optimistic version hints at the possibility of some new way of life, a best-of-both-worlds compromise between art and nature figured by a "middle landscape." This is a domain which was once thought by dreamers like Jefferson to lie somewhere between over-civilized Europe, with its excess of sophistication and suffering, and the underdeveloped terrain of the American West—threatening, barbaric, impulse-ridden. But of course the Jeffersonian dream of realizing the pastoral hope in a political order was not fulfilled, and our writers reverted to (so far as they ever had departed from) the usual literary way out. The only possible locus of a resolution, they seem to say, is in consciousness and, more specifically, in works of art. In the aesthetic closure, and only there, can we enjoy the pleasure of having it both ways.[5]

5. This is a telescoped version of the pastoral design described in detail in *The Machine in the Garden: Technology and the Pastoral Ideal in America* (New York: Oxford University Press, 1964), and in "Pastoral Ideals and City Troubles," Smithsonian Annual II, *The Fitness of Man's Environment* (New York, 1968).

I V

Coming back now to Sontag's *Trip to Hanoi,* the two sharp turns of feeling already mentioned provide the transitions analgous to those between the initial retreat, the exploration of a culture "closer to nature," and the return to the complex world. At first Sontag withdraws, in the usual westward direction, from a technologically advanced society (it is now militarized and in her view murderously aggressive) to the relatively simple world of its peasant victims. She is sympathetic with the Vietnamese, of course, but she finds that these admirable people are mentally much *too* "simple," *too* "close" to nature," for her taste. They seem to live in a two-dimensional world or, as she puts it, an "ethical fairy tale," endlessly repeating the same simplistic, Manichean account of their melancholy history. Their repetitive, sloganized, resolutely unironic discourse strikes her as a kind of pathetic "baby talk." Her feeling of superiority makes her anxious and guilty, but as an intellectual she is particularly sensitive to verbal crudity and oversimplification. For example, they refer to Americans as "imperialists" and "henchman" and "cruel thugs."

> Although . . . the quaintness of phrase makes me smile, that is just
> what they [the Americans] are—from the vantage point of helpless
> peasants being napalmed by swooping diving metal birds. Still . . .
> such language does make me uncomfortable. Whether because I am
> laggard or maybe just dissociated, I both assent to the unreserved
> moral judgment and shy away from it, too. I believe they are right.
> At the same time, nothing here can make me forget that events are
> much more complicated than the Vietnamese represent them. But
> exactly what complexities would I have them acknowledge? Isn't it
> enough that their struggle is, objectively, just? Can they afford sub-
> tleties when they need to mobilize every bit of energy to continue
> standing up to the American Goliath?

Sontag's ambivalent response to the crude political idiom of the Vietnamese is only one aspect of a larger, all-encompassing ambivalence. It derives in part from the monotonous single-mindedness of this beleagured socialist society. Granted that these people are virtuous, even noble, what is there here to occupy the mind of a Western intellectual?

"Of course I *could* live in Vietnam, or in an ethical society like this one," she reassures herself about the third day, "—but not without the loss of a big part of myself." There is something a bit comic about Sontag and her two American companions in Hanoi, all deeply alienated from the American cause, talking nostalgically about San Francisco rock groups and The *New York Review of Books*. It is comedy not unfamiliar to writers of pastoral:

Corin:            And how like you this shepherd's life, Master Touchstone?
Touchstone:   Truly shepherd, in respect of itself, it is a good life; but in respect that it is a shepherd's life, it is naught . . . Now, in respect it is in the fields, it pleaseth me well; but in respect it is not in the court, it is tedious. As it is a spare life, look you, it fits my humour well; but as there is no more plenty in it, it goes much against my stomach.[6]

The point is that Vietnamese society may be morally superior to American society (Sontag has no doubt about that), but from the standpoint of intellectual, psychological, or aesthetic variety and range of interest, it strikes her as manifestly inferior. But, again, this is a familiar bind of the artist, intellectual, or "complex" man, disclosed by pastoral: he looks at the rustic, worker, or "simple" man with what Empson calls a "double attitude." "I am better in one way," he says to himself, "but not so good in another." So with Sontag: ". . . while my consciousness does include theirs, or could, theirs could never include mine. They may be nobler, more heroic, more generous than I am, but I have more on my mind than they do—probably just what precludes my ever being that virtuous." The dilemma is painful. Hasn't she—haven't all American intellectuals—been morally disabled by what has been called the "high stimulant" quotient of our culture? She finds in herself the condescension of someone from a "big" rich culture visiting a "little" poor one. "My consciousness . . . is a creature with many organs accustomed to being fed by a stream of cultural goods, and infected by irony." Moral seriousness, as she conceives it, requires irony, an awareness of contradiction

6. *As You Like It,* III, ii.

and paradox—the complexity which has been ironed out of Vietnamese discourse. "Part of me," she confesses, "can't help regarding them as children—beautiful, patient, heroic, martyred, stubborn children." Discovering this double attitude in herself generated much of the disappointment and depression of her first few days in Hanoi. At the time the conflict seemed too deep ever to be resolved, and perhaps it was: "the gluttonous habits of my consciousness prevent me from being at home with what I most admire, and—for all my raging against America—firmly unite me with what I condemn."

She appears to have reached an impasse in her effort to develop a satisfactory relationship with the Vietnamese when, suddenly, her experience begins to change. This is the first turn. The anxiety-arousing retreat is over. Now the Vietnamese as "real people" and Vietnam as a "real place" come into view. She notes the callowness and stinginess of the first responses she had recorded in her journal. She supplants the journal form with a straight discursive style. What follows in the middle section of the book corresponds to the "exploration of nature," the search for an alternative way of life, in the usual design of American pastorals. In this case the result also is a kind of idyll, if only on the plane of the intellect. All the traits which she had found baffling now prove to be understandable and attractive. Even the simple language and the slogans acquire a remarkable resonance and grace.

> Take the saying of Ho, repeated to us so often: "Nothing is more precious than independence and liberty." Not until I'd heard the quote many many times did I actually consider it. But when I did, I thought, yes, it really does say a great deal. One could indeed, as the Vietnamese have, live spiritually from that simple sentence for a long time. The Vietnamese regard Ho not as a thinker but as a man of action; his words are for use.

In Vietnam, a society animated by revolutionary will, language serves a special, a different function. Because the Vietnamese don't suffer the isolation of the private self, or the discrepancy between private and public experience (a condition which nurtures irony), language is for them an instrumentality. It is not, as it is for Western literary intellectuals, a medium of consolation or of aesthetic pleasure or of resolving inner conflicts. In North Vietnam words, talk, literature are ancillary to

collective action. Once that is understood the words take on new meaning, new beauty.

Virtually all of Vietnamese behavior now appears to Sontag in a
similarly flattering light. She is impressed by their astonishing calm,
their lack of hate, their magnanimity toward America and Americans,
their habitual emotional tact, their almost universal capacity for heroic
renunciation. Somehow they manage to combine the martial spirit with
a civil life which "places great value on gentleness and the demands of
the heart." They really believe, she decides, in the goodness of man, and
in the possibility of achieving something like the pastoral ideal.

> It was my impression that the Vietnamese, as a culture, genuinely
> believe that life is simple. They also believe, incredible as it may
> seem considering their present situation, that life is full of joy. Joy
> is to be discerned behind what is already so remarkable: the ease
> and total lack of self-pity with which people worked a backbreaking
> number of hours, or daily faced the possibility of their own death
> and the death of those they love. The phenomena of existential
> agony, of alienation, just don't appear among the Vietnamese—
> probably in part because they lack our kind of "ego," and our en-
> dowment of free-floating guilt.

These are great, no doubt exaggerated claims, but as the last statement
indicates, they are not based merely on impressions. Sontag has con-
sulted the experts, and much of her analysis turns upon the distinction
between a culture founded on shame, like Vietnam, and a culture energized by explosive charges of guilt, like our own.

And yet, even if one grants the logic or plausibility of her argument,
it is hard to believe. It is hard to believe that people can be so lacking in
rancor or personal ambition. It is hard to believe they can be so self-
effacing, so controlled, so committed to a common cause, or, in a word,
so virtuous. Sontag relies upon the deep reserves of mistrust in us as
she builds up to the second turn. She talks about the virtues of the Vietnamese with shameless certitude and enthusiasm until, as I have said,
our credulity is near exhaustion. But then she discloses a similar failing
in herself, and we get the remarkable passage, already quoted at length,
in which she reports how a derisive inner voice accuses Susan Sontag,
the writer, of sentimentality and related literary offenses.

This passage is reminiscent of the "interrupted idyll" which recurs in American pastorals. What threatens to obliterate the vision of harmony in this case is not a machine, of course, it is merely a "voice" representing the magisterial Western idea of a self-contained literary culture. That idea comports with the high degree of specialization in our advanced technological system. The "voice" tells Sontag that the way of life she has been describing was invented by Theocritus and Virgil; it is a mode, a set of conventions, a cliché called "the pastoral ideal." It belongs to literature, not to life. Or does it? Has she been forcing her account of Vietnamese culture into this ancient literary mold? Or is it possible that what she has seen in Vietnam might serve to validate the germ of a truth about human possibilities which had always been there, buried, largely invisible or hedged about by irony? This is the crux we reached earlier with her statement: "If some of what I have written evokes the very cliché of the Western left-wing intellectual idealizing an agrarian revolution that I was so set on not being, I must reply . . ." The sentence ends: "that a cliché is a cliché, truth is truth, and direct experience is—well—something one repudiates at one's peril." She continues: "In the end I can only avow that, armed with these very self-suspicions, I found, through direct experience, North Vietnam to be a place which, in many respects, *deserves* to be idealized."

There it is. Although she immediately qualifies this affirmation, acknowledging certain "crimes committed by the present government" of North Vietnam, she never retracts it. She is compelled by her "direct experience" to put down that skeptical inner voice, and to *believe* that the Vietnamese are as virtuous as she has described them. The moment is an extraordinary one because writers working in the pastoral mode usually manage to avoid this ultimate crux. Is there any basis in reality for crediting such an extravagant display of virtue? For most writers the issue never has arisen. They have been protected by the well-known "artificiality" of the mode—its obtrusive and often simple-minded conventionality has precluded any need for moral seriousness. When they have pressed beyond the limits of its equivocal conventions, moreover, they invariably have opted for irony as a way out. Literary pastoral is a treasure-store of devices for having it both ways, even with respect to the nature of human nature. A characteristic solution is to use words, as Robert Frost would put it, which say one thing and mean another. The choice is thereby passed on to the reader. In this case, Sontag might have described what appeared to her to be the ideal character of the Vietnamese, but in language contrived to cast doubt on her judgment and to suggest the deceptive conventionality of her account. By invoking the criterion of "direct [i.e., not merely literary] experience," however, she aims to neutralize the cliché and so, in effect, to validate the hope which pastoral invests in the retreat from the world of power and sophistication.

What makes this passage all the more striking to anyone familiar with Sontag's earlier work is the evident turnabout in her ideas about the relation between art and reality. To my mind, at least, she had hitherto been a critic distinguished by a far greater interest in bold aesthetic effects than in the sense of life they presumably were intended to convey. The essays with which she had established her reputation as (in the words of a *New York Times* reviewer) "the most controversial critic writing in America today," had seemed to court notoriety by extreme statements of currently fashionable, resolutely apolitical notions about art as a highly specialized, cerebral enterprise comparable to symbolic logic in its degree of abstraction from the concerns of the common life. I am thinking especially of "Against Interpretation," "On Style," and her much discussed "Notes on 'Camp.'" Only the year before her visit to Hanoi, moreover, Sontag had alluded to the pastoral mode as a merely formal resource, a venerable body of conventions like that used in pornography. Her point about the pastoral in "The Pornographic Imagination" is that it "depicts relations between people that are certainly reductive, vapid, and unconvincing." That may be true about a great deal of writing in the pastoral mode, but it could not be further from the discoveries she makes in *Trip to Hanoi*. In this book, at least, she seems to abandon her cool aestheticism, as many writers and artists did under the pressure of that civil crisis. My point about the pivotal statement on "direct experience" is that there she seems to credit the incipient moral seriousness of the pastoral convention. So far from conveying a vapid and unconvincing idea of human relations, the pastoral mode now seems to embody an ethos one might conceivably live by in America today. What strikes us as an idealized account of Vietnam, she now claims, is not merely an expression of a stock literary attitude imported from the West; it has its origin in political reality, in the actual substance of the contrast between the Vietnamese and American ways of life.

But what is to be done with this new knowledge? Earlier she had invoked "the old severe rule: if you can't put your life where your head (heart) is, then what you think (feel) is a fraud." How can she possibly put her life where her head presently is? How can she cast her lot with these admirable people and their noble revolutionary cause? By "cast her lot" I don't mean to imply that she ever seriously considers remaining in Indochina. Of course she comes home on schedule. But the question that informs the closing pages of this book, as it does the "return" in all American pastorals, is: how will this withdrawal have changed her life? How might it, if we take it seriously enough, change ours?

v

It is hard to respond decisively to the conclusion of *Trip to Hanoi*. The ending, like the journal extracts at the beginning, is colored by a deep ambivalence. Indeed, the strongest appeal of the book is precisely its lucid expression of the dilemma confronting many Americans these days, particularly members of the professional middle class who are morally alienated from a society which so abundantly favors them. The issue, in the end, is what sort of re-entry Sontag contrives.

> I came back from Hanoi considerably chastened. Life here looks both uglier and more promising. To describe what is promising, it's perhaps imprudent to invoke the promiscuous ideal of revolution. Still, it would be a mistake to underestimate the amount of diffuse yearning for radical change pulsing through this society. Increasing numbers of people do realize that we must have a more generous, more humane way of being with each other; and great, probably convulsive, social changes are needed to create these psychic changes.

Imprudent or not, the conclusion of Sontag's pastoral essay manifestly rides on the ideal of "revolution." But just what does this ever-so-tentative avowal of revolutionary purpose mean? If "great, possibly convulsive social changes" are a necessary precondition of the psychic change she wants, then would not the pastoral ethos of disengagement and a "return to nature" be irrelevant at best and an "infantile" diversion at worst? The way she describes social change (as "convulsive") harks back to her orthodox Marxist past. On the other hand, her goal—"a more generous, more humane way of being with each other"—catches the pastoral feeling which pervades the counterculture nowadays.

True to her own conflicting emotions, Sontag provides abundant evidence for the harsh skeptic who would reject this ideal of revolution, either on political or literary grounds, as a neat bit of self-serving evasiveness.

Politically speaking, her Vietnam experience would seem to be of little or no help to an American who is drawn to the prospect of revolution. In spite of the boldness with which she affirms the ideal aspect of North Vietnam and its citizens, she admits that a Southeast Asian peasant society struggling for national independence hardly can provide a model for American radicals. How can we possibly emulate the behavior of the Vietnamese? An even more troubling question is whether highly favored, white, middle-class intellectuals like Sontag could ever adapt to some hypothetical equivalent of that morally superior society. Early in the book she had raised the question herself:

> Of course I *could* live in Vietnam, or an ethical society like this one—but not without the loss of a big part of myself. Though I believe incorporation into such a society will greatly improve the lives of most people in the world (and therefore support the advent of such societies), I imagine it will in many ways impoverish mine. I live in an unethical society that coarsens the sensibilities and thwarts the capacities for goodness of most people but makes available for minority consumption an astonishing array of intellectual and aesthetic pleasure.

What this means is that members of the intelligentsia of Europe and the United States like herself probably are too privileged, have too much to lose, ever to commit themselves wholeheartedly to an authentic revolutionary cause. True, some will adopt radical opinions; like Sontag, they will "support the advent of such societies" (how abstract and remote she makes it sound!), but are they likely to summon much passion or will for a cause that almost certainly would, if successful, deprive them of so many pleasures? Whatever their opinions, whatever kind of society they "support the advent of," the truth is that most such indulged intellectuals are likely to find themselves aligned, in a crisis, with those who would preserve the system whose benefits they enjoy. In those dismal first days in Vietnam Sontag acknowledged as much about herself. It was her "mental appetitiveness" and her lust for intellectual and aesthetic variety which seemed to disqualify her from entering into the spirit of the place. She might have added the seductive prerogative that an advanced bourgeois society bestows upon artists and intellectuals by supplying them with astonishingly specialized roles. One obvious reason for her ambivalence, and her relatively accommodating re-entry, is her desire to be "Susan Sontag"—critic, novelist, moviemaker, radical. Perhaps this is not so much a matter of fame or notoriety as it is the opportunity for an individual to acquire a unique combination of talents. In the light of the commonplace notion that advanced industrial technology, with its standardizing tendencies, is a threat to individualism, this may seem something of a paradox. North Vietnam is a much smaller country with a far less demanding and intricate technology, but it is unlikely to produce anyone as individualized as Sontag. She is a distinctive product of a culture which exalts the individual performance of the most highly specialized skills. Of all the ways in which our society rewards its intellectuals, perhaps none is more effective as a solvent of the radical will.

From a literary viewpoint, also, *Trip to Hanoi* may seem to end with an easy, conventional compromise. It seems to follow an old familiar pattern for resolving the pastoral opposition between complex and simple ways of life. Sontag returns to the corrupt world of power and wealth, and to all of the pleasurable possibilities she had found missing from the rarefied moral environment of North Vietnam. At the same time, by invoking the ideal of revolution, she testifies to the spiritual change wrought in her by the retreat. A skeptical Empsonian critic also might observe that this vague political affirmation could help to assuage her guilt. It is like the rustic's posture Frost adopts, and so cagily satirizes, at the end of "New Hampshire," when the farmer-poet is challenged by a New York sophisticate:

> Well, if I had to choose one or the other
> I choose to be a plain New Hampshire farmer

With an income in cash of say a thousand
(From say a publisher in New York City).

One might conclude that *Trip to Hanoi* merely illustrates, once again, how well the pastoral mode can serve the writer who wants nothing less than the best of both worlds.

My own sense of the matter, however, is somewhat different. It would be a mistake, I believe, to dismiss Sontag's measured claim, at the end, that she came back from Vietnam with a fresh conception of what a radical political commitment might entail for privileged Americans like herself.

Soon after leaving Indochina she is in Paris hearing from French acquaintances about their recent experience in the abortive May revolution. What strikes her is the fact that they are still possessed by the new feelings they had discovered when, for a few weeks, "vast numbers of ordinarily suspicious, cynical urban people, workers and students, behaved with unprecedented generosity and warmth and spontaneity toward each other." In Paris they had known a change of heart like the one she had undergone in Vietnam. At first she too had been cynical and suspicious, unable to credit the self-effacing solidarity and simplicity of the Vietnamese. But then, with the suddenness of a conversion, she had begun to enjoy a brief but exhilarating reprieve from the inhibitions on love and trust enforced by our competitive, individualistic culture. Later she again was compelled to overcome the same inhibitions, although now they took the form of literary scruples—scruples about invoking what our literary culture would assume to be the mere pastoral cliché "of the Western left-wing intellectual idealizing an agrarian revolution." But this time she breaks free, allowing herself to move beyond the limits we habitually set on our trust in human motives. One consequence of this psychic liberation, it seems, was to free her from the block she formerly had had against writing about her political convictions. It is as if she suddenly had regained confidence in the compatibility of her aesthetic and political aspirations. In Vietnam, as in Paris, the "revolution" had made possible a notable widening of the boundaries of human sympathy.

In many ways, then, *Trip to Hanoi* exemplifies the recent, though as yet imperfect, assimilation of American pastoralism to the politics of protest and radical aspiration. An inchoate thrust toward such a politics has been latent in the writing of native pastoralists since Thoreau's time. The retreat in the direction of nature has always had for its aim an amplified conception of human nature. By disengaging from the dominant bourgeois-Protestant culture with its constricting norms of work and success, sexual identity and family life, pastoralists then and now have been seeking alternatives to the shallow personality type encouraged and rewarded in our society. It is worth recalling, moreover, that in the classic American fables of the nineteenth century the "exploration of nature" often involves an inspiriting contact with representatives of non-Western culture. The young radicals of the Vietnam era, in their refusal to pursue conventional careers, gained the chance to imagine, and sometimes to enact, a simpler, less specialized, more spontaneous and affectionate way of life. What made their pastoralism different, however, is the degree to which it was informed by a heightened political awareness. In contemporary American society, the old-fashioned return, with its emphasis upon private accommodation and aesthetic consolation, no longer seems adequate or even possible. To be sure, only a visionary capable of denying the realities of political power would dream that such a creed of renunciation and its privileged adherents could, in and of themselves, transform the basic structure of this complex and powerful society.

Until now the contribution of the new pastoralists to revolutionary politics, therefore, has been chiefly exemplary. By enlarging the scope of feeling they exemplify all of those affective possibilities now foreclosed by industrial capitalism. They herald the eventual emergence of a politics responsive, in ways that were inconceivable in the era of scarcity, to aesthetic motives. If such a program is compatible with a revolutionary ideology, it is because, first, it prefigures the transformation of the dominant culture and, second, because it provides a model for a transformation of human nature not unlike that which has always been the ultimate concern of both pastoralism and left radicalism. Whether the pastoral ethos ever can be made to appeal to a larger, less privileged segment of the population, is of course doubtful. One of the chief claims I would make for Sontag's New Left version of pastoral is, indeed, the vividness with which she discloses the limitations of the ethos at its center. That disclosure is not theoretical or abstract; it is evoked directly by her candid account of the inner resistance with which she herself met the prospect of a more ethical, egalitarian society. She thereby compels us to recognize what rare qualities of mind and will, a capacity for virtual self-transcendence, would be required of those favored Americans who presume, under late twentieth-century circumstances, to call themselves revolutionaries.

# The American Revolution and
the American Landscape

Although my subject is unusual, it is not wholly unfamiliar. I say unusual because we do not ordinarily think of landscape as having political
consequences. A landscape, after all, is an image of topography. Does
it make any sense to attribute revolutionary force to a topographical
image? How would the image acquire such force? To my knowledge,
no political philosopher has addressed these questions.

But if the subject seems unusual when considered in the abstract, the
specific title—"The American Revolution and the American Landscape"—
sounds familiar. If anything it has a conventional schoolroom air about
it, like an idea of revolution that we learned in the first grade along
with the words to "America the Beautiful." The oddity of the concept
of a revolutionary landscape seems to fade when we specify the *American* Revolution and the *American* landscape. To indicate what I mean,
let us suppose for a moment that we are not now assembled in Char-
lottesville, Virginia,* on a university campus designed by Mr. Jefferson, but in Paris, in a setting designed, say, for Louis XIV; and let us
suppose that the revolution we are preparing to celebrate is not the one
that began on the village green of Lexington in April 1775, but rather

* This lecture in celebration of the Bicentennial of the United States was delivered in Cabell Hall at the University of Virginia, March 27, 1974.

the one that began at the Bastille in July 1789. Is it conceivable that we would have gathered to discuss "The French Revolution and the French Landscape"? I think not.

The point is that our subject is not only peculiar but, as we used to say with more pride than we can easily muster nowadays, peculiarly American. This is not to deny that the French mind, like that of any self-conscious people, has in a degree been shaped by the place it inhabits. As Americans, however, we seem to be particularly receptive to the idea that the native landscape has had a specially important part in the formation of our national identity. The reason is obvious. From the time they first saw the New World, Europeans conceived of it symbolically, as a possible setting for a new beginning. "All these islands are very beautiful," wrote Columbus, describing his first landfall,

> and distinguished by a diversity of scenery; they are filled with a great variety of trees of immense height . . . there are mountains of very great size and beauty, vast plains, groves, and very fruitful fields, admirably adapted for tillage, pasture and habitation. The convenience and excellence of the harbours in this island, and the abundance of the rivers, so indispensable to the health of man, surpass anything that would be believed by one who had not seen it.[1]

Even here, in this letter dated March 14, 1493, the landscape has begun to work its characteristic influence upon the imagination. Of course we know that Europeans long had cherished the fantasy of disengagement from a constricted world, and a chance to begin life anew in an unspoiled landscape. It is true that the tacit invitation that we hear in Columbus's letter—the invitation to come away and enjoy a better life—is like the invitation that had been given expression in Europe's pastoral literature since Theocritus and Virgil. But the difference in this instance is important too. This time the place to which we are being invited is not an imaginary Arcadia, but a real land with real pastures and real trees.

More than any other quality, then, it is the unique tangibility of this ideal landscape, so unspoiled, so rich, so beautiful—in a word, so inviting—that accounts for its exceptionally powerful hold upon the imag-

1. Christopher Columbus, *Four Voyages to the New World,* ed., R. H. Major (New York: Corinth Books, 1961), pp. 5-6.

ination. The power of this imagery is reflected in the work of our classic American writers (Cooper, Emerson, Thoreau, Hawthorne, Melville, Whitman, Mark Twain, Frost, Faulkner, Hemingway), where the landscape is no mere setting or backdrop, but an active shaping force in the consciousness of men and women. If our imaginative writers are correct, the landscape may be a decisive clue to the special character of American thought and behavior. Let me illustrate with a familiar example, F. Scott Fitzgerald's *The Great Gatsby,* which happens to be enjoying a conspicuous vogue right now. Today we tend to read *Gatsby* as a tragic fable written in the peculiar hybrid mode of pastoral-romance developed by American writers. But it also can be read as a kind of mystery story. I want to call attention to the mystery, which inheres (as it turns out) in the national character itself, and to the remarkable device that Fitzgerald uses, finally, to dispel the mystery.

Gatsby's story is told, you will recall, by Nick Carraway, a young man from Minnesota who comes East in the spring of 1922 to make his fortune in Wall Street. The novel turns on Nick's effort to understand the behavior of his legendary, mysterious neighbor—the former James Gatz of North Dakota. To Nick, Gatsby represents, as he says, "everything for which I have unaffected scorn." What he scorns is Gatsby's vulgar display of wealth (exemplified by his ostentatious parties and his burnished, cream-colored car), not to mention his ruthless and even criminal methods of making money. And yet Nick cannot help admiring the man. Above all, he admires Gatsby's single-minded devotion to one ideal, his absolute commitment to winning back Daisy, his first love. It is the man's "extraordinary gift for hope," his belief in the possibility of erasing the past (the five years since the end of his rhapsodic affair with Daisy), that leads Nick to tell Gatsby, "You're worth the whole damn bunch put together." But until the very end Nick is unable to make up his mind about Gatsby. He cannot fathom the man's strange blend of moral obtuseness and idealism, and so throughout his telling of the story he wavers between scorn and admiration. It is only when the summer is over, after Gatsby has been murdered, that Nick finally discovers the missing clue. Just before going back to Minnesota, his trunk packed, he returns to the shore near Gatsby's house for a final look. It is evening, and in the moonlight he sees the landscape as he imagines it once had appeared to arriving Europeans. Only then does he recognize the origin of Gatsby's contradictory and self-destructive behavior.

> Most of the big shore places were closed now and there were hardly any lights except the shadowy, moving glow of a ferryboat across the Sound. And as the moon rose higher the inessential houses began to melt away until gradually I became aware of the old island here that flowered once for Dutch sailor's eyes—a fresh, green breast of the new world. Its vanished trees, the trees that had made way for Gatsby's house, had once pandered in whispers to the last and greatest of all human dreams; for a transitory enchanted moment man must have held his breath in the presence of this continent, compelled into an aesthetic contemplation he neither understood nor desired, face to face for the last time in history with something commensurate to his capacity for wonder.[2]

What this extraordinarily resonant passage implies is nothing less than an explanation of the formation of an American character and, by extension, of certain aspects of our national behavior. It says that what happened to Gatsby, both how he came to be the man he was and how he brought on his own defeat, can only be understood in the light of the special way that Europeans perceived the New World. The sight of an unspoiled, unstoried green continent nurtured certain propensities of thought and action which are still operative five centuries after Columbus's first landfall. It is important to notice, also, that Nick describes that flowering landscape, back to the momentarily vanished houses, as having "pandered" to the dreams of his prototypical American. With that one devastating word, Fitzgerald quietly insinuates a dark view of the effect of the landscape upon the native consciousness. I will return to that theme. Here it is only necessary to emphasize the importance of this retrospective image of the unspoiled American continent. Without it, Fitzgerald tells us, Nick could not have penetrated the mystery of Gatsby and his ambiguous greatness. I do not know any work of literature that invests an image of landscape with greater significance, and in fact it is difficult to imagine how one could.

But there also is something anomalous about the notion that Americans are, or have been, uniquely responsive to their natural surround-

2. *The Great Gatsby* (New York: Charles Scribner's Sons, 1953), pp. 2, 154, 182.

ings. Compared with other peoples, surely, we have not been distinguished for cherishing the environment. If there is anything distinctive about the American experience of the land, it is the brevity of our tenure and the fact that we often made the land a commodity before using it as a habitation. "The land was ours," in Robert Frost's words, "before we were the land's."[3] So, far from having a particularly enduring and affectionate attachment to the places we inhabit, Americans probably are the least rooted, the most casually nomadic of modern peoples. Moreover, the nation's record as a user of forests, grasslands, wildlife, and water sources has been, in the judgment of one knowledgeable observer, "the most violent and the most destructive of any written in the long history of civilization."[4]

No, the unique significance of the landscape in the American consciousness is not to be confused with reverence for the land as such. Rather, as Fitzgerald understood, its significance is chiefly symbolic. It is a central feature of our myth of national origins. According to one version of that myth, it is the landscape that initially invited Europeans to disengage themselves from a constricted social environment and to begin a simpler, freer, more fulfilling life in the unstoried terrain of North America. When Nick gazes at the shore in the moonlight, when he summons an image of the way it looked to the first Europeans, he suddenly recognizes the source of Gatsby's "heightened sensitivity to the promises of life." Once the landscape had been the embodiment of those promises. Like Columbus or the Dutch sailors or the millions who followed them, Gatsby had believed that tomorrow, any tomorrow, he could have erased the past and begun a new life—the sort of life that only exceptional beauty, wealth, and freedom make possible. If Americans have a peculiar inclination to experience the world in this way, it is because the idea of a new beginning once had, or at least seemed to have had, a credible basis in topographical reality. That unspoiled continent once had been there, a tangible landscape of limitless possibilities, and it informed everything that Europeans did when they came to America.

3. "The Gift Outright," *Complete Poems of Robert Frost* (New York: Henry Holt, 1959), p. 467.
4. Fairfield Osborn, *Our Plundered Planet* (New York: Little Brown, 1948), p. 175.

And this brings me back to our subject, for in politics the only action that can be described as a genuine new beginning is a revolution. It is fitting, therefore, that the first successful large-scale modern revolution—"successful" in the sense that it led to the establishment of a wholly new polity—was enacted by Americans. I want to suggest some of the ways in which the topographical image of a fresh start lent an impetus to the revolutionary spirit, and how it may help to account for the unusual character of the American Revolution, as well as for our subsequent failure to abide by its principles. I shall discuss four specific attributes of the New World landscape: its significance as an image of space, of time, of wealth, and of the ultimate values presumed to be inherent in nature.

II

To Europeans the most important physical attribute of the American landscape no doubt was space itself—real, open, seemingly boundless and unclaimed space. It is worth recalling that modern Europeans first began to take an interest in landscape as an aesthetic subject, exemplified by the painting of landscape for its own sake, during the age of exploration.[5] Before that time European art and literature seems to reflect a sense of being hemmed in—of being confined to old, used, closed spaces. When the idealizing imagination of Europeans had taken flight, it had tended to move in time rather than space. Such dreams of felicity as we identify with the Golden Age or with Eden or Arcadia draw most of their vitality from their location in time. It is their temporal distance, their "pastness," rather than a particular topography, that invests these ideal worlds with most of their power. A similar point can be made about the future-oriented utopias of the Renaissance. But the availability of space outside of Europe, and particularly in the hospitable climate of North America, changed all that. Here was usable space that enabled Europeans to act out that most ancient primordial urge to get away, to take a trip, to begin life again in an unspoiled landscape.

Of the many versions of the redemptive journey into the wilderness known to the revolutionary generation of Americans, perhaps the most

5. Kenneth Clark, *Landscape into Art* (Edinburgh: Penguin Books, 1956).

vivid was the migration of the people of Israel, or its individual counterpart, the retreat of the Old Testament prophet, into the desert. Such
withdrawals from the world into nature made possible a spiritual redemption, a new sense of righteous purpose and commitment, a zeal for
the triumph of justice like that of the American patriots. Thus John
Adams explains the inspiriting force of the analogy in a letter to his
wife, Abigail, dated June 11, 1775. He is in Philadelphia as a delegate
to the Second Continental Congress, and he has just come from hearing
a Mr. Duffield preach. "His discourse," writes Adams, "was a kind of
exposition on the thirty-fifth chapter of Isaiah. America was the wilderness and the solitary place, and he said it would be glad, 'rejoice and
blossom as the rose.' " Adams then paraphrases the sermon on points of
similarity between the prophecies of Isaiah and the prospects of the
embattled Americans: " 'No lion shall be there, nor any ravenous beast
shall go up thereon, but the redeemed shall walk there.' " In essence
the analogy is topographical. It works only so far as the colonists are
prepared to see themselves, like the Hebrew prophet, as having been
redeemed by their journey into desert places. (The "deserts of North
America" was a stock phrase of the period.) In his letter Adams testifies to the emotional power of the metaphor. The preacher, he says,
"applied the whole prophecy to this country, and gave us as animating
an entertainment as I ever heard. He filled and swelled the bosom of
every hearer."[6] From the viewpoint of an Adams, of course, the application was bound to be effective. It comported with the New England-
er's millennial conception of American history. Had not the Puritan
ancestors of John Adams, as he wrote elsewhere, "resolved to fly to the
wilderness for refuge from the temporal and spiritual principalities and
powers, and plagues and scourges of their native country"?[7]

But the idea of the special, almost sacred character of North American space did not appeal only to sons of the Puritans. When Tom Paine
wrote *Common Sense,* late in 1775, he had been in the colonies for
only one year. Yet that remarkably effective revolutionary pamphlet is
steeped in a similar geographical awareness. "The Reformation," Paine

6. *Familiar Letters of John Adams and His Wife Abigail Adams, During the Revolution,* ed., Charles Francis Adams (Freeport, N.Y.: Books for Libraries Press, 1970), p. 65.
7. "On the Feudal and the Canon Law," in Gordon S. Wood, ed., *The Rising Glory of America, 1760-1820* (New York: George Braziller, 1971), p. 28.

writes, "was preceded by the discovery of America: As if the Almighty graciously meant to open a sanctuary to the persecuted in future years, when home should afford neither friendship nor safety." In addition to the seeming emptiness of American space (hence its availability as an asylum for the oppressed), Paine emphasized the monumental dimensions of this virgin landscape. Throughout he writes as if there were some necessary affinity between great size, the sheer extent of the continental terrain, and the great merit of the American cause. "The sun never shone on a cause of greater worth. 'Tis not the affair of a city, a county, a province, or a kingdom; but of a continent—of at least one eighth part of the habitable globe."[8]

The degree to which the idea of revolution was nurtured by the topographical awareness of the colonists cannot be established with any precision. It is the kind of link between feeling and action which the actors seldom make explicit, and for evidence the historian must attend to innovations or shifts in language. When Paine relates the worth of the American cause to the fact that it is the affair, not of a mere political unit, like a city or a kingdom, but of a topographical entity—a continent—he is giving voice to a pervasive if amorphous feeling. As the revolutionary fervor of the Americans rose between 1774 and 1776, they invoked the words *continent* and *continental* more and more often. When the delegates to the first Congress assembled, in September 1774, they did not call themselves the "Continental Congress"; but before it was over, that term, along with terms like "continental currency" and "continental army," had come into use. The identification of the revolutionary cause with the huge North American land mass was a source of courage and hope. It was obviously reassuring for John Adams to be able to write, in another letter to his wife, this curious sentence: "The continent is really in earnest, in defending the country."[9] In retrospect there is a certain pathos, along with the unmistakable brag, about the popularity of the word "continent" in 1776. One hundred and fifty

8. *The Complete Writings of Thomas Paine,* ed., Philip S. Foner, 2 vols. (New York: The Citadel Press, 1945), I, 21, 17.

9. *Familiar Letters,* June 17, 1775, p. 65. No historian I have read has explained the sudden vogue of the word "continental." It may have originated in the British Parliament, when members wanted to distinguish between the West Indian island colonies, which remained loyal to the Crown, and the rebellious American colonies. It seems likely that the Americans then took up the seemingly invidious distinction as a taunt and a boast.

years had passed since settlement began, and yet here were the spokesmen for a thin line of colonies, still largely confined to a narrow strip
along the eastern seaboard, describing themselves as an entire *continent*
in revolt.

It was not difficult for a brilliant polemicist like Paine to invest the
American landscape with revolutionary significance. In *Common Sense*
he repeatedly translates indisputable geographical facts into arguments
for independence. " 'Tis repugnant to reason," he writes, "to the universal order of things, to all examples from former ages, to suppose
that this continent can long remain subject to any external power. . . .
Reconciliation is *now* a fallacious dream. Nature has deserted the connection, and art cannot supply her place." A large part of what Paine
meant by "common sense" was a simple environmentalism, an assumption that people's interests inevitably are determined by the place they
inhabit. It is folly to argue, Paine writes, that Americans should accept
the royal veto merely because British subjects living in England do. Geography makes all the difference:

> England being the king's residence, and America not so, makes
> quite another case. The king's negative here is ten times more dan-
> gerous and fatal than it can be in England; for there he will scarcely
> refuse his consent to a bill for putting England into as strong a state
> of defense as possible, and in America he would never suffer such
> a bill to be passed.

Like Franklin, Paine loved to taunt the British with their presumptuous
smallness. "There is something absurd," he writes, "in supposing a
Continent to be perpetually governed by an island." Topography, after
all, is a visible embodiment of those laws of nature to which the Declaration will appeal as a sanction for revolution. "In no instance,"
Paine wrote, "hath nature made the satellite larger than its primary
planet; and as England and America, with respect to each other, reverse
the common order of nature, it is evident that they belong to different
systems. England to Europe; America to itself."[10]

Turning now to the second attribute of the American landscape, its
seeming timelessness, I want to suggest how it too contributed to the
idea of a revolutionary new beginning. But I would add that the spatial

10. *Complete Writings,* vol. 1, pp. 23, 26, and 24.

and temporal characteristics of the landscape lent credibility to the cause of revolution in opposite ways. The vast forests, mountains, rivers, prairies, and plains of North America provided tangible images of boundlessness. These physical objects served to represent ideal space. But the same virgin landscape divested time of its usual landmarks. Compared to the terrain of Britain or Western Europe, with its cities, roads, monuments and ruins, the American landscape was a blank. It was unmarked by the usual traces of history—or at least what the white men of Europe considered to be history. (The fact that the Native Americans seemed to lack a written record of the past was one of the many reasons that Europeans assigned them to the realm of raw nature, or "savagery," rather than to human civilization.) During the revolutionary era Americans often referred to their country as an "asylum," by which they meant a sanctuary from the forms of constraint and repression bequeathed by the past. It was a landscape that invited adjectives like "virgin" and "unstoried" and "immemorial," words that reveal how the native sense of place carried the mind beyond the usual limits of memory, tradition, and history. This unworked terrain turned thought from the past to the future. It implied that here at least the grip of the past upon the present was not a fixed condition of human existence, hence a fresh start was possible. By 1776 this potentially radical idea had been translated into a specific program for dissolving the political bands which connected Americans to the past. It issued in a revolutionary act of separation.

But if the unhistoried landscape reinforced the separatist or centrifugal aspect of the American Revolution, it also lent an impetus to its political corollary: the idea of founding an entirely new republic. A landscape untouched by history also could be perceived as a threatening "hideous wilderness," and it inevitably aroused fears of lawlessness. The instinctive response of many Englishmen was to go back to first principles and establish a new political order. Beginning with the Mayflower Compact, drawn up on board ship in 1620, this habit of laying political foundations by setting forth basic, higher, or fundamental law was repeated in hundreds of convenanting acts for small towns as well as religious congregations, cities, and states during the colonial period. As Hannah Arendt has suggested, this penchant for the act of founding may be the feature of the American Revolution which chiefly distinguishes it from all others. She notes that not only do we call the men of our Revolution "Founding Fathers," but they actually thought of themselves that way.[11] In all thirteen colonies, moreover, the Declaration of Independence was accompanied by the framing of new constitutions—as if bringing to the surface a doctrine of the sovereignty of the people which had been present, in fact if not in theory, for a long while. Although seldom formulated as an abstract principle, the idea of popular sovereignty had been a practical reality at the level of local government. (In New England alone there were more than 550 organized townships by the time independence was declared.) Many historians have noted the sudden and seemingly inexplicable transformation of colonial opinion on the eve of the Revolution. After having argued exclusively for the restoration of their traditional rights as British subjects, the colonists in 1775 and 1776 abruptly adopted the radical idea of founding a new republic in which power and authority derived from the people. It is as if the idea of new beginnings, having been nurtured by the act of settling a wilderness and having given rise to hundreds of lesser acts of founding, had by then sunk deep roots in the native consciousness.

Much of the success that we claim for the American Revolution can be attributed to the fact that it took place in an undeveloped landscape. Most revolutionary movements, no matter how much they have aspired to anti-authoritarian ideals, have had to struggle against entrenched power and authority, and in the course of the struggle they often have been compelled to recreate the kind of centralized power they initially had repudiated. But for the most part the old order against which the American revolutionists were fighting was located across the Atlantic. Besides, the very newness of the colonies tended to diminish the influence of the wealth, status, and power that some Americans had acquired by 1776. Hence the American Revolution was won without generating the degree of class hatred, fanaticism, absolutism, and violence that has often undermined revolutionary idealism. Unlike the French, Russian, or Chinese revolutionists, the Americans did not have to build their new order on the ruins of an old one. Even at the time the Americans understood why theirs had been a particularly fortunate revolution. When

---

11. *On Revolution* (New York: Viking Press, 1963), p. 204.

a group of French officers who had fought beside the Americans were embarking for their return to Europe, a Bostonian issued this warning:

> Do not let your hopes be inflamed by our triumphs on this virgin soil. You will carry our sentiments with you, but if you try to plant them in a country that has been corrupt for centuries, you will encounter obstacles more formidable than ours. Our liberty has been won with blood; you will have to shed it in torrents before liberty can take root in the old world.[12]

The third attribute of the North American landscape that contributed to the revolutionary spirit, along with its boundlessness and timelessness, was its promise of economic fulfillment. To gaze upon these "very fruitful fields, admirably adapted for tillage, pasture and habitation," as Columbus put it in his first letter, was to imagine an escape from the chronic scarcity which Europeans had assumed to be a permanent fact of life. It is ironic to recall that in the seventeenth and early eighteenth centuries European governments were disdainful of their North American colonies because, lacking abundant gold and silver, they were considered too poor to bother about. Whereas Central and South America were associated with fabulous wealth, North America came to be identified with a more modest comfort and economic sufficiency. By the time of the Revolution the dominant image of the American landscape was that of "improved nature," a happy middle state located between the over-civilization of *l'ancien régime* and the "savagery" of the frontier. To Crèvecoeur this middle state meant a "pleasing uniformity" of economic conditions. When an Englishman first lands on the East Coast, said Crèvecoeur, he "beholds fair cities, substantial villages, extensive fields, an immense country filled with decent houses, good roads, orchards, meadows and bridges where a hundred years ago all was wild, woody, and uncultivated!"[13]

This concept of the American economy as a kind of golden mean, a perfect blend of art and nature, comported with the prevailing eighteenth-century idea of the cyclical character of social development. All civilizations were thought, like living organisms, to go through an un-

---

12. Lord Acton, *Lectures on the French Revolution* (London: Macmillan, 1925), p. 32.
13. *Letters from an American Farmer*, ed., Albert E. Stone (New York: New American Library, 1963), pp. 60-61.

varying cycle of youth, maturity, and inevitable decline. By 1750 it was widely assumed that European societies were overripe; so far as they still could generate any vitality or creativity, it would manifest itself in America. No one gave more vivid expression to this popular idea than did Bishop Berkeley in his "Verses on the Prospect of Planting Arts and Learning in America." The poem is about the emigration of the Muse, "disgusted" with the barrenness and decay of Europe, to a landscape that epitomizes freshness, youth, and hope:

> . . . happy climes, where from the genial sun
> And virgin earth such scenes ensue,
> The force of art by nature seems outdone,
> And fancied beauties by the true:

Here again it is the topography of North America, the "happy climes" and "virgin earth," that the poet relies upon for the credibility of his prophetic vision of "another golden age" and for the conviction with which he finally declares: "Westward the course of empire takes its way."[14]

It is difficult to exaggerate what this sense of the inevitability of American growth and development, symbolized by the beckoning landscape, meant for the morale of the revolutionary cause. By 1776 the idea of freedom from want in America was no mere promise; the colonies already had become the world's leading example of a society without poverty. In economic terms they were fulfilling precisely the ideal that was figured by the landscape of the middle state—neither too much development nor too little, neither too wealthy nor too poor. In Jefferson's language, the unique thing about America was the "lovely equality which the poor enjoy with the rich." Our term "middle class" lacks the resonance of this eighteenth-century "middle state." For the men of the Revolution it had moral, cultural, and political as well as economic implications, and they all were figured by the image of a terrain midway between a decadent Europe and a savage frontier. The republic of the middle state was to be an essentially classless—almost pastoral—society of small property holders, men who would be satisfied to fulfill

14. *Berkeley's Complete Works,* ed., A. C. Fraser, 4 vols. (Oxford: Clarendon Press, 1901), IV, 365-66.

the austere neoclassic ideal of economic sufficiency. This idea of the good life makes itself felt in the Declaration of Independence, and particularly in Jefferson's substitution of the "pursuit of happiness" for property in the Lockean trilogy of unalienable rights.[15] It is this moderate sensibility which distinguishes the revolutionists of 1776 from the men who made most other revolutions. No other revolution has been fought by a people in so little danger of real deprivation or so undisturbed by a guilty awareness of desperate poverty in close proximity to great wealth. Just as the American landscape represented freedom from constraint in space and in time, so it represented the scarcely credible possibility of freedom from want.

But of all the implications of the American landscape which nurtured the revolutionary spirit of a new beginning, the most profoundly effective (if also the most elusive) was philosophical. Here I refer to the capacity of the landscape to represent the norm of nature itself. When Europeans journeyed into the wilderness to establish new communities, they were beginning again, returning to nature, in a quite literal sense. And when in 1776 the Congress voted to declare the independence of the colonies, they faced the issue of beginning again in an abstract, political, and philosophical sense. How would they justify breaking the law and resorting to violence? This was the bedrock philosophic issue with which the Congress confronted the Committee of Five (Jefferson, Adams, Franklin, Sherman, and Livingston) when it directed them to draw up the official proclamation of independence. In effect these men were asked to provide a reasoned case on behalf of behavior which they themselves would have described, not long before, as criminal. They were asked to justify acts which they knew would be regarded by many of their contemporaries as unmitigated treason and murder. But the fact is that they had very little difficulty in marshalling their arguments. They announced to the world that they were *entitled* to make a revolution, to alter or abolish the existing government, by (in the familiar yet seldom understood phrase) "the Laws of Nature and of Nature's God."

15. Caroline Robbins, *The Pursuit of Happiness* (Washington, D.C.: American Enterprise Institute, 1974), and Cecelia Kenyon, "Republicanism and Radicalism in the American Revolution: An Old-Fashioned Interpretation," *William and Mary Quarterly,* third series, vol. 19 (1962), 153-82.

This is not to suggest that the idea had resulted directly from their experience of the native landscape. It was ready at hand, as everyone knows, in the language of the natural rights philosophy so effectively propounded by John Locke and others almost a century before. To justify an unlawful seizure of power, Locke had asked Englishmen to suppose a hypothetical situation in which they found themselves living outside politically defined, or social, space—in what he called a "state of nature." His brilliant notion was that when we imagine such a return to a presocialized setting, we will be more likely to see the purpose of government in proper perspective. We will then recognize that government is not a natural or biological necessity, like air, food, water, clothing, or shelter. Rather, men form governments for self-protection, and it follows that governments exist to serve men rather than men to serve governments. When a government ceases to provide protection, men have a right, derived from their essential being, from that initial "state of nature," to alter or abolish that government. They have a "natural right" to organize a revolution. In making this argument Locke came close to deifying the idea of nature, by which he meant a set of abstract principles or laws governing the universe and accessible to human reason. That such laws exist had been proved beyond all doubt by the astonishing discoveries of Galileo, Kepler, and Newton. Although science had discovered the physical principles of natural order and harmony, their political counterparts had yet to be fully apprehended. Locke's theory of the natural right of revolution was intended to fill that gap.

But if Englishmen of the eighteenth century were responsive to the doctrine of natural rights, consider how much more it meant to their colonial relatives. For a century and a half the colonists had been accustomed to think of themselves as living, if not in a state of nature, at least at a considerable distance from the centers of urbane civilization. The colonists were indisputably and irrevocably provincials, and although earlier they may have been embarrassed by the idea, during the Revolution they embraced it. The pervasive environmentalism of the age enabled them to make a virtue of provinciality. For if thought and behavior is in large measure determined by the environment, and if the ultimate principles of order lie hidden behind the mask of nature, then an American obviously was far more likely to gain access to those principles than a Londoner or a Parisian. Thus the American landscape effected a virtual religious conversion. When Englishmen set foot on American soil, said Crèvecoeur, they experienced a kind of "resurrection"—they became new men. This idea accorded perfectly with the criticism of a corrupt society developed by disaffected Englishmen at home. Adapted to American needs, the fashionable neoclassic and radical Whig social criticism meant that coarse native homespun, like provincial manners, was more natural, honest, and virtuous than imported silk or London coffeehouse sophistication. In republican America, as in republican Rome, access to a "natural" rural setting was thought to be conducive to sound anti-monarchical views. At a time when Englishmen believed that the simple life, repose, and contemplation in the countryside helped to breed republican manners, the American landscape inevitably was perceived as a seedbed of republican virtue.

What I have been trying to suggest is that the topographical awareness of Americans converged with John Locke's philosophical argument on behalf of revolution. Even in the seventeenth century Locke had had a glimpse of this truth. "In the beginning," he wrote, speaking of the willingness of men in a state of nature to be satisfied with the conveniences of life, "all the world was America."[16] When Englishmen migrated they in effect were approximating a return to that natural state in which men are best able to perceive self-evident truths. The Lockean doctrine of natural rights thus provided a philosophical confirmation of a viewpoint that seemed to arise, almost spontaneously, from American soil. If the four attributes of the native landscape I have been discussing have a common significance it is, most simply put, that they reinforce the idea of freedom from constraint. The apparent limitlessness of space, the seeming absence of history, the promise of abundance, the accessibility of Nature's God—all of these were made visible, tangible, literally available (or so it seemed) by the American landscape. This was the green beacon that attracted millions of English and European migrants to America. The white colonists who rebelled against Britain in 1776 constituted a self-selected population of men and women with a special responsiveness to the idea of a fresh start.

16. "An Essay Concerning . . . Civil Government," ed., E. A. Burtt, *The English Philosophers from Bacon to Mill* (New York: The Modern Library, 1939), p. 422.

With few exceptions, either they themselves or their ancestors had at some point chosen to leave an old and organized society and to begin a new life in the fresh green terrain of the New World.

### III

In conclusion, let us briefly reconsider the idea of a political new beginning to which the American landscape lent so much credibility. What has happened to the native spirit of revolution since 1776? One answer to that question is implicit in F. Scott Fitzgerald's image of the continental landscape with which I began. When Nick Carraway, the narrator of *The Great Gatsby,* imagines seeing the New World as it had flowered once for Dutch sailors' eyes, he says that the landscape had *"pandered* in whispers to the last and greatest of all human dreams. . . ." With that one shocking verb he intimates a somber view of the eventual effect of the landscape upon the American consciousness. To pander is to minister to base passions. If the virgin land helps to explain Gatsby's "extraordinary gift for hope," it also helps to explain the corruption of that hope. In 1776, as we have seen, the landscape had reinforced an inspiriting vision of political possibilities—indeed a revolutionary commitment to a new kind of republic aimed at securing three fundamental "natural" (hence egalitarian) rights: life, liberty, and the pursuit of happiness. Today, however, it seems evident that those very attributes of the landscape which once had inspired revolutionary idealism also ministered to the passions which dissipated it.

The movement of Europeans into a wilderness perceived as boundless, empty space served as a solvent for old assumptions about the fixity of class and status. It encouraged the rebels of 1776 to dedicate themselves to the proposition, in Lincoln's words, that all men are created equal. But of course this image of an unstoried and unpeopled landscape was a distortion of reality. In it there was no place for the Native Americans and their culture, and the image thereby helped to justify removing them from their land, along with the trees that made way for Gatsby's palatial house. It is worth noting, incidentally, that it was protesting black Americans, spokesmen for the civil rights movement of the 1960s, who reminded us of the unmistakably (if inadvertently) eth-

nocentric history lesson we teach our children with that simple statement about our beginning, "Columbus discovered America"—as if no
one had lived here before 1492! The fact is that for all its egalitarian
implications, the spatial image of America pandered to ethnocentric and
potentially racist passions. If there was no place in the myth of national
origins for Native Americans neither was there a place in it for blacks.
They crossed the Atlantic not in order to be free but in order to be en-
slaved. In practice the more ample life for all people allegedly provided
by American space has meant, above all, a more ample life for white
males of British and European origin.

By the same token, the idea of escape from historical time into the
immemorial North American terrain had destructive as well as creative
consequences. The image of an unstoried landscape evoked in the native consciousness a sense of unique political possibilities, but it also
encouraged an excessive confidence in the ability of European colonists
to throw off constraints, both external and internal, inherited from the
past. In its most extravagant form the idea of a new beginning in time
has proved to be as delusive as the image of limitless space. It has encouraged an excessive reliance upon strategies of disengagement as a
means of solving problems. There is a telling moment in *The Great
Gatsby* when Nick tries to persuade Gatsby that he cannot expect Daisy
simply to erase the five years she has been married to Tom Buchanan.
" 'You cannot repeat the past,' " Nick says. " 'Can't repeat the past?'
he [Gatsby] cried incredulously. 'Why of course you can! . . . I'm
going to fix everything just the way it was before. . . .' "[17] This habit
of mind—the illusion that at any moment it is possible to erase time,
to recapture a relatively ideal untainted past in order to begin again—
is traceable to our myth of national origins. It accounts for the often
noted American propensity for tactics of avoidance and denial. When
the trees or other natural resources in a place have been used up, when
a river is polluted or a city made unlivable, the instinctive native reflex
has been to move out and start again somewhere else. A contemporary
sociologist, Philip Slater, has called this notion that complicated problems simply can be flushed away the "Toilet Assumption" of American

17. *Gatsby*, p. 111.

thought.[18] It is a self-deluding tendency, one that has served to deflect attention, energy, and imagination from the unavoidable problems that would have to be confronted in order to realize the aspirations of the Founding Fathers.

So, too, the promise of abundance represented by the American landscape has had the unforeseen effect of diminishing revolutionary hopes. The patriots of 1776 envisaged a nation that might make possible, for the first time in history, universal freedom from want. They hoped to achieve a relative equality of condition, a society in which none would be too rich or too poor. But the appetite for personal wealth, sharpened by the radical individualism that emerged after 1776, turned out to be more powerful than the egalitarian ideals. Well before the middle of the nineteenth century the acquisitive and competitive ethos of capitalism had begun to subvert the spirit of democratic revolution. While continuing to affirm the democratic principles of their Revolution, Americans in fact were reproducing a modified version of the stratified European social structure, marked by increasingly distinct class divisions, a system of minority ownership and control of the means of production, and an uneven distribution of wealth and power. The seemingly inexaustible riches symbolized by the landscape stimulated a passion for an endlessly rising rate of production and consumption, a goal at variance with the sober eighteenth-century ideal of economic sufficiency.

The first lecturer in this series, Professor Irving Kristol, has affirmed the compatibility of America's democratic ideals and the capitalist program of economic growth. In the opinion of the American revolutionists, he says, "poverty is abolished by economic growth, not by economic redistribution—there is never enough to redistribute."[19] Quite apart from the question of what the Founding Fathers believed—surely Jefferson cannot without qualification be included in that generalization—I would argue that it is precisely the reliance upon corporate economic growth as a means of abolishing poverty that accounts for the

18. *The Pursuit of Loneliness: American Culture at the Breaking Point* (Boston: Beacon Press, 1970), p. 15ff.

19. *The American Revolution as a Successful Revolution* (Washington, D.C.: American Enterprise Institute, 1973), pp. 13-14.

shameful and unnecessary persistence of poverty in what was until recently the richest of industrial nations. Our vast natural wealth has ministered to those very passions the Founding Fathers had identified with a decadent European aristocracy: greed, arrogance, and the enjoyment of wasteful luxury in the presence of acute deprivation. A primary source of the disenchantment with American society that informs so much of contemporary literature is indicated by Fitzgerald's savage description of the narrow self-serving behavior of the very rich in *The Great Gatsby*. "They were careless people," Nick says of Tom and Daisy, "—they smashed up things and creatures and then retreated back into their vast carelessness, or whatever it was that kept them together, and let other people clean up the mess they had made. . . ."[20]

But of all the dubious passions to which the landscape pandered, perhaps the most destructive has been the national appetite for illusory notions of American virtue. It was only a short step from the exhilarating revolutionary spirit, with its justifiable sense of the republic's rare good fortune, to an exaggerated and self-righteous sense of the unique benevolence of the national character. When Europeans crossed the Atlantic, they presumably gained access to the "state of nature" itself—that is, to ultimate, sacred, redeeming values. According to the myth, the landscape of the New World was a repository of virtue formerly attributed to the deity. Freedom from the constraints of European institutions, manners, and scarcity made possible the emergence of a "new man"— an American Adam who proved to be more spontaneous, forthright, easy, good-hearted, or (in a word) more natural than people elsewhere. The identification of the national character with Nature had the effect of sacralizing national aspirations. Hence any purpose adopted by Americans was likely to be perceived, like Jay Gatsby's desire to win back Daisy, "as the following of a grail." This quasi-religious belief, needless to say, no more jibed with the facts than did the belief in an escape from history into boundless space. Although the physical attributes of the landscape had encouraged Americans to believe in the uniqueness of their new republic, with its stirring dedication to the principle of equality, those same attributes also enabled them to re-

20. *Gatsby,* pp. 180-81.

create many of the conditions of European society which violated that principle.

IV

As we approach the bicentennial of the Revolution, we have an obligation to acknowledge the ways in which the republic of 1976 falls short of the revolutionary goals of 1776. If the green light at the end of Daisy's dock is a sadly diminished emblem of the possibilities once made available by the landscape of the New World, it also may be said to represent a diminished commitment to our own revolutionary ideals. For at least a century after 1776 the United States was the inspiration of people struggling for freedom everywhere. But today, in many parts of the world, rebels with aspirations not unlike those of the American patriots regard our government (and with good reason) as an enemy of revolutionary egalitarianism. Within the United States, moreover, attitudes toward the idea of revolution also have been changing. In recent years the word itself has regained a measure of its appeal for numbers of disaffected citizens. Once again some Americans are thinking about revolution as a conceivable recourse, a means of achieving democratic objectives, but the dismaying fact is that the revolution they contemplate would be directed against American institutions.

All of these reflections bring me back, finally, to the way Fitzgerald unlocks the mystery of Jay Gatsby's violent death. It is from the landscape that Nick learns what destroyed Gatsby. In the end he realizes that Gatsby's dream of ecstatic fulfillment, like the national vision of possibilities, also had helped to destroy the dreamer. To be sure, the myth always had fostered extravagant hopes, but in the early phase of American history, while the land was being settled, those hopes had had a far more credible basis in fact than they do in the twentieth century.

> And as I sat there [says Nick], brooding on the old unknown world, I thought of Gatsby's wonder when he first picked out the green light at the end of Daisy's dock. He had come a long way to this blue lawn, and his dream must have seemed so close that he could hardly fail to grasp it.

And just here, in the pause between sentences, Nick finally grasps the reason for Gatsby's failure. He now knows something that Gatsby had not known. "He did not know," says Nick of Gatsby, "that it [the dream] was already behind him, somewhere back in that vast obscurity beyond the city, where the dark fields of the republic rolled on under the night."

We may take this to mean that the dream of felicity figured by the American landscape, if it ever was attainable, was closer to attainment when the Republic was founded. Although the idea of America as a new beginning no longer corresponds with the facts, many Americans (like Gatsby) have continued to behave as if it did. What this means, in political terms, is that the revolutionary content of the myth has been dissipated, but the form—the habit of mind it nurtured—is with us still. In preparation for 1976, therefore, it is instructive to read *The Great Gatsby* as a cautionary fable. It helps to explain why and how we became distracted from those generous revolutionary ideals once represented by the native landscape. Perhaps that knowledge may yet encourage us to change direction and complete our uncompleted revolution.

# Irving Howe: The Pathos of the Left in the Reagan Era

> Individualism, at first, only saps the virtues of public life; but in the long run it attacks and destroys all others and is at length absorbed in downright selfishness.
>
> ALEXIS DE TOCQUEVILLE

Probably no impression Tocqueville had during his 1831–32 tour of the United States was more provocative—or dismaying—than the prospect of a society in which, as he puts it, "every man seeks for his opinions within himself," and turns "all his feelings . . . towards himself alone." But he takes pains, in *Democracy in America*, to distinguish this "vice" from ordinary selfishness or *égoïsme*, a passionate and exaggerated love of self that is not characteristic of any particular form of society. Far from being a psychological abnormality, the unusual self-centeredness of Americans is of democratic origin: a calm, mature, socially authorized feeling, and so novel that it has given birth, he writes, to "a novel expression."

The expression is *individualisme*, and the fact that Tocqueville required this new word to represent the ways of Americans gives credence to what has been, and probably remains, the most widely accepted theory of "American exceptionalism."[1] According to this view, the absence in the United States of traditional European institutions—monarchy, aristocracy, an established church—made possible the extraordinary de-

---

1. The word's appearance in *La Démocratie en Amérique*, Vol. II (book 2, ch. 2) is one of the first in any language, and the translation is one of the first significant appearances in English.

gree of individual freedom enjoyed by each (white male) citizen. Later this theory would be invoked to account for the fact that relatively few Americans, in striking contrast to the citizens of other advanced capitalist societies, were drawn to the idea of socialism.[2]

While the young French aristocrat was touring the States, Emerson was going through the crisis of belief that led him to resign his Unitarian pastorate and to adopt the radically individualistic creed of the God within. But Tocqueville had introduced "individualism" as a descriptive term for a social actuality, whereas Emerson intended his variant, "self-reliance," as a spiritual prescription for his politically liberated but religiously and morally conformist countrymen. "Let me admonish you, first of all," he told his Harvard Divinity School audience in 1838, "to go alone; to refuse the good models, even those which are sacred in the imagination of men, and dare to love God without mediator or veil." He exhorted each American to assert his personal independence as forthrightly as the rebels of 1776 had asserted their collective independence. "In all my lectures," he wrote in 1840, referring to the influential addresses he had delivered in the aftermath of his conversion to the new faith—"The American Scholar," the "Address" to the Divinity School, and "Self-Reliance"—"I have taught one doctrine, namely, the infinitude of the private man."

In *The American Newness,* a graceful, engaging essay based on the Massey Lectures he gave at Harvard in 1985, Irving Howe takes the distinctiveness of American individualism as an unexamined premise. At the outset he simply asserts that the essence of the national culture—"a thin but strong presence: a mist, a cloud, a climate"—is Emersonian. To capture that essence, first given expression during "the newness" (as Emerson and others referred to the expansionary, exuberant spirit of the American 1830s and 1840s), Howe raises such questions as: "What were they up to, Emerson and his disciples?" and "What can they still mean to us?" Coming from Howe, a staunch socialist, editor of *Dissent,* and lifelong member of the anticommunist left, these questions have an obvious political timeliness. They point to the *sauve-*

2. Like other plausible versions of exceptionalism, this one is a hypothesis about national distinctiveness, not uniqueness; Tocqueville did not claim that the political culture of the United States was uniquely conducive to individualism, only that it was more conducive than that of any other Western nation.

*qui-peut* moral climate of the Reagan era and, more specifically, to the refurbished laissez-faire economic creed; the cult of the inspired entre-preneur; the sorry, demoralized state of the left; and—a less conspicu-ous sign of the times—the Emerson revival now under way in the Amer-ican academy.

"During the last twenty years," Harold Bloom announced not long ago, "Emerson has returned, burying his undertakers."[3] He means that Emerson now has recovered from the disfavor into which he had fallen with American literary intellectuals between, roughly, 1915 and 1965, the heyday, successively, of aesthetic modernism and the academic New Criticism. To Bloom the current revival is a significant turning point in our cultural history, and by way of explanation he notes that it began just as "the Age of Eliot" waned. He credits T. S. Eliot, avatar of the New Criticism and unabashed exponent of cultural hierarchy, with having inspired the almost successful effort (joined by such other anti-romantic critics as Yvor Winters and Allen Tate) to bury the sage of Concord. By the early 1960s Emerson's influence had reached its nadir. Since then, however, a number of gifted scholars, among them a few eccentric philosophers and political theorists as well as literary his-torians and critics, have rediscovered the power and the pertinence of Emerson's radical individualism.[4]

But it should be said that the Emerson now being revived is not that remote Victorian essayist and poet (1803–1882) who has long occupied a central place in the history of American arts and letters; nor is he the Yankee religionist without a church who was read by undergraduates in American literature courses, the secular theist whose devoted follow-ers included Thoreau and Whitman, who provoked the strong contra-puntal responses of Hawthorne and Melville, and whose ideas helped shape the work of Emily Dickinson, Henry and William James, John Dewey, Robert Frost, Wallace Stevens, Louis Sullivan, Frank Lloyd Wright, and Charles Ives. *That* Emerson, the historical figure whose importance is measured largely by the influence he exerted upon other

3. "Mr. America," *The New York Review* (November 22, 1984).
4. In addition to Harold Bloom, the participants in the revival include Jona-than Bishop, Stanley Cavell, James Cox, William Gass, George Kateb, Barbara Packer, Joel Porte, and Richard Poirier. By "eccentric" I mean only that the work of many of these scholars is not typical of work being done nowadays in their respective fields.

writers and artists, cannot be said to have "returned," for he never departed—never was displaced from the anthologies or university courses. No, the Emerson whose resurrection Bloom asks us to celebrate is our virtual contemporary, a skeptical theorist of culture whose apotheosis of the individual will-to-power so impressed Nietzsche, and who once again is, or soon will become, as active a presence in our cultural life as the original Ralph Waldo Emerson was until about 1915. "I prophesy," Bloom declares in the revival's unofficial manifesto,

> that . . . [Emerson], rather than Marx or Heidegger, will be the guiding spirit of our imaginative literature and our criticism for some time to come. . . . Individualism, whatever damages its American ruggedness continues to inflict on our politics and social economy, is more than ever the only hope for our imaginative lives.

That Howe does not share Bloom's conception of our "only hope" is not surprising. In twentieth-century America "individualism" has been an almost exclusively conservative rallying cry, and adherents of the left habitually have dismissed the idea with an adjective, as in "bourgeois individualism." This device, meant to imply that individualism is only a euphemism for class privilege, has been a standard feature of socialist rhetoric for a long time. "You must, therefore, confess," wrote Marx and Engels in *The Communist Manifesto,* "that by 'individual' you mean no other person than the bourgeois, than the middle-class owner of property." But Howe, breaking with that tradition, asks whether individualism is indeed incompatible with the ideals of the left. "A central difficulty in Emersonian thought," he writes, ". . . [is] the tendency toward a tragic sundering between democratic sentiment and individualist aggrandizement."

*The American Newness* is about Howe's effort to overcome that difficulty, and in the process he canvasses just about every conceivable objection to Emersonianism. He deftly notes the idiosyncratic, even deformed aspect it has been given by some of Emerson's most devoted disciples—by Thoreau, for example, "who drives to an extreme a version of individualism that . . . later . . . would lend itself to conservative bullying and radical posturing"; or by Whitman, the "new world flaneur" who finally leaves behind, "as any New Yorker would have to, Emerson's cool sense of separateness." He considers the objections both of writers who were responding directly to Emerson, like Hawthorne and Melville, and of others, among them F. H. Bradley, Karl Marx, and J. G. A. Pocock, who were not. He observes that certain strong yet distinct arguments against individualism, like those of Bradley, the philosophic idealist, and Marx, the materialist, lead to much the same conclusion. Bradley unequivocally asserts that "the 'individual' apart from the community is an abstraction," that there is no such thing as a self-contained consciousness, and Marx curtly dismisses the bourgeois idea of the individual as a product of nature—rather than of history—as an "illusion . . . characteristic of every new epoch."

Although Howe treats many of these arguments with respect, he never gets around to incorporating them in a summary assessment of his own. When he does pose the issues in his own voice, moreover, he is strangely diffident. "Is there not something unsatisfying," he asks, "in that view of human experience which proposes an all-but-absolute self-sufficiency of each individual and makes 'self-reliance' the primary value? Something deeply impoverishing in the linked view that contents itself with individualism as ideology?" Well, yes, one wants to reply, there is, but isn't there something oddly conceding about this way of casting the question? Something dangerously subjective, not to say individualistic, about the very notion of judging a "view of human experience" according to the degree of satisfaction or enrichment it affords those who hold it? Doesn't this criterion encourage the "downright selfishness" Tocqueville predicted? Mustn't the adequacy of any large view of life be tested, finally, by its capacity to convey truths about the world?

Although Howe does not join Bloom in accepting Emerson as a spiritual guide, his intermittently acquiescent tone suggests that he may be closer to doing so than he admits. We can be sure, in any event, that he now is much closer than he once was. At one time, he tells us in his 1982 intellectual autobiography, *A Margin of Hope,* he thought of Emerson's philosophy as "pale, disabling, genteel, an individualism of vaporous spirituality." Like most of the other "New York intellectuals," Howe then regarded the classic American writers, especially Emerson and Thoreau, as "deficient in those historical entanglements that seemed essential to literature because inescapable in life." Exactly when he recanted is not clear, but: "Now," he says, "I know better, or think I do." He revised his opinion because of his realization that almost every "major American writer bears the stamp of Emerson. To evade Emerson was to evade both America and its literature."

Yet even before that change of heart, Howe seems to have been attracted to the Emersonian ideal of the critic's vocation. One of the leitmotifs of *A Margin of Hope* is his admiration for Edmund Wilson, whom he first read when he was sixteen, and whom he avowedly took as his intellectual model. What elicited his admiration was Wilson's moral gravity, the breadth of his interests, his lucidity, and his disdain for academicism—especially the academic critics' preoccupation with methodological problems. Howe, who has been a member of university faculties during most of his professional life, does not conceal his envy of Wilson's success in avoiding university jobs. The truth is that Wilson, perhaps more than any American writer since Emerson himself, embodied the qualities of the self-sufficient critic of culture Emerson described in "The American Scholar." The undefined and largely unacknowledged attraction to Emersonian ideas that makes itself felt in *The American Newness* becomes more understandable once we recognize that Emerson's exemplary "scholar"—the independent, unaffiliated, all-around man of letters—is precisely the kind of writer Howe always wanted to be.

What is lacking in Howe's book is a sense of Emerson's power. Except for the abstract argument about his Americanness, Howe never really accounts for Emerson's astonishing capacity to seize the imagination of other writers and artists. It would have been useful had Howe noticed that Emerson begins his central essay, "Self-Reliance," with an aesthetic distinction: "I read the other day some verses by an eminent painter which were original and not conventional," and that the main argument is composed of repeated unfurlings of that same distinction. Step by step the argument takes on moral, social, political meanings, and in the end it comes to seem an all-encompassing view of life. "Originality" for Emerson is what distinguishes the spirit from the form, protestantism from Christian orthodoxy, a democratic from a hierarchical social order, the New World from the Old, and indeed all fresh intuitions from derivative tuitions.

The appeal of Emerson's doctrine to artists and intellectuals derives in large measure from the identification of creativity with "self-reliance." To do original work of any kind, he argues, it is first necessary to clear a channel to the aboriginal self. Because of our craven conformity, however, the channel usually is clogged with cultural detritus: moribund forms, received opinions, stock responses, clichés, in short, all conventionalities. The universal antidote is to believe that "nothing is at last sacred but the integrity of your own mind." However imperfect this doctrine may be as a general philosophy, it is hard to imagine a more tonic formula to offer aspiring writers, artists, theoretical scientists, philosophers, intellectuals—anyone indeed whose work depends on original insights.

Most people do not do that kind of work, however, and Emerson's radical individualism is more compelling as a credo for intellectuals than as a general social philosophy. This point Howe only acknowledges indirectly, in his survey of objections to Emerson's social views. Of these objections, the most persuasive, I think, is directed against Emerson's tacit assumption that society consists of little more than the sum of individual wills. As early as 1840, Orestes Brownson, the New England writer and sometime transcendentalist, exposed the unreality of this conception with its quietistic belief in "self-culture," or the alteration of the individual consciousness, as the most effective way to accomplish fundamental changes in society. In his incisive polemic, "The Laboring Classes," Brownson observed that evils like poverty are "not merely individual in character," but are "inherent in all our social arrangements, and cannot be cured without a radical change of those arrangements." Hence the fundamental difference between religionists who want a change of heart and radical democrats whose primary goal is to change class relations and institutions. This is a telling—to my mind incontrovertible—argument against individualism as a theory of political practice.

But Howe dismisses Brownson's argument, on the ground that nowadays we are "inclined to reject a simple dichotomy between social transformation and individual regeneration," in favor of the Gramscian sense of their interdependence. I think this is beside the point, because Brownson does not insist upon that dichotomy; he merely states that a change in the consciousness of individuals, however desirable, cannot possibly transform society unless it accompanies a concerted effort to change social arrangements. Neither Brownson nor Gramsci was so foolish as to believe that a program of fundamental social reform can be effected without changing the minds of a good many people. But Howe fails to distinguish between that prerequisite for social change and the belief in the regeneration of individuals as a sufficient means of transforming society.

This question—whether to concentrate on changing hearts or structures of power—has continued to be a vexing one for the American left. During the 1960s it was a major issue between the New and the Old Left, and, within the New Left, between the advocates of "cultural" and "political" rebellion. At the time Howe, standing firm on Old Left principles of organization, rationality, and ideological consistency, was an outspoken opponent of rebellious students and the counterculture. But he also has changed his mind on this issue. Now, he writes in *A Margin of Hope*, he is more willing to "recognize what might be genuinely revolutionary in that strand of Emerson's thought which placed a central value on a shared vision of personal autonomy." This change helps to explain why, in his discussion of Brownson, as elsewhere in *The American Newness,* he pulls back just as he seems on the verge of acknowledging the need to choose between an absolute individualism and the democratic politics to which he has been committed all of his life.

Here the contrast with Harold Bloom, who exhibits no such reluctance, is illuminating. "Emerson," Bloom writes, "is more than prepared to give up on the great masses that constitute humankind. His hope . . . is that a small community of the spirit can come into existence." This is Howe's rejoinder:

> Now it is true you can find almost anything you want in Emerson's writings, and by, say, the 1850s he might have been ready to settle for a "small community of the spirit." Every democratic idealist, his goal not yet reached, must at times settle provisionally for something like that. But no democrat can give up "on the great masses" and remain a democrat.

This last assertion is the firmest political judgment Howe makes in *The American Newness,* the one place where he draws the line beyond which an adherent of the left cannot go in the direction of Emersonianism. One wishes he had brought a similar firmness to his overall analysis of that philosophy. In the event, however, he fails to distinguish between Emerson as a guide to an intellectual vocation and to a politics, and he ultimately adopts a position of considered ambivalence. "The experience of our century," he writes, "both underscores the inadequacies of an absolutist individualism and the dangers of too sweeping an attack upon it."

One explanation for Howe's inconclusiveness is his own largely unacknowledged attraction to Emersonianism; a hint of another may be heard in the melancholy note he sounds in his rejoinder to Bloom. It is the lament of the "democratic idealist" compelled to settle for something like "a small community of the spirit," and it finally becomes the dominant emotional tone of *The American Newness*. We first hear it as the undertone of Howe's sardonic repudiation of Emerson's comforting belief in a universal principle of "compensation." To Emerson's notion that there "is always some levelling circumstance that puts down the overbearing, the strong, the rich, the fortunate, substantially on the same ground with others," Howe replies:

> Perhaps death does that; but short of death, what could Emerson have meant? As one who has spent a good part of his life looking for the "levelling circumstance" of which Emerson speaks, I can only report that thus far it has steadily eluded me.

Later, in a moving account of the end of "the newness," Howe underlines the theme of private disillusionment. In the decades of the 1830s and 1840s it was possible, he says, for otherwise sober people to believe that postrevolutionary America had disentangled itself from historical conditions; but then, as the slavery crisis deepened and "the country shuddered with foreknowledge," that optimism was abruptly dispelled. Howe pinpoints the change "in 1851, when Emerson, raging against the Fugitive Slave Law, finds it intolerable that 'this filthy enactment was made in the 19th century by people who could read and write. I will not obey it, by God.' "

Howe connects Emerson's sense of the impinging tyranny of circumstances to the marked shift in tone of the two powerful, Nietzsche-like essays, "Experience" and "Fate," which figure prominently in the current Emerson revival. In them we encounter an Emerson who no longer is the hopeful democratic idealist; he is a man "encoiled," twisting and turning at one moment, locked in a prison of glass at another. He prods and pricks himself. "Life is a bubble and a skepticism," he writes, "and a sleep within a sleep." It is as if, Howe says, Emerson had discovered in himself "the spiritual tokens of a nihilism that lurks at the bottom of everything."

> It is all astonishing, terrible, heartbreaking. Whoever has known the collapse of a large ideal will share Emerson's pain.

This is the most affecting—the climactic—moment in *The American Newness*. It expresses the pathos of the American left in the Reagan age. It brings to mind Howe's account of his own enervating service to the idea of socialism—the dreary meetings and sectarian squabbles and esoteric language—and it becomes apparent that his diffidence in criticizing individualism is in large part owing to a loss of confidence in the future of the left in America. The unspoken question that informs Howe's new-found respect for Emersonianism is one that he raised toward the end of his cool, unillusioned study, *Socialism and America* (1985):

> Does the socialist idea, even if rendered more sophisticated than it was in the past, still survive as a significant option? Has it outlived its historical moment? . . . Nowhere on the globe can one point to a free, developed socialist society. The proclaimed goal has not been reached, and as I write it does not seem close. Socialism has been shaken by failures, torn by doubts. Its language and symbols have been appropriated by parodic totalitarianism, and from this trauma we have still to recover. . . . Whether socialism can be revived as a living idea—which is something different from the mere survival of European social-democratic parties as established institutions—is by now very much a question.

If, as I believe, there is a muddle at the center of *The American Newness*, then it is—foolish as it sounds—a useful, which is to say a revealing, muddle. Like today's vigorous Emerson revival, it should help to remind the intellectual left in this country of the need to come to terms with the individualism of Americans. This means taking account of several implications of Howe's admirably unguarded meditation, beginning with the obvious fact that individualism is not one thing, but many, and that in addition to distinguishing among its various forms we must decide which are reconcilable with a further extension of democracy, whether socialist or otherwise, and which are not.

# Acknowledgments

Several of the pieces reprinted above were written many years ago, and I could not possibly name or even recall all of the debts I incurred in writing them. But I owe a particular gratitude to Bernard Bowron and Arnold Rose, with whom I collaborated in writing one of them, and to a few other friends—Ann and Warner Berthoff, George Kateb, Jane Marx, Henry May, Henry Nash Smith, John William Ward—who have read and commented upon many of them over the years. The introductory essay, the only one never published before, benefited from the comments of Brenda and Monroe Engel, Giles Gunn, Jane Marx, Michael McGerr, Sheldon Meyer, and Alan Trachtenberg. For a long while now I also have benefited from the example set for me—an indirect but mightily effective form of criticism and support—by my children, to whom this book is lovingly dedicated.

I want to thank the editors and others representing the following publications for granting permission to reprint the essays listed below.

*American Literature* and Duke University Press for "The Pilot and the Passenger: Landscape Conventions and the Style of *Huckleberry Finn.*"

*The Sewanee Review* and the University of the South for "Melville's Parable of the Walls."

*The New York Review of Books* for "The Two Thoreaus" and "A Visit to Mr. America."

*The New England Quarterly* and The Colonial Society of Massachusetts for "The Machine in the Garden."

*American Quarterly* and the American Studies Association for "Literature and Covert Culture."

*Science* and the American Association for the Advancement of Science for "American Institutions and Ecological Ideals."

*Daedalus* and the American Academy of Arts and Sciences for "Reflections on the Neo-Romantic Critique of Science."

Rutgers University Press and Rutgers, The State University of New Jersey, for "The Puzzle of Anti-Urbanism in American Literature."

*Monthly Review* and the Monthly Review Foundation for "The Teacher" and "Double Consciousness and the Cultural Politics of F. O. Matthiessen."

Holt, Rinehart and Winston for "Susan Sontag's 'New Left Pastoral': Notes on Revolutionary Pastoralism."

*The Massachusetts Review* for "Noble Shit: The Uncivil Response of American Writers to Civil Religion in America."

The American Enterprise Institute for Public Policy Research for "The American Revolution and the American Landscape."

# Index

Aaron, Daniel, ix
Abercrombie, Lascelles, 102
Acton, John, Lord, 326
Adams, Henry, 116, 117-18, 182-83,
    191, 195, 196, 197, 205, 234; *The
    Education of Henry Adams,* 179-
    81, 196
Adams, John, 321, 322, 328
Adorno, T. W., 256, 258
Aeschylus, 235
Alexander, Franz, 31
Althusser, Louis, 258-59
Anderson, Perry, 235, 258-59
Arendt, Hannah, 324-25
Arnold, Matthew, 181
Arvin, Newton, 55

Babbitt, Irving, 233, 244
Bakhtin, M. M., x, xi
Baldwin, James, 212
Beard, George Miller, 136-37
Beethoven, Ludwig van, 291
Bell, Daniel, xiv
Bellah, Robert, 262-63, 270, 278, 285
Bellamy, Gladys, 51
Bellow, Saul, 212

Benes, Eduard, 240-41
Benjamin, Walter, 256
Berkeley, George, 327
Bernstein, Leonard, 236
Bewley, Marius, 4, 9, 17
Bercovitch, Sacvan, xi, xiii
Bishop, Jonathan, 339
Blake, William, 122, 163, 168, 171
Bloom, Harold, 339, 340, 341, 344
Boone, Daniel, xii, 210
Bowron, Bernard, 127-38
Bradford, William, 3
Bradley, F. H., 341
Bridgman, Richard, 283
Brooks, Van Wyck, xviii, 212, 244
Brower, Reuben, 105
Brown, Harrison, 143
Brownson, Orestes, 343-44
Bruno, Giordano, 185
Bruss, Elizabeth W., 281
Bunyan, John, 81, 122
Burke, Kenneth, 256
Burroughs, John, 283
Byron, George, Lord, 60

Calverton, V. F., 248, 249

Carlyle, Thomas, 163, 165-67, 177, 181, 266
Carson, Rachel, 150
Cavell, Stanley, 91, 339
Cervantes, 132, 289
Chapin, F. Stuart, 130
Chase, Richard, 55, 209
Cheney, Russell, 242, 243, 250
Cicero, 196, 268
city, xviii, 12, 68, 202, 208-27
civil rights, 144, 145-46, 201, 203, 206, 292-93, 331-32
Clark, Kenneth, 320
Clemens, Samuel L. (pseud. Mark Twain), xv-xvi, 4, 8, 11-17, 37-53, 107, 139, 191-97, 205, 209, 250, 265, 277-83, 289, 317; *Adventures of Huckleberry Finn,* xi, xiv, xvi, 4, 6, 12-17, 18-36, 37-53, 99, 138, 189, 191-97, 221, 277-80, 282-83, 301; *The Adventures of Tom Sawyer,* 19, 24-25, 27, 33-34, 43, 47; *The Connecticut Yankee,* 17, 195; *Life on the Mississippi,* 19, 20, 22, 25-28, 30-31, 34-35, 194; "Old Times on the Mississippi," xv, xvii, 20, 22-24; *A Tramp Abroad,* 51
Cody, Richard, 294
Cohen, G. A., 253
Cohn, David L., 135
Coleridge, Samuel Taylor, 163, 171, 249-50, 266
Columbus, Christopher, 316, 318, 319, 326, 332
Commoner, Barry, 142-43
Cook, Bruce, 199, 200
Cooper, James Fenimore, 3, 11, 15, 99, 136, 137, 139, 152, 208, 210, 221, 317
Cox, James, 339
Crane, Hart, 265
Crane, Stephen, 212
Crèvecoeur, Michel Guillaume St. Jean de, 326, 330
Cunliffe, Marcus, 205

Dante, 81, 165

Darwin, Charles, xvii
Davies, W. H., 102
De Voto, Bernard, 25, 27, 38
Dewey, John, 339
Dickens, Charles, 181, 253
Dickinson, Emily, 339
Dos Passos, John, 212
Dostoevski, 216
Douglas, Ann, xi
Dreiser, Theodore, 212, 213, 231-34, 238, 265
Dubos, René, 143
Durkheim, Emile, 121, 128, 190

Eagleton, Terry, 252, 253
ecology, xiii, 139-59
Edel, Leon, 88
Edwards, Jonathan, 64, 266-67
egalitarianism, 8, 9, 16, 17, 152, 244, 262, 267, 273, 276-77, 285, 286, 287, 314, 331-33, 335
Ehrlich, Paul, 143
Eliot, T. S., 37-53, 101, 110, 121, 217, 243, 275, 339
Ellison, Ralph, 212, 283
Ellul, Jacques, 200
Emerson, Ralph Waldo, 9, 77-81, 86, 87, 89, 90, 92, 95, 96, 107, 113-18, 121, 122, 125, 136, 139, 141, 152, 163, 164-65, 167-68, 171, 175-76, 181, 192, 208, 221, 237-38, 244, 247-48, 249-50, 250-51, 255-56, 262, 265-75, 278-79, 286, 289, 317, 338-47; *Nature,* 99, 107-8, 125, 164, 219, 221
Empson, William, 293-94, 294-95, 296
Engels, Friedrich, 121, 251, 340
Enlightenment, 50, 172, 173, 175-76, 185
Epimetheus, 119
Erikson, Erik, 83-86
Ervin-Tripp, Susan, 281
Everett, Edward, 133-34

Fairbanks, Henry G., 137-38
Farrell, James T., 212

Faulkner, William, 99, 126, 209, 283, 317; *The Bear*, 11, 116, 197; *Go Down, Moses*, 301

Feidelson, Charles, 117, 212

Feuerbach, Ludwig, 255

Fields, James T., 77

Fishman, Joshua A., 283

Fitzgerald, F. Scott, 209, 250, 331; *The Great Gatsby*, 197, 221, 222-26, 317-18, 319, 331-32, 334-36

Flint, F. S., 102

Fluck, Winifried, 193

Forster, E. M., 37

Franklin, Benjamin, 184-85, 189, 192, 323, 328

Freud, Sigmund, 78, 86, 131, 135, 137, 259; *Civilization and Its Discontents*, 131

Fromm, Erich, 258

Frost, Robert, 99, 101-10, 152, 208, 294, 307, 317, 319, 339; *A Boy's Will*, 102, 109; *North of Boston*, 102, 106, 107; *A Witness Tree*, 109

Fuller, Margaret, 97

Galileo, 165, 185, 329

Gandhi, Mohandas, 83, 89

Gass, William, 339

Geertz, Clifford, x, 185

Geismar, Maxwell, 115

genteel tradition, xv, xvii, 15, 25, 37, 45-46, 51, 195, 232, 264-65, 274-75, 276, 281-82, 286, 287, 289, 341

Gibson, Wilfrid, 102

Ginsberg, Allen, 199, 202

Goethe, 121, 163

Goldmann, Lucien, 256

Goodman, Mitchell, 201, 293-94

Goodman, Paul, 284, 285

Gorky, Maxim, 291

Graham, Loren, 161

Gramsci, Antonio, 256, 343-44

great transformation, *see* industrialization

Green, Arnold W., 31

Gregg, Alan, 150

Gunn, Giles, 246

Halperin, David, 188

Hamilton, Alexander, 124, 154

Hansen, Chadwick, 44

Harding, Walter, 83

Hartz, Louis, x

Hawthorne, Nathaniel, 3, 9, 17, 27, 54, 63, 70, 73, 74, 99, 113, 115-16, 117-18, 119-26, 137-38, 208, 212-22, 238, 244, 245, 248, 249, 250, 317, 341; "Ethan Brand," 119-24, 125; *The House of Seven Gables*, 123, 212, 216, 217-18; *The Scarlet Letter*, 122, 213-22, 225, 250

Hays, S. P., 141

Hegel, 254, 255

Heidegger, Martin, 340

Hemingway, Ernest, 38, 99, 107, 152, 209, 279-80, 289, 317; *In Our Time*, 301; *A Farewell to Arms*, 279; *For Whom the Bell Tolls*, 280; *The Old Man and the Sea*, 11, 15, 17

Hickman, C. Addison, 129

Hicks, Granville, 248, 249

Hitler, Adolf, 240

Hobbes, Thomas, 198

Hofstadter, Richard, x

Holmes, Oliver Wendell, 244

Holton, Gerald, 167

Homer, 28-29, 188

Horney, Karen, 31

Houghton, Donald, 133

Howe, Irving, xvii, xviii, 241, 337-47

Howells, William, 212, 232

Huberman, Leo, 239-40

Hutchinson, Ann, 219

Hyde, Louis, 242, 243

industrial capitalism, *see* industrial society

Industrial Revolution, *see* industrialization

industrial society, x, xii, xvi, 26, 27,
    100, 123, 153, 155, 160, 171,
    172, 175, 179, 186, 192, 202,
    224, 225-26, 275, 294, 302, 313
industrialization, xii, 113-26, 132-38,
    148, 149, 153-55, 176-77, 185,
    190, 226, 251
Ives, Charles, 339

Jackson, Andrew, xiv, 289
James, Henry, 3, 4, 9, 17, 115, 209,
    221, 237, 238, 339
James, William, 92, 197, 238, 339
Jameson, Frederic, 254
Jefferson, Thomas, 141, 154, 189-90,
    302, 315, 328
Jung, Carl, 117, 131

Kaagen, Larry, 205
Kant, Immanuel, 121, 163, 248, 249,
    255-56, 266
Kateb, George, 339
Kautsky, Karl, 252
Kennedy, John F., 263
Kenyon, Cecilia, 328
Kepler, Johannes, 329
Kermode, Frank, 288
Kerouac, Jack, 199
Kerr, Clark, 198
Kesey, Ken, 199
Kirkland, Edward C., 113
Klingender, Francis, 122, 123
Kluckhohn, Clyde, 130
Kuhn, Manford H., 129
Kuklick, Bruce, ix

landscape, xii, xv-xvi, 3, 17, 18-36,
    99, 118, 120, 123, 138, 139, 147-
    48, 152-54, 158, 186, 190, 193,
    202, 206, 301, 315-36; middle
    landscape, 189, 302; wilderness,
    118, 136, 140, 147-48, 152, 187,
    210, 213, 219, 320-21, 324, 325,
    328, 331
Langley, Samuel, 180
Lanman, James H., 134, 137-38
Lawrence, D. H., 212, 221, 244
Leadbelly, 236

Lebeaux, Richard, 83-91, 93-100
Lenin, 281, 291, 295, 296
Levenson, J. C., 257
Levin, Harry, 243
Lewis, Anthony, 143
Lewis, R. W. B., ix, xiv
Lincoln, Abraham, 284-85, 286, 287,
    288
Livingston, Robert R., 328
Locke, John, 164, 165, 247, 328, 329,
    330
Longfellow, Henry Wadsworth, 4-8,
    10, 11, 15, 244, 274, 286
Louis XIV, 315-16
Low, Benjamin, 135
Lowell, James Russell, 244
Lukacs, George, 256
Lynn, Kenneth S., 193

machine, see technology
Mailer, Norman, 204, 263-65, 267,
    273, 276, 277, 279-80, 282-84,
    285, 286, 289; The Armies of the
    Night, 261, 283-84, 286; Canni-
    bals and Christians, 150, 289;
    Why Are We in Vietnam?, 11,
    197, 201
Marcuse, Herbert, 201, 258, 296-97
Marsh, George Perkins, 142
Marx, Karl, 97-98, 121, 201, 211, 251,
    252, 255, 296, 340, 341
Marx, Leo, x, xiii, 27, 117, 122, 138,
    151, 190, 197, 283, 302
Marxism, xiv, xvii, 97-98, 121, 190,
    195, 205, 238, 240, 245, 248,
    249, 251-60, 292, 296-97, 310
Masaryk, Jan, 241
Matthiessen, F. O., x, xvii, xviii, 71,
    117, 212, 231-60; American Re-
    naissance, xiv, 212, 236, 239, 244,
    246, 247, 248, 249, 255; From
    the Heart of Europe, 237, 241,
    247, 259
Melville, Herman, xvi, 23-24, 31, 54-
    75, 114-15, 117, 137, 139, 152,
    156, 181, 209, 216, 238, 244, 245,
    249, 250, 289-90, 317, 341; The
    Confidence Man, 216; Mardi, 62,

Melville, Herman (*Cont.*)
63; *Moby-Dick,* xi, 11, 23-24, 54-57, 59, 62, 70-75, 99, 119, 125-26, 152, 155, 221, 250, 288-90, 301; *Omoo,* 62; *Pierre,* 54, 56, 59, 62, 63, 72; *Redburn,* 62, 69; *Typee,* 55-56, 59, 73, 301; *White-Jacket,* 69
Mencken, H. L., 94, 244
Merton, Robert K., 130, 200
Meyer, Hans, 256
Meyers, Marvin, x
middle landscape, *see* landscape
Miller, Perry, x, xiv, 79, 94, 136, 217
Milton, John, 122, 165
Munro, Harold, 102
More, Paul Elmer, 244
Morris, William, 181, 254
Mumford, Lewis, xviii, 200, 204, 244
Murray, Henry A., 31
Mussolini, 240

Newman, Stanley, 283
Newton, 165, 185, 329
Nicholson, Marjorie Hope, 174
Niebuhr, Reinhold, 259
Nietzsche, Friedrich, 345
Nixon, Richard M., 145, 203, 286
Norris, Frank, 212, 265

O'Connor, Flannery, 283
Oliver, E. S., 55
Orwell, George, 265-66
Osborn, Fairfield, 142, 148, 319
Owen, Robert, 135

Packer, Barbara, 339
Paine, Albert Bigelow, 25
Paine, Thomas, 321-23
Panofsky, Erwin, 126
Parrington, V. L., x, xviii, 244, 248-49
pastoral, 82, 109, 152-53, 196-97, 222, 291-314, 316, 317
pastoralism, xii-xiii, xvii, xviii, 16, 20, 27, 72-74, 99, 107-8, 113-26, 151-59, 187-207, 220, 222-26, 291-314

Plato, 96, 192, 247, 294
Plekhanov, Georgi, 252
Pocock, J. G. A., 341
Poggioli, Renato, 187, 197
Poirier, Richard, 105, 264, 289, 339
Polanyi, Karl, 190
Pope, Alexander, 161, 185
Porte, Joel, 339
Pound, Ezra, 101, 102, 103, 179, 182
preindustrial society, *see* industrial society
Priestley, Joseph, 64
primitivism, 17, 72, 73, 82, 94, 173, 187-88, 300
Pritchard, William, 101-10
progress, xii, xiii, 32, 116, 132-38, 148, 154, 173, 176-77, 180, 185-207, 218; progressive world-view, 185, 186, 187, 190, 191; progressivism, 185, 191
progressive world-view, *see* progress
progressivism, *see* progress
Prometheus, 114, 118-19

Rackliffe, John, 243, 249
railroad, *see* technology
Reagan, Ronald: era of, 337, 339, 346
Reich, Charles, 201, 203, 292, 296
religion, x, xvii, 30, 37, 42, 45, 48, 49-50, 64, 79, 80, 81, 88, 91, 92, 93-94, 98, 107, 122-26, 128, 133, 137, 153, 161, 166, 171-73, 176, 180-81, 182, 184, 186, 188-89, 196, 210, 214-15, 216, 217, 218, 219, 225, 238, 239, 240, 246-47, 251, 252-55, 259-60, 302, 313, 321-22, 330, 334, 339, 342, 345
Revel, Jean-François, 201
Richards, I. A., 167-68, 170, 171, 243
Robbins, Caroline, 328
Roosevelt, Franklin D. and Theodore, 141
Rose, Arnold, 127-38
Roszak, Theodore, 160, 169-76, 201
Rourke, Constance, 9
Rousseau, Jean-Jacques, 262, 284, 285
Ruland, Richard, 244
Ruskin, John, 181

Sagarin, E., 283
Salinger, J. D., 283
Sandburg, Carl, 17
Sanford, Charles, ix
Santayana, George, xiv-xv, xvii, 37, 45-46, 51, 195, 264-65, 274, 281-82, 287, 290
Sapir, Edward, 130
Sarton, May, 243
Savio, Mario, 197-99, 204
Schaar, John, 284-85
Schlatter, Richard, 257
Schmidt, Paul Stewart, 18
Scott, Sir Walter, 3
Seelye, John, 280
Sewall, Ellen, 88
Shakespeare, William, 114, 118, 132, 235, 294, 304
Shaw, George Bernard, 235
Shelley, Percy, 163
Sherman, Stuart, 244, 328
Slater, Philip, 332-33
slavery, 4-6, 13, 16, 40, 45, 49, 50, 51, 99, 133, 268-71, 274-75, 278, 345
Slotkin, Richard, xi
Smith, Henry Nash, ix, 18, 23; *Mark Twain: The Development of a Writer*, 277, 283; *Virgin Land*, xi, xii, xiv, 118
Snow, C. P., 167
Snyder, Gary, 199, 294
Socrates, 96, 211
Solomon, Maynard, 256
Sontag, Susan, xvii, 284, 285, 292-314
Sparks, Jared, 97
Spenser, Edmund, 294
Stalinism, 240, 241, 252, 257, 258, 298
Stange, G. R., 257
Stanley, J. Lyndon, 82
Stein, William Bysshe, 115
Stern, Frederick, 246-47, 256, 258
Stevens, Wallace, 99, 101, 110, 208, 339
Sullivan, Louis, 339
Summers, Joseph H., 254
Sweezy, Paul, 239-40, 252, 253, 257
Swift, Jonathan, 161

Tasso, Torquato: *Aminta,* 294
Tate, Allen, 339
Taylor, George R., 113
technology, xvi, xvii, 113-26, 127, 133-38, 140, 146-47, 149-50, 152, 157-59, 160-61, 179-207, 303, 307, 311; machine, 113-26, 137-38, 165-67, 177-78, 180-86, 190-207, 307; railroad, 26, 29, 117, 122, 134-35, 137, 180, 185, 186, 218
Theocritus, 316
Thomas, Edward, 102
Thompson, E. P., 253, 254, 258-59
Thompson, Laura, 130
Thompson, Lawrance, 103-4
Thoreau, Cynthia, 84, 96
Thoreau, Helen, 84
Thoreau, Henry David, xvi, 55, 70, 76-100, 114, 125, 137, 139, 152, 153, 181, 199, 208, 221-22, 223, 244, 249-50, 317, 339, 340, 341; *Excursions,* 76-82; *Journal,* 85, 96-97; *Walden,* 23, 76, 77, 81-82, 90, 91-100, 116, 125, 152, 188-89, 197, 221, 222, 301; *A Week on the Concord and Merrimack Rivers,* 76, 77, 90
Thoreau, John (brother), 84, 85-86, 88-90
Thoreau, John (father), 84, 87
Thoreau, Sophia, 77, 84
Thorpe, T. B., 11
Tocqueville, Alexis de, 147, 186, 337-38, 341
Toliver, Harold E., 197, 222
Trachtenberg, Alan, ix, xiv
Trilling, Lionel, x, xiv, xvi, 37-53
Trotsky, Leon, 252
Turner, J. M. W., 123
Turner, Victor, x
Twain, Mark, *see* Clemens, Samuel
Tyler, Royall, 8-9

utopia, 133, 154, 211, 220, 254, 259, 320

Veblen, Thorstein, 149

vernacular, xv, xvi, xvii, 3-17, 19-20,
    27, 29, 32-33, 261-62, 265, 273,
    276-77, 277-90
vernacular style, see vernacular
vernacular tradition, see vernacular
Vetter, Harold J., 283
Vietnam, xvii, 11, 142, 144, 169, 183,
    197, 199, 201, 203, 205, 245, 271,
    280, 284, 292, 295-314
Vincent, Howard P., 125
Virgil, 165, 294, 316
Vogelback, A. L., 37

Wald, George, 143
Wallace, George, 286
Wallace, Henry, 237, 241, 258
Ward, John William, x, xii, xiv
Warner, Charles, 23
Weber, Max, 184, 190, 210, 217
Webster, Daniel, 133-34, 268-71
West, Nathanael, 197
Wharton, Edith, 212
White, George Abbott, 243, 246
White, Lynn Jr., 147, 166
White, Morton and Lucia, 208,
    222
Whitehead, Alfred North, 162-63,
    173, 178

Whitman, Walt, 4-11, 16, 17, 107,
    125, 139, 186, 199, 208-9, 244,
    247, 249-50, 265, 271-77, 285,
    286, 287, 289, 317, 339, 340;
    "Democratic Vistas," 9, 17, 275;
    Leaves of Grass, 9, 186, 271-72,
    275; "Song of Myself," 5-11, 99,
    125
Whittier, John Greenleaf, 244
Wiener, Philip P., 137
wilderness, see landscape
Williams, Raymond, 195, 253, 254
Williams, Tennessee, 283
Williams, William Carlos, 101, 110,
    199, 258, 283
Williamson, Rev. Bro. I. D., 133-34
Wilson, Edmund, 92, 115, 217, 295,
    342
Winner, Langdon, 182
Winters, Yvor, 244, 339
Winthrop, John, 210
Wolin, Sheldon, 177, 198, 203-5
Wordsworth, William, 9-10, 92, 155,
    163-64, 171, 266
Wright, Frank Lloyd, 212, 339

Yankelovich, Daniel, 205
Yeats, William, 102
Yeomans, John W., 115